always up to date

The law changes, but Nolo is on top of it! We offer several
ways to make sure you and your Nolo products are up to date:

1 **Nolo's Legal Updater**
We'll send you an email whenever a new edition of this book
is published! Sign up at **www.nolo.com/legalupdater**.

2 **Updates @ Nolo.com**
Check www.nolo.com/update to find recent changes
in the law that affect the current edition of your book.

3 **Nolo Customer Service**
To make sure that this edition of the book is the most
recent one, call us at **800-728-3555** and ask one of
our friendly customer service representatives.
Or find out at **www.nolo.com**.

please note

We believe accurate, plain-English legal information should help you solve many of your own legal problems. But this text is not a substitute for personalized advice from a knowledgeable lawyer. If you want the help of a trained professional—and we'll always point out situations in which we think that's a good idea—consult an attorney licensed to practice in your state.

12th edition

The California Landlord's Law Book:
Evictions

by Attorney David Brown

edited by Janet Portman

TWELFTH EDITION	FEBRUARY 2007
Editor	JANET PORTMAN
Book Design	TERRI HEARSH
Production	MARGARET LIVINGSTON
CD-ROM Preparation	ELLEN BITTER
Proofreading	ROBERT WELLS
Index	MICHAEL FERREIRA
Cover Photography	TONYA PERME (www.tonyaperme.com)
Printing	DELTA PRINTING SOLUTIONS, INC.

Brown, David Wayne, 1949-
    The California landlord's law book. Evictions / by David Brown ; edited by Janet
Portman.-- 12th ed.
        p. cm.
    ISBN-13: 978-1-4133-0570-8
    ISBN-10: 1-4133-0570-9
    1. Landlord and tenant--California--Popular works. 2. Eviction--California--Popular
works. I. Portman, Janet. II. Title. III. Title: Landlord's law book. IV. Title: Evictions.

KFC145.Z9B762 2007
346.79404'34--dc22

2006047126

Quantity sales: For information on bulk purchases or corporate premium sales, please contact
the Special Sales department. For academic sales or textbook adoptions, ask for Academic
Sales, 800-955-4775. Nolo, 950 Parker Street, Berkeley, CA 94710.

Acknowledgments

This book could not have been published without the generous assistance of many people. A special thank you to Mary Randolph, Steve Elias, Jake Warner, Marcia Stewart, Patricia Gima, and Janet Portman, who all tirelessly read the entire manuscript several times and made numerous helpful suggestions, nearly all of which were incorporated. If you find this book easy to follow and enjoyable to read (well, not like a novel), Mary, Steve, Jake, Marcia, Patricia, and Janet deserve most of the credit.

Thanks also to Robin Leonard, Amy Ihara, John O'Donnell, Barbara Hodovan, Kate Thill, Carol Pladsen, Stephanie Harolde, Julie Christianson, David Cole, Ann Heron, Jack Devaney, Susan Quinn, Alison Towle, and especially Toni Ihara and Terri Hearsh, who were responsible for the layout of this book. Ira Serkes, past president of the Rental Housing Association of Contra Costa County, read the manuscript and made helpful suggestions. Martin Dean, of Martin Dean Essential Publishers, Inc., generously gave us permission to reprint one of their forms.

About the Author

David Brown practices law in the Monterey, California, area, where he has represented both landlords and tenants in hundreds of court cases—most of which he felt could have been avoided if both sides were more fully informed about landlord/tenant law. Brown is a graduate of Stanford University (chemistry) and the University of Santa Clara Law School. He is the author of *Fight Your Ticket and Win in California* and *Beat Your Ticket* (national), and the coauthor of *The California Landlord's Law Book: Rights & Responsibilities* and *The Guardianship Book*, all published by Nolo.

Table of Contents

8 Contested Cases

9 Collecting Your Money Judgment

10 When a Tenant Files for Bankruptcy

Appendix 1

Rent Control Chart

Appendix 2

How to Use the CD-ROM

Appendix 3

Tear-Out Forms

Forms for ending the tenancy

Three-Day Notice to Pay Rent or Quit

30-Day Notice of Termination of Tenancy (Tenancy Less Than One Year)

60-Day Notice of Termination of Tenancy (Tenancy of One Year or Longer)

90-Day Notice of Termination of Tenancy (Subsidized Tenancies)

Three-Day Notice to Perform Covenant or Quit

Three-Day Notice to Quit (Improper Subletting, Nuisance, Waste, or Illegal Use)

Forms for filing an eviction lawsuit

Summons—Unlawful Detainer—Eviction

Complaint—Unlawful Detainer

Civil Case Cover Sheet

Civil Case Cover Sheet Addendum and Statement of Location

Proof of Service of Summons

Application and Order to Serve Summons by Posting for Unlawful Detainer

Prejudgment Claim to Right of Possession

Blank Pleading Paper

Forms for default judgments

Request for Entry of Default

Writ of Execution

Application for Issuance of Writ of Execution, Possession or Sale

Declaration in Support of Default Judgment for Rent, Damages, and Costs (3-, 30-, 60- or 90-Day Notice)

Declaration in Support of Default Judgment for Damages and Costs (Violation of Lease)

Declaration for Default Judgment by Court

Forms for contested evictions

Judgment—Unlawful Detainer

Stipulation for Entry of Judgment

Request/Counter-Request to Set Case for Trial—Unlawful Detainer

Notice of Motion for Summary Judgment; Plaintiff's Declaration; and Points and Authorities

Proof of Personal Service

Order Granting Motion for Summary Judgment

Judgment Following Granting of Motion for Summary Judgment

Judgment—Unlawful Detainer Attachment

Forms for collecting your money judgment

Application and Order for Appearance and Examination

Questionnaire for Judgment-Debtor Examination

Application for Earnings Withholding Order (Wage Garnishment)

Acknowledgment of Satisfaction of Judgment

Proof of Service by Mail

Index

Evictions in California: An Overview

Sometimes even the most sincere and professional attempts at conscientious landlording fail, and you have to consider evicting a tenant. This is a do-it-yourself eviction manual for California landlords. It shows you, step by step, how to file and conduct an uncontested eviction lawsuit against a residential tenant. It does not cover how to evict a hotel guest, a tenant in a mobile home park, or a commercial tenant. Neither does it show a new owner, who has just purchased property at a foreclosure sale, how to evict a former owner (or his tenant).

The Landlord's Role in Evictions

Strictly speaking, the word "evict" refers to the process of a sheriff or marshal ordering a tenant to get out or be forcibly removed. It is illegal for you to try to physically evict a tenant yourself. The sheriff or marshal will only evict a tenant pursuant to a court order known as an "unlawful detainer judgment." To get such a judgment, you must bring an eviction lawsuit, called an "unlawful detainer action," against the tenant.

The linchpin of an unlawful detainer suit is proper termination of the tenancy; you can't get a judgment without it. This usually means giving your tenant adequate written notice, in a specified way. The law sets out very detailed requirements for landlords who want to end a tenancy. If you don't meet them exactly, you will lose your suit even if your tenant has bounced checks, including your rent check, from here to Mandalay.

This legal strictness is not accidental; it reflects the law's bias in favor of tenants. The law used to be heavily weighted on the landowner's side, but attitudes have changed, and today the law puts more value on a tenant's right to shelter than a landlord's right to property. As one court put it, "Our courts were never intended to serve as rubber stamps for landlords seeking to evict their tenants, but rather to see that justice be done before a man is evicted from his home." (*Maldanado v. Superior Court* (1984) 162 Cal. App. 3d 1259, 1268-69.)

Because an eviction judgment means the tenant won't have a roof over his head (and his children's heads), judges are very demanding of the landlord. In addition, many California cities go beyond state law, which allows the termination of periodic tenancies at the will of the landlord, and require the landlord to show a "just cause" for eviction. In these cities, nonpayment of rent is still a straightforward ground for eviction, but there are few others.

Why do we emphasize the negatives of evicting a tenant? Because we want you to understand at the outset that even if you properly bring and conduct an unlawful detainer action, you are not assured of winning and having the tenant evicted if the tenant decides to file a defense. In other words, despite the merits of your position, you may face a judge who will hold you to every technicality and bend over backwards to sustain the tenant's position. A tenant can raise many substantive, as well as procedural, objections to an unlawful detainer suit. Essentially, any breach by you of any duty imposed on landlords by state or local law can be used by your tenant as a defense to your action. Simply put, unless you thoroughly know your legal rights and duties as a landlord before you go to court, and unless you dot every "i" and cross every "t," you may end up on the losing side. Our advice: Especially if your action is contested, be meticulous in your preparation.

Before you proceed with an unlawful detainer lawsuit, consider that even paying the tenant a few hundred dollars to leave right away may be cheaper in the long run. For example, paying a tenant $500 to leave right away (with payment made only as the tenant leaves and hands you the keys) may be cheaper than spending $100 to file suit and going without rent for three to eight weeks while the tenant contests the lawsuit and stays. The alternative of a several-month-long eviction lawsuit—during which you can't accept rent that you may be unable to collect even after winning a judgment—may, in the long run, be more expensive and frustrating than paying the tenant to leave and starting over with a better tenant quickly.

Note of Sanity. Between 80% and 90% of all unlawful detainer actions are won by landlords because the tenant fails to show up. So the odds favor relatively smooth sailing in your unlawful detainer action.

Proceed With Caution When Evicting a Tenant

The moment relations between you and one of your tenants begin to sour, you will be wise to remember a cardinal truth. Any activity by you that might be construed by your tenant as illegal, threatening, humiliating, abusive, or invasive of his privacy can potentially give rise to a lawsuit against you for big bucks. So, although the unlawful detainer procedure can be tedious, it's important to understand that it is the only game in town.

Shortcuts such as threats, intimidation, utility shutoffs, or attempts to physically remove a tenant are illegal and dangerous. If you resort to them, you may well find yourself on the wrong end of a lawsuit for such personal injuries as trespass, assault, battery, slander and libel, intentional infliction of emotional distress, and wrongful eviction. A San Francisco landlord was ordered to pay 23 tenants $1.48 million in 1988, after a jury found he had cut off tenants' water, invaded their privacy, and threatened to physically throw them out. (The verdict was reduced on appeal, to half a million dollars.) (*Balmoral Hotel Tenants Association v. Lee* (1990) 226 Cal. App. 3d 686, 276 Cal. Rptr. 640.)

To avoid such liability, we recommend that you avoid all unnecessary one-on-one personal contact with the tenant during the eviction process unless it occurs in a structured setting (for example, during mediation, at a neighborhood dispute resolution center, or in the presence of a neutral third party). Also keep your written communications to the point and as neutral as you can, even if you are boiling inside. Remember, any manifestations of anger on your part can come back to legally haunt you somewhere down the line. Finally, treat the tenant like she has a right to remain on the premises, even though it is your position that she doesn't. Until the day the sheriff or marshal shows up with a writ of possession, the tenant's home is legally her castle, and you may come to regret any actions on your part that don't recognize that fact.

When Not to Use This Book

Most of you fit within the most common eviction situation: You (or the owner, if you are a manager) own residential rental property which you operate as a business. You need to evict a tenant who has not paid the rent, has violated another important rental term or condition, or has held over past the expiration of his or her lease or rental agreement. This is the book for you, to use on your own or in conjunction with an attorney.

There are some situations, however, that this book doesn't address. Do not use this book, or its forms, if any of the following scenarios describe you.

You have bought the property at a foreclosure sale and need to evict the former owner, who has not moved out. If you now want to get rid of the former owner-occupant, you must use a special unlawful detainer complaint, unlike the forms contained in this book. You'll need to see a lawyer.

You have bought the property at a foreclosure sale and need to evict the tenant of the former owner. If the occupant is a tenant of the former owner, different procedures apply depending on whether the tenant's lease predated the mortgage or deed of trust foreclosed upon, and whether you accepted rent from the tenant after foreclosure. Here are the rules:

- If the tenant's lease or rental agreement began after the deed of trust was recorded (which will be true in most cases), the foreclosure sale has the effect of wiping out the lease or rental agreement. If you have not accepted rent from the former owner's tenant, there is a way to get the tenant out quickly—but you won't be able to use the Complaint forms in this book. You'll need to see a lawyer.
- If the tenant's lease began before the deed of trust was recorded, or if you have accepted rent from a tenant whose lease or rental agreement predates the deed of trust, you must honor his lease or rental agreement just as the former owner did. In short, you are now the tenant's landlord, and until the lease runs out (or you terminate a month-to-month tenancy with the proper amount of notice), or until the tenant otherwise violates the rental conditions, you are stuck with this tenant. If any of these events come to pass, however, you may use this book.

You have purchased the property and want to evict the former owner's tenant. When you purchase property at a normal sale, you "take" it subject to existing leases or rental agreements. This means that no matter how much you would like to move in yourself or install different tenants, you can't do so until the leases run out, you terminate a month-to-month with the proper amount of notice, or the tenant violates an important rental term or condition. When any of these conditions are met, however, you may go ahead and use this book and its forms.

You own commercial property and want to evict a tenant for nonpayment of rent or other lease violations. Commercial landlords should not use this book. Many commercial leases require tenants to pay for common-area maintenance, prorated property taxes, and utility charges, in addition to a set monthly sum. Because the exact rent amount is often not clear, a special termination notice (not supplied in this book) must be used. Also, many commercial leases provide for special types of notice periods and ways to serve notices, which are different from the ones specified in this book. Finally, since commercial leases often run for five or ten years and can be quite valuable to a tenant, a commercial tenant is much more likely than a residential tenant to contest an eviction—and judges are less likely to order an eviction for minor lease violations. In short, with all these possible complications, we suggest seeing an attorney to handle an eviction of a commercial tenant.

A Reason for Which You Must Evict: Drug Dealing

In cases of drug dealing, it's not a question of whether or not it's permissible to evict a tenant—it's imperative to do so. In fact, a landlord who fails to evict a tenant who deals illegal drugs on the property can face lawsuits from other tenants, neighbors, and local authorities. Many landlords have been held liable for tens of thousands of dollars in damages for failing to evict a drug-dealing tenant. A landlord can also face loss of the property.

When it's a month-to-month tenancy, terminate the tenancy with a 30-day notice (or 60-day notice if tenant has stayed a year or more—see Chapter 3 as soon as you suspect illegal drug activity by the tenant or any

members of the tenant's family. If the tenant has a fixed-term lease, you will have to follow the procedures in Chapter 4. Evictions for drug dealing may be a little more difficult in rent control cities with "just cause eviction" provisions in their rent control ordinances; even so, a landlord faced with a drug-dealing tenant should do everything he or she can to evict, and should begin gathering evidence against the drug dealer—including getting tenants and neighbors to keep records of heavy traffic in and out of the suspected tenant's home at odd hours.

Prosecutors May Evict for You—At a Price

The legislature has established a program for certain courts within Alameda, Los Angeles, and San Diego counties that authorizes the city attorney or district attorney to file an unlawful detainer action against tenants who are using rental property to sell, use, store, or make illegal drugs. (H&S § 11571.1.) The program applies to cases brought in certain cities in those counties, including the City of Los Angeles, Long Beach, San Diego, and Oakland. It will expire January 1, 2010, unless the legislature extends it.

Owners will be given 30 days' notice of the intended eviction lawsuit, and will be given 30 days to proceed with the eviction on their own. If they decline, they will be expected to furnish relevant information about the tenants and their activities and must assign their right to evict to the city. Owners may be asked to cover up to $600 worth of the city's litigation costs. If the owners don't cooperate or respond within the 30 days, the city can join the owners as defendants in the eviction lawsuit. And if the city has to go this route and wins, the owner will be ordered to pay the city for the entire cost of bringing the lawsuit. In Los Angeles, the District Attorney's office issues about 500 such eviction notices per year; 50 to 80 go to trial, and the city wins 98% of them. ("Law Would Give Oakland the Muscle to Oust Tenants," *San Francisco Daily Journal*, April 6, 2004.)

Heard enough? The message is clear: Take care of drug problems yourself, quickly. If you don't want to handle the eviction on your own, hire counsel. Don't end up footing the bill for the services of well-paid city attorneys.

Evictions in Certain Cities

Local ordinances in many California cities address evictions—specifying under what circumstances you may proceed, and how to proceed. Most of these cities also have rent control ordinances, but not all, as you'll see below.

Cities With Rent Control

If you think all local rent control laws do is control rents, you have a surprise coming. They also affect evictions in two important ways: First, many (but not all) rent control ordinances and regulations impose important restrictions or additional procedural requirements on evictions. For example, the ordinances of some cities require a landlord to have a "just cause" (good reason) to evict a tenant, sometimes even for rental units that are exempt from rent control. Local ordinances also commonly require tenancy termination notices and complaints to contain statements not required by state law.

Second, any violation of any provision of a rent control law may provide a tenant with a defense to your eviction lawsuit. Even failure to register your rental units with the local rent board, if that is required under the ordinance, may provide a tenant with a successful defense against an eviction suit. Appendix 1 in this book lists the requirements each rent control city imposes on eviction lawsuits—such as any applicable registration requirements or extra information required in three-day or other termination notices or in the eviction complaint itself.

No two cities' rent control ordinances are alike. Within the space of one book, we can only write instructions and forms for use by the majority of California landlords—those who do not have rent control. We cannot include 15 additional sets that are tailor-made for use in the 15 cities that have rent control and impose additional requirements when it comes to filling out forms. **But your rent control ordinance may affect almost every step in your eviction proceeding.** If you do not conform your notices and court filings to your ordinance's requirements, it's very likely that your case will be tossed out or lost, perhaps after you've spent considerable time and effort. We cannot say this strongly enough: **Read your rent control ordinance before you begin an unlawful detainer proceeding and before you use any of the forms in this book.** Begin by reading the overview in Appendix 1, which tells you what to look for and where to learn more (often, you can read the ordinance online).

Cities With Rent Control	
Some form of rent regulation now exists in fifteen California cities:	
Berkeley	Oakland
Beverly Hills	Palm Springs
Campbell (mediation only)*	San Francisco
East Palo Alto	San Jose*
Fremont (mediation only)*	Santa Monica
Hayward	Thousand Oaks
Los Angeles	West Hollywood
Los Gatos*	

*These rent control cities do not have just cause eviction provisions.

San Diego and Glendale

Two cities without rent control—San Diego and Glendale—also restrict evictions, though San Diego's ordinance applies only to tenancies lasting two years of more. These cities' rules do not affect the procedure for evicting with a three-day notice based on nonpayment of rent or other breach, or commission of waste or nuisance. They do affect evictions based 30-day or 60-day terminations of month-to-month tenancies. See "Checklist for 30- or 60-Day Notice Eviction" in Chapter 3.

Evicting Roommates

This book was written with the small property owner in mind, such as an owner of a modest apartment complex or a single-family rental.

However, some of our readers have used this book to evict a roommate. If you are thinking about evicting a roommate, we suggest that you read *The Landlord's Law Book: Rights & Responsibilities*, where we discuss the legal relationship between roommates.

If you want to use this book to evict a roommate, you must be the original tenant (or the one who has signed a lease or rental agreement with the landlord), and the roommate you want to evict must be your landlord's "subtenant." A "subtenant" is usually someone who is renting part of your place from you and paying rent to you instead of your landlord. In this relationship, you are the "landlord" and your roommate is your "tenant."

You can't evict a roommate if you and your roommate are "cotenants." You are cotenants if you and your roommate both signed the lease or rental agreement.

EXAMPLE: Marlena Mastertenant rents a two-bedroom house from Oscar Owner for $900 a month. Marlena rents one of the bedrooms (plus half the common areas such as kitchen, bathroom, and hallways) to Susie Subtenant for $400 a month. Marlena is the tenant and Susie is the subtenant. Marlena can use the procedures in this book to evict Susie if Susie doesn't pay her rent. In the unlawful detainer complaint (see "Preparing the Complaint," Item 3, in Chapter 6), Marlena should list herself as "lessee/sublessor."

Evicting a Lodger

A lodger, or roomer, is someone who rents a room in a house that you own and live in. The rules for evicting a lodger are covered by California Civil Code § 1946.5 and Penal Code §§ 602.3 and 837, and apply only if you rent to *one* lodger. (If you have two or more lodgers, you must use the unlawful detainer procedures described in this book.) In addition, you must have overall control of the dwelling unit and have retained a right of access to areas occupied by the lodger.

If your lodger is a month-to-month tenant and you want to terminate the tenancy, you can serve the lodger with a 30-day notice, as explained in Chapter 3. You may also use a shortcut (not available to landlords serving nonlodger tenants) and send the notice by certified or registered mail, restricted delivery, with a return receipt requested.

A lodger who doesn't leave at the end of the notice period is guilty of an infraction. Technically, this entitles you to do a citizen's arrest, which means that you can eject the lodger using reasonable, but not deadly, force. However, we strongly advise against this tactic, and instead suggest calling local law enforcement to handle the situation. Have a copy of your dated termination notice available. Be aware that many local police do not know the procedures for evicting lodgers or may not want to get involved, fearing potential liability for

improperly evicting a tenant. The police may insist that you go through the normal unlawful detainer lawsuit process—which will result in a court order authorizing the police or sheriff to evict the lodger. If the lodger has stayed for a year or more and the police won't evict on your 30-day notice, you will have to start all over with a 60-day notice according to a different law, Civ. § 1946.1. Check with your chief of police to find out how this issue is handled.

If you need to evict your lodger "for cause"—that is, for failing to pay the rent or violation of the rental agreement—you can serve him with a three-day notice, *but if he doesn't leave you will have to go through an unlawful detainer lawsuit as explained in this book.* You cannot hand your copy of the three-day notice to the local police and ask them to remove the lodger. For this reason, you may want to use the less complicated route of the 30-day notice, in hopes that, if the lodger refuses to budge, local law enforcement will honor your termination notice.

Finally, if your lodger has a lease, you cannot evict unless he has failed to pay the rent, violated a term of the lease, or engaged in illegal activity. In these situations you will need to use a 30-day or 60-day notice. If the lodger fails to vacate, you must file an unlawful detainer lawsuit in order to get him out.

EXAMPLE: Terry Tenant and Tillie Tenant (brother and sister) jointly rent a two-bedroom apartment from Lenny Landlord. They moved in at the same time and both of them signed the lease. They are both Lenny's tenants. Since neither Terry nor Tillie are each other's subtenant, they cannot use this book.

⚠️ The legal relationship between roommates is often unclear. For example, if one tenant moved in first, is the second occupant a subtenant because she negotiated with and rented from the first tenant, or a cotenant because she claims to have a separate verbal understanding with the owner regarding rent? If in doubt, see a lawyer before using this book to evict a roommate you claim is your subtenant.

Evicting a Resident Manager

If you fire a resident manager, or if he quits, you will often want him to move out of your property, particularly if he occupies a special manager's unit or if the firing or quitting has generated (or resulted from) ill will. Eviction lawsuits against former managers can be extremely complicated. This is especially true if the management agreement requires good cause for termination of employment or a certain period of notice. Such lawsuits can also be complicated where a single combined management/rental agreement is used or if local rent control laws impose special requirements. While all rent control cities do allow eviction of fired managers, some cities impose restrictions on it.

This section outlines some of the basic issues involved in evicting a resident manager. We do not, and cannot, provide you complete advice on how to evict a resident manager. In many cases, you will need an experienced attorney who specializes in landlord-tenant law to evict a former manager, particularly if the ex-manager questions whether the firing was legally effective or proper.

Separate Management and Rental Agreements

To evict a tenant-manager with whom you signed separate management and rental agreements (which allows you to terminate the employment at any time),

you will have to give a normal 30-day written termination notice, or a 60-day notice if the tenant-manager stayed for a year or more, subject in either case to any just cause eviction requirements in rent-control cities. (See Chapter 3.) If the tenant has a separate fixed-term lease, you cannot terminate the tenancy until the lease expires.

Single Management/Rental Agreement

What happens to the tenancy when you fire a manager (or he quits) depends on the kind of agreement you and the manager had.

If the Manager Occupied a Special Manager's Unit

If your manager occupies a specially constructed manager's unit (such as one with a reception area or built-in desk) which must be used by the manager, or if she receives an apartment rent-free as part or all of her compensation, your ability to evict the ex-manager depends on:

- the terms of the management/rental agreement, and
- local rent control provisions.

If the agreement says nothing about the tenancy continuing if the manager quits or is fired, termination of the employment also terminates the tenancy. You can insist that the ex-manager leave right away, without serving any three-day or other termination notice, and can file an eviction lawsuit the next day if the ex-manager refuses to leave. (See C.C.P. § 1161 (1) and *Lombard v. Santa Monica YMCA* (1985) 160 Cal. App. 3d 529.) (See the checklist in Chapter 5.)

The just cause eviction provisions of any applicable rent control law, however, may still require a separate notice or otherwise restrict your ability to evict a fired manager.

If the Manager Didn't Occupy a Manager's Unit

If the manager was simply compensated by a rent reduction, and there is no separate employment agreement, there may be confusion as to whether the rent can be "increased" after the manager is fired.

If an ex-manager refuses to pay the full rent, you will have to serve a Three-Day Notice to Pay Rent or Quit, demanding the unpaid rent. If she still won't pay, you'll have to follow up with an eviction lawsuit. (See Chapter 2.)

Attorneys and Eviction Services

While you can do most evictions yourself, there are a few circumstances when you may want to consult an attorney who specializes in landlord-tenant law:

- The property you own is too far from where you live. Since you must file an eviction lawsuit where the property is located, the time and travel involved in representing yourself may be great.
- Your tenant is already represented by a lawyer, even before you proceed with an eviction.
- Your property is subject to rent control and local ordinances governing evictions.
- The tenant you are evicting is an ex-manager whom you have fired. (See above.)
- Your tenant contests the eviction in court. (See Chapter 8 for more details on hiring an attorney in contested cases.)
- Your tenant files for bankruptcy. (See Chapter 10.)

If you simply want someone to handle the paperwork and eviction details, you can use an "eviction service." (Check the Yellow Pages under this heading.) Because eviction services cannot represent you in court, however, they are not helpful where the tenant contests the eviction in court.

Eviction services must be registered as "unlawful detainer assistants" with the county in which they operate, and must also be bonded or insured. (Bus. & Prof. Code §§ 6400-6415.) In additional, all court papers filed by an unlawful detainer assistant must indicate that person's name, address and country registration number.

How to Use This Book

This book is a companion volume to *The California Landlord's Law Book: Rights & Responsibilities*, which discusses the legal rules of renting residential real property, with an eye toward avoiding legal problems and fostering good tenant relations. Although you can use this book as a self-contained do-it-yourself eviction manual, we strongly recommend that you use it along with *The California Landlord's Law Book: Rights & Responsibilities*. It's not just that we want to sell more books—*The California Landlord's Law Book: Rights & Responsibilities* provides crucial information on the substance of landlord-tenant law that you almost certainly will need to know to win a contested unlawful detainer lawsuit. For example it discusses leases, cotenants, subtenants, roommates, deposits, rent increases, rent control laws, privacy, discrimination, your duty to provide safe housing, and many more crucially important areas of landlord-tenant law. Even more important, *The California Landlord's Law Book: Rights & Responsibilities* provides a good overview of your duties as a landlord so that you can minimize the need to evict tenants as much as possible, or at least know in advance whether you're vulnerable to any of the commonly used tenant defenses.

Some material is necessarily repeated here and discussed in the eviction context. For example, information on three-day notices is important for both rent collection and for eviction. For the most part, however, this volume makes extensive references to *The California Landlord's Law Book: Rights & Responsibilities* for detailed discussions of substantive law instead of repeating them.

Now let's take a minute to get an overview of how this volume works. Chapters 2 through 5 explain the legal grounds for eviction. This entire lists looks like this:

- The tenant has failed to leave or pay the rent due within three days of having received from you a written Three-Day Notice to Pay Rent or Quit (Chapter 2).
- A month-to-month tenant has failed to leave within the time allowed after having received from you a written notice giving 30 days, or 60 days if the tenant rented for a year or more, or 90 days (certain government-subsidized tenancies.) (Chapter 3.)
- The tenant has failed to leave or comply with a provision of her lease or rental agreement within three days after having received your written three-day notice to correct the violation or quit (Chapter 4).
- The tenant has sublet the property contrary to the lease or rental agreement, has caused or allowed a nuisance or serious damage to the property, or has used the property for an illegal purpose, and has failed to leave within three days of having received from you an unconditional three-day notice to vacate (Chapter 4).
- A tenant whose fixed-term lease has expired and has not been renewed has failed to leave (Chapter 5).

- A month-to-month tenant has failed to leave within the stated time after having given you a written 30-day or 60-day notice terminating the tenancy (Chapter 5).

After the tenancy is terminated (in almost all cases, by a three-day or other notice), most of the procedures in unlawful detainer lawsuits are the same no matter which reason your suit is based on. Thus, after you read either Chapter 2, 3, 4, or 5, depending on the way you're terminating the tenancy, go next to the chapters that explain the court procedures. These begin with Chapter 6 on filing a complaint to begin your unlawful detainer lawsuit.

If your tenant doesn't contest the lawsuit within five days after being served with a copy of your complaint, you will go next to Chapter 7 on getting an eviction judgment by default.

If the tenant does contest your unlawful detainer suit, you will proceed directly to Chapter 8, which tells you how to handle contested actions and when the services of a lawyer are advisable. Chapter 10 discusses your options when a tenant files for bankruptcy.

Chapter 9, on collecting your money judgment, will be your last stop after you win the lawsuit.

The whole eviction process typically takes from one to two months.

If you live in a city with a rent control ordinance, you will be referred to Appendix 1 from time to time for more detailed information on your locality's ordinance.

Here are two examples of common pathways through this book:

EXAMPLE: A tenant in your Los Angeles apartment building, Roy, doesn't pay the rent when it's due on the first of the month. A few days pass, and you decide he's probably never going to pay it. You turn to Chapter 2 on nonpayment of rent. Following the instructions, you serve Roy with a three-day notice to pay rent or quit (after checking Appendix 1 in this book and a copy of the current Los Angeles rent control ordinance to see if there are any special requirements you should know about).

Roy neither pays the rent nor moves in three days. You then turn to Chapter 6, which tells you how to begin an unlawful detainer suit by filing a complaint with the court and serving a copy of the complaint and a summons on the tenant. Roy does not respond to your complaint in five days,

and Chapter 6 steers you to Chapter 7 on how to get a default judgment. You are entitled to a default judgment when the other side does not do the things necessary to contest a case. After you successfully use Chapter 7 to take default judgments both for possession of the premises and the money Roy owes you, your final step is to turn to Chapter 9 for advice on how to collect the money.

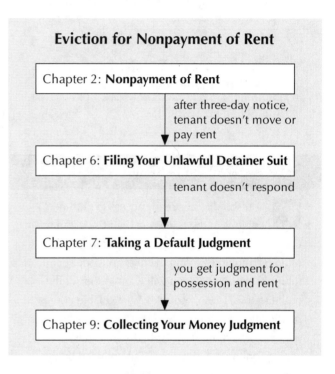

Eviction for Nonpayment of Rent

Chapter 2: **Nonpayment of Rent**

after three-day notice, tenant doesn't move or pay rent

Chapter 6: **Filing Your Unlawful Detainer Suit**

tenant doesn't respond

Chapter 7: **Taking a Default Judgment**

you get judgment for possession and rent

Chapter 9: **Collecting Your Money Judgment**

EXAMPLE: You decide that you want to move a new tenant into the house you rent out in Sacramento. The current tenant, Maria, occupies the house under a month-to-month rental agreement. She pays her rent on time, and you've never had any serious problems with her, but you would rather have your friend Jim live there. You turn to Chapter 3 and follow the instructions to prepare and serve a notice terminating Maria's tenancy—a 60-day notice because she's lived there more than a year. Maria doesn't leave after her 60 days are up, so you go to Chapter 6 for instructions on how to file your unlawful detainer suit. After you serve her with the summons and complaint, Maria files a written response with the court. You then go to Chapter 8 to read about contested lawsuits.

Eviction With 30-Day or 60-Day Notice

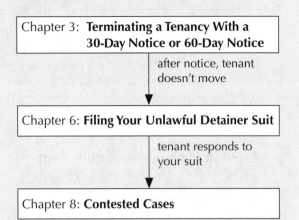

Chapter 3: **Terminating a Tenancy With a 30-Day Notice or 60-Day Notice**

↓ after notice, tenant doesn't move

Chapter 6: **Filing Your Unlawful Detainer Suit**

↓ tenant responds to your suit

Chapter 8: **Contested Cases**

Valuable Resources

 You should have ready access to current editions of the *California Civil Code* and the *California Code of Civil Procedure*. Although we often refer to and explain the relevant code sections, there are times when you will want to look at the entire statute. These resources are available at most public and all law libraries. You can also order the paperback versions from Nolo. To read California statutes online, see the website maintained by the Legislative Counsel at www.leginfo.ca.gov. Chapter 8 of *The California Landlord's Law Book: Rights & Responsibilities* shows you how to find and use statutes and other legal resources if you want to do more research on a particular subject.

To go further, we recommend *Legal Research: How to Find & Understand the Law*, by Stephen Elias and Susan Levinkind (Nolo), which gives easy-to-use, step-by-step instructions on how to find legal information. (See order information at the back of this book.)

Abbreviations Used in This Book

We use these standard abbreviations throughout this book for important statutes and court cases covering evictions.

California Codes

Bus. & Prof.	Business & Professions
Civ. Code	Civil
C.C.P.	Civil Procedure
Evid.	Evidence
Gov't.	Government
H. & S.	Health and Safety

Federal Laws

C.F.R.	Code of Federal Regulations
U.S.C.	United States Code

Cases

Cal. App.	California Court of Appeal
Cal.	California Supreme Court
F. Supp.	Federal District Court
F.2d or F.3d	Federal Court of Appeals
U.S.	United States Supreme Court

Icons Used in This Book

 Caution. This icon alerts you to potential problems.

See an Expert. This icon lets you know when you need the advice of an attorney or other expert.

 Fast Track. This icon lets you know when you can skip information that may not be relevant to your situation.

Recommended Reading. This icon refers you to other books or resources.

 Rent Control. This icon indicates special considerations for rent control cities.

Tip. This icon alerts you to a practical tip or good idea.

 Tear-out Forms and CD-ROM. This icon tells you that the form referred to in the text can be found as a tear-out in Appendix 3 and on the CD-ROM that is included with this book. Instructions for opening and using the CD are in Appendix 2.

2

Eviction for Nonpayment of Rent

Approximately nine out of ten unlawful detainer lawsuits are brought because of the tenant's failure to pay rent when due. Although you don't want to sue your tenants every time they're 20 minutes late with the rent, obviously it's unwise to let a tenant get very far behind. You have to use your own best judgment to decide how long to wait.

Once you've decided that your tenants either can't or won't pay the rent within a reasonable time (or move out), you will want to evict them as fast as possible. As we stressed in the previous chapter, the only legal way to do this is with an "unlawful detainer" lawsuit. This chapter shows you how to do this step by step.

Overview of the Process

Before you can file an unlawful detainer lawsuit against a tenant, the law requires that you terminate the tenancy. To properly terminate a tenancy for nonpayment of rent, you must give the tenant three days' written notice using a form called a Three-Day Notice to Pay Rent or Quit. This is normally referred to as a three-day notice.

If within three days after you properly serve the tenant with this notice (you don't count the first day) she offers you the entire rent demanded, the termination is ineffective and the tenant can legally stay. If, however, the tenant neither pays nor moves by the end of the third day (assuming the third day doesn't fall on a Saturday, Sunday, or holiday), you can begin your lawsuit.

You do not have to accept payment offered after the end of the third day (unless it falls on a Saturday, Sunday, or holiday, in which case the tenant has until the end of the next business day to pay up). If you do accept the rent, you no longer have the right to evict the tenant based on the three-day notice.

> **EXAMPLE:** Tillie's lease requires her to pay $600 rent to her landlord, Lenny, on the first day of each month in advance. Tillie fails to pay November's rent on November 1. By November 9, it's evident to Lenny that Tillie has no intention of paying the rent, so he serves her with a Three-Day Notice to Pay Rent or Quit following the instructions set out below. The day the notice is given doesn't count, and Tillie has three days, starting on the 10th, to pay. Tillie doesn't pay the rent on the 10th, 11th, or 12th. However, since the 12th is a Saturday, Tillie is not legally required to pay until the close of the next business day, which is November 15 (because November 13 is a Sunday and the 14th is a holiday—Veteran's Day). In other words, Lenny cannot bring his lawsuit until November 16.

> Lenny will be very lucky if he can get Tillie out by the end of the month, partly because he waited so long before giving her the three-day notice. If Lenny had given Tillie the notice on November 4, the third day after that would have been November 7. Lenny could have filed his suit on the 8th and gotten Tillie out a week sooner.

Checklist for Uncontested Three-Day Notice Eviction

Here are the steps involved in evicting on the grounds covered in this chapter, if the tenant defaults. We cover some of the subjects (for example, filing a complaint and default judgments) in later chapters. As you work your way through the book you may want to return to this chart to see where you are in the process.

Preparing the Three-Day Notice to Pay Rent or Quit

Pay very close attention to the formalities of preparing and giving the notice. Any mistake in the notice, however slight, may give your tenant (or her attorney) an excuse to contest the eviction lawsuit. At worst, a mistake in the three-day notice may render your unlawful detainer lawsuit "fatally defective"—which means you not only lose, but very likely will have to pay the tenant's court costs and attorney's fees if she is represented by a lawyer, and will have to start all over again with a correct three-day notice.

Requirements of a Three-Day Notice

In addition to stating the correct amount of past due rent and the dates for which it is due (see the next section), your three-day notice must contain all of the following:

Checklist for Uncontested Three-Day Notice Eviction

Step		Earliest Time to Do It
☐ 1.	Prepare the Summons (or Summonses, if there is more than one tenant) and Complaint and make copies. (Chapter 6)	Any day after the rent is due—for example, on or after the second of the month when the rent is due on the first. (If rent due date falls on Saturday, Sunday, or holiday, it's due the next business day.)
☐ 2.	Prepare and serve the three-day notice on the tenant.	Late in the third day after service of the three-day notice.
☐ 3.	File the Complaint at the courthouse and have the Summons(es) issued. (Chapter 6)	The fourth day after service of the three-day notice, or, if the third day after service falls on a Saturday, Sunday, or holiday, the second business day after that third day.
☐ 4.	Have the sheriff, the marshal, or a friend serve the Summons and Complaint. (Chapter 6)	As soon as possible after filing the Complaint and having the Summons(es) issued.
☐ 5.	Prepare Request for Entry of Default, Judgment, Declaration, and Writ of Possession. (Chapter 7)	While you're waiting for five-day (or 15-day, if Complaint not personally served) response time to pass.
☐ 6.	Call the court to find out whether or not tenant(s) has filed written response.	Just before closing on the fifth day after service of Summons, or early on the sixth day. (Do not count holidays that fall on weekdays, however. Also, if fifth day after service falls on weekend, or holiday, count the first business day after that as the fifth day.)
☐ 7.	Mail copy of Request for Entry of Default to tenant(s), file original at courthouse. Also file Declaration and Proof of Service, and have clerk issue Judgment and Writ for Possession for the property. (Chapter 7)	Sixth day after service of Summons and Complaint. (Again, count first business day after fifth day that falls on weekend or holiday.)
☐ 8.	Prepare letter of instruction for, and give writ and copies to, sheriff, or marshal. (Chapter 7)	As soon as possible after above step. Sheriff or marshal won't evict for at least five days after posting notice.
☐ 9.	Change locks after tenant vacates.	As soon as possible.
For Money Judgment		
☐ 10.	Prepare Request for Entry of Default, Judgment, and, if allowed by local rule, Declaration in Support of Default Judgment (or a Declaration in Lieu of Testimony). (Chapter 7)	As soon as possible after property is vacant.
☐ 11.	Mail Request for Entry of Default copy to tenant, file request at courthouse. If Declaration in Lieu of Testimony allowed, file that too, and give clerk judgment and writ forms for money part of judgment. If testimony required, ask clerk for default hearing. (Chapter 7)	As soon as possible after above.
☐ 12.	If testimony required, attend default hearing before judge, testify, and turn in your judgment form for entry of money judgment. (Chapter 7)	When scheduled by court clerk.
☐ 13.	Apply security deposit to cleaning and repair of property, and to any rent not accounted for in judgment, then apply balance to judgment amount. Notify tenant in writing of deductions, keeping a copy. Refund any balance remaining. If deposit does not cover entire judgment, collect balance of judgment. (Chapter 9)	As soon as possible after default hearing. Deposit must be accounted for within three weeks of when the tenants vacate.

- Your tenant(s)'s name(s).
- A description of the property: street address and apartment or unit number, city, county, and state.
- A demand that the tenant(s) pay the stated amount of rent due within three days or move. If you just demand the rent and do not set out the alternative of leaving, your notice is fatally defective.
- A statement that you will pursue legal action (or declare the lease/rental agreement "forfeited") if the tenant does not pay the entire rent due or move.
- Information on to whom, where, and how the rent is to be paid.
- An indication—such as a signature by you, your manager, or other person you authorize to sign three-day notices—that the notice is from you. You don't need to date the notice, but it doesn't hurt.

$ Some rent control ordinances require three-day notices to pay rent or quit to contain special warnings. Check Appendix 1 and your ordinance if your property is subject to rent control.

How to Determine the Amount of Rent Due

It's essential that you ask for the correct amount of rent in your three-day notice. That may seem easy, but a demand for an improper amount is the most common defect in a three-day notice. If, at trial, the court finds that the rent due at the time the three-day notice was served was less than the amount demanded in the notice (in other words, the notice overstated the rent), you will lose the lawsuit. (See *Ernst Enterprises, Inc. v. Sun Valley Gasoline, Inc.* (1983) 139 Cal. App. 3d 355 and *Nouratchan v. Miner* (1985) 169 Cal. App. 3d 746.)

To calculate the correct amount, follow these rules.

Rule 1: Never demand anything in a Three-Day Notice to Pay Rent or Quit other than the amount of the past due rent. Do not include late charges, check-bounce or other fees of any kind, interest, utility charges, or anything else, even if a written lease or rental agreement says you're entitled to them.

Does this mean that you cannot legally collect these charges? No. It simply means you can't legally include them in the Three-Day Notice to Pay Rent or Quit or recover them in an unlawful detainer lawsuit. You can

deduct these amounts from the security deposit or sue for them later in small claims court. (See Chapter 20 of *The California Landlord's Law Book: Rights & Responsibilities.*) You can evict a tenant for failure to pay legitimate utility or other nonrent charges, even though you can't recover or ask for those charges in an unlawful detainer lawsuit. (See "Using the Three-Day Notice to Perform Covenant or Quit" in Chapter 4.)

Rule 2: Assuming the rent is due once a month and the tenant simply does not pay the rent for the month, you are entitled to ask for the full month's rent in your notice. The amount of rent due is not based on the date the three-day notice is served, but on the whole rental period. Thus, if rent is due in advance the first of every month, and you serve a three-day notice on the 5th, you should ask for the whole month's rent—that's what's overdue.

Rule 3: If the tenancy is already scheduled to terminate because you have given a 30-day, 60-day, or other notice to that effect, you must prorate the rent due. For example, if the tenant's $900 monthly rent is due June 1, but you gave her a 30-day notice about three weeks earlier, on May 10, the tenancy is terminated effective June 10. Your three-day notice served after June 1 should demand only $300, the rent for June 1 through 10. Because this can get tricky, we don't recommend terminating a tenancy in the middle of the month or other rental period. If you serve a three-day notice after having served a 30-day or 60-day notice, you risk confusing the tenant and losing an unlawful detainer action. (See Chapter 3.)

Rule 4: To arrive at a daily rental amount, always divide the monthly rent by 30 (do this even in 28-, 29-, or 31-day months).

Rule 5: If the tenant has paid part of the rent due, your demand for rent must reflect the partial payment. For example, if the monthly rent is $800 and your tenant has paid $200 of that amount, your three-day notice must demand no more than the $600 balance owed.

Rule 6: You do not have to credit any part of a security deposit (even if you called it last month's rent) toward the amount of rent you ask for in the three-day notice. In other words, you have a right to wait until the tenant has moved, to see if you should apply the deposit to cover any necessary damages or cleaning. (See *Volume 1,* Chapter 5.) Even if you called the money "last month's rent," the tenant is entitled to have this credited—before termination of the tenancy—only if and when he has properly terminated the tenancy with a 30-day or 60-day notice, or has actually moved out.

Here are a few examples of how rent should be calculated for purposes of a three-day notice.

EXAMPLE: Tom has been paying $1,000 rent to Loretta on the first of each month, as provided by a written rental agreement. On October 6, Tom still hasn't paid his rent, and Loretta serves him with a three-day notice to pay the $1,000 or leave. (Loretta has, in effect, given Tom a five-day grace period; she could have given him the notice on October 2.) Even though the rental agreement provides for a $10 late charge after the second day, Loretta should not list that amount in the three-day notice.

EXAMPLE: Teresa's rent of $900 is due the 15th of each month for the period of the 15th through the 14th of the next month. Teresa's check for the period from October 15 through November 14 bounced, but Linda, her landlord, doesn't discover this until November 15. Now Teresa not only refuses to make good on the check, but also refuses to pay the rent due for November 15 through December 14. It's now November 20. Teresa owes Linda $1,800 for the two-month period of October 15–December 14, and that's what the notice should demand. Linda should not add check-bouncing charges or late fees to the amount. And even though Teresa promises to leave "in a few days," rent for the entire period of October 15 through December 14 is already past due, and Linda has the right to demand it.

EXAMPLE: Terri and her landlord, Leo, agree in writing that Terri will move out on July 20. Terri's $900 rent is due the first of each month, in advance for the entire month. Terri will only owe rent for the first 20 days of July, due on the first day of that month. If Terri doesn't pay up on July 1, the three-day notice Leo should serve her shortly thereafter should demand this 20 days' rent, or 1/30th of the monthly rent ($900/30 = $30/day) for each of the 20 days, a total of $600.

EXAMPLE: Tony pays $950 rent on the first of each month under a one-year lease that expires July 31. On June 30, he confirms to his landlord, Lana, that he'll be leaving at the end of July, and he asks her to consider his $1,000 security deposit as the last month's rent for July. Lana has no obligation to let Tony do this, and can serve him a three-day notice demanding July's rent of $950 on July 2, the day after it's due. As a practical matter, however, Lana might be wiser to ask Tony for permission to inspect the property to see if it's in good enough condition to justify the eventual return of the security deposit. If so, there's little to be gained by giving Tony a three-day notice and suing for unpaid rent, since by the time the case gets before a judge, Lana will have to return the security deposit. (This must be done within 21 days after Tony leaves. See *The California Landlord's Law Book: Rights & Responsibilities*, Chapter 20.)

Special Rules for Rent Control Cities

You can't evict a tenant for refusal to pay a rent increase that was illegal under a rent control ordinance, even if the tenant also refuses to pay the part of the rent that is legal under the ordinance.

EXAMPLE: Owsley rents out his Santa Monica two-bedroom apartments for a reasonable $650 per month. After a year of renting to Tina on a month-to-month basis, Owsley gave Tina a notice raising the rent to $750. When Tina refused to pay the increase, Owsley served her with a three-day notice demanding that she pay the additional $100 or move. Unfortunately for Owsley, Santa Monica's rent control board allowed only a 7% increase that year, so that the most Owsley can legally charge is $695. Since the three-day notice demanded more rent than was legally due (under the rent control ordinance), Tina will win any lawsuit based on the three-day notice.

EXAMPLE: Suppose Tina refused to pay any rent at all, in protest of the increase. Tina does owe Owsley the old and legal rent of $650. But since Owsley's three-day notice demanded $750, more rent than was legally due, the notice is defective. Owsley will lose any eviction lawsuit based on this defective notice, even though Tina refuses to pay even the legal portion of the rent, because the three-day notice must precisely demand the correct rent.

A three-day notice is also defective under a rent control ordinance if the landlord at any time collected rents in excess of those allowed under the ordinance and failed to credit the tenant with the overcharges, even though she now charges the correct rent and seeks to evict based only on nonpayment of the legal rent. Since the previously collected excess rents must be credited against unpaid legal rent, any three-day notice that doesn't give the tenant credit for previous overcharges is legally ineffective because it demands too much rent.

EXAMPLE: Lois rented the apartments in her Los Angeles building for $700 a month. In April, she served Taylor with a notice increasing the rent to $800, effective May 1. Taylor paid the increase (without complaint) in May and June. In July, when Taylor was unable to pay any rent at all, Lois learned, after checking with the Rent Adjustment Commission, that the maximum legal rent was $721. She therefore served Taylor with a three-day notice demanding this amount as the rent for July.

After filing an unlawful detainer complaint based on the nonpayment of this amount, Lois lost the case and had to pay Taylor's court costs and attorney's fees. Why? First, since her rent increase notice had demanded an illegally high rent, it was void. The legal rent therefore was still $700. Second, in May and June, Lois collected a total of $200 more than that legal rent, which had to be credited against the $700 Taylor did owe. Taylor therefore owed only $500. Since Lois' three-day notice demanded more than this, it was ineffective.

Some rent control ordinances impose special requirements on rent increase notices. Under state law for month-to-month tenancies, all that's required is a written, notice of 30 days (60 days for a rent increase of 10% or more over 12 months) that clearly states the address of the property and the new rent—see Chapter 14 of *The California Landlord's Law Book: Rights & Responsibilities*. Quite a few rent-controlled cities require rent increase notices to list a justification or itemization of rent increases and other information.

A rent increase notice that fails to comply with all requirements imposed by both state and local law is of no effect. Therefore, any later Three-Day Notice to Pay Rent or Quit based on the tenant's failure to pay the increased amount is void because, by definition, it demands payment of more rent than is legally owed, either by asking for the increased rent or by failing to credit previous "excess" payments. In short, a landlord will lose any eviction lawsuit based on this sort of defective notice.

EXAMPLE: When Opal raised the rent on her Beverly Hills apartment unit from $700 to $775, an increase allowed under that city's rent control ordinance, she thought everything was okay. When she prepared her 60-day rent increase notice, however, she forgot about the part of the ordinance requiring a landlord to justify and itemize the rent increase and state in the notice that her records were open to inspection by the tenant. Opal collected the $775 rent for three months. The next month, when her tenant Renee failed to pay rent, Opal served her with a three-day notice demanding $775. When the case got to court, the judge told Opal her rent increase notice hadn't complied with city requirements and was ineffective, leaving the legal rent at $700. Since Renee had paid the extra $75 for three months, she was entitled to a $225 credit against this amount, so that she owed $475. Since Opal's three-day notice demanded $775, it too was ineffective, and Renee won the eviction lawsuit.

These problems occur most often in cities with "moderate" to "strict" rent control ordinances, which set fixed rents that a landlord cannot legally exceed without board permission. (See *The California Landlord's Law Book: Rights & Responsibilities*, Chapter 4.) To remind you, moderate to strict rent control cities include Berkeley, Santa Monica, Palm Springs, East Palo Alto, Thousand Oaks, West Hollywood, Los Angeles, San Francisco, and Beverly Hills.

These problems are far less likely to occur in cities with "mild" rent control, including Oakland, San Jose, Hayward, and Los Gatos, where if the tenant fails to contest a rent increase, the increase is usually considered legally valid. Even if the tenant does contest the increase in these "mild" cities, the proper legal rent will be quickly decided by a hearing officer, making it less likely the landlord will be caught by surprise later if she has to evict for nonpayment of rent.

The moral of all this is simple: Pay close attention to any rent control ordinance in the city in which your property is located. Ask yourself the following questions:

- Have you owned the premises at all times when the tenant was living there?
- If not, did the previous owner fully comply with your rent control law?
- If so, have you fully complied with the notice requirements for rent increases and charged the correct rent?

If your answer is "no" to either of the last two questions, your tenant may be due a refund before you can evict for nonpayment of rent.

If your answer to these questions is "yes," have you fully complied with all other provisions of the rent control ordinance? If so, you are probably in a position to legally evict the tenant for nonpayment of rent.

Good-Faith Mistakes

Cities that require registration of rents (Berkeley, Santa Monica, East Palo Alto, Los Angeles, Palm Springs, Thousand Oaks, and West Hollywood) must limit the sanctions against landlords who make good-faith mistakes in the calculation of rents. (Civ. Code § 1947.7.)

How to Fill Out a Three-Day Notice

A sample Three-Day Notice to Pay Rent or Quit and instructions for filling it out appear below. A blank tear-out form is included in the forms section in the back of this book. You may tear out the form or use a photocopy. We recommend using a photocopy, because you will probably use this form more than once.

Appendix 3 contains a tear-out Three-Day Notice to Pay Rent or Quit. The CD-ROM that accompanies this book also includes this form. Instructions for using the CD and a list of file names are in Appendix 2.

Sign Pay or Quit Notices Yourself

A pay or quit notice signed by your lawyer may trigger the Fair Debt Collection Practices Act. This Act (15 U.S.C. §§ 1692 and following) governs debt collectors and requires, among other things, that debtors be given 30 days in which to respond to a demand for payment. A federal appellate court in New York has ruled that when an attorney signs a pay or quit notice, he or she is acting as a debt collector. Consequently, the tenant must have 30 days to pay or quit, regardless of the state's three-day provision. (*Romea v. Heiberger* 163 F.3d 111 (2d Cir. 1998).)

Although this ruling applies only to New York landlords, there is no reason why a tenant in California could not bring an identical lawsuit. To date, we are aware of none. To easily protect yourself (or avoid the dubious honor of being the test case), tell your lawyer that you want to sign pay or quit notices yourself.

Step 1: Fill In the Tenant's Name

The first blank is for the name(s) of the tenant(s) to whom the three-day notice is addressed. This normally should include the tenant(s) whose name(s) is (are) listed on a written lease or rental agreement, or with whom you orally entered into a rental agreement, plus the names, if known, of any other adult occupants of the property.

The California Supreme Court has ruled that in order to evict an adult who claims to be a tenant but is not on the lease or rental agreement, the landlord must provide the person with notice of the unlawful detainer action and an opportunity to be heard. This usually means naming the person as a defendant in the suit. For example, if a married couple occupies an apartment but only the husband signed the lease, the landlord must still name both the husband and wife as defendants. Although this rule technically only applies to unlawful detainer complaints (see Chapter 6), not necessarily to the three-day notice, it's still a good idea to follow it here as well and name all adult occupants in the notice. (C.C.P. § 1174.25; *Arrieta v. Mahon* (1982) 31 Cal. 3d 381, 182 Cal. Rptr. 770.)

Step 2: Fill In the Address

The next spaces are for the address of the premises. Include the street address, city and county, and apartment number if your tenant lives in an apartment or condominium unit.

In the unlikely event the unit has no street address, use the legal description of the premises from your deed to the property, along with an ordinary understandable description of where the place is located (for example, "the small log cabin behind the first gas station going north on River Road from Pokeyville"). You can retype the notice to make room for the legal description or staple a separate property description as an attachment to the notice and type "the property described in the attachment to this notice" in place of the address.

Step 3: Fill In the Rent Due

The next space is for the amount of rent due and the dates for which it is due. You must state this figure accurately. (See "How to Determine the Amount of Rent Due," above.)

Step 4. Fill In Payment Information

The next spaces tell the tenant to whom, where, and how to pay the rent, as follows.

Under "RENT IS TO BE PAID TO," check the box next to "the undersigned" if the person who signs the notice (such as the manager or owner) will receive the rent. If someone else will receive the rent, check the box next to "the following" and list the name of that person.

Under "AT THE FOLLOWING ADDRESS," give the address where the rent should be paid (do not list a post office box unless you want the rent to be mailed to one). Give the telephone number of the person who will accept the rent.

Under "IN THE FOLLOWING MANNER," check one or more boxes indicating how the rent will be accepted. If you check "in person," be sure to list the days and hours when someone will be present to accept the rent. For example, the office hours for a resident manager might be "Monday through Friday, 9:00 AM through 5:00 PM." If you check "by mail …" only, rent is legally paid when mailed, regardless of when you receive it.

Do not omit any information on your three-day notice. Failure to include all of the information called for on the form may make the notice legally ineffective. If your tenant refuses to move and you attempt to evict on the basis of a legally defective three-day notice, you'll be tossed out of court and will have to begin all over, with a new three-day notice.

Step 5: Sign and Date the Notice and Make Copies

The "ultimatum" language—that the tenant either pay the rent within three days or move out, or you'll bring legal action—and the "forfeiture" language are already included in our printed form. All you need to add are your signature and the date you signed it. The date is not legally required, but it helps to clarify when the rent was demanded. This date must not be the same day the rent was due, but at least one day later.

Be sure to make several photocopies for your records; the original goes to the tenant. If you serve a notice on more than one tenant (see the next section), you can give the others copies.

Step 6: Complete the Proof of Service Box on Your Copy

At the bottom of the Three-Day Notice to Pay Rent or Quit is a "Proof of Service," which indicates the name of the person served, the manner of service, and the date(s) of service. You or whoever served the notice on the tenant should fill out the Proof of Service on your copy of the three-day notice and sign it. You do not fill out the Proof of Service on the original notice that is given to the tenant. If more than one person is served with the notice, there should be a separate Proof of Service (on a copy of the notice) for each person served. Save the filled-out Proof(s) of Service—you'll need this information when you fill out the Complaint and other eviction forms.

Serving the Three-Day Notice on the Tenant

The law is very strict about when and how the Three-Day Notice to Pay Rent or Quit must be given to ("served on") your tenant(s). Even a slight departure from the rules may cause the loss of your unlawful detainer

Three-Day Notice to Pay Rent or Quit

To: ___Tyrone Tenant_____,

(name)

Tenant(s) in possession of the premises at ___123 Market Street, Apartment 4_____,

(street address)

City of ___San Diego_____, County of ___San Diego_____, California.

Please take notice that the rent on these premises occupied by you, in the amount of $ ___400_____, for the period

from ___June 1, 20xx_____ to ___June 30, 20xx_____, is now due and payable.

YOU ARE HEREBY REQUIRED to pay this amount within THREE (3) days from the date of service on you of this notice or to vacate and surrender possession of the premises. In the event you fail to do so, legal proceedings will be instituted against you to recover possession of the premises, declare the forfeiture of the rental agreement or lease under which you occupy the premises, and recover rents, damages, and costs of suit.

RENT IS TO BE PAID TO:

☒ the undersigned, or

☐ the following person: _____

AT THE FOLLOWING ADDRESS: ___123 Maple Street, La Mesa_____

_____, California, phone: (_619_) _123-4567_____;

IN THE FOLLOWING MANNER:

☒ In person. Usual days and hours for rent collection are: ___3 p.m. to 8 p.m. Monday through Saturday___

☐ by mail to the person and address indicated above

☐ by deposit to account _____ at _____, a financial institution

   located within 5 miles of your rental at , _____ California

☐ by electronic funds transfer procedure previously established.

Date: ___June 5, 20xx_____   *Lou Landlord*_____

Owner/Manager

- -

Proof of Service

I, the undersigned, being at least 18 years of age, served this notice, of which this is a true copy, on _____,

_____, one of the occupants listed above as follows:

☐ On _____, _____, I delivered the notice to the occupant personally.

☐ On _____, _____, I delivered the notice to a person of suitable age and discretion at the
   occupant's residence/business after having attempted personal service at the occupant's residence, and business, if known. On
   _____, _____, I mailed a second copy to the occupant at his or her residence.

☐ On _____, _____, I posted the notice in a conspicuous place on the property, after having
   attempted personal service at the occupant's residence, and business, if known, and after having been unable to find there a
   person of suitable age and discretion. On _____, _____, I mailed a second copy to the occupant
   at the property.

I declare under penalty of perjury under the laws of the State of California that the foregoing is true and correct.

Date: _____   _____

Signature

lawsuit if it is contested. As ever, if your property is covered by a local rent control ordinance, be sure to check for any special requirements, such as mandatory language to be included in the notice, before using the forms in this book.

When to Serve the Notice

The three-day notice can be given to your tenant any day after the rent is due, but not on the day it is due. For example, if the rent is due on the first day of each month, a notice given to the tenant on that day has no legal effect. If the due date falls on a Saturday, Sunday, or holiday, rent is still due on that day, unless your lease or rental agreement specifies that it will be due on the next business day. The three-day notice cannot be given until the day after that.

> **EXAMPLE:** Tyson pays monthly rent, due in advance on the first of each month. If the first falls on a Monday holiday, and since Tyson's lease states that rent is due on the next business day when the date falls on a Saturday, Sunday, or holiday, Tyson's rent is not legally due until Tuesday. This means the three-day notice cannot be served until Wednesday.

This is one of the many technicalities of eviction law that can haunt an unlawful detainer action from the very beginning. Bizarre as it sounds, if you give the notice only a day prematurely, and the tenant still doesn't pay the rent during the two to three weeks he contests the lawsuit, you may still lose the case if the tenant spots your mistake.

> **EXAMPLE:** When Tiffany didn't pay her $400 rent to Leslie on Friday, January 1, Leslie prepared a Three-Day Notice to Pay Rent or Quit, giving it to Tiffany the next day. Unfortunately for Leslie, she forgot that her lease included a clause that specified that when the rent due date falls on a Saturday, Sunday, or holiday, the rent would be due on the next business day. Therefore, the rent wasn't actually due until January 4, even though Tiffany's lease said it was due on the first, because January 1, New Year's Day, was a legal holiday; January 2 was a Saturday; and January 3 was a Sunday. Oblivious to all this, Leslie waited the three days, and, as Tiffany still hadn't paid the rent, Leslie filed her unlawful

detainer suit on January 6. Tiffany contested it, and the case finally went to court on February 5. Even though Tiffany clearly owed Leslie the rent for January and February, Leslie lost the lawsuit because she gave Tiffany the three-day notice before the rent was legally past due. Now Leslie will have to pay Tiffany's court costs as well as her own. Assuming Tiffany has still not paid the rent, Leslie can, of course, serve a new three-day notice and begin the eviction procedure again, poorer but wiser.

In *LaManna v. Vognar* (1993) 4 Cal. App. 4th Supp. 4, 22 Cal. Rptr. 2d 501, a landlord lost a case for the same reason illustrated in the example above. The three-day notice was served on a Wednesday. The third day after that was a Saturday. The tenant had until the end of the following Tuesday to pay the rent because Saturday and Sunday were not business days and Monday was a legal holiday, Memorial Day. The landlord could not legally file the eviction lawsuit until Wednesday. Unfortunately, he filed one day early, on Tuesday, and lost the case as a result.

If You Routinely Accept Late Rent

There is no law that gives tenants a five-day or any other grace period when it comes to paying the rent. If, however, you regularly allow your tenant to pay rent several days or even weeks late, you may have problems evicting the tenant. If your three-day notice demands the rent sooner than the tenant is accustomed to paying it, the tenant might be able to successfully defend an eviction based on that three-day notice.

> **EXAMPLE:** You routinely allowed the tenant to pay by the fifth of the month, even though the rental agreement states that the rent is due on the first. If you now serve a notice on the second or third day of the month, the tenant may be able to convince a judge that you served the notice too early.

This is called an "estoppel defense" in legalese. This means that one person (you) who consistently fails to insist on strict compliance with the terms of an agreement (in this case, prepayment of rent on time) may be prevented or stopped ("estopped") from insisting on strict compliance at a later time.

To avoid problems, wait until after any traditional grace period (that is, one that you've given regularly in the past) has expired before serving the three-day notice. Or, if the tenancy is one from month to month, and the rental agreement requires that rent be paid on the first of the month, you can reinstate the original payment terms with a 30-day written notice. Doing so allows you to insist that rent be paid on the first of the month, regardless of past custom. (See *The California Landlord's Law Book: Rights & Responsibilities*, Chapter 3, for more information on and Sample Notice of Reinstatement of Terms of Tenancy.)

Grace periods. Rent is due on a certain day under many rental agreements (usually on the first of the month), but late charges aren't usually imposed until several days later. Even so, the rent is still "due" on the date the rental agreement or lease says it's due, and the Three-day Notice to Pay Rent or Quit can be served the day after that (taking into account extension of the due date by Saturdays, Sundays, and holidays). Any so-called grace period, after which late charges kick in, has no effect on when the three-day notice can be served.

> EXAMPLE: Under the lease between Tom Tenant and Lisa Landlady, Tom's $900 rent is due on the first day of each month, with a $25 late charge if paid after the 5th. Despite this so-called five-day grace period, the three-day notice can be served on the day after the first of the month, assuming the first doesn't fall on a Saturday, Sunday, or holiday.

Despite the above, it generally isn't a good idea to serve a three-day notice before any late charge comes due, for two reasons: First, if the rental agreement or lease provides for a grace period and you never made a habit of insisting on the rent before the late charge came due, the tenant may be able to successfully defend against the three-day notice if he or she was not accustomed to paying it on time. (See "If You Routinely Accept Late Rent," above.)

Second, it isn't a good business practice to serve a three-day notice right away. It breeds unnecessary tenant resentment and, in effect, gives the tenant a three-day grace period anyway.

Who Should Serve the Three-Day Notice

Anyone at least 18 years old (including you) can legally give the three-day notice to the tenant. It's often best to have it served by someone else. That way, if the tenant refuses to pay the rent and contests the resulting eviction suit by falsely claiming he didn't receive the notice (this is rare), at trial you can present the testimony of someone not a party to the lawsuit who is more likely to be believed by a judge. Of course, you must weigh this advantage against any time, trouble, or expense it takes to get someone else to accomplish the service and, if necessary, appear in court.

Who Should Receive the Notice

Ideally, each person named on the three-day notice should be personally handed a copy of it. This isn't always possible, though, and under certain circumstances it isn't necessary. If you rented your property to just one tenant, whose name alone appears on any written rental agreement or lease, serve that person with the three-day notice. (However, as discussed below in the next section, you can sometimes actually give the notice to a co-occupant of the property who isn't listed on the lease if you can't locate the tenant who is listed on the lease.)

If you rented to two or more tenants whose names are all on the lease or rental agreement, it is legally sufficient to serve just one. *(University of Southern California v. Weiss* (1962) 208 Cal. App. 2d 759, 769, 25 Cal. Rptr. 475.) If your agreement is only with one tenant and that tenant has a roommate who is not on the agreement, the notice should be served on both. (See *Briggs v. Electronic Memories & Magnetics Corp.* (1975) 53 Cal. App. 3d 900.) We recommend doing this to minimize the possibility that a nonserved tenant will try to defend against any subsequent eviction lawsuit on the ground that he didn't receive the notice.

You normally have no obligation to serve the three-day notice on occupants who are not named in the written rental agreement or lease and with whom you've had no dealings in renting the property. (See *Chinese Hospital Foundation Fund v. Patterson* (1969) 1 Cal. App. 3d 627, 632, 8 Cal. Rptr. 795, and *Four Seas Investment Corp. v. International Hotel Tenants Ass'n* (1978) 81 Cal. App. 3d 604.) However, as discussed above, it's best to serve all adult occupants of the premises.

How to Serve the Three-Day Notice on the Tenant

The law is very strict on how the three-day notice must be served on the tenant. It is not enough that you mail the notice or simply post it on the door. There are three legal methods of service for a three-day notice.

Personal Service

The best method of service of a three-day notice is to simply have someone over 18 hand your tenant the notice.

If the tenant refuses to accept the notice, it is sufficient to drop or lay it at his feet. It is unnecessary and possibly illegal to force it on the tenant's person. If the tenant slams the door in your face before you can leave it at her feet, or talks to you through the door while refusing to open it, it's okay to slide it under the door or shout, "I'm leaving a notice on your doormat" while doing so.

Handing the notice to any other person, such as someone who lives with your tenant but is not listed as a cotenant on the written rental agreement, is not sufficient except as described just below under "Substituted Service on Another Person."

Substituted Service on Another Person

If the tenant to whom you're attempting to give the three-day notice never seems to be home, and you know where she is employed, you should try to personally serve her there. If you are unable to locate the tenant at either place, the law allows you to use "substituted service" in lieu of personally giving the notice to the tenant. In order to serve the notice this way, you must:

1. Make at least one attempt to personally serve the tenant at her home, but not succeed and
2. Make one attempt to serve her with the notice at work, but still not succeed, and
3. Leave the notice, preferably with an adult, at the tenant's home or workplace. (Although one California court ruled that a 16-year-old boy (but not a younger child) could be served a three-day notice on behalf of the tenant, the ruling is not binding on all California courts (*Lehr v. Crosby* (1981) 123 Cal. App. 3d Supp.7), and

4. Mail a copy of the notice to the tenant at home by ordinary first-class mail. (C.C.P. § 1162(2).)

Ask for the name of the person with whom you leave the notice; you'll need to include it in the complaint you'll file to begin your lawsuit (Chapter 6). If you can't get a name, you can just put a description of the person.

Accomplishing Substituted Service. Substituted service of the notice is not completed, and the three-day period specified in the notice does not start running, until you have left the copy with the "substitute" person and mailed the second copy to the tenant at home. The first day of the notice's three-day period is the day after both these steps are accomplished.

EXAMPLE: Tad should have paid you his rent on the first of the month. By the fifth, you're ready to serve him with a Three-Day Notice to Pay Rent or Quit. When you try to personally serve it on him at home, a somewhat hostile buddy of Tad's answers the door, saying he's not home. Your next step is to try his workplace—the one listed on the rental application he filled out when he moved in. You go there only to find that Tad called in sick that day. You can give the notice to one of his coworkers or to his friend at home, with instructions to give it to Tad when they see him. After that, you must mail another copy of the notice to Tad at home by ordinary first-class mail. Substituted service is complete only after both steps have been accomplished.

"Posting-and-Mailing" Service

If you can't find the tenant or anyone else at her home or work (or if you don't know where she is employed), you may serve the three-day notice through a procedure known as "posting and mailing" (often referred to as "nail-and-mail"). To serve the notice this way, you must do the following, in the order indicated:

1. Make at least one unsuccessful attempt to personally serve the tenant at home
2. If you know where the tenant works, try unsuccessfully to serve her at work
3. Post a copy of the notice on the tenant's front door, and
4. Mail another copy to the tenant at home by first-class mail. (C.C.P. § 1162(3) and *Hozz v. Lewis* (1989) 215 Cal. App. 3d 314.)

You may want to send the letter by certified mail and save the mailing receipt the Postal Service gives you. You can send it return receipt requested, so you know when the tenant received it; on the other hand, some people routinely refuse to sign for and accept certified mail.

Another way around this problem is to talk to the tenant—before you file an eviction lawsuit—and pin her down as to having received the notice. (Don't ask, "Did you get my three-day notice?" Ask, "When are you going to pay the rent I asked for in the three-day notice I left you?")

> EXAMPLE: Tyler's rent is due on the 15th of each month, but he still hasn't paid Lyle, his landlord, by the 20th. Lyle can seldom find Tyler (or anyone else) at home, and doesn't know where (or if) Tyler works. Since that leaves no one to personally or substitute serve with the three-day notice, Lyle has only the "posting-and-mailing" alternative. Lyle can tape one copy to the door of the property and mail a second copy to Tyler at that address by first-class mail. Lyle should begin counting the three days the day after both of these tasks are accomplished. The three-day period after which Lyle can bring an unlawful detainer lawsuit is counted the same way as if the notice were served personally.

Proof of Service. Be sure the person who serves the three-day notice completes the Proof of Service at the bottom on an extra copy of the notice. (See above.)

After the Three-Day Notice Is Served

Your course of action after the three-day notice is served depends on whether or not the tenant pays the rent in full and whether the tenant stays or leaves.

The Tenant Stays

If the tenant offers the rent in full any time before the end of the three-day period, you must accept it if it's offered in cash, certified check, or money order. If you've routinely accepted rent payments by personal check, you must accept a personal check in response to a three-day notice unless you notified the tenant otherwise in the notice itself. If you refuse to accept the rent (or if you insist on more money than demanded in the notice, such as late charges) and file your lawsuit anyway, your tenant will be able to contest it and win. (The only way to evict a month-to-month tenant who never pays until threatened with a three-day notice is to terminate his tenancy with a 30-day or 60-day notice—see Chapter 3.)

If a properly notified tenant doesn't pay before the notice period passes, the tenancy is terminated. You then have a legal right to the property, which you can enforce by bringing an unlawful detainer action. (See below and Chapter 6.)

⚠ **You do not have to accept rent after the end of the notice period.** In fact, if you do accept rent (even part payments), you reinstate the tenancy and waive your right to evict based on the three-day notice. For example, if on the third day after service of a three-day notice demanding $300 rent you accept $100, along with a promise to pay the remaining $200 "in a few days," you will have to start over again with a three-day notice demanding only the balance of $200, and base your lawsuit on that. If you proceed with the lawsuit based on the three-day notice demanding all the rent, the tenant may be able to successfully defend the lawsuit on the ground that you waived the three-day notice by accepting part of the rent. Of course, you may want the partial payment badly enough to be willing to serve a new notice. In that case, accept it with one hand and serve a three-day notice for the remaining unpaid amount.

The Tenant Moves Out

Once in a great while, a tenant will respond to a Three-Day Notice to Pay Rent or Quit by actually moving out within the three days. If the tenant doesn't pay the rent, but simply moves after receiving the three-day notice, he still owes you a full month's rent since rent is due in advance. The tenant's security deposit may cover all or most of the rent owed. If not, you may decide to sue the tenant in small claims court for the balance.

📖 Nolo's book *Everybody's Guide to Small Claims Court in California*, by Ralph Warner, shows how to sue in small claims court.

What if the tenant simply sneaks out within the three-day period, but doesn't give you the keys or otherwise make it clear he's turning over possession of the property to you? In that case, you can't legally enter and take possession unless you either use a procedure called "abandonment" or file an eviction suit anyway. If you file suit, you must serve the summons and complaint by posting and mailing, as described in "Serving the Papers on the Defendant" in Chapter 6, and obtain a judgment. For more information on the abandonment alternative, and to decide whether it may be suitable under your circumstances, see *The California Landlord's Law Book: Rights & Responsibilities*, Chapter 19.

When to File Your Lawsuit

As we have stressed, you cannot begin your unlawful detainer lawsuit until the three-day notice period expires. The rules for counting the days are as follows:

- Service is complete when you personally serve the three-day notice or, if you serve the notice by "substituted service" or "posting-and-mailing" service, three days after you have both (1) mailed the notice and (2) either given it to another adult or posted it (as described above).

- If you serve more than one tenant with notices, but not all on the same day, start counting only after the last tenant is served.

- Do not count the day of service as the first day. The first day to count is the day after service of the notice was completed.

- Do not file your lawsuit on the third day after service is complete. The tenant must have three full days after service to pay the rent or leave before you file suit.

- If the third day is a business day, you may file your lawsuit on the next business day after that.

- If the third day falls on a Saturday, Sunday, or legal holiday, the tenant has until the end of the next business day to pay the rent. You cannot file your suit on that business day, but must wait until the day after that. (*LaManna v. Vognar* (1993) 4 Cal. App. 4th Supp. 4, 22 Cal. Rptr. 2d 510.)

In the past, some judges (particularly some in Los Angeles County) ruled that if you served your three-day notice by posting-and-mailing or by "substituted service" on another person—both of which involve mailing a second copy to the tenant—you have to wait an extra five days for the tenant to pay or move, before filing suit. Now, however, the law is clear. You do not have to wait an extra five days before filing your complaint. (*Losornio v. Motta* (1998) 67 Cal. App. 4th 110, 78 Cal. Rptr. 2d 799.) You should be prepared to bring this to the attention of the judge during any default hearing or trial if the judge or tenant raises the issue. (See "Getting a Money Judgment for Rent and Costs" in Chapter 7 and "The Trial" in Chapter 8.)

EXAMPLE: Toni failed to pay the rent due on Monday, November 1. On November 11, Les personally served Toni with the three-day notice at home. The first day after service is Friday the 12th, the second day is Saturday the 13th, and the third day is Sunday the 14th. Since third day falls on a Sunday, Toni has until the end of the next business day—Monday the 15th—to pay the rent or leave. Only on the 16th can Les file suit. ∎

Eviction by 30-Day or 60-Day Notice

The second most common basis for unlawful detainer lawsuits (after failure to pay rent) is the tenant's failure to move after receiving a 30-day notice terminating the tenant's month-to-month tenancy.

Overview of the Process

Before you can file an unlawful detainer lawsuit against a tenant, you must legally terminate the tenancy. If the tenant has a month-to-month tenancy, you can use a 30-day notice to terminate the tenancy if the tenant has occupied the rental for less than a year. In most cases, you must give a tenant 60 days' notice if he or she has lived in the property a year or more. (See "30-Day, 60-Day, and 90-Day Notices," below.) Also, a 90-day notice is required to terminate certain government-subsidized tenancies. In most circumstances, you don't have to state a reason for terminating the tenancy. This general rule, however, has some very important exceptions, discussed below.

If the tenant doesn't leave by the end of the 30 (or 60) days, you can file your lawsuit to evict the tenant.

Checklist for 30- or 60-Day Notice Eviction

Below is an overview of steps involved in evicting on the grounds covered in this chapter, assuming that the tenant defaults. We cover some of the subjects (for example, filing a complaint and default judgment) in later chapters. As you work your way through the book, you may want to return to this chart to see where you are in the process.

When a Tenancy May Be Terminated With a 30-Day or 60-Day Notice

There are basically two types of residential tenancies. The first is a "fixed-term" tenancy, where the property is rented to the tenant for a fixed period of time, usually a year or more, and which is normally formalized with a written lease. During this period, the landlord may not raise the rent and may not terminate the tenancy except for cause, such as the tenant's failure to pay the rent or violation of other lease terms. This type of tenancy may not be terminated by a 30- or 60-day notice.

Negotiating With Tenants

If a lease is in effect and for some important reason, such as your need to sell or demolish the building, you want the tenants out, you might try to negotiate with them. For example, offer them a month or two of free or reduced rent if they'll move out before their lease expires. Of course, any agreement you reach should be put in writing.

The second type of tenancy is a "periodic tenancy," a tenancy for an unspecified time in which the rent is paid every "period"—month, week, every other week, and so on. A "periodic tenancy" that goes from month to month may be terminated with a 30-day notice (subject to the two restrictions introduced earlier). If the rental period is shorter than one month, the notice period can be shorter, too. The point is that the notice must only be as long as the rental period.

Because the overwhelming majority of residential tenancies are month to month, we assume 30 or 60 days is the correct notice period for terminating a periodic tenancy using the procedures in this chapter.

How do you tell if your tenancy is month to month? If you have been accepting monthly rent from your tenant without a written agreement or if you have a written rental agreement that either is noncommittal about a fixed term or specifically provides for 30 days' notice to terminate the tenancy, the tenancy is from month to month. It is also a month-to-month tenancy if you (or the owner from whom you purchased the property) continued to accept rent on a monthly basis from a tenant whose lease had expired.

Impermissible Reasons to Evict

A landlord can evict a tenant without a reason, but not for the wrong reason. This means you can't evict a tenant:

- because of race, marital status, religion, sex, having children, national origin, or age (Unruh Civil Rights Act, Civ. Code §§ 51–53)
- if the tenant exercised the "repair-and-deduct" remedy (by deducting the cost of habitability-related repairs from the rent) within the past six

Checklist for 30- or 60-Day Notice Eviction

Step	Earliest Time to Do It
☐ 1. Prepare and serve the 30- or 60-day notice on the tenant.	Any time. Immediately after receipt of rent is best.
☐ 2. Prepare the Summons (or Summonses, if there is more than one tenant) and Complaint and make copies. (Chapter 6)	The 30th or 60th day after service of the 30-day or 60-day notice is complete.
☐ 3. File the Complaint at the courthouse and have the Summons(es) issued. (Chapter 6)	The first day after the notice period expires.
☐ 4. Have the sheriff, the marshal, or a friend serve the Summons and Complaint. (Chapter 6)	As soon as possible after filing the Complaint and having the Summons(es) issued.
☐ 5. Prepare Request for Entry of Default, Judgment, Declaration, and Writ of Possession. (Chapter 7)	While you're waiting for five-day (or 15-day, if Complaint not personally served) response time to pass.
☐ 6. Call the court to find out whether or not tenant(s) have filed written response.	Just before closing on the fifth day after service of Summons, or early on the sixth day. (Do not count holidays that fall on weekdays, however. Also, if fifth day after service falls on weekend or holiday, count the first business day after that as the fifth day.)
☐ 7. Mail copy of Request for Entry of Default to tenant(s), file original at courthouse. Also file Declaration and Proof of Service, and have clerk issue Judgment and Writ for Possession for the property. (Chapter 7)	Sixth day after service of Summons and Complaint. (Again, count first business day after fifth day that falls on weekend or holiday.)
☐ 8. Prepare letter of instruction for, and give writ and copies to, sheriff or marshal. (Chapter 7)	As soon as possible after above step. Sheriff or marshal won't evict for at least five days after posting notice.
☐ 9. Change locks after tenant vacates.	As soon as possible.
For Money Judgment	
☐ 10. Prepare Request for Entry of Default, Judgment, and, if allowed by local rule, Declaration in Lieu of Testimony. (Chapter 7)	As soon as possible after property is vacant.
☐ 11. Mail Request for Entry of Default copy to tenant, file request at courthouse. If Declaration in Lieu of Testimony allowed, file that too, and give clerk judgment and writ forms for money part of judgment. If testimony required, ask clerk for default hearing. (Chapter 7)	As soon as possible after above.
☐ 12. If testimony required, attend default hearing before judge, testify, and turn in your judgment form for entry of money judgment. (Chapter 7)	When scheduled by court clerk.
☐ 13. Apply security deposit to cleaning and repair of property, and to any rent not accounted for in judgment, then apply balance to judgment amount. Notify tenant in writing of deductions, keeping a copy. Refund any balance remaining. If deposit does not cover entire judgment, collect balance of judgment. (Chapter 9)	As soon as possible after default hearing. Deposit must be accounted for within three weeks of when the tenants vacate.

months, unless the notice states a valid reason for terminating the tenancy

- because he complained about the premises to local authorities, exercised rights given to tenants by law, or engaged in behavior protected by the First Amendment—for example, organizing other tenants. (See *The California Landlord's Law Book: Rights & Responsibilities*, Chapter 15.)

If you evict for an illegal reason, or if it looks like you are trying to, your tenant can defend the unlawful detainer lawsuit or sue you later for damages. Generally, if any of the elements listed below are present, you should think twice about evicting with a 30-day or 60-day notice that doesn't state a valid reason. Even though you state a valid reason, the tenant can still sue if she believes the eviction was illegally motivated. Conversely, even if you state no reason, your eviction will be upheld if you prevail over the tenant's defense. The main reason to state a valid reason (except in rent control areas where the reason must be stated) is to convince the tenant not to be paranoid.

Think twice about evicting with such a notice and without a valid business reason when any of the following are true:

- The tenant is a member of a racial, ethnic, or religious minority group.
- The tenant is gay.
- The tenant has children and your other tenants don't.
- The tenant has recently (say within a year) complained to the authorities about the premises.
- The tenant has recently (within six months) lawfully withheld rent.
- The tenant has organized a tenants' union.
- The tenant is handicapped.
- The tenant is elderly.
- The tenant receives public assistance.

If none of these factors is present (and the premises are not covered by a rent control ordinance or rented under a government-subsidized program), you will probably have no problem using a 30-day or 60-day notice, without specifying a reason, to terminate a tenancy.

Federal Housing Programs

"Section 8" refers to Section 8 of the United States Housing Act of 1937 (42 U.S.C. § 1437f), and "Section 236" refers to Section 236 of the National Housing Act of 1949 (12 U.S.C. § 1517z-1). Both are federal laws providing government housing assistance to low-income families. For additional information about the more stringent requirements for eviction from government-subsidized rentals, see Civ. Code § 1954.535 and the following cases: *Appel v. Beyer* (1974) 39 Cal. App. 3d Supp. 7; *Gallman v. Pierce* (1986, N.D. Cal.) 639 F. Supp. 472; *Mitchell v. Poole* (1988) 203 Cal. App. 3d Supp. 1; *Gersten Companies v. Deloney* (1989) 212 Cal. App. 3d 1119; and 24 C.F.R. §§ 450 and following, §§ 882 and following.

30-Day, 60-Day, and 90-Day Notices

To terminate a month-to-month tenancy, you must give written notice to the tenant. You need give only 30 days' notice if your tenant has occupied the property for less than a year, 60 days' notice if the tenant has been in the property a year or more, and 90 days' notice for certain government-subsidized tenancies. Regardless of which notice is required, you must comply with any just-cause eviction provisions of any applicable rent control ordinances—which usually includes listing the reason for the termination of tenancy.

30-Day Notice for Tenancies of Less Than a Year

If your tenant has occupied your property for less than a year, you must give him 30 days' notice to terminate a residential month-to-month tenancy. (Civ. Code § 1946.1(c).) This is true even for tenancies of shorter periodic length, such as tenancies from week to week. (However, the *tenant* need give only a week's notice to terminate a week-to-week tenancy, and so forth.) Of course, you can give the tenant *more* than 30 days' notice if you want to. The requirement is that you give at least 30 days' written notice.

⚠ **Landlords cannot reduce their notice period to less than 30 days.** Although agreements reducing the landlord's notice period to as few as seven days were previously legal under Civ. Code § 1946, termination of residential tenancies, as opposed to commercial ones, is now governed by the newer Section 1946.1, which does not refer to the possibility of such a reduced notice period. We believe Civ. Code § 1946, with its language allowing the parties to agree in writing to a shorter notice period, no longer applies to residential tenancies.

One final word of caution: The "less than a year" requirement refers to how long the tenant has actually lived in the property, not the length of the most recent lease term. For example, if your tenant has lived in your rental house for the past year and a half, but signed a new six-month lease eight months ago (so that the lease expired and the tenancy is now month to month), you must give 60 days' notice. (See Section 2, below.) In other words, you start counting as of the date the tenant started living in the unit, not when you both signed the most recent lease or rental agreement.

60-Day Notices for Tenancies of a Year or More

If your tenant has occupied the premises for a year or more, you must deliver a 60-day notice to terminate a month-to-month tenancy. (Civ. Code § 1946.1.) Again, this is true even for periodic tenancies of shorter duration, such as week to week, and regardless of any provision in your rental agreement that specifies a shorter notice period.

This 60-day notice requirement does not work both ways. A month-to-month residential tenant who has occupied your property for a year or more does not have to give you 60 days' notice. The tenant need give you only 30 days' notice to terminate the tenancy.

If you give your tenant a 60-day notice, the tenant has the right to give *you* a written 30-day (or more) notice, which (as long as it's less than your 60-day notice) will terminate the tenancy sooner than the expiration of the 60-day notice that you delivered.

EXAMPLE: Lois Landlord has rented to Terri Tenant for over a year. On March 1, Lois serves Terri with a 60-day notice, terminating her tenancy effective April 29. Terri, however, quickly finds a new place and now wants to leave sooner than that. So, on March 10, she gives Lois a written 30-day notice, which terminates her tenancy on April 9. Assuming she vacates on or before that date, she won't be responsible for any rent past April 9.

There is one extremely narrow exception to the rule that a landlord must give a tenant 60 days' notice of termination of a month-to-month tenancy, where the tenant has lived in the property a year or more. This is where the landlord is in the process of selling the property to an individual who is going to live in it. Even if the tenant has occupied the property for a year or more, the landlord can terminate the tenant's month-to-month tenancy with a 30-day notice if all the following are true:

- The property is a single-family home or condominium unit (as opposed to an apartment unit).
- You are selling the property to an actual ("bona fide") purchaser (as opposed to transferring it to a relative for less than fair market price, for example).
- The buyer is an individual (not a corporation, partnership, or LLC) who intends to occupy the property for a year.
- You and the buyer have opened an escrow for the sale to be consummated.
- You give the 30-day notice within 120 days of opening the escrow.
- You have never previously invoked this exception, with respect to this property.

Unless all the above things are true, you must give the tenant at least 60 days' written notice to terminate a month-to-month or other periodic tenancy, if the tenant has occupied the property for a year or more.

90-Day Notices to Terminate Government-Subsidized Tenancies

If you receive rent or other subsidies from federal, state, or local governments, you may evict only for certain reasons. Acceptable reasons for termination are usually listed in the form lease drafted by the agency or in the agency's regulations. If your tenants receive assistance from a local housing authority under a "Section 8" or other similar program of a federal, state, or local agency, you must very specifically state the reasons for termination in the 90-day notice, *not* a 30-day or 60-day notice, saying what acts the tenant did, and when, that violated the lease or otherwise constitute good cause for eviction. (Civ. Code § 1953.545; *Wasatch Property Management v. Del Grate*, 35 Cal. 4th 1111 (2005).) Allowable reasons for eviction are contained in the standard form leases the housing authority requires the landlord to use.

If you decide to terminate a Section 8 tenant because you no longer wish to participate in the program, simply say so on the termination form. Keep in mind, however, that you cannot terminate for this reason until that tenant's initial rental term has elapsed. In addition, during the 90-day period prior to termination, you cannot increase the rent or otherwise require any subsidized tenant to pay more than he or she paid under the subsidy.

Rent Control and Just Cause Eviction Ordinances

"Just cause" requirements for evictions severely limit the reasons for which landlords can evict tenants. Landlords are authorized to terminate a month-to-month tenancy only for the reasons specifically listed in the particular ordinance. Most just cause provisions also require that the reason be clearly and specifically stated on the notice (see below) as well as in a subsequent unlawful detainer complaint.

Cities That Require Just Cause for Eviction

Berkeley	Hayward	San Francisco
Beverly Hills	Los Angeles	Santa Monica
East Palo Alto	Oakland	Thousand Oaks
Glendale	San Diego	West Hollywood
	(2+ years' tenancy)	

If your property is in a city that requires just cause, the usual rules for 30- or 60-day notice evictions simply do not apply. Even if an eviction is authorized under state law, a stricter local rent control ordinance may forbid it. For example, San Francisco's rent control ordinance, which does not permit eviction of a tenant solely on the basis of a change in ownership, has been held to prevail over state law, which allows eviction for this reason if the tenancy is month to month. (*Gross v. Superior Court* (1985) 171 Cal. App. 3d 265.)

> **EXAMPLE:** You wish to terminate the month-to-month tenancy of a tenant who won't let you in the premises to make repairs, even though you have given reasonable notice (all ordinances consider this a just cause for eviction). You must give the tenant a 30-day (or 60-day) notice that complies with state law and that also states in detail the reason for the termination, listing specifics, such as dates the tenant refused to allow you in on reasonable notice. If the tenant refuses to leave and you bring an unlawful detainer suit, the complaint must also state the reason for eviction (this is usually done by referring to an attached copy of the 30-day or 60-day notice). If the tenant contests the lawsuit, you must prove at trial that the tenant repeatedly refused you access, as stated in the notice.

Before you start an eviction by giving a 30-day or 60-day notice, you should check Appendix 1, which lists the just cause requirements of each city with rent control, and a current copy of your ordinance. (For a more thorough discussion of rent control, see *The California Landlord's Law Book: Rights & Responsibilities*, Chapter 4.) Do this carefully. If you are confused, talk to your local landlords' association or an attorney in your area who regularly practices in this field.

Although cities' ordinances differ in detail, the basic reasons that constitute "just cause" are pretty much the same in all of them. Most rent control ordinances allow the following justifications for terminating a month-to-month tenancy with a 30-day or 60-day notice.

Just Cause Protection in San Diego and Glendale

Two non-rent-control California cities—San Diego and Glendale—require a landlord in certain cases to have "just cause" to terminate a tenancy, even one from month-to-month. In your termination notice, you must state which reason justifies your actions.

San Diego. San Diego's just-cause-eviction rules apply only where the tenant has lived in the property for two years. (San Diego Municipal Code §§ 98.0701 through 98.0760.) With such tenants, the landlord may terminate the tenancy only for the following reasons:

- Nonpayment of rent, violation of "a lawful and material obligation or covenant of the tenancy," commission of a nuisance, or illegal use of the premises. These grounds duplicate those in state law. You may use the three-day notice to pay rent or quit, notice to cure covenant or quit, or unconditional notice to quit (nuisance or illegal use) in the forms appendix in this book when terminating such tenancies.

- Refusal to give the landlord reasonable access to the rental unit for the purpose of making repairs or improvements, or for the purpose of inspection as permitted or required by the lease or by law, or for the purpose of showing the rental unit to a prospective purchaser or mortgagee. If the lease or rental agreement has a clause requiring the tenant to allow access, you may use a three-day notice to cure the covenant or quit. If the tenancy is month to month, you may also choose an unconditional 60-day notice of termination.

- Refusal "after written request of a landlord" to sign a lease renewal "for a further term of like duration with similar provisions."

- To make necessary repairs or construction when removing the tenant is reasonably necessary to do the job, provided the landlord has obtained all necessary permits from the city.

- When the landlord intends to withdraw all rental units in all buildings or structures on a parcel of land from the rental market, or when the landlord, a spouse, parent, grandparent, brother, sister, child, grandchild, or a resident manager plans to occupy the rental unit. These grounds may be used only if the tenancy is month to month (under state law, you must give 60 days' written notice).

Glendale. Glendale's just-cause-eviction rules (Glendale Municipal Code §§ 9.30.010 through 9.30.100) allow eviction in the following situations (all termination notices must be in writing and state the landlord's reasons for terminating):

- Nonpayment of rent, breach of a "lawful obligation or covenant," nuisance, or illegal use of the premises or permitting any illegal use within 1,000 feet of the unit. "Illegal use" specifically includes all offenses involving illegal drugs, such as marijuana (without a doctor's prescription). In these situations, you may use a three-day notice.

- When an unauthorized subtenant not approved by the landlord is in possession at the end of a lease term.

- When a tenant refuses to allow the landlord access "as permitted or required by the lease or by law." If the lease or rental agreement has a clause requiring the tenant to allow access, you might use a three-day notice to cure covenant or quit, or an unconditional 60-day notice of termination of tenancy if the tenancy is month-to-month.

- When the landlord offers a lease renewal of at least one year, serves a notice on the tenant of the offer at least 90 days before the current lease expires, and the tenant fails to accept within 30 days.

- When the landlord plans to demolish the unit or perform work on it that costs at least eight times the monthly rent, and the tenant's absence is necessary for the repairs; or when the landlord is removing the property from the rental market, or seeks to have a spouse, grandparent, brother, sister, in-law, child, or resident manager (if there is no alternate unit available) move into the unit. Under state law, these grounds may be used only if the tenancy is month-to-month, and 30 or 60 days' written notice is given. The landlord must pay the tenant relocation expenses of two months' rent for a comparable unit plus $1,000.

Don't Get Tripped Up by Rent Control Violations

Any violation of a rent control ordinance by you can be used by a tenant to avoid eviction—even if the part of the ordinance you violated has nothing to do with the basis for eviction. For example, in many "strict" rent control cities, as well as in Los Angeles, where ordinances require landlords to register their properties with rent boards, a landlord who fails to register all the properties in a particular building cannot evict any tenant in any of the units for any reason—even if that particular unit is registered. In these cities, a tenant could be months behind in the rent and destroying his apartment, but the landlord would be legally unable to evict because he hadn't registered some other apartment in the same building with the rent board.

Similarly, a landlord's minor violation, such as failing to keep a tenant's security deposit in a separate account (if required), can be used by a tenant to defend an eviction based on the tenant's repeated loud parties. Problems of this sort can be avoided if you comply with every aspect of your city's ordinance.

Nonpayment of Rent

Although you can use a 30-day or 60-day notice to evict a tenant who doesn't pay the rent, you should almost always use a three-day notice (see Chapter 2) instead. A longer notice will delay the eviction, and you can't sue for back rent in your unlawful detainer action. (*Saberi v. Bakhtiari* (1985) 169 Cal. App. 3d 509, 215 Cal. Rptr. 359.) It is, however, arguable that if you use a longer notice based on nonpayment of rent, you deprive the tenant of her right to a conditional notice that gives her the chance to stay if she pays the rent. Although the long notice gives more time, it's unconditional, unlike a three-day notice to pay rent or quit.

Refusal to Allow Access

If, following receipt of a written warning from you, the tenant continues to refuse you or your agent access to the property (assuming you give the tenant reasonable notice of your need to enter—see *The California Land-lord's Law Book: Rights & Responsibilities*, Chapter 13) to show it to prospective buyers or to repair or maintain it, you may evict the tenant.

Most ordinances require that tenants be given a written warning before their tenancy is terminated by notice. Thus, if the tenant refuses you entry, you should serve, at least three days before you give the tenant a 30-day or 60-day notice, a written demand that the tenant grant access. Check your ordinance to make sure you comply with its requirements for such a notice. Before you begin an eviction on this ground, you should answer "yes" to all the following questions:

- Was your request to enter based on one of the reasons allowed by statute, such as to make repairs or show the property? (See *The California Landlord's Law Book: Rights & Responsibilities*, Chapter 13, for more on this.)
- Did you give your tenant adequate time to comply with the notice?
- Did you send a final notice setting out the tenant's failure to allow access and clearly stating your intent to evict if access was not granted?

You should use a 30-day or 60-day notice to evict on this ground, if the tenancy is month to month. If the tenant rents under a lease, you can use only a three-day notice to evict, and then only if the lease has a clause specifically requiring the tenant to give you access to the property.

Relatives

A landlord who wants the premises to live in herself (or for her spouse, parent, or child) may use a 30-day or 60-day notice to ask the existing tenants to leave, provided the tenancy is month to month.

Some ordinances also allow landlords to evict tenants so that other relatives of the landlord (such as step-children, grandchildren, grandparents, or siblings) may move in. Because some landlords have abused this reason for eviction—for example, by falsely claiming that a relative is moving in—most cities strictly limit this option by requiring the termination notice to include detailed information, such as the name, current address, and phone number of the relative who will be moving in.

In addition, severe rent control cities forbid the use of this ground if there are comparable vacant units in the building into which the landlord or relative could move. Some cities allow only one unit per building to be occupied this way, and most cities do not allow nonindividual landlords (corporations or partnerships) or persons with less than a 50% interest in the building to use this reason. Los Angeles, West Hollywood, and a few other cities go so far as to require landlords evicting for this reason to compensate the tenant who must move out. (See Appendix 1.)

Finally, rent control ordinances and state law ordinances now provide for heavy penalties against landlords who use a phony-relative ploy. State law requires that in rent control cities that mandate registration, landlords who evict tenants on the basis of wanting to move a relative (or the landlord) into the property must have their relative actually live there for six continuous months. (Civ. Code § 1947.10.) Individual cities may require a longer stay (San Francisco specifies 36 months). If this doesn't happen, the tenant can sue the landlord in court for actual and punitive damages caused by the eviction.

If a court determines that the landlord or relative never intended to stay in the unit, the tenant can move back in. The court can also award the tenant three times the increase in rent she paid while living somewhere else and three times the cost of moving back in. If the tenant decides not to move back into the old unit, the court can award her three times the amount of one month's rent of the old unit and three times the costs she incurred moving out of it. The tenant can also recover attorney fees and costs. (Civ. Code § 1947.10.) A court awarded one San Francisco tenant $200,000 for a wrongful eviction based on a phony-relative ploy. (*Beeman v. Burling* (1990) 216 Cal. App. 3d 1586, 265 Cal. Rptr. 719.)

If you are planning to evict on the ground of renting the premises to a family member, you should answer "yes" to all the following questions:

- Are you an "owner" as that term is described in your ordinance for the purpose of defining who has the right to possession?
- If a relative is moving in, does he qualify under the ordinance?
- Will the person remain on the premises long enough to preclude a later action against you by the tenant?
- Does your notice provide the specific information required by the ordinance?

- Are you prepared to pay the tenant compensation, if required by your local ordinance?

Remodeling

A landlord who wants possession of the property to conduct remodeling or extensive repairs can use a 30-day or 60-day notice to evict tenants in some circumstances if the tenancy is month to month. Because of the ease with which this ground for eviction can be abused, most cities severely limit its use. For instance, the Los Angeles ordinance requires that at least $10,000 or more per unit (depending on the size of the property) be spent on the repairs or remodeling before eviction on this ground is allowed, and some ordinances (for example, those in Berkeley and Santa Monica) allow this ground only where the repairs are designed to correct local health or building code violations. In some cities, the landlord, once the repairs are made, must give the evicted tenant the right of "first refusal" to re-rent the property. All cities with just cause eviction provisions require that the landlord obtain all necessary building and other permits before eviction. Finally, most cities allow the tenant to sue the landlord for wrongful eviction if the work isn't accomplished within a reasonable time (usually six months) after the tenant leaves.

If you plan to evict using this ground, you should answer "yes" to all the following questions:

- Is the remodeling really so extensive that it requires the tenant to vacate the property?
- Have you obtained all necessary permits from the city?
- Are you prepared to pay the tenant compensation if required by ordinance?
- Have you made all necessary arrangements with financing institutions, contractors, and so on, in order to make sure the work will be finished within the period required by the ordinance?
- Have you met all other requirements of your local ordinance, such as giving proper notice to the tenant, offering the tenant the right to relocate into any vacant comparable unit, or giving the tenant the opportunity to move back in once the apartment is remodeled?

Condominium Conversion or Demolition

A landlord may evict to permanently remove the property from the rental market by means of condominium conversion or "good faith" demolition (not motivated by the existence of the rent control ordinance). But the notice of termination (which must specify the reason) is only the last step in a very complicated process. (In addition, the tenancy must be month to month.) All cities allow this ground to be used only after the landlord has obtained all the necessary permits and approvals. Most cities have very stringent condominium-conversion or antidemolition ordinances that require all sorts of preliminary notices to tenants. A state statute, the Ellis Act, allows this ground for eviction, but cities can (and do) restrict application of the law, including requiring notice periods of more than 30 or even 60 days—in some cases, as much as 120 days or even a year. In recent years, the legislature has considered bills that would affect the removal of residential rental property from the market. (One proposal would limit the landlord's right to demolish residential rental property occupied by low-income tenants; another would limit the ability of individual cities to impose restrictions on condominium conversions.) Be sure to check for new legislation, on the state and local levels, if your eviction is a first step toward hoped-for condominium conversion.

Violation of Rental Agreement

If the tenant violates a significant provision of the rental agreement, you can use a 30-day or 60-day notice to initiate an eviction if the tenancy is month to month. This ground also justifies evicting with a three-day notice, but if one is used, the tenant must, in some cases, be given the opportunity to correct the violation. (See Chapter 4.) As a general rule, however, you should use a 30-day or 60-day notice if the tenancy is month to month. (See below.)

$ Violation of New Terms. Some cities prohibit eviction for violation of a rental agreement provision that was added to the original rental agreement, either by means of a notice of change in terms of tenancy or by virtue of a new rental agreement signed after the original one expired.

Even in places without rent control, judges are reluctant to evict based on breaches other than nonpayment of rent. First, the breach must be considered "substantial"—that is, very serious. Second, you should be able to prove the violation with convincing testimony from a fairly impartial person, such as a tenant in the same building who is willing to testify in court. If you're unable to produce any witnesses who saw (or heard) the violation, or who heard the tenant admit to it, forget it.

Before you begin an eviction on this ground, you should answer "yes" to the following questions:

- Was the violated provision part of the original rental agreement?
- If the provision was added later, does your ordinance allow eviction on this ground?
- Can you definitely prove the violation?
- Was the violated provision legal under state law and the ordinance? (See *The California Landlord's Law Book: Rights & Responsibilities*, Chapter 2.)

Damage to the Premises

If the tenant is disturbing other tenants or seriously damaging the property, you can use a 30-day or 60-day notice to initiate an eviction procedure. Under state law, a three-day notice to quit that doesn't give the tenant the option of correcting the problem may also be used. Some rent control cities (Berkeley, East Palo Alto, and Hayward) require that a landlord give the tenant a chance to correct the violation. (See Chapter 4.)

Illegal Activity on the Premises

If the tenant has committed (or, in some cities, been convicted of) serious illegal activity on the premises, a landlord may initiate an eviction by using a 30-day or 60-day notice if the tenancy is month to month. This ground also justifies using a three-day notice, but you should use the longer one if possible. (See Chapter 4.) You should document the illegal activity thoroughly (see Chapter 4), keeping a record of your complaints to police and the names of the persons with whom you spoke. And although not required by ordinance, it's often a good idea to first give the tenant written notice to cease the illegal activity. If he fails to do so, the fact that you gave notice should help establish that there's a serious and continuing problem.

⚠ **Drug-Dealing Tenants.** As stated earlier, it is essential to do everything you can to evict any tenant who you strongly suspect is dealing illegal drugs on the property. A landlord who ignores this sort of problem can face severe liability.

Should You Use a Three-Day, 30-Day, or 60-Day Notice?

As we have pointed out, some reasons for eviction under a 30-day or 60-day notice, such as making too much noise or damaging the property, also justify evicting with a three-day notice, as described in Chapter 4. If you can evict a tenant by using a three-day notice, why give the tenant a break by using a 30-day or 60-day notice? Simply because a tenant is more likely to contest an eviction lawsuit that accuses her of misconduct and gives her a lot less time to look for another place to live. In places where you don't have to show just cause to give a 30-day or 60-day notice, you also avoid having to prove your reason for evicting (unless you must overcome a tenant's defense based on your supposed retaliation or discrimination).

Finally, if you base the three-day notice on trivial violations, such as a tenant's having a goldfish or parakeet contrary to a no-pets clause in the rental agreement, but you really want her out because she can't get along with you, the manager, or other tenants, you are likely to lose your unlawful detainer suit. Judges are not eager to let a tenant be evicted, with only three days' notice, for a minor breach of the rental agreement or causing an insignificant nuisance or damage. If, on the other hand, you use a 30-day or 60-day notice and rent in an area that does not require just cause to evict, you don't have to state a reason. In other words, by following this approach, you have one less significant problem to deal with.

On the other hand, if your tenant has an unexpired fixed-term lease, you cannot use an unconditional 30-day or 60-day notice to evict. You then can only evict if the tenant violates the lease; in that case, the three-day notice must usually give the tenant the option of correcting the violation and staying in the premises.

Finally, you should use a three-day notice if your reason for evicting a month-to-month tenant is nonpayment of rent (and you want the rent). That's because you won't be able to sue for back rent in an unlawful detainer lawsuit based on a 30-day or 60-day notice (you'll have to bring a separate, small claims court suit to get the rent). Unless you are prepared to go to two courts (or want to forgo the back rent in favor of not having to prove a reason for the termination), you'll need to use a three-day notice. (*Saberi v. Bakhtiari,* (1985) 169 Cal. App. 3d 509, 215 Cal. Rptr. 359.)

Preparing the 30-Day or 60-Day Notice

A sample Notice of Termination of Tenancy, with instructions, appears below. As you can see, filling in the notice requires little more than setting out the name of the tenant, the address of the property, the date, and your signature.

List the names of all adult occupants of the premises, even if their names aren't on the rental agreement.

💿 Blank, tear-out versions of the Notice of Termination of Tenancy are in Appendix 3. The CD-ROM also includes these forms. Instructions for using the CD are in Appendix 2.

💲 As mentioned above, some rent control ordinances that require just cause for eviction require special additions to 30-day or 60-day notices. For example, San Francisco's ordinance requires that every notice on which an eviction lawsuit is based tell the tenant that she may obtain assistance from that city's rent control board. Also, San Francisco's Rent Board regulations require that the 30-day notice quote the Section that authorizes evictions for the particular reason listed.

In addition, many rent control ordinances require that the reason for eviction be stated specifically in the notice (state law doesn't require any statement of a reason). For example, under most just cause provisions, a notice based on the tenant's repeated refusal to allow the landlord access to the property on reasonable notice must state at least the dates and times of the refusals. And for terminations based on wanting to move in a relative or remodel the property, extra notice requirements are specified in detail in the ordinance or in regulations adopted by the rent control board. Check Appendix 1 for general information, and be sure to get a current copy of your rent control ordinance and follow it carefully.

30-Day Notice of Termination of Tenancy

(Tenancy Less Than One Year)

To: _____ **fill in tenant's name(s)** _____,
                        (name)

Tenant(s) in possession of the premises at _____ **list street address, including apartment number** _____,
                                        (street address)

City of _____, County of _____, California.

YOU ARE HEREBY NOTIFIED that effective 30 DAYS from the date of service on you of this notice, the periodic tenancy by which you hold possession of the premises is terminated, at which time you are required to vacate and surrender possession of the premises. If you fail to do so, legal proceedings will be instituted against you to recover possession of the premises, damages, and costs of suit.

if you are in a rent control city or are otherwise required by law to state a reason for terminating a tenancy, insert it here

_____

_____

_____

_____

_____

_____

Date: _____ **date of notice** _____   _____ **owner's or manager's signature** _____
                                       Owner/Manager

the instructions for completing the Proof of Service are the same as those described under the Three-Day Notice to Pay Rent or Quit (Chapter 2) with one exception—service by certified mail may be used

Proof of Service

I, the undersigned, being at least 18 years of age, served this notice, of which this is a true copy, on _____, _____, one of the occupants listed above as follows:

☐ On _____, _____, I delivered the notice to the occupant personally.

☐ On _____, _____, I delivered the notice to a person of suitable age and discretion at the occupant's residence/business after having attempted personal service at the occupant's residence, and business, if known. On _____, _____, I mailed a second copy to the occupant at his or her residence.

☐ On _____, _____, I posted the notice in a conspicuous place on the property, after having attempted personal service at the occupant's residence, and business, if known, and after having been unable to find there a person of suitable age and discretion. On _____, _____, I mailed a second copy to the occupant at the property.

I declare under penalty of perjury under the laws of the State of California that the foregoing is true and correct.

Date: _____   _____
                                    Signature

30-Day Notice of Termination of Tenancy

(Tenancy Less Than One Year)

To: _____Rhoda D. Renter_____ ,
(name)

Tenant(s) in possession of the premises at _____950 Parker Street_____ ,
(street address)

City of _____Palo Alto_____ , County of _____Santa Clara_____ , California.

YOU ARE HEREBY NOTIFIED that effective 30 DAYS from the date of service on you of this notice, the periodic tenancy by which you hold possession of the premises is terminated, at which time you are required to vacate and surrender possession of the premises. If you fail to do so, legal proceedings will be instituted against you to recover possession of the premises, damages, and costs of suit.

_____

_____

_____

_____

_____

_____

_____

Date: _____August 3, 20xx_____   *Lani Landlord*_____
                                                   Owner/Manager

- -

Proof of Service

I, the undersigned, being at least 18 years of age, served this notice, of which this is a true copy, on _____ , _____ , one of the occupants listed above as follows:

☐ On _____ , _____ , I delivered the notice to the occupant personally.

☐ On _____ , _____ , I delivered the notice to a person of suitable age and discretion at the occupant's residence/business after having attempted personal service at the occupant's residence, and business, if known. On _____ , _____ , I mailed a second copy to the occupant at his or her residence.

☐ On _____ , _____ , I posted the notice in a conspicuous place on the property, after having attempted personal service at the occupant's residence, and business, if known, and after having been unable to find there a person of suitable age and discretion. On _____ , _____ , I mailed a second copy to the occupant at the property.

I declare under penalty of perjury under the laws of the State of California that the foregoing is true and correct.

Date: _____   _____
                                      Signature

Also, if your tenant has made a complaint to you or a local government agency, withheld rent because of a claimed defect in the property, or participated in tenant-organizing activity, your notice should state legitimate, nonretaliatory reasons for terminating the tenancy. (Civ. Code § 1942.5(c); *Western Land Office, Inc. v. Cervantes* (1985) 174 Cal. App. 3d 724.)

You should not list the reason for the termination unless you are in a high-risk situation as described in "Impermissible Reasons to Evict," above, or the local rent control ordinance or government regulation (for subsidized housing) requires it. If you do have to include the reason, you may wish to check with an attorney or other knowledgeable person in your area to make sure you state it properly and with specificity; this will help assure that your tenant cannot complain that the notice is too vague or void under local law.

Serving the Notice

The law sets out detailed requirements for serving a 30-day or 60-day notice on a tenant. If you don't comply with them, you could lose your unlawful detainer lawsuit.

When the Notice Should Be Served

A 30-day or 60-day notice can be served on the tenant on any day of the month. For example, a 60-day notice served on March 17 terminates the tenancy 60 days later, on May 16. (Remember to count 60 days, regardless of whether any intervening month has 28, 29, or 31 days.) This is true even if rent is paid for the period from the first to the last day of each month. There's one exception: if your lease or rental agreement requires notice to be served on a certain day, such as the first of the month.

The best time to serve the notice is shortly after you receive and cash a rent check. Assuming the tenant paid on time, this means the notice is given toward the beginning of the month or rental period, so that the last day of the tenancy will fall only one or two days into the next month. The advantage is that you will already have the rent for almost all of the time the tenant can (legally) remain on the premises. If the tenant refuses to pay any more rent (for the day or two in the

next month), you can just deduct it from the security deposit. (See Chapter 9.)

EXAMPLE: Tess has been habitually late with the rent for the last five months of her seven-month occupancy, usually paying on the third day after receiving your three-day notice. On October 2 you knock on Tess's door and ask for the rent. If you luck out and get her to pay this time, cash the check and then serve Tess with a 30-day notice. The last day of the tenancy will be November 1, and she'll owe you only one day's rent. You can deduct this amount from the deposit before you return it, assuming you give the tenant proper written notice of what you are doing.

Of course, if Tess doesn't pay her rent on the 2nd, you can resort to the usual three-day notice. If she still doesn't pay within three days, you can sue for nonpayment of rent as described in Chapter 2.

If you've already collected "last month's rent," you can serve the 30-day notice (assuming the tenancy has lasted less than a year) on the first day of the last month without worrying about collecting rent first. Do not, however, serve it so that the tenancy ends before the end of the period (the last month) for which you have collected rent. Accepting rent for a period beyond the date you set in the 30-day notice for termination of the tenancy is inconsistent with the notice and means you effectively cancel it. (See *Highland Plastics, Inc. v. Enders* (1980) 109 Cal. App. 3d Supp.1, 167 Cal. Rptr. 353.)

If you serve the 30-day or 60-day notice in the middle of the month, your tenant may not be eager, when the next month comes around, to pay rent for the part of a subsequent month before the tenancy ends. If this happens and you can't settle the issue by talking to your tenant, you can take the prorated rent for the last portion of a month out of the security deposit. (See Chapter 9.) You could also serve the tenant with a three-day notice to pay rent or quit for the prorated rent due. We recommend against this, unless you've given a 60-day notice and the tenant refuses to pay the rent for the following full month. Using two notices increases the chances that you will make a procedural mistake. It complicates the eviction, increases hostility, and probably won't get the tenant out any faster.

If you are giving less than 30 days' notice because your rental agreement allows it but you collect your rent once a month, be sure that the notice doesn't terminate the tenancy during a period for which you've already collected rent. For example, if you collected the rent for August on August 1, serving a seven-day notice any sooner than August 24 would improperly purport to end the tenancy before the end of the paid-for rental period, August 31.

Who Should Serve the Notice

The 30-day notice may be served by any person over age 18. (See Chapter 2.) Although you can legally serve the notice yourself, it's often better to have someone else serve it. That way, if the tenant refuses to pay the rent and contests the eviction lawsuit by claiming he didn't receive the notice, you can present the testimony of someone not a party to the lawsuit who is more likely to be believed by a judge. Of course, you must weigh this advantage against any time, trouble or expense it takes to get someone else to accomplish the service and, if necessary, appear in court.

Whom to Serve

As with three-day notices, you should try to serve a copy of the 30-day or 60-day notice on each tenant to whom you originally rented the property. (See Chapter 2.)

How to Serve the Notice on the Tenant

The notice may be served in any of the ways three-day notices can be served (see Chapter 2):

- by personal delivery to the tenant
- by substituted service on another person, plus mailing, or
- by posting and mailing.

In addition, the notice can be served by certified mail. The statute does not require that it be sent return receipt requested. The return receipt gives you proof that the tenant received the notice, but it also entails a risk, because a tenant can refuse the letter by refusing to sign the receipt. In any case, the post office gives you a receipt when you send anything by certified mail.

If you serve the notice by certified mail, we suggest that you give the tenant an extra five days (in addition to the 30 or 60 days) before filing suit. You may be wondering why, since you do *not* need to add the extra five days if you serve a three-day or other notice by substituted service plus mailing or by posting and mailing. (In Chapter 2, see "When to File Your Lawsuit" and its explanation of the *Losornio* case that established this rule.) The answer is that, in both a substituted service plus mailing situation and a posting plus mailing situation, there is a chance that the tenant will, in fact, get the benefit of the full period (the person you've served may give the tenant the notice, or the tenant may pick up the posted notice, within the three or 30 or 60 days). When you serve using certified mail only, however, there is no way that the tenant can get the benefit of the full 30 or 60 days, since the notice will necessarily sit in the post office and the mailbag for a day or two at least, and there is no alternative way to receive the notice. For this reason, we think that you should add the five days to service accomplished via certified mail only, although plausible arguments can be made to the contrary. It's best to take the time to serve the 30-day notice personally.

 Remember:

- Do not accept any rent whatsoever for any period beyond the day your tenant should be out of the premises under your notice.
- Accept only rent prorated by the day up until the last day of tenancy, or you'll void your notice and have to start all over again with a new one.
- If you've given a 30-day notice, don't accept any rent at all if you collected "last month's rent" from the tenant, since that's what you apply to the tenant's last month or part of a month.
- Be sure the person serving the notice completes a Proof of Service at the bottom of an extra copy of the notice, indicating when and how the notice was served. (See "Preparing the Three-Day Notice to Pay Rent or Quit" in Chapter 2.)

When to File Your Lawsuit

Once your 30-day or 60-day notice is properly served, you must wait 30 or 35 (or 60 or 65) days before taking any further action. If you file an unlawful detainer complaint prematurely, you will lose the lawsuit and have to start all over again. Here's how to figure out how long you have to wait:

- Service is complete when you personally serve the notice, or after you have mailed it following substituted service or posting. If you serve it by certified mail, though, you should wait an extra five days before filing suit.
- If you serve more than one tenant with notices, but not all on the same day, start counting only after the last tenant is served.
- Do not count the day of service as the first day. The first day to count is the day after service of the notice was completed.
- The tenant gets 30 or 60 full days after service. Do not file your lawsuit until at least the 31st day (plus any five-day extension on account of serving by certified mail) after service is complete.
- If the 30th or 60th day is a business day, you may file your lawsuit on the next business day after that.
- If the 30th or 60th day falls on a Saturday, Sunday, or legal holiday, the tenant can stay until the end of the next business day. You cannot file your suit on that business day, but must wait until the day after that.

EXAMPLE: You personally served Tanya with her 30-day notice on June 3 (the day after she paid you the rent). June 4 is the first day after service, and July 3 is the 30th day. But July 3 is a Sunday, and July 4 is a holiday. This means Tanya has until the end of the next business day, July 5, to vacate. The first day you can file your suit is July 6.

If you had served Tanya on June 3 using any other method of service, she would have an additional five days to leave, and you could file suit on July 11 (or later if July 10 were a Saturday, Sunday, or holiday).

Once you have waited the requisite period, and the tenant has failed to leave, you can proceed to the next phase, which is filing an eviction complaint. We tell you how to do this in Chapter 6. ■

CHAPTER

4

Eviction for Lease Violations, Property Damage, or Nuisance

This chapter is about evicting tenants who:

- engage in highly disruptive activity (for example, making unreasonable noise, creating a nuisance, threatening neighbors)
- destroy part or all of the premises
- clearly violate the lease or rental agreement (for example, keeping a pet or subleasing without permission)
- make illegal use of the premises (for example, selling drugs), or
- fail to make a payment (other than rent) that is required under the lease or rental agreement (for example, late fee, security deposit upgrade, utility surcharge). (If you want to evict the tenant for nonpayment of rent, use Chapter 2.)

When to Use This Chapter

Surprising as it may seem, you may prefer to use a 30-day or 60-day notice to terminate a month-to-month tenancy instead of the three-day notice allowed under these circumstances. Why would you want to take the slower route? First, if you use a three-day notice, you will have to prove your reason for eviction (the tenant's misconduct) in court, whereas with a 30-day or 60-day notice you don't have to (except in cities with rent control that require just cause; see Appendix 1). Second, a tenant who receives a three-day notice for misconduct is a lot more likely to defend the suit. He may want to vindicate his reputation, or get back at you, or simply want some additional time to move. By contrast, if you terminate a month-to-month tenancy with a 30-day or 60-day notice, the tenant has time both to move and to cool off emotionally, and will probably exit quietly without finding it necessary to shoot a hole in your water heater.

Also, to use a three-day notice successfully, the problem you're complaining about must be truly serious. A judge will not order an eviction based on a three-day notice for minor rental agreement violations or property damage. For example, if you base a three-day notice eviction on the fact that your tenant's parakeet constitutes a serious violation of the no-pets clause in the lease, or that one or two noisy parties or the tenant's loud stereo is a sufficient nuisance to justify immediate eviction, you may well lose. The point is

simple: Any time you use a three-day notice short of an extreme situation, your eviction attempt becomes highly dependent on the judge's predilections, and therefore at least somewhat uncertain.

For these reasons, you should resort to three-day notice evictions based on something other than nonpayment of rent only when the problem is serious and time is very important.

Drug Dealing. If the tenant is dealing illegal drugs on the property, the problem is serious. A landlord who hesitates to evict a drug-dealing tenant (1) faces lawsuits from other tenants, neighbors, and local authorities; (2) may wind up liable for tens of thousands of dollars in damages; and (3) may even lose the property. Fortunately, you won't be in the ridiculous position of having to argue about the seriousness of drug dealing. California law identifies such activity as an illegal nuisance per se. (C.C.P. § 1161(4).)

It's easier to evict drug-dealing tenants with a 30-day or 60-day notice, especially in cities without rent control. However, if the tenant has a fixed-term lease (which can't be terminated with a 30-day or 60-day notice), you will have no choice but to follow the procedures set forth in this chapter by using a three-day notice to quit. (See "Using and Preparing an Unconditional Three-Day Notice to Quit," below.) You should start by getting other tenants, and neighbors, if possible, to document heavy traffic in and out of the tenant's home at odd hours. Under these circumstances, an attorney is recommended.

Checklist for Uncontested Nonrent Three-Day Notice Eviction

Here are the steps involved in evicting on the grounds covered in this chapter, if the tenant defaults (doesn't contest the eviction). We cover some of the subjects (for example, filing a complaint and default judgments) in later chapters. As you work your way through the book, you may want to return to this chart to see where you are in the process.

The Two Types of Three-Day Notices

Two kinds of three-day notices are covered here. The first is called a Notice to Perform Covenant or Quit and is like the three-day notice used for nonpayment of rent

Checklist for Uncontested Nonrent Three-Day Notice Eviction

Step		Earliest Time to Do It
☐	1. Prepare and serve the three-day notice on the tenant.	Any day the tenant is in violation of the lease, has damaged the property, or has created a nuisance.
☐	2. Prepare the Summons (or Summonses, if there is more than one tenant) and Complaint and make copies. (Chapter 6)	When it's apparent the tenant(s) won't leave on time; don't sign and date it until the day indicated below in Step 3.
☐	3. File the Complaint at the courthouse and have the Summons(es) issued. (Chapter 6)	The first day after the lease term or tenant's notice period expires.
☐	4. Have the sheriff, the marshal, or a friend serve the Summons and Complaint. (Chapter 6)	As soon as possible after filing the Complaint and having the Summons(es) issued.
☐	5. Prepare Request for Entry of Default, Judgment, Declaration, and Writ of Possession. (Chapter 7)	While you're waiting for five-day (or 15-day, if Complaint not personally served) response time to pass.
☐	6. Call the court to find out whether or not tenant(s) has filed written response.	Just before closing on the fifth day after service of Summons, or early on the sixth day. (Do not count holidays that fall on weekdays, however. Also, if fifth day after service falls on weekend or holiday, count the first business day after that as the fifth day.)
☐	7. Mail copy of Request for Entry of Default to tenant(s), file original at courthouse. Also file Summons and Declaration and have clerk issue judgment and writ for possession of the property. (Chapter 7)	Sixth day after service of Summons and Complaint. (Again, count first business day after fifth day that falls on weekend or holiday.)
☐	8. Prepare letter of instruction for, and give writ and copies to, sheriff or marshal. (Chapter 7)	As soon as possible after above step. Sheriff or marshal won't evict for at least five days after posting notice.
☐	9. Change locks after tenant vacates.	As soon as possible.
For Money Judgment		
☐	10. Prepare Request for Entry of Default, Judgment, and, if allowed by local rule, Declaration in Lieu of Testimony. (Chapter 7)	As soon as possible after property is vacant.
☐	11. Mail Request for Entry of Default copy to tenant, file request at courthouse. If Declaration in Lieu of Testimony allowed, file that, too, and give clerk judgment and writ forms for money part of judgment. If testimony required, ask clerk for default hearing. (Chapter 7)	As soon as possible after above.
☐	12. If testimony required, attend default hearing before judge, testify, and turn in your judgment form for entry of money judgment. (Chapter 7)	When scheduled by court clerk.
☐	13. Apply security deposit to cleaning and repair of property, and to any rent not accounted for in judgment, then apply balance to judgment amount. Notify tenant in writing of deductions, keeping a copy. Refund any balance remaining. If deposit does not cover entire judgment, collect balance of judgment. (Chapter 9)	As soon as possible after default hearing. Deposit must be accounted for within three weeks of when the tenants vacate.

(see Chapter 2) in that it gives the tenant the option of staying if he corrects his behavior within the three-day period. If he doesn't, then the tenancy is considered terminated. Most three-day notices fit into this category.

The other type of three-day notice simply tells the tenant to move out in three days. There is no option to correct the behavior. This kind of unconditional notice is allowed only in certain circumstances described below.

We strongly recommend that you use the conditional notice if any guesswork is involved. The consequences of using the unconditional notice can be drastic if the judge later disagrees with you and thinks that the situation called for a conditional notice. In that event, the judge will rule that your unconditional three-day notice was void; you will lose the lawsuit, be liable for the tenant's court costs and attorney's fees, and have to start all over again with a new notice.

Using the Three-Day Notice to Perform Covenant or Quit

In most situations, you'll use a conditional three-day notice, giving the tenant the option of correcting the violation or moving out.

When to Use a Conditional Notice

If a tenant who has violated a provision of the lease or rental agreement can correct her behavior, your three-day notice must give her that option. As mentioned, most lease violations are correctable. For instance:

- The tenant who violates a "no-pets" clause can get rid of the pet.
- The tenant who has failed to pay separate charges for utilities, legitimate late charges, or an installment toward an agreed-on security deposit can make the payment.
- The tenant who violates a lease clause requiring him to allow you reasonable access to the property (on proper notice—see *Volume 1*, Chapter 13) can let you in.

The list of potentially correctable lease violations is endless. As a general rule, if the violation isn't of the type listed below, it's probably correctable, and you should use a three-day notice giving the tenant the option of correcting the violation.

Rent control ordinances that require just cause for eviction (many don't) often dictate what kind of notice must be used. For example, Berkeley's ordinance allows eviction of a tenant who damages the property only after she's been given a notice giving her a chance to stop and to pay for the damage. State law does not require the landlord to give any warning, but rather authorizes an unconditional three-day notice to quit in such a circumstance. These two sources of law can be reconciled by giving the tenant two notices—first, the warning or "cease and desist" notice required by the local ordinance, followed by an unconditional three-day notice to quit under state law. This can be very tricky, so if you're unsure about applicable eviction regulations or have any doubt about the validity of your grounds for eviction, a consultation with a landlord-tenant specialist will be well worth the price.

If you attempt to evict a tenant in violation of a city's ordinance, you may be facing more than an unsuccessful eviction. Depending on the circumstances and the city, the tenant may come back at you with a suit of her own, alleging any number of personal injuries—even if the tenant defaults or loses in the underlying eviction action. (*Brossard v. Stotter* (1984) 160 Cal. App. 3d 1067.) And, as always, if you are not in compliance with the entire ordinance, a tenant in an eviction lawsuit may successfully defend on that basis.

Also, some rent control cities preclude eviction for violations of a lease provision if the provision was added to the original agreement, either by means of a notice of change of terms in tenancy or by virtue of a new lease signed by the tenant after the previous one expired. In such cities, a landlord who, for example, rented to a tenant with a pet couldn't later change the terms of the rental agreement with a 30-day notice saying no pets are allowed, then evict for violation of that term after it goes into effect. (Los Angeles's ordinance specifically forbids just this sort of eviction.) This would allow the landlord without grounds for eviction to evade the just cause requirement by changing the terms to assure the tenant's breach. Even in cities that do permit eviction based on after-added clauses, the clauses still must be legal and reasonable. Also, every city's ordinance makes it illegal for a landlord to attempt to evade its provisions. An unreasonable change in the rental agreement that assures a tenant's breach will most likely be considered an attempt to circumvent any just cause requirement, and will not be enforced.

If your property is located in a rent control city that provides for just cause eviction (see Chapter 3), be sure to check Appendix 1 and a current copy of your ordinance for additional eviction and notice requirements that may apply.

Before using the violation-of-lease ground to evict a tenant, ask yourself the following questions:

- Was the violated provision part of the original lease or rental agreement?
- If the provision was added later, does a rent control ordinance in your city preclude eviction on this ground?
- If the violation is correctable (most are), does your three-day notice give the tenant an option to cure the defect?
- Does your city's rent control ordinance impose special requirements on the notice, such as a requirement that it state the violation very specifically, be preceded by a "cease-and-desist" notice, or include a notation that assistance is available from the rent board?

Preparing a Conditional Three-Day Notice

If you opt for the conditional notice, your three-day notice to perform the lease provision (often termed a covenant or promise) or quit should contain all of the following:

- The tenant's name. List the names of all adult occupants of the premises, even if they did not sign the original rental agreement or lease.
- The property's address, including apartment number if applicable.
- A very specific statement as to which lease or rental agreement provision has been violated, and how.

    EXAMPLE: "You have violated the Rules and Regulations incorporated by paragraph 15 of the lease, prohibiting work on motor vehicles in the parking stalls, in the following manner: by keeping a partially dismantled motor vehicle in your parking stall."

- A demand that within three days the tenant either comply with the lease or rental agreement provision or leave the premises.

- A statement that you will pursue legal action or declare the lease or rental agreement "forfeited" if the tenant does not cure the violation or move within three days.
- The date and your (or your manager's) signature.

Two sample Three-Day Notices to Perform Covenant or Quit appear below. The instructions for completing the Proof of Service are the same as those described under the Three-Day Notice to Pay Rent or Quit. (See Chapter 2.)

 A blank, tear-out version of the Three-Day Notice to Perform Covenant or Quit is in Appendix 3. The CD-ROM also includes this form. Instructions for using the CD are in Appendix 2.

Using and Preparing an Unconditional Three-Day Notice to Quit

As noted above, under certain circumstances, the three-day notice need not give the tenant the option of correcting the problem. This is true in four kinds of situations:

1. The tenant has sublet all or part of the premises to someone else, contrary to the rental agreement or lease.
2. The tenant is causing a legal nuisance on the premises. This means that he is seriously interfering with his neighbors' ability to live normally in their homes, for example, by repeatedly playing excessively loud music late at night, or by selling illegal drugs on the premises.

    If you are tempted to use this ground, be sure that you can prove the problems with convincing testimony from a fairly impartial person, such as a tenant in the same building who is willing to testify in court. If you're unable to produce any witnesses, forget it.
3. The tenant is causing a great deal of damage ("waste," in legalese) to the property. Forget about evicting on this ground for run-of-the-mill damage caused by carelessness. It will work only in extreme cases such as where a tenant shatters numerous windows, punches large holes in walls, or the like. Again, you must be able to prove the damage convincingly.

Three-Day Notice to Perform Covenant or Quit

To: _Tammy Tenant_ ,
　　　　　　　　　　　(name)

Tenant(s) in possession of the premises at _1234 4th Street_ ,
　　　　　　　　　　　　　　　　　　　　　　　(street address)

City of _Monterey_ , County of _Monterey_ , California.

YOU ARE HEREBY NOTIFIED that you are in violation of the lease or rental agreement under which you occupy these premises because you have violated the covenant to:

pay agreed installments of the security deposit in the amount of $50 per month on the first day of each
month (in addition to the rent) until paid

in the following manner:

failing to pay the $50 on the first day of the month of September 20xx

YOU ARE HEREBY REQUIRED within THREE (3) DAYS from the date of service on you of this notice to remedy the violation and perform the covenant or to vacate and surrender possession of the premises.

If you fail to do so, legal proceedings will be instituted against you to recover possession of the premises, declare the forfeiture of the rental agreement or lease under which you occupy the premises, and recover damages and court costs.

Date: _Sept. 25, 20xx_ 　　　　_Leo Landlord_
　　　　　　　　　　　　　　　　　　Owner/Manager

- -

Proof of Service

I, the undersigned, being at least 18 years of age, served this notice, of which this is a true copy, on _____ , _____ , one of the occupants listed above as follows:

☐ On _____ , _____ , I delivered the notice to the occupant personally.

☐ On _____ , _____ , I delivered the notice to a person of suitable age and discretion at the occupant's residence/business after having attempted personal service at the occupant's residence, and business, if known. On _____ , _____ , I mailed a second copy to the occupant at his or her residence.

☐ On _____ , _____ , I posted the notice in a conspicuous place on the property, after having attempted personal service at the occupant's residence, and business, if known, and after having been unable to find there a person of suitable age and discretion. On _____ , _____ , I mailed a second copy to the occupant at the property.

I declare under penalty of perjury under the laws of the State of California that the foregoing is true and correct.

Date: _____ 　　　　_____
　　　　　　　　　　　　　　　Signature

Three-Day Notice to Perform Covenant or Quit

To: _Lester Lessee_ ,
                                                 (name)

Tenant(s) in possession of the premises at _123 Main Street, Apartment 4_ ,
                                                                (street address)

City of _San Jose_ , County of _Santa Clara_ , California.

YOU ARE HEREBY NOTIFIED that you are in violation of the lease or rental agreement under which you occupy these premises because you have violated the covenant to:

refrain from keeping a pet on the premises

in the following manner:

by having a dog and two cats on premises

YOU ARE HEREBY REQUIRED within THREE (3) DAYS from the date of service on you of this notice to remedy the violation and perform the covenant or to vacate and surrender possession of the premises.

If you fail to do so, legal proceedings will be instituted against you to recover possession of the premises, declare the forfeiture of the rental agreement or lease under which you occupy the premises, and recover damages and court costs.

Date: _November 6, 20xx_   _Linda Landlord_
                                                      Owner/Manager

- -

Proof of Service

I, the undersigned, being at least 18 years of age, served this notice, of which this is a true copy, on _____ ,
_____ , one of the occupants listed above as follows:

☐ On _____ , _____ , I delivered the notice to the occupant personally.

☐ On _____ , _____ , I delivered the notice to a person of suitable age and discretion at the occupant's residence/business after having attempted personal service at the occupant's residence, and business, if known. On _____ , _____ , I mailed a second copy to the occupant at his or her residence.

☐ On _____ , _____ , I posted the notice in a conspicuous place on the property, after having attempted personal service at the occupant's residence, and business, if known, and after having been unable to find there a person of suitable age and discretion. On _____ , _____ , I mailed a second copy to the occupant at the property.

I declare under penalty of perjury under the laws of the State of California that the foregoing is true and correct.

Date: _____   _____
                                                      Signature

$ Some rent control cities (for example, Berkeley, East Palo Alto, and Hayward) require that the tenant be given a written notice directing her to stop damaging the property and pay the estimated cost of repairs before you can evict using this ground. This requirement can be satisfied by either a Three-Day Notice to Perform Covenant or Quit, or a "cease and desist" notice followed by a Three-Day Notice to Quit.

4. The tenant is using the property for an illegal purpose (running a house of prostitution, dealing drugs, or operating a legitimate business clearly in violation of local zoning laws). You probably can't evict for minor transgressions such as smoking marijuana on the premises. It is unclear just how serious illegal activity must be to justify eviction; there are very few court decisions dealing with this question.

Because local police—or at least health department employees—may be interested in the tenant's illegal conduct, make sure to make appropriate complaints to them first. Keep a record of the dates and times of your complaints, and the name(s) of the person(s) with whom you spoke. And, although not required by ordinance, your record of having given the tenant written notice to cease the illegal activity should also help establish that there's a problem.

$ No rent control ordinance requires the tenant be given a chance to correct illegal use of property. Some cities, however, allow eviction on this ground only if the tenant is convicted of illegal activity. (See Appendix 1.)

The notice must contain:
- The tenant's name. List the names of all adult occupants of the premises, even if they didn't sign the original lease or rental agreement.
- The property's address.
- A specific statement as to how and approximately when the tenant violated the rental agreement or lease in a way that can't be corrected—for example, if the tenant illegally sublet, created a nuisance, damaged the premises, or illegally used the premises. This is the most important part of the notice, and must be drafted very carefully to clearly tell the tenant what she is doing wrong. Failure to be very specific regarding dates, times,

and conduct could render the notice void— another reason why a 30-day or 60-day eviction or, at least, a conditional three-day notice is usually preferable.

$ Again, many rent control ordinances that provide for just cause for eviction require that the reason to use an unconditional three-day notice be stated even more specifically than is required under state law. Check your ordinance.

- A demand that the tenant leave the premises within three days.
- An unequivocal statement that the lease is forfeited and that you will take legal action to remove the tenant if she fails to vacate within three days.
- The date and your (or your manager's) signature.

Two sample unconditional Three-Day Notices to Quit appear below. The instructions for completing the Proof of Service are the same as those described under the Three-Day Notice to Pay Rent or Quit. (See Chapter 2.)

⊙ A blank, tear-out version of the Three-Day Notice to Quit is in Appendix 3. The CD-ROM also includes this form. Instructions for using the CD are in Appendix 2.

Serving the Three-Day Notice (Either Type)

A three-day notice telling a tenant to either comply with a lease provision or vacate can be served any day the tenant is in violation of the lease, but not before. For example, if your tenant informs you of his intent to move in a pet Doberman in violation of the "no pets" clause in the lease, you can serve him with a conditional three-day notice only as soon as he gets the dog. You can't get the jump on him by anticipating the violation. The same is true of an unconditional Three-Day Notice to Quit. You can serve the notice any time after the tenant has illegally sublet, caused a nuisance, severely damaged the property, or used the property for an illegal purpose.

When to Serve Notice

What happens if you've accepted rent for a whole month and then want to give your tenant a three-day notice? Should you wait awhile? Here are some general rules about when to serve your tenants with three-day notices:

- Serve a conditional notice right after you receive the rent. That way, you won't be out the rent during the first month the eviction lawsuit is pending. It's perfectly reasonable to accept the rent for the month and then demand, for example, that the tenant get rid of her pet, anticipating that she will comply.

- Serve an unconditional notice as close as possible to the end of a rental period. If you serve the notice right after you've collected the rent in advance for a whole month, the tenant may claim that by accepting the rent (assuming you knew about the problem) you gave up your right to complain. However, if you can prove that you became aware of a noncorrectable violation only a few days after having accepted rent, don't worry. If you get the tenant out within the month for which the tenant has already paid rent, the tenant does not get a refund for the days he paid for but didn't get to stay. By breaching the lease or rental agreement, the tenant forfeited his right to occupy the premises, even though he'd already paid the rent.

- Never give a tenant an unconditional Three-Day Notice to Quit concurrently with a Three-Day Notice to Pay Rent or Quit. The two are contradictory, one telling the tenant he can stay if he pays the rent, the other telling the tenant to move no matter what. Also, do not give the tenant an unconditional Three-Day Notice to Quit along with a 30-day or 60-day Notice of Termination of Tenancy. These two are contradictory as well, giving two different time periods within which the tenant must leave unconditionally.

Who Should Serve the Three-Day Notice

As with a Three-Day Notice to Pay Rent or Quit, anyone over 18 can serve the notice, including you. (See Chapter 2.)

Whom to Serve

As with other three-day notices, you should try to serve a copy of the notice on each tenant to whom you originally rented the property. (See Chapter 2.)

How to Serve the Notice

The three-day notice must be served in one of three ways:

- personal service on the tenant
- substituted service and mailing, or
- posting-and-mailing.

You may not serve the notice by certified mail, which may be used only for 30-day or 60-day notices terminating month-to-month tenancies. Chapter 2 explains how to accomplish service.

Accepting Rent After the Notice Is Served

With conditional three-day notices, don't accept any rent unless the tenant has cured the violation within three days—in which case you can't evict, and the tenant can stay. If the tenant doesn't correct the violation within three days, don't accept any rent unless you want to forget about evicting for the reason stated in the notice.

Don't accept rent after you've served an unconditional three-day notice unless you want to forget about the eviction. Acceptance of the rent will be considered a legal admission that you decided to forgive the violation and go on collecting rent rather than complain about the problem.

> **EXAMPLE:** You collected a month's rent from Peter on March 1. On March 15, Peter threw an extremely boisterous and loud party that lasted until 3 a.m. Despite your warnings the next day, he threw an identical one that night. He did the same on the weekend of March 22-23. You served him an unconditional Three-Day Notice to Quit on the 25th of the month, but he didn't leave and you therefore have to bring suit. The rent for March is already paid, but you can't accept rent for April or you'll give up your legal right to evict on the basis of the March parties. However, you can get a court judgment for the equivalent of this rent in the form of "damages" equal to one day's rent for each day from April 1 until Peter leaves or you get a judgment.

Three-Day Notice to Quit
(Improper Subletting, Nuisance, Waste, or Illegal Use)

To: _Ronald Rockland_____ ,

                                            (name)

Tenant(s) in possession of the premises at _1234 Diego Street, Apartment 5_____ ,

                                                                              (street address)

City of _San Diego_____ , County of _San Diego_____ , California.

YOU ARE HEREBY NOTIFIED that you are required within THREE (3) DAYS from the date of service on you of this notice to vacate and surrender possession of the premises because you have committed the following nuisance, waste, unlawful use, or unlawful subletting:

You committed a nuisance on the premises by reason of loud boisterous parties at which music was
played at an extremely loud volume, and at which intoxicated guests milled about outside the front
door to the premises and shouted obscenities at passersby every night from February 26th through
_28th, 20xx._

As a result of your having committed the foregoing act(s), the lease or rental agreement under which you occupy these premises is terminated. If you fail to vacate and surrender possession of the premises within three days, legal proceedings will be instituted against you to recover possession of the premises, damages, and court costs.

Date: _____March 1, 20xx_____   _Laura Landlord_____

                                                              Owner/Manager

- -

Proof of Service

I, the undersigned, being at least 18 years of age, served this notice, of which this is a true copy, on _____ , _____ , one of the occupants listed above as follows:

☐ On _____ , _____ , I delivered the notice to the occupant personally.

☐ On _____ , _____ , I delivered the notice to a person of suitable age and discretion at the occupant's residence/business after having attempted personal service at the occupant's residence, and business, if known. On _____ , _____ , I mailed a second copy to the occupant at his or her residence.

☐ On _____ , _____ , I posted the notice in a conspicuous place on the property, after having attempted personal service at the occupant's residence, and business, if known, and after having been unable to find there a person of suitable age and discretion. On _____ , _____ , I mailed a second copy to the occupant at the property.

I declare under penalty of perjury under the laws of the State of California that the foregoing is true and correct.

Date: _____   _____

                                                             Signature

Three-Day Notice to Quit

(Improper Subletting, Nuisance, Waste, or Illegal Use)

To: _Leslie D. Lessee_____ ,

(name)

Tenant(s) in possession of the premises at _____2468 Alameda Street_____ ,

(street address)

City of _____San Jose_____ , County of _____Santa Clara_____ , California.

YOU ARE HEREBY NOTIFIED that you are required within THREE (3) DAYS from the date of service on you of this notice to vacate and surrender possession of the premises because you have committed the following nuisance, waste, unlawful use, or unlawful subletting:

You have unlawfully sublet a portion of the premises to another person who now lives on the premises

_with you, contrary to the provisions of your lease._____

_____

_____

_____

As a result of your having committed the foregoing act(s), the lease or rental agreement under which you occupy these premises is terminated. If you fail to vacate and surrender possession of the premises within three days, legal proceedings will be instituted against you to recover possession of the premises, damages, and court costs.

Date: _____March 3, 20xx_____   _Mel Manager_____

Owner/Manager

- -

Proof of Service

I, the undersigned, being at least 18 years of age, served this notice, of which this is a true copy, on _____ ,
_____ , one of the occupants listed above as follows:

☐ On _____ , _____ , I delivered the notice to the occupant personally.

☐ On _____ , _____ , I delivered the notice to a person of suitable age and discretion at the occupant's residence/business after having attempted personal service at the occupant's residence, and business, if known. On _____ , _____ , I mailed a second copy to the occupant at his or her residence.

☐ On _____ , _____ , I posted the notice in a conspicuous place on the property, after having attempted personal service at the occupant's residence, and business, if known, and after having been unable to find there a person of suitable age and discretion. On _____ , _____ , I mailed a second copy to the occupant at the property.

I declare under penalty of perjury under the laws of the State of California that the foregoing is true and correct.

Date: _____   _____

Signature

When to File Your Lawsuit

Once you have properly served the notice you will need to wait for the appropriate number of days to pass before you take the next step, filing your lawsuit. Here is how to compute this period:

- If you serve more than one tenant with notices, but not all on the same day, start counting only after the last tenant is served.
- Do not count the day of service as the first day. The first day to count is the day after service of the notice was completed.
- Do not file your lawsuit on the third day after service is complete. The tenant must have three full days after service before you file suit.
- If the third day is a business day, you may file your lawsuit on the next business day after that.
- If the third day falls on a Saturday, Sunday, or legal holiday, the tenant has until the end of the next business day to correct the violation (if the notice was conditional) or move. You cannot file your suit on that business day, but must wait until the day after that.

EXAMPLE: On November 11, Manuel personally served Maria with a conditional three-day notice at home. The first day after service is Friday the 12th, the second day is Saturday the 13th, and the third day is Sunday the 14th. Since the third day falls on a Sunday, Maria has until the end of the next business day—Monday the 15th—to correct the lease violation or leave. Only on the 16th can Manuel file suit.

Once you have waited the requisite period, and the tenant has failed to leave (or correct the violation if your notice was conditional), you can proceed to the next phase, which is filing an eviction complaint. We tell you how to do this in Chapter 6. ■

5

Eviction Without a Three-Day or Other Termination Notice

There are just two situations in which you may file an eviction lawsuit against a tenant without first giving a written three-day, 30-day, or 60-day notice. They are:

- when the tenant refuses to leave after a fixed-term lease expires, and you haven't renewed it or converted it into a month-to-month tenancy by accepting rent after expiration of the lease term, and

- when your month-to-month tenant terminates the tenancy by giving you a 30-day notice, but then refuses to move out as promised.

Rent control ordinances requiring just cause for eviction in many cities limit evictions or add requirements for eviction. Be sure to check the Rent Control Chart in Appendix 1 and a copy of your city's rent control ordinance if your property is subject to rent control.

Lease Expiration

Unlike a month-to-month tenancy, a fixed-term tenancy ends on a definite date, stated in the lease. No further notice is necessary. However, unless you are careful you may find yourself inadvertently renewing the lease or converting it into a month-to-month tenancy. Here are the basic rules:

- If you simply continue to accept monthly rent after the termination date, the fixed-term tenancy is automatically converted to a month-to-month tenancy. (Civ. Code § 1945.) It must be terminated with a 30-day or 60-day notice. (See Chapter 3.)

- If the lease has a renewal provision, your acceptance of rent may automatically operate to renew the lease for another full term.

EXAMPLE: Masao rented his house to Yuko under a six-month lease for January 1 through June 30. Although Masao assumed Yuko would leave on June 30, Yuko is still there the next day. When she offers Masao the rent on July 1, Masao accepts it, believing this is preferable to filing an eviction lawsuit, but tells Yuko she can stay only a month more. At the end of July, however, Yuko's lawyer tells Masao that Yuko is entitled to stay under her now month-to-month tenancy until and unless Masao terminates it with a proper 30-day notice. Masao gives Yuko a written 30-day notice on July 31, which means Yuko doesn't have to move until August 30.

In this example, Masao could have given Yuko a one-month extension without turning the tenancy into one from month to month. He need only have insisted that Yuko, as a condition of staying the extra month, sign a lease for a fixed term of one month, beginning on July 1 and ending on July 31.

Reminding the Tenant Before the Lease Expires

To avoid an inadvertent extension of the lease or its conversion into a month-to-month tenancy, it is always a good idea to inform a fixed-term tenant, in writing and well in advance, that you don't intend to renew the lease. While not required, such a notice will prevent a tenant from claiming that a verbal extension was granted. A fixed-term tenant who knows a month or two in advance that you want her out at the end of a lease term is obviously in a good position to leave on time. A tenant who realizes that the lease is up only when you refuse her rent and demand that she leave immediately is not. Your letter might look something like this.

Notice to Tenant That Lease Will Not Be Renewed

November 3, 20xx
950 Parker Street
Berkeley, CA 94710

Leo D. Leaseholder
123 Main Street, Apt. #4
Oakland, CA 94567

Dear Mr. Leaseholder:

As you know, the lease you and I entered into on January 1 of this year for the rental of the premises at 123 Main Street, Apartment 4, Oakland, is due to expire on December 31, slightly less than two months from now.

I have decided not to extend the lease for any period of time, even on a month-to-month basis. Accordingly, I will expect you and your family to vacate the premises on or before December 31. You have the right to request an initial move-out inspection, and to be present at that inspection, provided you request it no more than two weeks prior to your move-out date. I will return your security deposit to you in the manner prescribed by Section 1950.5 of the California Civil Code, within three weeks after you move out. If I deduct you also have the right to receive copies of invoices or receipts for work needed to remedy damage beyond normal wear and tear or to perform necessary cleaning.

Sincerely,

Lenny D. Landlord

Lenny D. Landlord

The letter isn't a legally required notice, but is just sent to show your intent to assert your right to possession of the property at the expiration of the lease. (However, the part of the letter telling the tenant of her right to an initial move-out inspection and to be present at it *is* legally required, as is the part concerning the tenant's right to invoices and receipts. See *The California Landlord's Law Book: Rights and Responsibilities*, Chapters 5 and 18.) It doesn't have to be served in any particular way. It can be mailed first class. However, if you're afraid the tenant will claim she never received the letter, you may want to send it certified mail, return receipt requested.

Is the Tenancy for a Fixed Term?

If you want to evict a tenant who stays after her lease expires, the first question to ask yourself is whether or not the tenant actually did have a lease—or, more accurately, a fixed-term tenancy. Since the titles of standard rental forms are often misleading (a rental agreement may be called a "lease" or vice versa), you should look at the substantive provisions of the document if you are in doubt. (We discuss this in detail in *Volume 1*, Chapter 2.)

To summarize, if the agreement lists either a specific expiration date or the total amount of rent to be collected over the term, chances are it's a lease. For example, a clearly written lease might use this language:

The term of this rental shall begin on _____, 20__, and shall continue for a period of _____ months, expiring on _____, 20__.

As discussed above, the big exception to the rule that no notice is required to end a fixed-term tenancy is when you have, by word or action, allowed the lease to be renewed, either for another full term (if there's a clause to that effect in the lease) or as a month-to-month tenancy (if you continued to accept monthly rent after the end of the term).

Must You Have a Reason for Not Renewing a Lease?

A landlord's reason for refusing to renew a lease is treated the same way as is a landlord's reason for terminating a month-to-month tenancy with a 30-day or 60-day notice. (See Chapter 3.) The general rule is that (except in certain cities with rent control) you don't have to give a reason for refusing to renew the lease. (If you're in a rent control city that requires just cause for eviction, read Chapter 3.) However, your refusal may not be based on retaliatory or discriminatory motives. Laws against illegal discrimination apply to nonrenewal of fixed-term tenancies to the same extent that they apply to termination of month-to-month tenancies.

In rent control cities with just cause ordinances, expiration of a fixed-term lease is generally not a basis for eviction, unless the tenant refuses to sign a new one on essentially the same terms and conditions. Most ordinances don't require you to give the tenant any specific kind of notice, although San Francisco, Thousand Oaks, and West Hollywood require that the tenant be requested in writing to sign the new lease. (See Appendix 1.)

The best practice is to personally hand the tenant a letter, at least 30 days before the lease expires, requesting that she sign the new lease (attached to the letter) and return it to you before the current one expires. Be sure to keep a copy of the letter and proposed new lease for your own records. Even if all this isn't required by your city, it will make for convincing documentation if the tenant refuses to sign and you choose to evict for this reason.

How to Proceed

You may begin an unlawful detainer suit immediately if all of the following are true:

- You conclude that your tenant's fixed-term tenancy has expired.
- You have not accepted rent for any period beyond the expiration date.
- The tenant refuses to move.

Instructions on how to begin the suit are set out in Chapter 6.

Termination by the Tenant

You can also evict a tenant without written notice when the tenant terminates a month-to-month tenancy by serving you with a legally valid 30-day notice but refuses to leave after the 30 days. (As we saw in Chapter 3, although you must give 60 days' notice of termination of tenancy to a tenant who has lived in the premises a year or more, he or she need only give you 30 days' notice.) Again, if you accept rent for a period after the time the tenant is supposed to leave, you've recreated the tenancy on a month-to-month basis and cannot use this chapter.

If only one of several cotenants (see *The California Landlord's Law Book: Rights & Responsibilities*, Chapter 10) terminates the tenancy, the others may stay unless the tenant who signed the notice was acting on their behalf as well.

Because the tenant's notice may be unclear in this respect or may be invalid for other reasons (such as failure to give a full 30 days' notice), some landlords follow a tenant's questionable termination notice with a definite 30-day notice of their own. This avoids the problem of relying on a tenant's notice, rerenting the property and then finding, after the tenant has changed her mind and decided to stay, that the notice is not legally sufficient to terminate the tenancy. However, this technique is no longer possible if the tenant has stayed a year or more, in which case a 60-day notice is required.

If you choose not to serve your own 30-day or 60-day notice and instead want to evict on the basis that the tenant has not vacated in accordance with her 30-day notice, proceed to Chapter 6 for how to file an unlawful detainer complaint. If you do decide to serve a 30-day or 60-day notice of your own, turn to Chapter 3.

Checklist for Uncontested "No-Notice" Eviction

Here are the steps required in this type of eviction, assuming the tenant does not answer your unlawful detainer complaint (that is, the tenant defaults). At this point, much of the outline may not make sense to you, as you have not yet read the chapters on filing the unlawful detainer complaint, taking a default judgment, or enforcing the judgment. As you proceed through those chapters (or Chapter 8, if the tenant contests your action), you may want to return to this chapter to keep in touch as to where you are in the process.

Checklist for Uncontested "No-Notice" Eviction

Step		Earliest Time to Do It
☐ 1.	Prepare the Summons(es) and Complaint and make copies. (Chapter 6)	When it's apparent the tenant(s) won't leave on time; don't sign and date it until the day indicated below in Step 3.
☐ 2.	File the Complaint at the courthouse and have the Summons(es) issued. (Chapter 6)	The first day after the lease term or tenant's notice period expires.
☐ 3.	Have the sheriff, the marshal, or a friend serve the Summons and Complaint. (Chapter 6)	As soon as possible after filing the Complaint and having the Summons(es) issued.
☐ 4.	Prepare Request for Entry of Default, Judgment, Declaration, and Writ of Possession. (Chapter 7)	While you're waiting for five-day (or 15-day, if Complaint not personally served) response time to pass.
☐ 5.	Call the court to find out whether or not tenant(s) has filed written response.	Just before closing on the fifth day after service of Summons, or early on the sixth day. (Do not count holidays that fall on weekdays, however. Also, if fifth day after service falls on weekend or holiday, count the first business day after that as the fifth day.)
☐ 6.	Mail copy of Request for Entry of Default to tenant(s), file original at courthouse. Also file Declaration and have clerk issue judgment and writ for possession of the property. (Chapter 7)	Sixth day after service of Summons and Complaint. (Again, count first business day after fifth day that falls on weekend or holiday.)
☐ 7.	Prepare letter of instruction for, and give writ and copies to, sheriff or marshal. (Chapter 7)	Sixth day after service of Summons and Complaint. (Again, count first business day after fifth day that falls on weekend or holiday.)
☐ 8.	Change locks.	As soon as tenant vacates.
For Money Judgment		
☐ 9.	Prepare Request for Entry of Default, Judgment, and, if allowed by local rule, Declaration in Lieu of Testimony. (Chapter 7)	As soon as possible after property is vacant.
☐ 10.	Mail Request for Entry of Default copy to tenant, file request at courthouse. If Declaration in Lieu of Testimony allowed, file that, too, and give clerk judgment and writ forms for money part of judgment. If testimony required, ask clerk for default hearing. (Chapter 7)	As soon as possible after above.
☐ 11.	If testimony required, attend default hearing before judge, testify, and turn in your judgment form for entry of money judgment. (Chapter 7)	When scheduled by court clerk.
☐ 12.	Apply security deposit to cleaning and repair of property, and to any rent not accounted for in judgment, then apply balance to judgment amount. Notify tenant in writing of deductions, keeping a copy. Refund any balance remaining. If deposit does not cover entire judgment, attempt to collect balance of judgment. (Chapter 9)	As soon as possible after default hearing. Deposit must be accounted for within three weeks of when the tenants vacate.

6

Filing and Serving Your Unlawful Detainer Complaint

After you have legally terminated your tenant's tenancy by properly serving the appropriate termination notice (or the tenancy has ended because a lease expired or the tenant terminated it himself), you can begin an unlawful detainer lawsuit to evict the tenant. This chapter tells you how to prepare and file a Complaint and Summons, the documents that initiate your lawsuit.

How to Use This Chapter

The reason you're evicting (nonpayment of rent, for example) and the kind of notice you use to terminate the tenancy (Three-Day Notice to Pay Rent or Quit, for example) determine the actual wording of your unlawful detainer Complaint. To keep you from getting confused, we label the parts of our discussion that apply to each type of eviction.

As you go through the instructions on how to fill out the Complaint, simply look for the number of your "home" chapter (the one you used to prepare the termination notice) and start reading. You needn't pay any attention to the material following the other symbols.

Key to Symbols in This Chapter

 Evictions based on nonpayment of rent—Three-Day Notice to Pay Rent or Quit (Chapter 2)

 Evictions based on a 30-day or 60-day notice (Chapter 3)

 Evictions based on lease violations, damage, or nuisance—Three-Day Notice to Quit or Three-Day Notice to Perform Covenant or Quit (Chapter 4)

 Evictions based on termination of tenancy without notice (Chapter 5).

If a paragraph is relevant only to certain types of evictions, only the appropriate symbols will appear. In addition, we occasionally refer you to the chapter you started with (for example, Chapter 2 for evictions based on nonpayment of rent). We also alert you to the special requirements of rent control ordinances.

Okay, let's start.

When to File Your Unlawful Detainer Complaint

   If you terminated the tenancy with a three-day, 30-day, or 60-day notice, you can file your unlawful detainer Complaint when the notice period expires. You must be careful not to file prematurely. If you file before the notice period is over, there is no basis for the suit because the tenancy was never properly terminated, and if the tenant files a written response to your lawsuit, you will lose.

It is therefore very important to correctly calculate the length of the notice period. We explained how to do this in the chapter you started out in (for example, Chapter 2 for evictions based on nonpayment of rent, Chapter 3 for evictions based on a 30-day notice). If necessary, go back to the chapter covering your type of eviction and review how to determine when the notice period ends. Then return here for instructions on how to fill in and file your unlawful detainer Complaint.

 If, as discussed in Chapter 5, the tenancy has already ended without a three-, 30-, or 60-day notice, that is, if a lease has expired or the tenant terminated the tenancy with a proper notice to you, you may file your Complaint at any time.

Where to File Suit

Until recently, California had two levels of civil trial courts: Municipal Courts, which heard cases involving less than $25,000, and Superior Courts, which handled cases over that amount. Because all residential evictions for nonpayment of rent involved much less than $25,000, they were heard in Municipal Court.

In November 1998, the voters amended the California Constitution to allow each county to abolish its Municipal Courts and consolidate them with the Superior Courts. All California counties have done so. Now, there are no more "Municipal" courts, only Superior Courts and their various "branches" or "divisions," some of which were formerly Municipal Courts. (Because this change is relatively new, some branches and divisions continue to have "Municipal Court" building signs and telephone listings.)

Court Locations

Most large counties divide their Superior Courts into "divisions" or "branches." (A notable exception is San Francisco, whose Superior Court has no divisions or branches.)

All California courts have Internet websites. You can reach them by going to a central website: www. courtinfo.ca.gov/courts/trial. Once you get to this main website, you'll see links to the superior courts.

File your lawsuit in the division or district where the property is located. To make sure you have the right court (some handle only criminal matters), call the civil clerk of the superior court for the division or district in which you think your rental property is located. You can also find the court's address and phone number in the telephone book under "courts" or "superior court."

Other Courts

In the past, unlawful detainer lawsuits were sometimes filed in small claims courts and justice courts. This is no longer true. Small claims courts do not hear eviction cases. (C.C.P. § 116.220.) In November 1994, the State Constitution was amended to rename justice courts as municipal courts (Const. Art. VI, § 5), all of which are also now Superior Courts.

Preparing the Summons

The first legal form that you'll need to start your lawsuit is the Summons. The Summons is a message from the court to each defendant (person being sued). It states that you have filed a Complaint (see "Preparing the Complaint," below) against the defendant, and that if there is no written response to the Complaint within five days, the court may grant you judgment for eviction and money damages.

A blank, tear-out version of the Summons and Proof of Service is in Appendix 3. The CD-ROM also includes this form. Instructions for using the CD are in Appendix 2.

If you photocopy the tear-out form in Appendix 3 and use both sides of the paper, or make a double-sided print from the CD-ROM, be sure that the front and back are in the same upside down relation to each other as is the form in the back of this book. The form is filled out in the same way no matter what the ground for the eviction you are using. Using a typewriter, fill it out as follows:

Step 1: "NOTICE TO DEFENDANT _____."

You should name as defendants the following individuals:

- All adults who live in the property, whether or not you made any agreement with them; and
- Any tenants who entered into the original rental agreement and have since sublet the property. (Such tenants are still legally in possession of the property through their subtenants.) If none of the original tenants is there, however, the current tenants are probably "assignees," not subtenants, and you shouldn't name the original tenants as defendants. (See *The California Landlord's Law Book: Rights & Responsibilities*, Chapter 10, for more discussion of the subtenant/assignee distinction.)

It is not enough to name the person you think of as the "main" tenant. For example, if a husband and wife reside on the property and are listed as tenants in your lease, and the wife's brother also lives there, you must list all three as defendants. The sheriff or marshal will not evict any occupant not named as defendant who claims to have moved in before you filed suit. You may then have to go back to court to evict the person you forgot to sue. (Meanwhile, this person will be free to invite the evicted tenants back as "guests.")

Also, below the defendants' names, type "DOES 1 to 5." This phrase indicates that you are also naming unknown defendants in your lawsuit, just in case you later find out that there are unauthorized occupants living on the premises in addition to the known tenants. We discuss this in more detail in "Preparing the Complaint," Item 5.

Step 2: "YOU ARE BEING SUED BY PLAINTIFF _____."

Type in the name of the plaintiff, or person suing. Here are the rules to figure out who this should be:

1. If you are the sole owner of the property, you must be listed as plaintiff (but see rule (4), below).
2. If there are several owners, they don't all have to be listed—the co-owner who rented to the tenant,

or who primarily deals with the manager, if there is one, should be listed.

3. The plaintiff must be an owner of the property (such as your spouse) or have some ownership interest, such as a lease-option. A nonowner manager or property management firm cannot be a plaintiff. (See C.C.P. § 367.) Some property managers and management companies have successfully brought unlawful detainer actions in their own behalf, without being called on it by a judge. Still, a competent tenant's attorney may raise this issue on occasion and win, perhaps even getting a judgment against the manager or management company for court costs and attorney's fees.

4. If the lease or rental agreement lists a fictitious business name (for example, "Pine Street Apartments") as the landlord, you cannot sue (either under that name or under your own name) unless the business name is registered with the county. (See Bus. & Prof. Code § 17910 and following.) If the name is registered, list it as the plaintiff if the property is owned by a partnership. If you own the property alone but use the business name, put your name followed by "dba Pine Street Apartments." (The dba means "doing business as.") If the name isn't registered, go down to the courthouse and get the process started. This involves filling out a form, paying a fee, and arranging to have the name published.

> EXAMPLE: Jack Johnson and Jill Smith, a partnership named "Jack & Jill Partnership," own a five-unit apartment building they call "Whispering Elms." Their rental agreements list Whispering Elms as the landlord, and the name is properly registered with the county as a fictitious business name. They should enter "Jack Johnson and Jill Smith, a partnership, dba Whispering Elms" as the plaintiff.

> EXAMPLE: Jill Smith owns the building herself, but her rental agreements list Whispering Elms as the landlord, and the name is on file with the county. The plaintiff in her eviction suit should be "Jill Smith, dba Whispering Elms."

5. If a corporation is the owner of the property, the corporation itself must be named as plaintiff and represented by an attorney. Even if you're president and sole shareholder of a corporation that owns the property, unless you're a lawyer you cannot represent the corporation in court. (Although C.C.P. § 87 seems to allow this, this statute was declared unconstitutional in *Merco Construction Engineers, Inc. v. Municipal Court* (1978) 21 Cal. 3d 724, 147 Cal. Rptr. 631.)

Step 3: (item 1 on the form) "The name and address of the court is _____."

Put the name and street address of the court, "SUPERIOR COURT OF CALIFORNIA," the county, and the division or branch in which your rental property is located. (See above.)

> EXAMPLE: Your property is located in the City of Oakland, in Alameda County. Oakland is in the "Oakland-Piedmont-Emeryville" division, whose Superior Court is located at 600 Washington Street, Oakland. You should type in:
> SUPERIOR COURT OF CALIFORNIA
> COUNTY OF ALAMEDA
> OAKLAND-PIEDMONT-EMERYVILLE DIVISION
> 600 Washington Street
> Oakland, CA 94607

Step 4: "CASE NUMBER _____."

Leave this space blank. The court clerk will fill in the case number when you file your papers.

Step 5: (item 2) "The name, address, and telephone number of plaintiff's attorney, or plaintiff without an attorney, is _____."

Place your name and mailing address along with a telephone number at which you can be reached.

Since your tenant will receive a copy of the Summons, he will see this address (to which the tenant must mail a copy of any written response) and telephone number. You may prefer to list a business address or post office box and/or a business telephone number.

SUM-130

SUMMONS
(CITACION JUDICIAL)
UNLAWFUL DETAINER—EVICTION
(RETENCIÓN ILÍCITA DE UN INMUEBLE—DESALOJO)

NOTICE TO DEFENDANT:
(AVISO AL DEMANDADO): TERRANCE D. TENANT,
TILLIE D. TENANT, and
DOES 1 through 5

YOU ARE BEING SUED BY PLAINTIFF:
(LO ESTÁ DEMANDANDO EL DEMANDANTE):
LENNY D. LANDLORD

FOR COURT USE ONLY
(SOLO PARA USO DE LA CORTE)

You have **5 CALENDAR DAYS** after this summons and legal papers are served on you to file a written response at this court and have a copy served on the plaintiff. (To calculate the five days, count Saturday and Sunday, but do not count other court holidays. If the last day falls on a Saturday, Sunday, or a court holiday then you have the next court day to file a written response.) A letter or phone call will not protect you. Your written response must be in proper legal form if you want the court to hear your case. There may be a court form that you can use for your response. You can find these court forms and more information at the California Courts Online Self-Help Center (www.courtinfo.ca.gov/selfhelp), your county law library, or the courthouse nearest you. If you cannot pay the filing fee, ask the court clerk for a fee waiver form. If you do not file your response on time, you may lose the case by default, and your wages, money, and property may be taken without further warning from the court.

There are other legal requirements. You may want to call an attorney right away. If you do not know an attorney, you may want to call an attorney referral service. If you cannot afford an attorney, you may be eligible for free legal services from a nonprofit legal services program. You can locate these nonprofit groups at the California Legal Services Web site (www.lawhelpcalifornia.org), the California Courts Online Self-Help Center (www.courtinfo.ca.gov/selfhelp), or by contacting your local court or county bar association.

Tiene 5 DÍAS DE CALENDARIO después de que le entreguen esta citación y papeles legales para presentar una respuesta por escrito en esta corte y hacer que se entregue una copia al demandante. (Para calcular los cinco días, cuente los sábados y los domingos pero no los otros días feriados de la corte. Si el último día cae en sábado o domingo, o en un día en que la corte esté cerrada, tiene hasta el próximo día de corte para presentar una respuesta por escrito). Una carta o una llamada telefónica no lo protegen. Su respuesta por escrito tiene que estar en formato legal correcto si desea que procesen su caso en la corte. Es posible que haya un formulario que usted pueda usar para su respuesta. Puede encontrar estos formularios de la corte y más información en el Centro de Ayuda de las Cortes de California (www.courtinfo.ca.gov/selfhelp/espanol/), en la biblioteca de leyes de su condado o en la corte que le quede más cerca. Si no puede pagar la cuota de presentación, pida al secretario de la corte que le dé un formulario de exención de pago de cuotas. Si no presenta su respuesta a tiempo, puede perder el caso por incumplimiento y la corte le podrá quitar su sueldo, dinero y bienes sin más advertencia.

Hay otros requisitos legales. Es recomendable que llame a un abogado inmediatamente. Si no conoce a un abogado, puede llamar a un servicio de remisión a abogados. Si no puede pagar a un abogado, es posible que cumpla con los requisitos para obtener servicios legales gratuitos de un programa de servicios legales sin fines de lucro. Puede encontrar estos grupos sin fines de lucro en el sitio web de California Legal Services, (www.lawhelpcalifornia.org), en el Centro de Ayuda de las Cortes de California, (www.courtinfo.ca.gov/selfhelp/espanol/) o poniéndose en contacto con la corte o el colegio de abogados locales.

1. The name and address of the court is:
   (El nombre y dirección de la corte es): SUPERIOR COURT OF CALIFORNIA,
   COUNTY OF LOS ANGELES,
   110 N. Grand Avenue, Los Angeles, CA 90012

CASE NUMBER:
(Número del caso):

2. The name, address, and telephone number of plaintiff's attorney, or plaintiff without an attorney, is:
   (El nombre, la dirección y el número de teléfono del abogado del demandante, o del demandante que no tiene abogado, es):

   LENNY D. LANDLORD, 12345 Angeleno St., Los Angeles, CA 90010. 213-555-6789

3. *(Must be answered in all cases)* An **unlawful detainer assistant (Bus. & Prof. Code, §§ 6400–6415)** [X] did **not** [ ] did for compensation give advice or assistance with this form. *(If plaintiff has received **any** help or advice for pay from an unlawful detainer assistant, complete item 6 on the next page.)*

Date: Clerk, by _____, Deputy
(Fecha)   *(Secretario)*   *(Adjunto)*

(For proof of service of this summons, use Proof of Service of Summons (form POS-010).)
(Para prueba de entrega de esta citación use el formulario Proof of Service of Summons, (POS-010)).

[SEAL]

4. **NOTICE TO THE PERSON SERVED:** You are served
   a. [X] as an individual defendant.
   b. [ ] as the person sued under the fictitious name of *(specify):*
   c. [ ] as an occupant
   d. [ ] on behalf of *(specify):*
      under: [ ] CCP 416.10 (corporation)   [ ] CCP 416.60 (minor)
             [ ] CCP 416.20 (defunct corporation)   [ ] CCP 416.70 (conservatee)
             [ ] CCP 416.40 (association or partnership) [ ] CCP 416.90 (authorized person)
             [ ] CCP 415.46 (occupant)   [ ] other *(specify):*
5. [ ] by personal delivery on *(date):*

Page 1 of 2

Form Adopted for Mandatory Use
Judicial Council of California
SUM-130 [Rev. January 1, 2004]

SUMMONS—UNLAWFUL DETAINER—EVICTION

Code of Civil Procedure, §§ 412.20, 415.456. 1167

SUM-130

PLAINTIFF *(Name):*	LENNY D. LANDLORD	CASE NUMBER:
DEFENDANT *(Name):*	TERRANCE D. TENANT, et al	

6. **Unlawful detainer assistant** *(complete if plaintiff has received any help or advice for pay from an unlawful detainer assistant):*

a. Assistant's name:

b. Telephone no.:

c. Street address, city, and ZIP:

d. County of registration:

e. Registration no.:

f. Registration expires on *(date)*:

Step 6: (item 3)

"An unlawful detainer assistant (B&P 6400-6415) ☐ did not ☐ did for compensation give advice or assistance with this form."

A nonattorney who is paid to fill out unlawful detainer paperwork must be registered and bonded. This law does not apply, however, to property owners or to managers who prepare such forms for their employer in the ordinary course of their duties (neither does it apply to attorneys). If you are such a property manager or owner, put an X next to the words "did not," and leave Item 6, on the second page, blank (but complete the Caption, as explained below). If you are paying a paralegal or other person to fill out or otherwise process your papers (other than just having a process server serve them), or to advise you on filling out the forms, he or she must be registered with the county and bonded, and the "did" box must be checked. That person's name, address, phone number, and registration information must then be listed on the next page of the Summons form. Provide the information requested, and fill out the box at the top of the page by entering the plaintiff's and defendants' names, as you did at the top of the summons. You will need to file both pages of the Summons, even if page 2 is blank except for the Caption (which will be the case for those who did not use an assistant).

Step 7: (item 4)

"NOTICE TO THE PERSON SERVED: You are served…"

This part of the Summons is for the process server to complete. The server needs to identify the defendant as an individual or as someone who represents a business entity. In residential eviction proceedings, the defendant will always be an individual, so we have gone ahead and preprinted the form with an X in Box 1. The process server will complete the rest of the form when he or she completes the service. (See below for more information on serving the Summons and completing this part of the form.)

Step 8: Complete the Caption on Page Two.

Enter the names of the plaintiff(s) and defendant(s), just as you did when filling out the top of the form on page one. Do so even if you won't be filling out Item 6 on this page (see instructions for Step 9).

Step 9: (Item 6)

If you used an unlawful detainer assistant, supply the information called for.

Leave these items blank if you did not use an assistant.

Preparing the Complaint

In the unlawful detainer Complaint, you allege why the tenant should be evicted. The Complaint also formally requests a judgment for possession of the premises and any sums which you may be owed as back rent (in nonpayment of rent evictions), damages, court costs, and attorney fees. The original of your unlawful detainer Complaint is filed with the court. A copy is given to (served on) each defendant along with a copy of the Summons. (See below.) Together, filing and serving the Complaint and Summons initiate the lawsuit.

To fill out the Complaint correctly, you need to know whether or not your property is located in an area covered by rent control. To find this out, consult the list of rent control cities in the Rent Control Chart in Appendix 1. Many rent control ordinances that require just cause for eviction require that the Complaint (as well as the three-, or 30-, or 60-day notice) include a specific statement of reasons for the eviction. This requirement is satisfied by attaching a copy of the notice to the Complaint and by making an allegation (that is, checking a box; see Item 6c, below) in the Complaint that all statements in the notice are true. Some ordinances also require Complaints to allege compliance with the rent control ordinance. If you don't comply with these requirements, the tenant can defend the unlawful detainer suit on that basis.

Although many of these specific rent control requirements are listed in Appendix 1, we can't detail all the rent control ordinance subtleties, and we can't guarantee that your ordinance hasn't been changed since this book was printed. Therefore, it is absolutely essential that you have a current copy of your ordinance and rent board regulations at the ready when you're planning an eviction in a rent control city.

As with the Summons, the unlawful detainer Complaint is completed by filling in a standard form, which is fairly straightforward. But don't let this lull you into a false sense of security. If you make even a seemingly minor mistake, such as forgetting to check a box, checking one you shouldn't, or filling in wrong or contradictory information, it will increase the chances that your tenant can and will successfully contest the action, costing you time and money. Pay very close attention to the following instructions. This chapter includes directions on filling in each item of the Complaint plus a completed sample form.

   A blank, tear-out version of the Complaint is in Appendix 3. The CD-ROM also includes this form. Instructions for using the CD are in Appendix 2.

If you make a double-sided photocopy of the tear-out Complaint, or make a double-sided print using the CD-ROM, be sure that the copies you make have the front and back in the same seeming upside-down relation to one another as the forms in the back of this book, or a fussy court clerk may refuse to accept your papers for filing.

At the top of the form, type your name, address, and telephone number in the first box that says Attorney or Party Without Attorney. After the words "Attorney For," we have preprinted the form to say "Plaintiff in Pro Per," to indicate that you're representing yourself. In the second box, you will need to fill in the county, division, and court address, the same as you put on the front of the Summons. In the third box, fill in the plaintiff's (your) and defendants' names in capital letters. As with the Summons, leave blank the boxes entitled "FOR COURT USE ONLY" and "CASE NUMBER."

Put an X in the box next to the space labeled "DOES 1 to _____ ," and put "5" in the space after that. This allows you to name five more defendants later, if, for example, you find out the names of unauthorized occupants of the premises.

If you want to name more defendants later, you can amend (change) your Complaint and add the names of the new defendants in exchange for each of your

fictional "Doe" defendants.

Put an X in the two boxes next to the words "ACTION IS A LIMITED CIVIL CASE" and the words "does not exceed $10,000." Do not check any other boxes in this area. This tells the clerk to charge you the lower filing fee (around $140) for a case involving a relatively small amount of money. (If you don't check these boxes, or check the wrong ones, you could be charged up to $275.)

Item 1: PLAINTIFF and DEFENDANT Names

    Type your name after the words "PLAINTIFF (names each):" and type the defendants' names after the words "DEFENDANT (names each):," using upper case for the first letter of each name and lower case for the remainder (Joe Smith).

Item 2: Plaintiff Type

    Item 2a: State whether the plaintiff is an individual, a public agency, a partnership, or a corporation. If, as in most cases, the plaintiff is an adult individual—you—who is an owner of the property, type an X in box (1) next to the words "an individual over the age of 18 years."

Do not check the box next to the words "a partnership" unless you listed the partnership as the plaintiff on the Summons. (See Step 2 in "Preparing the Summons," above.)

Do not check the box next to the words "a corporation." Corporate landlords must be represented by an attorney—in which case you should not be doing the eviction lawsuit yourself. (See above.)

    Item 2b: Type an X in the box if you included a fictitious business name when you identified the plaintiff in the Summons (see Step 2 in "Preparing the Summons," above). Type the fictitious business name in the space provided.

Item 3: Address of Rental Property

    List the street address of the rental property, including apartment number if applicable, and the city and county in which it is located.

EXAMPLE: 123 Main Street, Apartment 4, San Jose, County of Santa Clara.

Item 4: Plaintiff's Interest

    If you are an owner of the property, type an X in the box next to the words "as owner." If you have a lease-option on the property and rent it to the tenants, check the "other" box and type in "Lessor."

Item 5: Unknown Defendants

  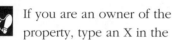 You don't need to do anything here. This allegation applies only if there are unauthorized subtenants or long-term "guests" in the property, but you don't know their names. If you later learn the real name of a "John Doe," this allegation makes it easier for you to file an "amended" Complaint, giving the correct name(s). Filing an amended Complaint gets a bit tricky. If you need help, contact a lawyer to help you.

Item 6: Landlord and Tenant's Agreement

    Item 6a: This item calls for basic information about the terms of the tenancy.

On the first line (beginning with "On or about"), fill in the date on which you agreed to rent the property to your tenant. This is the date the agreement was made, not the date the tenant moved in. If a written lease or rental agreement is involved, the date should be somewhere on it. If it's an oral agreement and you can't remember the exact date, don't worry. The approximate date is okay.

It's very common for tenants with leases to stay beyond the lease expiration date, with the full knowledge and blessing of the landlord. When the landlord continues to accept rent, these tenants become month-

to-month tenants, subject to the same terms and conditions of the original lease. If the tenant you're evicting stayed on in this way, use the date that the original lease was signed. If you asked this tenant to sign a new lease when the old one expired (this is the better practice), use the date that the latest lease was signed, and refer to this lease for all other information that's called for in the Complaint.

Then, on the same line, fill in the names of the persons with whom you made the oral agreement or who signed a written agreement or lease. In the case of an oral agreement, list the name(s) of the person(s) with whom you or a manager or other agent originally dealt in renting the property. Don't worry if the list of people with whom the oral or written agreement was made does not include all the current adult occupants. Occupants who didn't make the original agreement are subtenants or assignees (see *The California Landlord's Law Book: Rights & Responsibilities*, Chapter 10) and are accounted for in Item 6c (below).

If some of the original tenants have moved out, they should not be listed in Item 6a, since you are not permitted to name them as defendants. You list here only those person(s) who entered into the rental agreement *and* still live in the property.

The boxes after line "(1)" of Item 6a (beginning with the words "agreed to rent the premises as a") indicate the type of tenancy you and your tenant(s) originally entered into.

- If the tenancy was from month to month (see Chapter 3) check that box.
- If the tenancy was not originally month to month, type an X in the "other tenancy" box.
- For a fixed-term tenancy, type "fixed-term tenancy for _____ months," indicating the number of months the lease was to last.
- The "other tenancy" box can also be used to indicate periodic tenancies other than from month to month such as week-to-week tenancies.
- If the tenancy began for a fixed period (one year is common), but the term has expired and the tenancy is now month to month, indicate it as it originally was (fixed-term). You can note in Item 6d (see below) that the tenancy subsequently changed to month to month.

The boxes after line "(2)" in Item 6a (beginning with the words "agreed to pay rent of") has a space for

UD-100

ATTORNEY OR PARTY WITHOUT ATTORNEY *(Name, State Bar number, and address):*

LENNY D. LANDLORD
12345 ANGELENO STREET
LOS ANGELES, CA 90010
TELEPHONE NO.: 213-555-6789   FAX NO. *(Optional):*
E-MAIL ADDRESS *(Optional):*
ATTORNEY FOR *(Name):*   Plaintiff in Pro Per

SUPERIOR COURT OF CALIFORNIA, COUNTY OF   LOS ANGELES
STREET ADDRESS: 110 North Grand Avenue
MAILING ADDRESS: same
CITY AND ZIP CODE: Los Angeles, CA 90012
BRANCH NAME: CENTRAL DISTRICT/DOWNTOWN BRANCH

PLAINTIFF: LENNY D. LANDLORD

DEFENDANT: TERRENCE D. TENANT, TILLIE D. TENANT

[X] DOES 1 TO _5_

COMPLAINT — UNLAWFUL DETAINER*

[X] COMPLAINT   [ ] AMENDED COMPLAINT *(Amendment Number):* _____

CASE NUMBER:

Jurisdiction *(check all that apply):*
[X] **ACTION IS A LIMITED CIVIL CASE**
Amount demanded   [X]   **does not exceed $10,000**
                  [ ]   **exceeds $10,000 but does not exceed $25,000**

[ ] **ACTION IS AN UNLIMITED CIVIL CASE (amount demanded exceeds $25,000)**
[ ] **ACTION IS RECLASSIFIED by this amended complaint or cross-complaint** *(check all that apply):*
      [ ] from unlawful detainer to general unlimited civil (possession not in issue)   [ ] from limited to unlimited
      [ ] from unlawful detainer to general limited civil (possession not in issue)   [ ] from unlimited to limited

1. PLAINTIFF *(name each):*   Lenny D. Landlord

    alleges causes of action against DEFENDANT *(name each):*   Terrence D. Tenant, Tillie D. Tenant

2. a. Plaintiff is   (1) [X] an individual over the age of 18 years.   (4) [ ] a partnership.
                       (2) [ ] a public agency.   (5) [ ] a corporation.
                       (3) [ ] other *(specify):*

    b. [ ] Plaintiff has complied with the fictitious business name laws and is doing business under the fictitious name of *(specify):*

3. Defendant named above is in possession of the premises located at *(street address, apt. no., city, zip code, and county):*
    6789 Angel Blvd. Apt. 10, Los Angeles, 90010, Los Angeles County

4. Plaintiff's interest in the premises is   [X] as owner   [ ] other *(specify):*
5. The true names and capacities of defendants sued as Does are unknown to plaintiff.
6. a. On or about *(date):* Jan. 1, 2002   defendant *(name each):*   Terrence D. Tenant, Tillie D. Tenant

        (1) agreed to rent the premises as a [X] month-to-month tenancy [ ] other tenancy *(specify):*
        (2) agreed to pay rent of $ 850.00   payable [X] monthly [ ] other *(specify frequency):*
        (3) agreed to pay rent on the [X] first of the month [ ] other day *(specify):*
    b. This [X] written [ ] oral   agreement was made with
        (1) [X] plaintiff.   (3) [ ] plaintiff's predecessor in interest.
        (2) [ ] plaintiff's agent.   (4) [ ] other *(specify):*

    * NOTE: Do not use this form for evictions after sale (Code Civ. Proc., § 1161a).

Page 1 of 3

Form Approved for Optional Use
Judicial Council of California
UD–100 [Rev. July 1, 2005]

COMPLAINT—UNLAWFUL DETAINER

Civil Code, § 1940 et seq.
Code of Civil Procedure §§ 425.12, 1166
www.courtinfo.ca.gov

American LegalNet, Inc.
www.USCourtForms.com

you to fill in the amount of the rent when the tenant originally rented the premises. If the rent has increased since then, say so in Item 6d (see below). Next indicate how often the rent was payable (again, when the tenancy began; changes since then should be indicated in Item 6d). In the rare cases where the rent was not payable monthly, put an X in the "other" box and type in the appropriate period (for example, weekly or bimonthly).

At line "(3)" of Item 6a, check "first of the month" if the rent was payable then. If it was payable on any other day (for example, on the 15th of each month, or every Monday), instead check the box next to "other day (specify):" and type in when the rent did come due.

 Item 6b: This item tells whether the rental agreement or lease was oral or written and whether you, an agent, or a previous owner entered into it with the tenant. Check either the "written" box or the "oral" box on the first line. If there was a written agreement with the first tenants, but only an oral agreement with subsequent occupants, the latter are most likely subtenants under the written agreement. So you need only check the "written" box.

Also put an X in one of the four boxes below it. Check the box labeled "plaintiff" if you—the plaintiff—signed the written rental agreement or lease or made the oral agreement with the tenant. If a manager, agent, or other person did this, check the box labeled "plaintiff's agent" instead. If the tenant was renting the property before you owned it, and you didn't have her sign a new rental agreement or lease, she is there because of some sort of agreement with the previous owner—in legalese, your "predecessor in interest"—and you should check that box.

 PLAINTIFF and DEFENDANT. At the top of the reverse side of the Complaint is a large box labeled "PLAINTIFF (Name):" and "DEFENDANT (Name):." Here, type in capital letters the names of the first-listed plaintiff and defendant the same way their names are listed on the front Caption under "PLAINTIFF" and "DEFENDANT." Where there are multiple plaintiffs or defendants, you

list only the first one here, followed by "ET AL."

 Item 6c: If the occupants you're trying to evict are all named in Item 6a (because you entered into a written or oral rental agreement or lease with them), leave box c blank and go on to Item 6d.

If, however, some of the persons you named as defendants were not named in Item 6a (for example, adults who later moved in without your permission), check box c and one of the three boxes below it to indicate whether these defendants are "subtenants" (usually) or "assignees" (rarely). (See *The California Landlord's Law Book: Rights & Responsibilities,* Chapter 10, for a discussion of these terms.)

Here's a brief explanation.

Subtenants. If any of the original tenants listed in Item 6a still live in the premises with these defendants, check the "subtenants" box, because these people are essentially renting from the original tenants, not from you.

> **EXAMPLE:** Larry rented to Tim and Twyla ten years ago. Tim and Twyla signed a month-to-month rental agreement that is still in effect (though Larry has increased the rent since then). Last year, Twyla moved out and Twinka moved in with Tim. Larry never had Twinka sign a new rental agreement.

What is the current status of Tim and Twinka? Tim is still renting from Larry under the old rental agreement, but Twinka is actually renting from Tim—even if she pays the rent to Larry herself. Twinka is a subtenant and should be listed under Item 6c. Tim and Twyla, the original tenants, are listed in Item 6a.

Assignees. On the other hand, if none of the original tenants lives on the premises and you don't expect any of them to return, chances are that the current occupants are "assignees"—unless you had them sign or enter into a new rental agreement. An assignee is someone to whom the former tenants have, in effect, turned over all of their legal rights under the lease.

> **EXAMPLE:** Lana rented one of her apartments to Toby and Toni five years ago. Three years ago, Toby and Toni left and, without telling Lana, had Toby's cousin Todd move in. Although Lana could have objected under the rental agreement clause prohibiting subletting and assignment, she didn't.

She accepted rent from Todd, but never had Todd sign a new rental agreement, so he's an "assignee" of Toby's and Toni's. In this situation, Lana would name only Todd as defendant, but list Toby and Toni as the persons in Item 6a to whom she originally rented. (This is true even though Item 6a asks you to list "defendants." Toby and Toni aren't actually defendants, because they no longer live there; the form isn't perfectly designed for every situation.) In Item 6c, you should check the "assignees" box to indicate that Todd, not named in 6a, is an assignee of the persons who are named.

 Item 6d: Box d should be checked if there was a change in any of information provided in Item 6a since the original tenancy began. For instance, if the rent is higher now than it was at first, this is the place for you to say so, especially if your eviction is for nonpayment of rent and you are seeking unpaid rent. If there have been several rent increases, list them all, in chronological order.

EXAMPLE: Leon rented his property on a month-to-month basis to Teresa on January 1, 2007, for $800 per month. (This date and former rent amount should be listed in Item 6a.) On July 1, 2007, Leon gave Teresa a 60-day notice (required for rent increases of more than 10%), that her rent would be increased from $800 to $900 effective September 1, 2007. Leon should check box d under Item 6 and after the words "The agreement was later changed as follows (specify):" type the following:

"On July 1, 2007, Plaintiff notified defendant in writing that effective September 1, 2007, the rent would be increased to $900 each month."

EXAMPLE: Teresa's neighbor, Juan, moved into one of Leon's apartments on January 1, 2007. On December 1, Leon told Juan his rent would go from $650 to $700, effective January 1, 2008. However, Leon forgot to give Juan the required written 30-day notice. (See *The California Landlord's Law Book: Rights and Responsibilities*, Chapter 14.) Still, Juan paid the increased rent for several months, beginning in January 2008. Even though Leon hould have raised the rent with a written notice,

Juan effectively "waived" or gave up his right to a written notice by paying the increase anyway. (Note: This may not be true in a rent control city, especially if the increased rent exceeds the legal rent for the property.) Now, in June 2008, Juan won't pay the rent (or move) and Leon has to sue him. Check box d under Item 6 and type in the following:

"On December 1, 2007, plaintiff notified defendant that effective January 1, 2008, the rent due would be increased to $700 each month, and defendant agreed to and did pay the increased rent on its effective date."

Another common event that should be recorded in Item 6d is any change in the type of tenancy (for example, from a fixed-term lease to a month-to-month tenancy).

EXAMPLE: On June 1, you rented your property to Leroy for one year under a written lease. Leroy didn't leave on June 1 of the following year and paid you the usual rent of $900, which you accepted. Although the original tenancy was one for a fixed term, as should be indicated in Item 6a, it is now month to month. (See Chapter 5.) Check box d in Item 6 and type the following:

"On June 1, 2007, after expiration of the lease term, defendant remained in possession and paid $900 rent, which plaintiff accepted, so as to continue the tenancy on a month-to-month basis."

Item 6d should also be filled out for changes in the rental period (for example, from bimonthly to monthly) and changes in the date when the rent was due (for example, from the 15th of the month to the first). Simply put, Item 6d is your chance to bring the court up to date as to your current arrangements with your tenants.

You may find that there isn't enough space on the Complaint form to type in all the required information for this item. If you can't fit it in with three typewritten lines that go right up against each margin, type the words "see attachment 6d" and add all the necessary information on a sheet of white typing paper labeled "Attachment 6d." This attachment is stapled to the

Complaint, along with the "Exhibit" copies of the lease/ rental agreement and three-day, 30-day, or 60-day notice discussed below. (Be sure to add one more page to the number of pages listed in Item 1 if you do this.)

    Item 6e: If the rental agreement is oral, skip this box and Item 6f, and go on to Item 7. If the rental agreement or lease is in writing, put an X in this box if you have the original or a copy of it. Attach a photocopy (not a signed duplicate) of the lease or rental agreement to the Complaint (unless you can't find an original or copy). Write "EXHIBIT 1" on the bottom of the copy. (If you and the tenants signed a new lease or rental agreement after having signed an older version, you need only attach a copy of the most recent lease or rental agreement.) You must include copies of any written amendments or addenda. Finally, keep track of the correct number of pages attached to the Complaint, which you'll need to list in Item 18 (count two printed sides of one page as two pages).

 If you're seeking to evict because of nonpayment of rent, you aren't legally required to attach a copy, but we think it's a good practice. If the tenant contests the lawsuit, the judge who hears the case will be more favorably impressed with the way you put your case together if you've taken the extra step to attach all relevant documents.

   Item 6f: This question asks you to explain why, if there is a written rental agreement or lease, you have not attached a copy of it to the Complaint. (You're not required to do so in rent-nonpayment cases even if you have a copy, though we suggest that you do if you have one.) If your rental agreement is oral, skip this item and go to Item 7. Also skip it if you are attaching a copy of the rental agreement or lease.

If you haven't attached a copy of a lease or rental agreement, put an X in the box next to Item 6f. Also put an X either in box (1) if you simply don't have an original or copy of the lease or rental agreement, or in box (2) if your lawsuit is based on nonpayment of rent, and (against our advice) you decide not to attach a copy.

    PLAINTIFF and DEFENDANT. At the top of the reverse side of the Complaint is a large box labeled "PLAINTIFF (Name):" and "DEFENDANT (Name):" Here, type in capital letters the names of the first-listed plaintiff and defendant the same way their names are listed on the front Caption under "PLAINTIFF" and "DEFENDANT." Where there are multiple plaintiffs or defendants, you list only the first one here, followed by "ET AL."

Item 7: Notice

  Check the box immediately following the number 7 to indicate that a notice to quit was served on at least one of the tenants, and fill in the name of the defendant to whom the notice was given. If you served more than one defendant, list all of their names. You will also list the other names and method of service in Items 7b and 7c, below.

 Leave Items 7 and 7a through 7f blank if your eviction is being brought under Chapter 5 of this book (that is, if no notice was given the tenant).

 Item 7a: Check box "(1)," labeled "3-day notice to pay rent or quit."

 Item 7a: Check box "(2)" labeled "30-day notice to quit" if that is what you used because the tenancy was for less than a year. (See Chapter 3.) If you had to give a 60-day notice because your tenant occupied the premises for a year or more, check box "(3)" next to the words "other (specify):" and type the words "60-day notice to quit."

If you used a 90-day notice of termination of tenancy because the tenancy was government-subsidized, check box "(6)" next to the words "Other (specify):" and type the words "90-day notice to quit."

Item 7a: Check either the box labeled "3-day notice to perform covenants or quit" "(4)" (the conditional notice), or "3-day notice to quit" "(5)" (the unconditional notice), depending on which type of notice you served.

Item 7b: List the date the period provided in your three-day notice expired. This is the third day, not counting the day the notice was served, after the three-day notice was personally served (eighth day for substituted service), except that when the third (or eighth) day falls on a weekend or legal holiday, the last day is the next business day. (See Chapters 2 and 4 for several detailed examples.) If you used substituted service for your notice or are unsure of your notice's expiration date, return to your "home" chapter (Chapter 2 or 4) and compute the correct expiration date in accordance with our instructions.

 Item 7b: List the date the period provided in your 30-day or 60-day notice expired. This is the 30th day (or the 60th day) after the notice was personally served (don't count the day the notice was served), except that when the 30th or 60th day falls on a weekend or legal holiday, the last day is the next business day. (See the detailed examples in Chapter 3 to get a better handle on this.) If you used substituted service or are unsure of the proper expiration date, return to Chapter 3 and compute the proper expiration date in accordance with our instructions.

Don't file until the three, 30, or 60 days have expired.

   Be sure you do not file your papers with the court (see below) until after the date you indicate in Item 7b. Otherwise, the Complaint will be premature, and you may lose the case and have to pay the tenant's court costs.

   Item 7c: You don't need to fill in a box or add information on this one, which just says that everything in the notice you served (a copy of which you will attach to the Complaint) is true.

  Item 7d: Put an X in this box. This indicates that your three-day notice contained an "election of forfeiture"—legalese for a statement in the notice that the tenancy is ended if the notice is not obeyed. The form notices in this book include a forfeiture statement.

 Item 7d: Leave this item blank, since 30-day and 60-day notices do not require a notice of forfeiture.

  Item 7e: Check this box. Label the bottom of your copy of the three- or 30-day notice "EXHIBIT 2" (even if you don't have an Exhibit 1), and remember to staple it to your Complaint. This is essential.

   Item 7f: Put an X in box 7f only if (1) there are two or more defendants, *and* (2) you served *two* or more of them with the notice on a different date or in a different manner. (Although the form contemplates checking this box also if two or more defendants were served with different notices, we do not recommend such a procedure.) For example, if Tillie Tenant and Sam Subtenant were each served with a three-day notice on a different day, or if one was served personally and the other served by substituted service and mailing (see Chapter 2), then Lenny Landlord would check this box. However, do not check the box if the two or more defendants are all cotenants on a written lease or rental agreement and you served just one of them on behalf of all tenants.

If you check Item 7f, you should also put an X in Item 8c on the reverse side of the Complaint form. At this point, the information in Items 8a through 8e on content and service of the notice will apply only to the person(s) whose name(s) is listed in Item 7a. You will have to state on a separate page labeled "Attachment 7f/8c," how any other persons were served in a different manner or on a different date. Before doing that, however, you should turn the Complaint form over and complete Items 8a and 8b.

 Item 7f: Leave Item 7f blank if your eviction is being brought under Chapter 5 of this book— that is, if no notice was served on any tenant.

Item 8: Service of Notice

   This part of the eviction form asks for the details on how you performed service of process. You have a choice: You can complete Items 8a through 8c as explained below, or you can demonstrate your service compliance by checking Item 8d and supplying as Exhibit 3 a written, signed proof of service indicating when and how the notice was served. Which method is preferable? We suggest using Items 8a through 8c, because these questions prompt you to give the detailed information (especially important in cases of substituted service or service by posting and mailing) that a judge needs to determine whether service was proper. Remember, if you have multiple defendants served different ways, you'll need to add separate attachment pages for each. On the other hand, you may find it easier to simply check Item 8d and attach multiple proofs of service for multiple defendants who were served in different ways or on different dates, instead of filling out Items 8a–8c and adding separate attachments. Put an X in the box after 8a to indicate that a notice was served on your tenant.

 Leave Items 8, 8a and 8b and 8c blank, since no notice was served on your tenant.

 Item 8a: If the defendant listed in Item 7a was personally served with the notice, check the first box (next to the words "by personally handing a copy to defendant on (date):") "(1)," and type the date she was handed the notice. Then go on to Item 8b.

The second box in Item 8a, next to "by leaving a copy with ..." "(2)," should be checked instead only if you used "substituted service," that is, you gave the notice to someone at the tenant's home or workplace and mailed a second copy. On the same line, list the name (or physical description if name is unknown) of the person to whom the notice was given. On the next two lines, fill in the date you delivered the notice, check a box to indicate whether the notice was served at the residence or business address, and list the date the second copy was mailed to the residence address. Then go on to Item 8b.

If you had to resort to "posting and mailing" service because you couldn't find anyone at the defendant's home or place of employment, check the third box next to the words "by posting a copy on the premises on (date):" "(3)" and insert the date the notice was posted. Ignore the box by the words "and giving a copy to a person found residing at the premises." Below that,

list the date the copy of the notice was mailed to the residence address. Next, check one of the two boxes (in front of phrases beginning with "because") to indicate why you used posting-and-mailing service. In almost all residential cases you should check the second box, next to the phrase "because no person of suitable age or discretion can be found there." Leave blank the box next to the phrase "because defendant's residence and usual place of business cannot be ascertained"—after all, you always know the defendant's residence address in a residential eviction.

 The fourth box in Item 8a, followed by the words *"not for 3-day notice"* in parentheses, obviously should be used only if your eviction was preceded by a 30-day or 60-day notice (see Chapter 3) which you served by certified or registered mail.

 Item 8a: The last (fifth) box in Item 8a should not be checked. It applies only to some commercial tenancies—a subject beyond the scope of this book.

 Item 8b: Put an X in this box and again list the name(s) of any defendant you served with a termination notice (as you did in Item 7a), only if all of the following are true: (1) there are two or more defendants, (2) two or more of the defendants both signed the written lease or rental agreement, and (3) you did not serve all of the signers of the lease or rental agreement with a notice. For example, Tillie Tenant and Terrence Tenant both signed the rental agreement, and although your Three-Day Notice to Pay Rent or Quit mentioned them both, you only served Terrence. (This is permitted under the case of *University of Southern California v. Weiss* (1962) 208 Cal. App. 2d 759, 769; 25 Cal. Rptr. 475.) In that case, Item 7a on the front should list "Terrence Tenant" as the one served with a notice, Item 6f should not be checked and Item 8b should be checked. At Item 8b, "Terrence Tenant" should again be listed as the person who was served on behalf of the other tenant(s) on the lease or rental agreement.

 Item 8c: If you put an X in box 7f, you did so because (1) there are two or more defendants, *and* (2) you served two or

PLAINTIFF *(Name):* LENNY D. LANDLORD	CASE NUMBER:
DEFENDANT*(Name):* TERRENCE D. TENANT, ET AL	

6. c. [X] The defendants not named in item 6a are   Terrence Tenant

    (1) [X] subtenants.

    (2) [ ] assignees.

    (3) [ ] other *(specify):*

  d. [X] The agreement was later changed as follows *(specify):* On Jan. 1, 20xx, plaintiff notified defendants in writing that effective Feb. 1, 20xx, the rent would be $900.00

  e. [X] A copy of the written agreement, including any addenda or attachments that form the basis of this complaint, is attached and labeled Exhibit 1. *(Required for residential property, unless item 6f is checked. See Code Civ. Proc., § 1166.)*

  f. [ ] *(For residential property)* A copy of the written agreement is **not** attached because *(specify reason):*

    (1) [ ] the written agreement is not in the possession of the landlord or the landlord's employees or agents.

    (2) [ ] this action is solely for nonpayment of rent (Code Civ. Proc., § 1161(2)).

7. [X] a. Defendant *(name each):*

    TERRANCE D. TENANT

    was served the following notice on the same date and in the same manner:

    (1) [X] 3-day notice to pay rent or quit   (4) [ ] 3-day notice to perform covenants or quit

    (2) [ ] 30-day notice to quit   (5) [ ] 3-day notice to quit

    (3) [ ] 60-day notice to quit   (6) [ ] Other *(specify):*

  b. (1) On *(date):* August 8, 20xx   the period stated in the notice expired at the end of the day.

    (2) Defendants failed to comply with the requirements of the notice by that date.

  c. All facts stated in the notice are true.

  d. [ ] The notice included an election of forfeiture.

  e. [X] A copy of the notice is attached and labeled Exhibit 2. *(Required for residential property. See Code Civ. Proc., § 1166.)*

  f. [X] One or more defendants were served (1) with a different notice, (2) on a different date, or (3) in a different manner, as stated in Attachment 8c. *(Check item 8c and attach a statement providing the information required by items 7a–e and 8 for each defendant.)*

8. a. [X] The notice in item 7a was served on the defendant named in item 7a as follows:

    (1) [X] by personally handing a copy to defendant on *(date):*   August 5, 20xx

    (2) [ ] by leaving a copy with *(name or description):*

        a person of suitable age and discretion, on *(date):*   at defendant's

        [ ] residence [ ] business AND mailing a copy to defendant at defendant's place of residence on

        (date):   because defendant cannot be found at defendant's residence or usual place of business.

    (3) [ ] by posting a copy on the premises on *(date):*   [ ] AND giving a copy to a person found residing at the premises AND mailing a copy to defendant at the premises on

        (date):

        (a) [ ] because defendant's residence and usual place of business cannot be ascertained OR

        (b) [ ] because no person of suitable age or discretion can be found there.

    (4) [ ] *(Not for 3-day notice; see Civil Code, § 1946 before using)* by sending a copy by certified or registered mail addressed to defendant on *(date):*

    (5) [ ] *(Not for residential tenancies; see Civil Code, § 1953 before using)* in the manner specified in a written commercial lease between the parties.

  b. [X] *(Name):*   TERRANCE D. TENNANT

    was served on behalf of all defendants who signed a joint written rental agreement.

  c. [ ] Information about service of notice on the defendants alleged in item 7f is stated in Attachment 8c.

  d. [ ] Proof of service of the notice in item 7a is attached and labeled Exhibit 3.

COMPLAINT—UNLAWFUL DETAINER

more defendants with the same notice on a different date or in a different manner. (You generally will not check box 7f or 8c if you checked box 8b to indicate you served one cotenant, but not other written-lease cotenants.) If you did put an X in box 7f, do so in box 8c also. You will then also need to add an extra piece of typing paper titled "Attachment 7f/8c to Complaint— Unlawful Detainer." On that attachment, you need to explain how the defendant(s) other than the one whose name is mentioned in Item 7a was served in a different manner or on a different date. Use the format of the wording in Item 8a(1), (2), (3), (4), or (5) [certified mail service of 30-day or 60-day notice only]. For example, where Items 7 and 8 show you served Tara Tenant personally with a three-day notice to pay rent or quit on September 4, and you served Sam Subtenant on September 6 by substituted service, boxes 7f and 8c should be checked, and Attachment 8c would state, "Defendant Sam Subtenant was served the three-day notice to pay rent or quit, alleged in Item 7, by leaving a copy with Tara Tenant, a person of suitable age and discretion, on September 6, 20xx, at his residence, and by mailing a copy to him on September 7, 20xx, because he could not be found at his residence or place of business."

  Item 8d: If you wish, you may check this box to indicate that instead of using Items 8a through 8c above to describe how the notice was served, you're attaching as Exhibit 3 a written, signed proof of service indicating when and how the notice was served. See the discussion at the beginning of Item 8 for the pros and cons of using Item 8d.

    PLAINTIFF and DEFENDANT At the top of the third page of the complaint (new second sheet) is another large box just like the one at the top of the second page (reverse side of first sheet) of the complaint, labeled "PLAINTIFF (name):" and "DEFENDANT (name):" As before, type the names of the first-listed plaintiff, and first-listed defendant, followed by "et al" if there's more than one.

Item 9: Expiration of Lease

   Do not use this box. It does not apply in evictions based on three-day, 30-day, or 60-day notices.

 Check this box if you are proceeding under Chapter 5 on the grounds that your fixed-term lease expired. Do not check it if the reason for the eviction is that the tenant failed to vacate on time after serving you with a 30-day notice.

Item 10: Rent Due

 Put an X in box 10. At the end of the sentence following the box, put the amount of rent you demanded in the three-day notice.

Your Complaint will be susceptible to a delaying motion if it ambiguously states that the rent due was something other than that stated on the attached three-day notice, so do not under any circumstances list a different amount.

   Leave this box blank. It is solely for evictions based on a Three-Day Notice to Pay Rent or Quit. (See Chapter 2).

Item 11: Daily Rental Value

    Check box 11 and list the daily prorated rent. This is the monthly rent divided by 30 or, if the rent is paid weekly, the weekly rent divided by seven. For example, if the rent is $450 per month, the daily rental value is $450/30, or $15. Round the answer off to the nearest penny if it doesn't come out even. This figure is the measure of the "damages" you suffer each day the tenant stays after the end of the rental period.

   PLAINTIFF and DEFENDANT At the top of the third page of the complaint (new second sheet) is another large box just like the one at the top of the second page (reverse side of first sheet) of the complaint, labeled "PLAINTIFF (name):" and "DEFENDANT (name):" As before, type the names of the first-listed plaintiff, and first-listed defendant, followed by "et al" if there's more than one.

Rent vs. Damages

The difference between "rent" and "damages" is illustrated as follows: On February 1, Tim doesn't pay his landlord Lenny the monthly $900 rent. On February 6, Lenny serves Tim a three-day notice. After the three days have elapsed, and Tim still hasn't paid the rent, the tenancy is terminated. Lenny brings an unlawful detainer action to enforce that termination, and gets a judgment against Tim on March 10. Lenny is still entitled to the $900 rent for February, since it was all due as rent before the tenancy was terminated.

Since the termination of the tenancy was effective in February, Tim owes no "rent" as such for his stay during March. What Tim does owe Lenny for those ten days is money to compensate Lenny for being unable to rerent the property during that time. Assuming that Lenny could have gotten the same rent from a new tenant, namely $900 per month or $30 per day, the "damages" for those ten days would be $300 in addition to the $900 rent, for total rent and damages of $1,200.

Item 12: Landlord's Right to Statutory Damages

   We normally recommend this box be left blank. By checking it, you allege in the Complaint that the tenant is being "malicious" in staying when he or she should leave, and you are asking for up to $600 in punitive damages in addition to the rent. (The law does not allow you to ask for more. Before 1994, a landlord could recover "treble damages," or three times the rent the tenant owed, but now you can recover only $600 if you can convince a judge the tenant acted maliciously.) If you do check this box, you must then add an Attachment 11 in which you state—in very specific detail—the acts of the tenant which you think show a malicious intent. Because only $600 of a probably uncollectible judgment is at stake, because the requirements for alleging and proving malicious intent are very technical, and because judges seldom award these types of extra damages, we do not recommend seeking this sum. Also, demanding extra money based on the tenant's maliciousness may provoke a delaying response on the part of the tenant. You're probably better off leaving item 12 blank.

Item 13: Attorney Fees

    Put an X in this box only if you have a written rental agreement or lease (a copy of which should be attached to the Complaint—see Item 6e)—and it has a clause specifically providing that you (or the prevailing party in a lawsuit) are entitled to attorney's fees. A clause referring only to "costs" or "court costs" isn't enough.

To be entitled to a court judgment for attorney's fees, you must also be represented by an attorney. Since you're representing yourself, you won't be entitled to attorney's fees even if you win. Still, you should fill in this part just in case your tenant contests the lawsuit and you later hire a lawyer.

Item 14: Rent/Eviction Control Ordinance

    This box should be checked only if your property is subject to a local rent control law or just cause eviction ordinance. (See "Rent Control and Just Cause Evictions" in Chapter 3 for a list.) When you put an X in this box, you declare under penalty of perjury that you have complied with all rent ceiling, registration, and other applicable requirements under the ordinance. Be sure you have. If you haven't, or if you're not sure, do some research. (See *The California Landlord's Law Book: Rights & Responsibilities*, Chapter 4.)

Once you're sure you are in compliance, type in the name of the city or county, the title of the ordinance, and the date it went into effect. Much of this information is listed in the Rent Control Chart in Appendix 1 of this volume (as well as *The California Landlord's Law Book: Rights & Responsibilities*, Chapter 4), but because rent control ordinances are constantly changing, you should also call the local rent control board for the latest information.

Item 15: Other Allegations

   This box does not have to be checked in cases based on three-day, 30-day, or 60-day notices.

Check this box if you're suing a tenant who won't leave after having terminated a month-to-month tenancy by giving you at least 30 days' written notice. You'll have to add an extra paper titled "Attachment 15" to the Complaint. Using a blank sheet of typing paper, type a statement based on this model:

> Attachment 15
>
> On _____*(date)*_____, 20__, defendants served plaintiff a written notice terminating their month-to-month tenancy no sooner than 30 days from the date of service of the notice, for the termination to be effective on _____*(date)*_____, 20__. That period has elapsed, and defendants have failed and refused to vacate the premises.

 Extra Required Allegations. Some rent control cities require landlords to make additional allegations. For example, Berkeley requires landlords to allege that they are in compliance with the "implied warranty of habitability." Attachment 15 can also be used for this sort of required allegation. The landlord might allege, "Plaintiff is in full compliance with the implied warranty to provide habitable premises with respect to the subject property."

Item 16: Jurisdictional Limit of the Court

 This statement just means you are not asking for more money than the court has the power to give.

Item 17: Landlord's Requests

 Here you list what you want the court to grant. Since you want "possession of the premises" and court costs such as court filing fees, in any unlawful detainer action, there is no box to check for "a" or "b." Put Xs in boxes c, e, and f. Also, put an X in box d if your lease or rental agreement has an attorney fees clause. (See Item 13.)

Fill in the amount of past due rent in the space provided following box c, again making sure this is the same amount stated in Item 10 and in the three-day notice. In the space after the word "(date)": to the lower right of box f, list the date for the next day following the rental period for which the rent is due.

EXAMPLE: Larry Landlord served Tanya Tenant with a three-day notice, demanding $900 rent for the month of September, or September 1 through 30. The first day after that rental period is October 1, 20xx. Larry should put that date after "(date:)" in box f, to ask the court to award him 1/30th of the monthly rent ($30) for each day after October 1st that Tanya stays.

EXAMPLE: Louise Landowner served Tom Tenant with a three-day notice, demanding $1,000 monthly rent that was due on July 15. Since this rent is due in advance, it covers July 15th through August 14. Louise should put the next day after that, August 15, 20xx, after "(date):" in box f.

 Put X's in boxes e and f for evictions based on both conditional three-day notices to perform covenant or quit and unconditional three day notices. In the space after the word "(date):" below box f, list the *day after* the three-day notice expiration date you listed in Item 7b(1). Don't check box c, since you can only collect back rent in evictions for nonpayment of rent. You may, however, put an X in box d if your lease or rental agreement has an attorney fees clause. (See Item 13.)

 Put an X in box f only. In the space after the word "(date):" below box f, list the *day after* the 30-day notice expiration date, or the *day after* the fixed-term lease expired. For example, if you or the tenant gave a 30-day notice on July 1, the last day the tenant could legally stay was July 31, and you list August 1, 2007, here. Or, if the tenant's lease expired on December 31, 2007 (and you didn't accept rent after that), list the next day, January 1, 2007.

Don't check box c, since it only applies in evictions for nonpayment of rent. Don't check box e, which only applies in evictions based on three-day notices to quit. (See Chapters 2 and 4.) You may, however, put an X in box d if your lease or rental agreement has an attorney's fees clause. (See item 13.)

 Do not check box g unless you insist on asking for extra "statutory damages" of up to $600 on account of the tenant's malicious conduct, in which case you will have also checked Item 12. (Once again, we do not recommend doing this.)

 Do not check box h.

Item 18: Number of Pages Attached

 List the number of pages to be attached to the Complaint, counting each page of every copy of a rental agreement or lease (Exhibit 1) and three-day, 30-day, or 60-day notice (Exhibit 2), as well as any attachments. (Count each printed side of a piece of paper as a page.) Do not count the pages of the Complaint. Thus, for a Complaint that attached a one-page lease and a one-page three-day, 30-day, or 60-day notice, the number of added pages should be "2."

Item 19: Unlawful Detainer Assistant

 The law requires that a non-attorney who is paid to fill out unlawful detainer paperwork must be registered and bonded. This law does not apply, however, to property owners or to managers who prepare such forms for their employer in the ordinary course of their duties (neither does it apply to attorneys). If you are such a property manager or owner, put an X next to the words "did not" in Item 18, and leave the rest of the item blank. If you are paying a paralegal or other person to fill out or otherwise process your papers (other than just having a process server serve them), or to advise you on filling out the forms, he or she must be registered with the county and bonded, and the "did" box must be checked on Item 18. That person's name, address, phone number, and registration information must then be listed on Item 19 of the Complaint form. (If you let an unregistered person prepare your forms for a fee and he or she filled out the "did not" box, remember, *you're* the one declaring, under penalty of perjury, to the truth of the form when you sign it!)

Verification and Plaintiffs' Names, Dates, and Signatures

Type your name in the spaces indicated below Item 19 and, under the heading "VERIFICATION," type in the date and sign the Complaint in both places.

 The two lines side by side above the word "Verification" are the first of two places to sign and type the name(s) of the plaintiff(s). The name of each person who is listed on the Complaint (and Summons) as a plaintiff should be typed in the space to the left. Their signatures go on the space to the right. For more than one plaintiff, it's okay to either separate the names and signatures by commas, with all names on one line, or to list one above the other.

Under the "Verification" heading you state under penalty of perjury that all the allegations in the Complaint are true. A name and signature—but only of one plaintiff even if there are several—is required here, too. The plaintiff with the most knowledge about the matter should type her name and the date in the space to the left and sign in the space at the right.

 Be sure the date you sign is at least one day after the date in Item 7b of the Complaint—the date the notice period legally expired.

If a partnership is named as plaintiff, the verification printed on the form must be modified. You can do this by using correction fluid to "white out" the line of instructions in parentheses just below the word "Verification," and typing over it "I am a partner of the partnership which is." Then, on the next line, white out the words "I am." The verification should then begin "I am a partner of the partnership which is the plaintiff in this proceeding ...."

Preparing the Civil Case Cover Sheet

This form must be filed with the court at the same time as your Complaint. Its purpose is to tell the court what kind of a civil case you're filing, and it's used when filing any type of civil case. (The second page is full of information and instructions that are either irrelevant to your case or unnecessary in light of the information you're getting from this book.) We've preprinted this form with all the information needed to tell the court clerk you're filing an unlawful detainer action to evict the tenant from a residence (as opposed to a commercial building). You need only type in the following information:

PLAINTIFF (Name):	LENNY D. LANDLORD	CASE NUMBER:
DEFENDANT(Name):	TERRENCE D. TENANT, ET AL	

9. ☐ Plaintiff demands possession from each defendant because of expiration of a fixed-term lease.

10. ☒ At the time the 3-day notice to pay rent or quit was served, the amount of **rent due** was $ 900.00

11. ☒ The fair rental value of the premises is $ 30   per day.

12. ☐ Defendant's continued possession is malicious, and plaintiff is entitled to statutory damages under Code of Civil Procedure section 1174(b). *(State specific facts supporting a claim up to $600 in Attachment 12.)*

13. ☒ A written agreement between the parties provides for attorney fees.

14. ☒ Defendant's tenancy is subject to the local rent control or eviction control ordinance of *(city or county, title of ordinance, and date of passage):*

     City of Los Angeles, Rent Stabilization Ordinance, enacted April 12, 1979.

     Plaintiff has met all applicable requirements of the ordinances.

15. ☐ Other allegations are stated in Attachment 15.

16. Plaintiff accepts the jurisdictional limit, if any, of the court.

17. **PLAINTIFF REQUESTS**

   a. possession of the premises.

   b. costs incurred in this proceeding:

   c. ☒ past-due rent of $900.00

   d. ☒ reasonable attorney fees.

   e. ☒ forfeiture of the agreement.

   f. ☒ damages at the rate stated in item 11 from *(date):* September 1, 20xx   for each day that defendants remain in possession through entry of judgment.

   g. ☐ statutory damages up to $600 for the conduct alleged in item 12.

   h. ☐ other *(specify):*

18. ☒ Number of pages attached *(specify):* 3

UNLAWFUL DETAINER ASSISTANT (Bus. & Prof. Code, §§ 6400–6415)

19. *(Complete in all cases.)* An unlawful detainer assistant ☒ did **not** ☐ did for compensation give advice or assistance with this form. *(If plaintiff has received **any** help or advice for pay from an unlawful detainer assistant, state:)*

   a. Assistant's name:

   b. Street address, city, and zip code:

   c. Telephone No.:

   d. County of registration:

   e. Registration No.:

   f. Expires on *(date):*

Date: August 10, 20xx

LENNY D. LANDLORD   ▶*Lenny D. Landlord*

(TYPE OR PRINT NAME)   (SIGNATURE OF PLAINTIFF OR ATTORNEY)

VERIFICATION

(Use a different verification form if the verification is by an attorney or for a corporation or partnership.)

I am the plaintiff in this proceeding and have read this complaint. I declare under penalty of perjury under the laws of the State of California that the foregoing is true and correct.

Date: August 10, 20xx

LENNY D. LANDLORD   ▶*Lenny D. Landlord*

(TYPE OR PRINT NAME)   (SIGNATURE OF PLAINTIFF)

- Type your name, address, and telephone number in the box at the left top of the page, and the court's name, including division, and address in the box below that.

- In the third box near the top of the page, entitled "CASE NAME," type in capital letters the last name of the first plaintiff (you) before the "vs." and the last name of the first defendant after the "vs." For example, if Leslie Smith and Laura Smith-Jones are suing Don Brown and Debra Miller, the case name is "SMITH vs. BROWN."

- Leave the CASE NUMBER box blank. As for Items 1 through 4 on this form, we have filled this information in for you. (It is always the same for residential unlawful detainer actions.)

- In Item 5, check "is not" (your eviction case won't be a class action lawsuit). Ignore Item 6 (it's highly unlikely that you'll have another, related case ongoing when you file your eviction lawsuit).

- Put the date and type your name in capital letters, in the spaces provided (labeled "Date:" and "(TYPE OR PRINT NAME)"). Then sign the form at the lower right in the space provided.

- You will need to make only one copy for your records, which the court clerk will date-stamp and return to you. You do not need to serve any copies on the tenant(s) along with copies of the Summons and Complaint.

A blank, tear-out version of the Civil Case Cover Sheet is in Appendix 3. The CD-ROM also includes this form. Instructions for using the CD are in Appendix 2.

In Los Angeles County, you'll also need to complete the Civil Case Cover Sheet Addendum and Statement of Location, which you'll file with your regular cover sheet. This form tells the court what kind of unlawful detainer action you're commencing (if the eviction is based on the tenant's drug use or sales, your case will proceed quickly), and why you've chosen this courthouse location. Complete the "Short Title" information at the top of each page by listing your name and the last name of the first defendant (for example, Landlord vs. Tenant). On the second page under column two, check box A6020 (Unlawful Detainer—Residential) or A6022 (Unlawful Detainer—Drugs). Under column three, circle reason 6 (the

rental property should be within the area served by the courthouse you've chosen). On page 4, under Item III, check box 6 and include the rental property's address.

Use the Internet to identify the correct court branch in L.A. Go to the L.A. County Superior Court website (www.lasuperiorcourt.org) and choose "Locations" under "About The Court." Then select the "Filing Court Locator." After entering the Zip code of the rental property, you'll learn the proper courthouse for your case.

Getting the Complaint and Summons Ready to File

Now that you have filled out the Complaint, go through the instructions again and double-check each step, using the sample Complaint form set out on the preceding few pages as a guide.

Finally, place the pages of the Complaint in the following order:

1. unlawful detainer Complaint (front facing you, on top)
2. attachments, in numerical order if there are more than one
3. Exhibit 1 (copy of written rental agreement) if applicable
4. Exhibit 2 (copy of three-day, 30-day, or 60-day notice) if notice was served.

Fasten them with a paper clip for now.

Before you take the Summons, Civil Case Cover Sheet, and Complaint to court for filing and stamping, you need to:

- Make one copy of the Complaint (together with attachments and exhibits) for your records, plus one copy to be served on each defendant. The original will be filed with the court. Make sure to copy both sides of the Complaint, using a two-sided copying process if possible. Be sure that the front and back of the Complaint you submit to the court are in the same upside down relation to each other as is the form in the back of this book.

- Make two copies of the Summons for each defendant and one for your records. For example, if you named three defendants in your Complaint, make seven copies of the Summons.

CM-010

ATTORNEY OR PARTY WITHOUT ATTORNEY *(Name, State Bar number, and address)*:	FOR COURT USE ONLY

ATTORNEY OR PARTY WITHOUT ATTORNEY *(Name, State Bar number, and address)*:

LENNY D. LANDLORD
12345 Angeleno Street
Los Angeles, CA 90010
TELEPHONE NO.: 213-555-6789   FAX NO.: 213-555-5678
ATTORNEY FOR *(Name)*: Plaintiff in Pro Per

SUPERIOR COURT OF CALIFORNIA, COUNTY OF LOS ANGELES
STREET ADDRESS: 110 North Grand Avenue
MAILING ADDRESS: Same
CITY AND ZIP CODE: Los Angeles, CA 90012
BRANCH NAME: CENTRAL DISTRICT/DOWNTOWN BRANCH

CASE NAME: LANDLORD vs. TENANT

CIVIL CASE COVER SHEET		Complex Case Designation		CASE NUMBER:
☐ **Unlimited** (Amount demanded exceeds $25,000)	☒ **Limited** (Amount demanded is $25,000 or less)	☐ **Counter** ☐ **Joinder** Filed with first appearance by defendant (Cal. Rules of Court, rule 3.402)		JUDGE:
				DEPT:

Items 1–5 below must be completed (see instructions on page 2).

1. Check **one** box below for the case type that best describes this case:

Auto Tort
☐ Auto (22)
☐ Uninsured motorist (46)

Other PI/PD/WD (Personal Injury/Property Damage/Wrongful Death) Tort
☐ Asbestos (04)
☐ Product liability (24)
☐ Medical malpractice (45)
☐ Other PI/PD/WD (23)

Non-PI/PD/WD (Other) Tort
☐ Business tort/unfair business practice (07)
☐ Civil rights (08)
☐ Defamation (13)
☐ Fraud (16)
☐ Intellectual property (19)
☐ Professional negligence (25)
☐ Other non-PI/PD/WD tort (35)

Employment
☐ Wrongful termination (36)
☐ Other employment (15)

Contract
☐ Breach of contract/warranty (06)
☐ Collections (09)
☐ Insurance coverage (18)
☐ Other contract (37)

Real Property
☐ Eminent domain/Inverse condemnation (14)
☐ Wrongful eviction (33)
☐ Other real property (26)

Unlawful Detainer
☐ Commercial (31)
☒ Residential (32)
☐ Drugs (38)

Judicial Review
☐ Asset forfeiture (05)
☐ Petition re: arbitration award (11)
☐ Writ of mandate (02)
☐ Other judicial review (39)

Provisionally Complex Civil Litigation (Cal. Rules of Court, rules 3.400–3.403)
☐ Antitrust/Trade regulation (03)
☐ Construction defect (10)
☐ Mass tort (40)
☐ Securities litigation (28)
☐ Environmental/Toxic tort (30)
☐ Insurance coverage claims arising from the above listed provisionally complex case types (41)

Enforcement of Judgment
☐ Enforcement of judgment (20)

Miscellaneous Civil Complaint
☐ RICO (27)
☐ Other complaint *(not specified above)* (42)

Miscellaneous Civil Petition
☐ Partnership and corporate governance (21)
☐ Other petition *(not specified above)* (43)

2. This case ☐ is ☒ is not complex under rule 3.400 of the California Rules of Court. If the case is complex, mark the factors requiring exceptional judicial management:
   a. ☐ Large number of separately represented parties
   b. ☐ Extensive motion practice raising difficult or novel issues that will be time-consuming to resolve
   c. ☐ Substantial amount of documentary evidence
   d. ☐ Large number of witnesses
   e. ☐ Coordination with related actions pending in one or more courts in other counties, states, or countries, or in a federal court
   f. ☐ Substantial postjudgment judicial supervision

3. Type of remedies sought *(check all that apply)*:
   a. ☒ monetary   b. ☒ nonmonetary; declaratory or injunctive relief   c. ☐ punitive

4. Number of causes of action *(specify)*:

5. This case ☐ is ☒ is not a class action suit.

6. If there are any known related cases, file and serve a notice of related case. *(You may use form CM-015.)*

Date: August 10, 20xx

Lenny D. Landlord
(TYPE OR PRINT NAME)

► *Lenny D. Landlord*
(SIGNATURE OF PARTY OR ATTORNEY FOR PARTY)

NOTICE
- Plaintiff must file this cover sheet with the first paper filed in the action or proceeding (except small claims cases or cases filed under the Probate Code, Family Code, or Welfare and Institutions Code). (Cal. Rules of Court, rule 3.220.) Failure to file may result in sanctions.
- File this cover sheet in addition to any cover sheet required by local court rule.
- If this case is complex under rule 3.400 et seq. of the California Rules of Court, you must serve a copy of this cover sheet on **all** other parties to the action or proceeding.
- Unless this is a complex case, this cover sheet will be used for statistical purposes only.

Page 1 of 2

Form Adopted for Mandatory Use Judicial Council of California CM-010 [Rev. January 1, 2007]	**CIVIL CASE COVER SHEET**	Cal. Rules of Court, rules 3.220, 3.400–3.403; Standards of Judicial Administration, § 19 *www.courtinfo.ca.gov*

- Make one copy of the Civil Case Cover Sheet for your records. Since this form is not served on the defendant, you don't need to make any more.

Filing Your Complaint and Getting Summonses Issued

To file your unlawful detainer Complaint, follow these steps.

Step 1: Take the originals and all the copies of your papers to the court's "civil" filing window at the courthouse and tell the clerk you want to file an unlawful detainer action.

Step 2: Give the clerk the original Civil Case Cover Sheet and Complaint to be filed with the court. Ask the clerk to "file-stamp" each of your copies and give them back to you. He will rubber-stamp each of the copies with the date, the word "FILED," and a case number.

Step 3: Give the clerk one copy of the Summons per defendant and ask him to "issue" a Summons for each. The clerk will stamp the court seal on each of these Summonses and fill in the date of issuance; these are now original Summonses, and the clerk gives them back to you.

Step 4: Give the clerk the other copies of the Summons, telling him they are copies to be "conformed." He will stamp them with the date, but not the court seal. Staple one of these Summons copies to the front of each Complaint copy. Both are to be served on the defendants at the same time. (The original Summonses are returned to the clerk after the copies are served—see below.)

Step 5: Pay the court filing fee of around $140, though the exact amount varies, depending on the county.

Serving the Papers on the Defendant

After you've filed your unlawful detainer Complaint and had the Summonses issued, a copy of the Summons and of the Complaint must be served on each person you're suing. This is called "service of process," and it's an essential part of your lawsuit. The reason for this is simple: A person being sued is constitutionally entitled to be notified of the nature of the lawsuit against him and how he may defend himself.

The Summons tells a defendant that he must file a written response to the allegations in your Complaint within five days of the date of service or lose by "default." Unlike service of notices to quit, where service on one tenant is often considered service on others, each person sued must be separately served with copies of the Summons and Complaint.

If you don't follow service rules to the letter, you lose. For example, a "shortcut" service of Summons and Complaint, where the papers are given to the first person who answers the door at the property, instead of being properly handed to the defendant himself, is not valid. This is true even if the papers nevertheless are eventually given to the right person. (If the defendant cannot be found, the strict requirements of "substituted service"—discussed in "Substituted Service on Another Person," below—including repeated attempts to personally serve, followed by mailing a second copy, must be followed.)

Who Must Be Served

Each defendant listed in the Summons and Complaint must be served. It doesn't matter that the defendants may live under the same roof or be married. If you don't serve a particular defendant, it's just as if you never sued her in the first place; the court can't enter a judgment against her, and she cannot be evicted when the sheriff or marshal comes later on. She not only will be allowed to stay, but may even be free to invite the evicted codefendants back in as "guests." (Minor children are evicted along with their parents, without the necessity of naming them as defendants and serving them with Complaints.)

Service on Unknown Occupants (Optional)

If you don't serve copies of the Summons and Complaint on everyone residing in the property as of the date you filed the Complaint, the eviction may be delayed even after you've gotten a judgment and arranged for the sheriff or marshal to evict. That's because occupants who weren't served with the Summons and Complaint were never really sued in the first place. After you get a court order for possession and the sheriff posts the property with a notice advising the occupants they have five days to move or be bodily evicted, the unserved occupants can file a Claim of Right to Possession with the sheriff and stop the eviction until you redo your lawsuit to get a judgment against them. (C.C.P. § 1174.3.) Coping with this problem is difficult, time-consuming, and beyond the scope of this book, and a lawyer is almost a necessity.

How can you avoid this? State law gives you an option: A sheriff, marshal, or registered process server, when serving the Summons and Complaint on the named defendants, can ask whether there are any other occupants of the property that haven't been named. If there are occupants who aren't named, the sheriff, marshal, or registered process server can then serve each of them, too, with a blank Prejudgment Claim of Right to Possession form and an extra copy of the Summons and Complaint, and indicate this on the proof of service. The unnamed occupants have ten days from the date of service to file any Claim of Right to Possession; they can't file it later when the sheriff is about to evict. If anyone does file a claim, he or she is automatically added as a defendant. (The court clerk is supposed to do that and notify you of such by mail.) The person filing a claim then has five days to respond to the Summons and Complaint. If they don't, you can obtain a default judgment for possession (see Chapter 7) that includes the new claimant as well as the other named defendants.

With this optional procedure, an unknown occupant will be less likely to file such a claim, since the threat of eviction is not as immediate as when the sheriff offers this opportunity only days before the actual eviction. (C.C.P. §§ 415.46, 1174.25.) On the other hand, this optional procedure may not be necessary if you have no reason to believe there are occupants of the property whose names you don't know. Because only a sheriff, marshal, or private process server can serve the papers when you follow this procedure, the eviction may be more costly or proceed more slowly. Also, if you use this option, you will have to wait ten days from service, rather than the usual five, to obtain a judgment that would include unnamed occupants.

A blank, tear-out version of the Prejudgment Claim to Right of Possession is in Appendix 3. The CD-ROM also includes this form. Instructions for using the CD are in Appendix 2.

If you want to have any unknown occupants served, you will need to make as many extra copies of the Summons and Complaint and claim form as you anticipate need to be served on unknown occupants. Fill out the caption boxes at the top of the Prejudgment Claim of Right to Possession form as you have on your other court forms, and leave the rest of it blank. Your instructions to the process server, sheriff, or marshal should include a statement something like this: "Enclosed are two additional sets of copies of the Summons and Complaint, together with a blank Prejudgment Claim of Right to Possession form; please serve the same on any unnamed occupants of the premises pursuant to C.C.P. § 415.46. Please indicate this type of service on your Proof of Service."

Who May Serve the Papers

The law forbids you (the plaintiff) from serving a Summons and Complaint yourself, but any other person 18 or older and not named as a plaintiff or defendant in the lawsuit can do it. You can have a marshal or sheriff's deputy, a professional process server, or just an acquaintance or employee serve the papers. (If you have a friend or employee serve the papers, have him read the part of this chapter on how to serve the papers and fill out the "Proof of Service" on the original Summons.) However, if you use the optional procedure shown in the section above for serving a Claim of Right to Possession on any unnamed occupants, you must use a marshal or sheriff's deputy or registered process server. An ordinary individual cannot serve the Claim of Right to Possession.

What about having your spouse serve the papers? Although no statute or case law specifically disallows spouses not named in the Complaint from serving papers for the named spouse, this isn't a good idea. Since spouses almost always share an ownership interest in real estate (even if the property is only in one spouse's name), a judge could rule, if the tenant contests service, that the unnamed spouse is a "party" because he or she partly owns the property.

Some landlords prefer to have a marshal or deputy sheriff serve the papers to intimidate the tenant and give the impression, however false, that the forces of the law favor the eviction. Not all counties provide this service, however, and in those that do, sheriff's deputies and marshals are occasionally slow and sometimes don't try very hard to serve a person who is avoiding service by hiding or saying she is someone other than the defendant. To have a marshal or deputy serve the Summons and Complaint, go to the marshal's office or the civil division of the county sheriff's office, pay a $26 fee for each defendant to be served, and fill out a form giving such information as the best hours to find the defendant at home or work, general physical descriptions, and so on.

Professional process serving firms are commonly faster and are often a lot more resourceful at serving evasive persons. They are also a little more expensive, but the money you'll save in having the papers served faster (and therefore in being able to evict sooner) may justify the extra expense. If you have an attorney, ask her to recommend a good process serving firm, or check the Yellow Pages for process servers in the area where the tenant lives or works.

Marshals and Sheriffs

Marshals are the enforcement officers for the courts. They serve court papers, enforce civil court judgments, and physically evict tenants who refuse to leave the property following a judgment of eviction. Los Angeles County and some others have marshal's offices separate from sheriff's offices, but in many other counties—especially in Northern California—the sheriff is designated as the marshal.

How the Summons and Complaint Copies Are Served

 If you use a sheriff, marshal, or professional process server, you can skip this section.

There are only three ways to serve a defendant legally. Again, pay close attention to the rules for the method you use.

Remember that only copies of the Summons, and not the originals with the court seals, should be served on the defendant. If you mistakenly serve the original, you'll have to prepare a Declaration of Lost Summons.

Personal Service

For personal service, the copy of the Summons and of the Complaint must be handed to the defendant by the server. The person serving the papers can't simply leave them at the defendant's workplace or in the mailbox. If the defendant refuses to take the paper, acts hostile, or attempts to run away, the process server should simply put the papers on the ground as close as possible to the defendant's feet and leave. The person serving the papers should never try to force a defendant to take them—it's unnecessary and may subject the process server (or even you) to a lawsuit for battery.

Personal service of the papers is best; if you have to resort to either of the other two methods, the law allows the defendant an extra ten days (15 days instead of five) to file a written response to the Complaint. It is therefore worthwhile to make several attempts at personal service at the defendant's home or workplace.

Before personally serving the papers, the process server must check boxes 1 and 4 on the bottom front of the Summons copies to be served and fill in the date of service in the space following box 4. A sample is shown below. It's better for the process server to fill the information in on the Summons copy in pencil before service—so it can be changed later if service isn't effected that way or on that date. This is also less awkward than doing it right there just as you've located the angry defendant.

Some individuals have developed avoidance of the process server into a high (but silly) art. It is permissible, and may be necessary, for the person serving the papers to use trickery to get the defendant to open the door or come out of an office and identify himself. One method that works well is for the process server to carry a wrapped (but empty) package and a clipboard, saying he has a "delivery" for the defendant and requires her signature on a receipt. The delivery, of course, is of the Summons and Complaint. If all else fails, your process server may have to resort to a "stakeout" and wait for the defendant to appear. It's obviously not necessary to serve the defendant inside his home or workplace. The parking lot is just as good.

When serving more than one defendant, it's sometimes difficult to serve the remaining defendant after having served one. For example, if one adult in the family customarily answers the door and is served the papers, it's unlikely that she will cooperate by

POS-010

ATTORNEY OR PARTY WITHOUT ATTORNEY *(Name, State Bar number, and address):*
LENNY D. LANDLORD
12345 ANGELENO STREET
LOS ANGELES, CA 90010
TELEPHONE NO.: 213-555-6789   FAX NO. *(Optional):*
E-MAIL ADDRESS *(Optional):*
ATTORNEY FOR *(Name):* Plaintiff in Pro Per

FOR COURT USE ONLY

SUPERIOR COURT OF CALIFORNIA, COUNTY OF LOS ANGELES
STREET ADDRESS: 110 North Grand Avenue
MAILING ADDRESS: Same
CITY AND ZIP CODE: Los Angeles, CA 90012
BRANCH NAME: CENTRAL DISTRICT/DOWNTOWN BRANCH

PLAINTIFF/PETITIONER: LENNY D. LANDLORD

DEFENDANT/RESPONDENT: TERRANCE D. TENANT, TILLIE D. TENANT

CASE NUMBER:

| **PROOF OF SERVICE OF SUMMONS** | Ref. No. or File No.: |

(Separate proof of service is required for each party served.)

1. At the time of service I was at least 18 years of age and not a party to this action.

2. I served copies of:

   a. ☐ summons

   b. ☒ complaint

   c. ☐ Alternative Dispute Resolution (ADR) package

   d. ☐ Civil Case Cover Sheet *(served in complex cases only)*

   e. ☐ cross-complaint

   f. ☐ other *(specify documents):*

3. a. Party served *(specify name of party as shown on documents served):*
   TERRANCE D. TENANT

   b. ☐ Person (other than the party in item 3a) served on behalf of an entity or as an authorized agent (and not a person under item 5b on whom substituted service was made) *(specify name and relationship to the party named in item 3a):*

4. Address where the party was served: 6789 Angel Blvd., Apt. 10, Los Angeles, CA 90010

5. I served the party *(check proper box)*

   a. ☒ **by personal service.** I personally delivered the documents listed in item 2 to the party or person authorized to receive service of process for the party (1) on *(date):* September 11, 20xx (2) at *(time):* 2:15 PM

   b. ☐ **by substituted service.** On *(date):*   at *(time):*   I left the documents listed in item 2 with or in the presence of *(name and title or relationship to person indicated in item 3):*

      (1) ☐ **(business)** a person at least 18 years of age apparently in charge at the office or usual place of business of the person to be served. I informed him or her of the general nature of the papers.

      (2) ☐ **(home)** a competent member of the household (at least 18 years of age) at the dwelling house or usual place of abode of the party. I informed him or her of the general nature of the papers.

      (3) ☐ **(physical address unknown)** a person at least 18 years of age apparently in charge at the usual mailing address of the person to be served, other than a United States Postal Service post office box. I informed him or her of the general nature of the papers.

      (4) ☐ I thereafter mailed (by first-class, postage prepaid) copies of the documents to the person to be served at the place where the copies were left (Code Civ. Proc., § 415.20). I mailed the documents on
      (date):   from *(city):*   **or** ☐ a declaration of mailing is attached.

      (5) ☐ I attach a **declaration of diligence** stating actions taken first to attempt personal service.

Page 1 of 2

calling the other defendant to the door so that your process server can serve that person too. So, when one person answers the door, the process server should ask whether the other person is at home. Usually the defendant who answers the door will stay there until the other person comes to the door—at which time your process server can serve them both by handing the papers to each individual or laying them at their feet.

Substituted Service on Another Person

If your process server makes three unsuccessful attempts to serve a defendant at home, at times you would reasonably expect the defendant to be there, he can give the papers to another person at the defendant's home, workplace, or usual mailing address (other than a U.S. Postal Service mailbox) with instructions to that person to give papers to the defendant.

If the papers are left at the defendant's home, they must be given to "a competent member of the household" who is at least 18 years old. In addition, the server must mail a second copy of the Summons and Complaint to the defendant at the place where the Summons was left. (C.C.P. § 415.20(b).) This is called "substituted service."

There are two disadvantages to this method. First, several unsuccessful attempts to find the defendant have to be made and must be documented in a separate form (discussed below). The second disadvantage is that the law allows the defendant ten extra days (or 15 days) to respond to a Summons and Complaint served this way. So using this method instead of personal service means that the eviction will be delayed ten days.

In most instances, unless your process server can serve a defendant at home, it's better to get a professional process server to make substituted service. If you send a relative or friend to try to serve a tenant at work, you could regret it, as service at work is likely to create a lot of hostility. It may even prompt the tenant to go out and get herself a lawyer, when she otherwise might have simply moved out.

Post Office Boxes

A tenant who is never home to be served (and no one ever answers the door at the tenant's home) *cannot* be served at a "usual mailing address" if that address happens to be a post office box at a U.S. Postal Service public post office. However, if the tenant rents a box at a *private* post office (such as Mailboxes, Etc.) and regularly uses that address and box, he may be served there by substituted service on the person in charge of the mail drop, followed by mailing a second copy of the Summons and Complaint (from a real U.S. Postal Service mailbox).

EXAMPLE: You name Daily and Baily as defendants. When your process server goes to serve the papers, only Daily is home. He serves Daily personally. Baily, however, has to be served before you can get a judgment against him. Two more attempts to serve Baily fail, when Daily answers the door and refuses to say where Baily is. The process server uses the substituted service technique and gives Daily another set of papers—for Baily—and mails still another set addressed to Baily. Service is not legally effective until the tenth day after giving the papers to Daily and mailing a second copy of the papers to Baily. This means that you'll have to wait these ten days, plus the five day "response time," (see "What Next?" below) for a total of 15 days, before you can take a default judgment against Baily.

Before serving the papers by substituted service, the process server should check box 3 on the bottom front of the Summons copy and also check the box next to "CCP 416.90 (individual)" and should write in the name of the defendant served this way (not the person to whom the papers are given) after the words "On behalf of." Of the boxes below box 3 and indented, check the box labeled "other" and add "C.C.P. § 415.20" after it to indicate that substituted service was used. As with personal service, check box 4 and fill in the date of delivery of the papers. A sample is shown below.

If the process server plans to serve a Prejudgment Claim to Right of Possession (see "Service on Unknown Occupants (Optional)," below), the server should check

PLAINTIFF/PETITIONER: LENNY D. LANDLORD	CASE NUMBER:
DEFENDANT/RESPONDENT: TERRANCE D. TENNANT	

5. c. ☐ **by mail and acknowledgment of receipt of service.** I mailed the documents listed in item 2 to the party, to the address shown in item 4, by first-class mail, postage prepaid,

    (1) on *(date):*   (2) from *(city):*

    (3) ☐ with two copies of the *Notice and Acknowledgment of Receipt* and a postage-paid return envelope addressed to me. *(Attach completed Notice and Acknowledgement of Receipt.)* (Code Civ. Proc., § 415.30.)

    (4) ☐ to an address outside California with return receipt requested. (Code Civ. Proc., § 415.40.)

  d. ☐ **by other means** *(specify means of service and authorizing code section):*

    ☐ Additional page describing service is attached.

6. The "Notice to the Person Served" (on the summons) was completed as follows:
  a. ☒ as an individual defendant.
  b. ☐ as the person sued under the fictitious name of *(specify):*
  c. ☐ as occupant.
  d. ☐ On behalf of *(specify):*
    under the following Code of Civil Procedure section:

    ☐ 416.10 (corporation)   ☐ 415.95 (business organization, form unknown)
    ☐ 416.20 (defunct corporation)   ☐ 416.60 (minor)
    ☐ 416.30 (joint stock company/association) ☐ 416.70 (ward or conservatee)
    ☐ 416.40 (association or partnership) ☐ 416.90 (authorized person)
    ☐ 416.50 (public entity)   ☐ 415.46 (occupant)
                      ☐ other:

7. **Person who served papers**
  a. Name: Sam D. Server
  b. Address: 1000 A Street, Los Angeles, CA 90010
  c. Telephone number: 213-444-7000
  d. **The fee** for service was: $ 50.00
  e. I am:

    (1) ☒ not a registered California process server.
    (2) ☐ exempt from registration under Business and Professions Code section 22350(b).
    (3) ☐ a registered California process server:
      (i) ☐ owner ☐ employee ☐ independent contractor.
      (ii) Registration No.:
      (iii) County:

8. ☒ **I declare** under penalty of perjury under the laws of the State of California that the foregoing is true and correct.

    or

9. ☐ **I am a California sheriff or marshal and I** certify that the foregoing is true and correct.

Date: September 11, 20xx

_____   ▶ *Sam D. Server* _____
Sam D. Server
(NAME OF PERSON WHO SERVED PAPERS/SHERIFF OR MARSHAL)   (SIGNATURE)

DECLARATION RE REASONABLE DILIGENCE FOR

SUBSTITUTED SERVICE OF SUMMONS ON INDIVIDUAL

I, SARAH SERVER, declare:

I am over the age of 18 years and not a party to this action.

On August 13, 20xx, I served the Summons and Complaint on defendant Terrence Tenant by leaving true copies thereof with Teresa Tenant at defendant's place of residence and mailing a second set of copies thereof addressed to defendant at his place of residence.

Prior to using substituted service to serve defendant Terrence Tenant, I attempted on the following occasions to personally serve him:

1. On August 10, 20xx, at 5:30 P.M., I knocked on the front door of defendant's residence. A woman who identified herself as Teresa Tenant answered the door. I asked her whether I could see either Terrence or Tillie Tenant and she replied, "They're not at home."

2. On August 12, 20xx, at 3:00 P.M., I went to defendant Terrence Tenant's place of employment, Bob's Burgers, 123 Main Street, Los Angeles, and was told that defendant Terrence Tenant had recently been fired.

3. On August 13, 20xx, at 7:00 A.M., I again went to defendant's home. Again, Teresa Tenant answered the door and said that Terrence Tenant was not home. I then gave her the papers for Terrence Tenant.

I declare under penalty of perjury under the laws of the State of California that the foregoing is true and correct.

DATED: ___August 13, 20xx___   _Sarah Server_____
                                       SARAH SERVER

Declaration re Reasonable Diligence for Substituted Service of Summons on Individual

box c next to the words, "as an occupant," and also box d, next to "CCP 425.46 (occupant)."

The process server must fill out the Proof of Service of Summons (see below) and sign and date a declaration detailing her attempts to locate the defendant for personal service. This declaration is attached to the original Summons. A sample is shown below.

"Posting-and-Mailing" Service

Occasionally, a process server isn't able to use either personal or substituted service to serve a defendant with copies of the Summons and Complaint. For example, if your tenant lives alone and is deliberately avoiding service, and you don't know where he works (he's no longer at the job listed on his application several months ago), the law provides that your process server can post copies of the Summons and Complaint on his front door and mail a second set of copies.

As with substituted service, this "posting-and-mailing" method also gives the defendant an extra ten days to file a response with the court, and so ten more days (total of 15 days) must go by before you can get a default judgment.

Posting and mailing can be more complicated than it looks, and we strongly recommend that you let a process server or a lawyer handle it. There are just too many ways to make a mistake, and, if you do, your whole lawsuit will fail.

Before you can use posting and mailing, you must get written permission from a judge. Your process server must show that he has made at least two, and preferably three, unsuccessful attempts to serve the papers at reasonable times. For example, an attempt to serve an employed defendant at home at noon on a weekday, when she would most likely be at work, isn't reasonable. Attempts to serve at unreasonable hours may subject you to legal liability for invasion of privacy or intentional infliction of mental distress—another good reason to let someone experienced handle it. However, a sample form (Application and Order to Serve Summons by Posting for Unlawful Detainer) for getting permission from a judge for this type of service is shown below. Keep in mind, though, that this sample should be adapted to your own situation.

A blank, Application and Order to Serve Summons by Posting for Unlawful Detainer is in Appendix 3. The CD-ROM also includes this page. Instructions for using the CD are in Appendix 2.

Filling Out the Proof of Service of Summons Form

Once the process server has served the copies of the Summonses, the server must fill out a "Proof of Service of Summons" form and staple it to the original Summons. (Remember, there is one original Summons for each defendant.) If you use a sheriff, marshal, or registered process server, that person should do this for you. So, even where two or more defendants are served at the same time and place by the same process server, two separate Proofs of Service—each stapled to each original Summons—should be filled out. When this form is filled out and returned to the court clerk (see Chapter 7), it tells the clerk that the tenant received notice of the lawsuit, an essential element of your lawsuit. Here's how to complete the Proof of Service of Summons. The process server must fill out a Proof of Service of Summons for each defendant.

A blank, tear-out version of the Proof of Service of Summons is in Appendix 3. The CD-ROM also includes this form. Instructions for using the CD are in Appendix 2.

In the box at the top of the form, fill in the plaintiff's and defendant's names, and leave blank the box entitled "case number."

Item 2: Check the box next to "Complaint." If a sheriff, marshal, or registered process server served a Prejudgment Claim of Right to Possession using the optional procedure discussed above, that person should also check the box next to "other (specify documents)" and add, "Prejudgment Claim of Right to Possession."

Item 3a: Type the name of the defendant for whom this Summons was issued and on whom the copies were served.

Item 3b: Leave this box blank (it's for the unlikely event that your tenant has a designated agent who will accept service of process).

NAME, ADDRESS, AND TELEPHONE NUMBER OF ATTORNEY OR PARTY WITHOUT ATTORNEY:	STATE BAR NUMBER	Reserved for Clerk's File Stamp
LENNY D. LANDLORD 12345 Angeleno Street Los Angeles, CA 90010 Tel: 213-555-6789		

ATTORNEY FOR (Name): Plaintiff in Pro Per

SUPERIOR COURT OF CALIFORNIA, COUNTY OF

COURTHOUSE ADDRESS:
110 N. Grand Avenue, Los Angeles, CA 90012

PLAINTIFF:
LENNY D. LANDLORD

DEFENDANT:
TERRENCE D. TENANT, TILLIE D. TENANT

APPLICATION AND ORDER TO SERVE SUMMONS BY POSTING FOR UNLAWFUL DETAINER	CASE NUMBER: A-123456-B

1. I am the ☒ plaintiff ☐ plaintiff's attorney ☐ other (specify):_____

2. I apply for an order pursuant to Code of Civil Procedure section 415.45 to permit service by posting of the summons and complaint on defendant(s). *Specify name(s):* Terrence D. Tenant, Tillie D. Tenant _____

3. The complaint seeks possession of property location at: 6789 Angel Street, Apt. 10, Los Angeles, Los Angeles, County, California . The property is ☒ residential ☐ commercial.

4. The notice to quit, or pay rent or quit, was served by: ☐ personal service ☐ substituted service ☒ posting and mailing ☐ other (specify):_____

5. At least three attempts to serve in a manner specified in Code of Civil Procedure, Article 3, (other than posting or publication) are required. List attempts to serve, if made by declarant, or attach declaration(s) of process server(s) stating attempts to locate and serve the defendants. If service not made, please explain.

DATE	TIME	REASON SERVICE COULD NOT BE MADE/REMARKS
8/10/xx	5:30 p.m.	Minor daughter answered through door, refused to open and said her parents were not home.
8/12/xx	3:00 p.m.	Defendants not present at place of employment, manager said fired two weeks earlier.
8/13/xx	7:15 p.m.	No one answered the door, though lights on and both defendants' vehicles in driveway.

☒ Declaration(s) of process server stating attempts to locate and serve the defendant(s) is attached and incorporated into this application by reference

CIV 107 10-03
LASC Approved

APPLICATION AND ORDER TO SERVE SUMMONS BY POSTING FOR UNLAWFUL DETAINER

Code Civ. Proc., § 415.45
Page 1 of 2

Short Title	Case Number
LANDLORD V. TENANT	A-123456-B

6. Service ☒ has ☐ has not been attempted during regular business hours at the place(s) of employment of the defendant(s). If not, state reason: ☐ the place(s) of employment of the defendant(s) is not known.
    ☒ Other *(specify)*: Service was attempted 8/12/xx at defendants' former place of employment, but process server was advised that defendants were fired two weeks before.
    _____

7. Service ☒ has ☐ has not been attempted at the "residence" of the defendant(s). If not, state reasons: ☐ The place of residence of the defendant(s) is not known.
    ☐ Other *(specify)*: _____
    _____
    _____

8. Other: _____
    _____
    _____

9. Did the plaintiff pay for help from a registered unlawful detainer assistant (Bus. and Prof. Code, §§ 6400-5415) who helped prepare this form?   ☐ Yes   ☒ No If yes, complete the following information:
    Name of Unlawful Detainer Assistant: _____; Telephone Number: (   )
    _____ Address *(Mailing address, city and Zip code)*: _____
    _____
    Registration #: _____; County of Registration: _____.

I declare under penalty of perjury under the laws of the State of California, that the foregoing is true and correct.

Aug. 13, 20xx	LENNY D. LANDLORD	*Lenny D. Landlord*
DATE	TYPE OF PRINT DECLARANT'S NAME	DECLARANT'S SIGNATURE

FINDINGS AND ORDER

THE COURT FINDS:

1. The defendant(s) named in the application cannot with reasonable diligence be served in any manner specified in Code of Civil Procedure, Article 3.

2. (a) A cause of action exists against the defendant(s) named in the application; **and/or** (b) defendant(s) named in the application has or claims an interest in real property in California that is subject to the jurisdiction of the court; **and/or** (c) the relief demanded in the complaint consists wholly or partially in excluding the defendant(s) from any interest in the property.

THE COURT ORDERS:

The defendant(s) named in the application may be served by posting a copy of the summons and complaint on the premises in a manner most likely to give actual notice to the defendant(s), and by immediately mailing, by certified mail, a copy of the summons and complaint to the defendant(s) at his/her last known address.

Dated: _____   _____   _____
                              Judicial Officer   Div/Dept.

POS-010

ATTORNEY OR PARTY WITHOUT ATTORNEY *(Name, State Bar number, and address):* LENNY D. LANDLORD 12345 ANGELENO STREET LOS ANGELES, CA 90010 TELEPHONE NO.: 213-555-6789 FAX NO. *(Optional):* E-MAIL ADDRESS *(Optional):* ATTORNEY FOR *(Name):* Plaintiff in Pro Per	*FOR COURT USE ONLY*

SUPERIOR COURT OF CALIFORNIA, COUNTY OF LOS ANGELES STREET ADDRESS: 110 North Grand Avenue MAILING ADDRESS: Same CITY AND ZIP CODE: Los Angeles, CA 90012 BRANCH NAME: CENTRAL DISTRICT/DOWNTOWN BRANCH	
PLAINTIFF/PETITIONER: LENNY D. LANDLORD DEFENDANT/RESPONDENT: TERRENCE D. TENANT, TILLIE D. TENANT	CASE NUMBER:
PROOF OF SERVICE OF SUMMONS	Ref. No. or File No.:

(Separate proof of service is required for each party served.)

1. At the time of service I was at least 18 years of age and not a party to this action.

2. I served copies of:

    a. ☐   summons

    b. ☒   complaint

    c. ☐   Alternative Dispute Resolution (ADR) package

    d. ☐   Civil Case Cover Sheet *(served in complex cases only)*

    e. ☐   cross-complaint

    f. ☐   other *(specify documents):*

3. a. Party served *(specify name of party as shown on documents served):*
    TERRENCE D. TENANT

    b. ☐   Person (other than the party in item 3a) served on behalf of an entity or as an authorized agent (and not a person
    under item 5b on whom substituted service was made) *(specify name and relationship to the party named in item 3a):*

4. Address where the party was served: 6789 Angel Blvd., Apt. 10, Los Angeles, CA 90010

5. I served the party *(check proper box)*

    a. ☒   **by personal service.** I personally delivered the documents listed in item 2 to the party or person authorized to
    receive service of process for the party (1) on *(date):* September 10, 20xx (2) at *(time):* 2:15 PM

    b. ☐   **by substituted service.** On *(date):*   at *(time):*   I left the documents listed in item 2 with or
    in the presence of *(name and title or relationship to person indicated in item 3):*

      (1) ☐   **(business)** a person at least 18 years of age apparently in charge at the office or usual place of business
      of the person to be served. I informed him or her of the general nature of the papers.

      (2) ☐   **(home)** a competent member of the household (at least 18 years of age) at the dwelling house or usual
      place of abode of the party. I informed him or her of the general nature of the papers.

      (3) ☐   **(physical address unknown)** a person at least 18 years of age apparently in charge at the usual mailing
      address of the person to be served, other than a United States Postal Service post office box. I informed
      him or her of the general nature of the papers.

      (4) ☐   I thereafter mailed (by first-class, postage prepaid) copies of the documents to the person to be served
      at the place where the copies were left (Code Civ. Proc., § 415.20). I mailed the documents on
      (date):   from *(city):*   **or** ☐ a declaration of mailing is attached.

      (5) ☐   I attach a **declaration of diligence** stating actions taken first to attempt personal service.

Page 1 of 2

Form Adopted for Mandatory Use Judicial Council of California POS-010 [Rev. January 1, 2007]	**PROOF OF SERVICE OF SUMMONS**	Code of Civil Procedure, § 417.10

PLAINTIFF/PETITIONER: LENNY D. LANDLORD	CASE NUMBER:
DEFENDANT/RESPONDENT: TERRENCE D. TENNANT	

5. c. ☐ **by mail and acknowledgment of receipt of service.** I mailed the documents listed in item 2 to the party, to the address shown in item 4, by first-class mail, postage prepaid,

    (1) on *(date):*   (2) from *(city):*

    (3) ☐ with two copies of the *Notice and Acknowledgment of Receipt* and a postage-paid return envelope addressed to me. *(Attach completed* Notice and Acknowledgement of Receipt.*)* (Code Civ. Proc., § 415.30.)

    (4) ☐ to an address outside California with return receipt requested. (Code Civ. Proc., § 415.40.)

  d. ☐ **by other means** *(specify means of service and authorizing code section):*

    ☐ Additional page describing service is attached.

6. The "Notice to the Person Served" (on the summons) was completed as follows:
  a. ☒ as an individual defendant.
  b. ☐ as the person sued under the fictitious name of *(specify):*
  c. ☐ as occupant.
  d. ☐ On behalf of *(specify):*
    under the following Code of Civil Procedure section:

    ☐ 416.10 (corporation)   ☐ 415.95 (business organization, form unknown)
    ☐ 416.20 (defunct corporation)   ☐ 416.60 (minor)
    ☐ 416.30 (joint stock company/association)   ☐ 416.70 (ward or conservatee)
    ☐ 416.40 (association or partnership)   ☐ 416.90 (authorized person)
    ☐ 416.50 (public entity)   ☐ 415.46 (occupant)
                  ☐ other:

7. **Person who served papers**
  a. Name: Sam D. Server
  b. Address: 123 Serve Street, Los Angeles, CA 90010
  c. Telephone number: 213-555-1234
  d. **The fee** for service was: $ 30.00
  e. I am:
    (1) ☒ not a registered California process server.
    (2) ☐ exempt from registration under Business and Professions Code section 22350(b).
    (3) ☐ a registered California process server:
      (i) ☐ owner ☐ employee ☐ independent contractor.
      (ii) Registration No.:
      (iii) County:

8. ☒ **I declare** under penalty of perjury under the laws of the State of California that the foregoing is true and correct.

    or

9. ☐ **I am a California sheriff or marshal and I** certify that the foregoing is true and correct.

Date: September 10, 20xx

Sam D. Server   ▶   *Sam D. Server*
_____   _____
(NAME OF PERSON WHO SERVED PAPERS/SHERIFF OR MARSHAL)   (SIGNATURE)

Item 4: Type the address where the defendant (or the person given the papers by substituted service) was served.

Item 5: If the defendant was personally served, check box a and list the date and time of service on the same line in subitems (1) and (2).

If the defendant was served by substituted service on another person, check box b, list the date and time the papers were given to this other person, and type the name of that other person in the space just below the first two lines. If you don't know the name of that person, insert the word "co-occupant," "coworker," or whatever other word (such as "spouse of defendant") describes the relationship of the person to the defendant. Check the box in subitem (1) or (2) to indicate whether the papers were left with this other person at the defendant's business or home. Then, indicate in subitem (4) the date that additional copies of the Summons and Complaint were mailed to the defendant (at the home or business address where the papers were left), and the city (or nearest post office branch) from which the second set was mailed. Do not check subitem (3), but do check subitem (5). Be sure to attach the original Declaration re Reasonable Diligence signed and dated by the process server, to the Proof of Service of Summons.

If you used service by posting and mailing, after getting permission from a judge, check box d on the reverse side and after the words "by other means (specify means of service and authorizing code section)" enter the words "C.C.P. § 415.45 pursuant to Court's order, by posting copies of Summons and Complaint on front door to premises at [list full street address] on [list date posted], and mailing copies thereof on [list date of mailing, or words "same date" if applicable] by certified mail addressed to defendant at that address."

Item 6: The alphabetical boxes here (a through d)

are the same as those on Item 4 on the front of the Summons (however, box d includes more options).

If personal service was used, check box a.

If substituted service was used, check box c, and also the box next to "CCP 416.90 (authorized person)." Also type the name of the defendant served by substituted service (not the one to whom the papers were given) on line c.

For posting-and-mailing service, check box a.

Items 7–9, Date and Signature: In the blank spaces below Item 7, list the home or business address and telephone number of the process server. Next to "The Fee for Service," list the amount you paid, if applicable, to the person who served the Summons. Check box 1 to indicate that this person is not a registered process server. (If you do use a registered process server, they will fill out the Proof of Service of Summons for you.) Do not check box 2 unless the person who served the papers is an attorney or licensed private investigator, or an employee of either. Then, check box 8 and have the person who served the papers date and sign the Proof of Service of Summons at the bottom. Do not check box 9.

What Next?

Your tenant has two choices after he is properly served with your Summons and Complaint: He can do nothing and lose automatically (in legalese, default), or he can fight the suit. He must decide what to do within five days (15 days if he wasn't personally served with the Summons and Complaint).

If the tenant doesn't file some kind of written response with the court within five days, you can get a default judgment by filing a few documents with the court. No court hearing is necessary. Chapter 7 tells you how to do this. ■

Taking a Default Judgment

If your tenant does not contest the unlawful detainer lawsuit by filing a written response to your Complaint, you win the lawsuit almost automatically. The tenant is said to have "defaulted," and you are entitled to obtain a "default judgment" from the court clerk for possession of the property. Most unlawful detainer actions are uncontested and wind up as defaults. By submitting more papers and, where required, appearing before a judge, you can also obtain a separate default judgment for some or all of the money the tenant owes you.

You can obtain a default judgment if all of the following requirements are satisfied:

- The tenancy was properly terminated.
- The Summons and Complaint were properly served on all the tenants.
- At least five days (counting Saturday and Sunday but not other court holidays) have elapsed from the date the tenant was personally served with the Summons and Complaint (15 days if you used substituted service).
- The tenants have not filed a written response to your Complaint by the time you actually seek your default judgment.

This chapter tells you when and how you can obtain a default judgment. (Refer to the checklist in your "home" chapter for a step-by-step outline of the process.)

When Can You Take a Default?

If a defendant was personally served with the Summons and Complaint, the law gives her at least five days to respond to your unlawful detainer Complaint. You can't take a default judgment until this response period has passed. You will have to wait at least six days before you can get a default judgment from the court clerk. This is because you don't count the day of service or court holidays, which include statewide legal holidays. You do count Saturday or Sunday, however, unless the fifth day falls on Saturday or Sunday.

A tenant who was served with the Complaint and Summons by substituted or posting-and-mailing service has an extra ten days to respond. Thus, you must count 15 days from the date of mailing. If the 15th day falls on a weekend or legal state holiday, you must wait until after the next business day to take a default.

Because you don't want to give the tenant any more time to file a written response than you have to, you should be prepared to "take a default" against one or all of the defendants on the first day you can. If the defendant beats you to the courthouse and files an answer, you can't take a default.

How do you know whether or not the tenant has in fact defaulted? Although the tenant is supposed to mail you a copy of any response he files, he may not do so, or he may wait until the last day to file and mail you a copy. To find out if he has filed anything, call the court clerk on the last day of the response period, just before closing time. Give the clerk the case number stamped on the Summons and Complaint and ask if a response has been filed.

Most tenants don't file a written response. If no response has been filed, you can visit the courthouse when it opens the next day to obtain the default judgment.

If, however, you find to your dismay that the tenant or his lawyer has filed a response to your lawsuit, it will probably take you a few more weeks to evict. (See Chapter 8 on contested eviction lawsuits.)

EXAMPLE: Your process server personally served Hassan with the Summons and Complaint on Tuesday, August 2. You can take a default if Hassan doesn't file a response within five days, not counting the day of service. The first day after service is Wednesday, August 3, and the fifth day is August 7. Because August 7 falls on a Sunday, Hassan has until the end of Monday to file his response and prevent a default. If he hasn't filed by the end of that business day, you can get a default judgment against him the next day, Tuesday, August 9.

EXAMPLE: Angela is a codefendant with Hassan, but neither you nor your process server can locate her at home or work. She is served by substituted service on August 7, when the papers are given to Hassan to give to her, and a second set of papers is mailed to her. She has 15 days to answer. The 15th day after the day of service is Monday, August 22. If she doesn't file a response by the end of the business day, you can take a default against her on August 23. (As a practical matter, you should probably wait until the 23rd to take Hassan's default too, since you won't get Angela out and the property back any sooner by taking Hassan's default first—and it's more paperwork.)

⚠ **Don't accept rent now.** Do not accept any rent from your tenant during (or even after) the waiting period (also called "response time") unless you want to allow him to stay. This is true whether you are evicting for nonpayment of rent, termination by 30-day or 60-day notice, breach of the lease, or any other reason. If you do accept rent, you will "waive," or give up, your right to sue, and the tenant can assert that as a defense in his answer. In rent-nonpayment cases, if you care more about getting your rent than getting the tenant out, you should at least insist that the tenant pay all the rent plus the costs of your lawsuit, including any costs to serve papers. Don't be foolish enough to accept partial rent payment with a promise to pay more later. If you do, and it's not forthcoming, you will very likely have to start all over again with a new three-day notice and new lawsuit.

The Two-Step Default Judgment Process

As part of evicting a tenant, normally you will obtain two separate default judgments:

1. Default Judgment for Possession of property. It's fairly easy to get a Judgment for Possession of your property on the day after the tenant's response time passes by simply filing your default papers with the court clerk.

2. Default judgment for any money you are entitled to. Getting a default judgment for back rent, damages, and court costs you requested in your Complaint is more time-consuming; you have to either go before a judge or submit a declaration setting forth the facts of the case. (See below.) And because the judge can only award you damages (prorated rent) covering the period until the date of judgment, your money judgment won't include any days after you get the judgment and before the tenant is actually evicted. (*Cavanaugh v. High* (1960) 182 Cal. App. 2d 714, 723; 6 Cal. Rptr. 525.) For example, a judgment cannot

say, "$10 per day until defendant is evicted." Prorated daily damages end on the day of the money judgment. The actual eviction won't occur for at least a week after the possession default is entered unless, of course, the tenant leaves voluntarily before then.

For this reason, it's best to first get a clerk's default Judgment for Possession and then wait until the tenant leaves before you go back to court to get the money part of the judgment. If you do get the money part of the judgment before the tenant is evicted, you are still entitled to the prorated rent for the time between money judgment and eviction. You can deduct this amount from any security deposit the tenant paid you. This isn't quite as good as waiting, because it means less of the security deposit will be available if the place is damaged or dirty. If you wait to enter the default as to rent until after the tenant leaves, you can get a judgment for the entire amount of rent due and still leave the deposit available to take care of cleaning and repairs. (See *The California Landlord's Law Book: Rights & Responsibilities*, Chapter 20.)

Getting a Default Judgment for Possession

To obtain a default Judgment for Possession of the property, you must fill out and file three documents:

- a Request for Entry of Default
- a Clerk's Judgment for Possession, and
- a Writ of Possession for the property.

Because you want to get your tenant out as fast as possible, you might as well prepare the default judgment forms during your five-day (or 15-day) wait. If the tenant files a response in the meantime, you won't be able to obtain a default judgment, and this work will be wasted. However, the time it takes to prepare these forms is not great. And because of the high percentage of cases that end in defaults, it's a worthwhile gamble.

If the tenant voluntarily moved out after being served with the Summons and Complaint, he still is required to answer the Complaint within five days. Assuming he does not, you should still go ahead and get a money judgment for any rent owed, by skipping to "Getting a Money Judgment for Rent and Costs," below.

Preparing Your Request for Entry of Default for Possession

Your request for the clerk to enter a default and a Judgment for Possession of the premises is made on a standard form called a Request for Entry of Default. In it you list the names of the defendants against whom you're taking defaults and indicate that you want a "clerk's judgment" that says you are entitled to possession of the property.

If you're suing more than one occupant of the property, and they were all served with the Summons and Complaint on the same day, you can get a default judgment against them all on the same day, by filing one set of papers with all their names on each form.

On the other hand, if you're suing more than one person and they were served on different days (or by different methods), each will have a different date by which he must respond. Your best bet is to prepare one set of papers with all the defaulting defendants' names on them, wait until the response time has passed for all defendants, and take all the defaults simultaneously.

You can fill out a separate set of papers for each defendant and take each defendant's default as soon as the waiting period for each defendant has passed, but there's normally no reason to, unless the tenants with later response times have already moved out or there is something special about the tenants with earlier response times (for example, they have potential retaliation or discrimination claims) that makes it advisable to take their default as soon as possible and get them out of the case. More paperwork is involved, and a default judgment against one tenant won't usually help you get the property back any sooner—you still have the others to deal with.

A blank, tear-out version of the Request for Entry of Default is in Appendix 3. The CD-ROM also includes this form. Instructions for using the CD are in Appendix 2. You'll find a sample filled out below.

On the front of the form, fill in the caption boxes (name, address, phone, name and address of the court, name of plaintiff and defendants, and case number) just as they are filled out on the Complaint. Put Xs in the boxes next to the words "ENTRY OF DEFAULT" and "CLERK'S JUDGMENT." Then fill in the following items:

Item 1a: Enter the date you filed the Complaint. This should be stamped in the upper right corner of your file-stamped copy of the Complaint.

Item 1b: Type your name, since you're the plaintiff who filed the Complaint.

Item 1c: Put an X in the box and type in the names of all the defendants against whom you are having the defaults entered.

Item 1d: Leave this box blank.

Item 1e: Put an X in box e. This tells the clerk to enter Judgment for Possession of the property. If you used the optional procedure in Chapter 6, "Service on Unknown Occupants," by which a sheriff, marshal, or registered process server served a Prejudgment Claim of Right to Possession on unnamed occupants, also check the box (1). Leave boxes (2) and (3) blank.

Items 2a–2f: Because you're only asking for possession of the property at this point, don't fill in any dollar amounts. Just type "possession only" in the "Amount" and "Balance" columns.

Item 2g: Type the daily rental value, listed in Item 10 of the Complaint, in the space with the dollar sign in front of it. Then, enter the date you put in box 17.f of the Complaint.

> **EXAMPLE:** May Li's $900 June rent was due on June 1. On June 7, you served her a Three-Day Notice to Pay Rent or Quit, which demanded the rent for the entire month. Monthly rent of $900 is equivalent to $30 per day. List this amount in Item 2g of the Request for Entry of Default form. Then, since the last day of the rental period for which you demanded the $900 rent was June 30, type in the next day, July 1. That is the date the prorated daily "damages" begin, at $30 per day, and it should be listed in Complaint Item 16f and Item 2g of the Request for Entry of Default form.

> **EXAMPLE:** You terminated Mortimer's month-to-month tenancy by serving a 30-day notice on September 10. The 30th day after this is October 9. The day after that, October 10, is the day you are entitled to prorated daily rent. That date should be listed in Item 2g of the Request for Entry of Default form and in Complaint Item 16f. Since Mortimer's monthly rent was $750, the dollar figure is $750/30, or $25 per day. That amount should be listed here (Item 2g) as well as in Complaint Item 10.

	CIV-100

ATTORNEY OR PARTY WITHOUT ATTORNEY *(Name, State Bar number, and address):* Lenny D. Landlord 12345 Angeleno Street Los Angeles, CA 90010 TELEPHONE NO.: 213-555-6789 FAX NO. *(Optional):* 213-555-5678 E-MAIL ADDRESS *(Optional):* ATTORNEY FOR *(Name):* Plaintiff in Pro Per	**FOR COURT USE ONLY**

SUPERIOR COURT OF CALIFORNIA, COUNTY OF   LOS ANGELES

STREET ADDRESS:	110 North Grand Avenue
MAILING ADDRESS:	Same
CITY AND ZIP CODE:	Los Angeles, CA 90012
BRANCH NAME:	CENTRAL DISTRICT/DOWNTOWN BRANCH

PLAINTIFF/PETITIONER: LENNY D. LANDLORD
DEFENDANT/RESPONDENT: TERRENCE D. TENANT, TILLIE D. TENANT

REQUEST FOR **(Application)**	[X] **Entry of Default** [ ] **Clerk's Judgment** [ ] **Court Judgment**	CASE NUMBER: A-12345-B

1. **TO THE CLERK:** On the complaint or cross-complaint filed
 a. on *(date):*   August 10, 20xx
 b. by *(name):*   Lenny D. Landlord
 c. [X] Enter default of defendant *(names):*   TERRENCE D. TENANT, TILLIE D. TENANT

 d. [ ] I request a court judgment under Code of Civil Procedure sections 585(b), 585(c), 989, etc., against defendant *(names):*

> **check this box only if you had a Prejudgment Claim of Right of Possession served; otherwise, ignore it**

  (Testimony required. Apply to the clerk for a hearing date, unless the court will enter a judgment on an affidavit under Code Civ. Proc., § 585(d).)
 e. [X] Enter clerk's judgment
  (1) [•] for restitution of the premises only and issue a writ of execution on the judgment. Code of Civil Procedure section 1174(c) does not apply. (Code Civ. Proc., § 1169.)
    [ ] Include in the judgment all tenants, subtenants, named claimants, and other occupants of the premises. The *Prejudgment Claim of Right to Possession* was served in compliance with Code of Civil Procedure section 415.46.
  (2) [ ] under Code of Civil Procedure section 585(a). *(Complete the declaration under Code Civ. Proc., § 585.5 on the reverse (item 5).)*
  (3) [ ] for default previously entered on *(date):*

2. **Judgment to be entered.**

	Amount	Credits acknowledged	Balance
a. Demand of complaint	$ possession only	$	$ possession only
b. Statement of damages *			
(1) Special	$	$	$
(2) General	$	$	$
c. Interest	$	$	$
d. Costs *(see reverse)*	$	$	$
e. Attorney fees	$	$	$
f. **TOTALS**	$	$	$

 g. **Daily damages** were demanded in complaint at the rate of: $ 30.00   per day beginning *(date):* Sept. 1, 20xx
 (Personal injury or wrongful death actions; Code Civ. Proc., § 425.11.)*

3. [X] *(Check if filed in an unlawful detainer case)* **Legal document assistant or unlawful detainer assistant** information is on the reverse *(complete item 4).*

Date: August 16, 20xx

Lenny D. Landlord	▶ *Lenny D. Landlord*
(TYPE OR PRINT NAME)	(SIGNATURE OF PLAINTIFF OR ATTORNEY FOR PLAINTIFF)

FOR COURT USE ONLY	(1) [ ] Default entered as requested on *(date):* (2) [ ] Default NOT entered as requested *(state reason):* Clerk, by _____, Deputy

Page 1 of 2

CIV-100

PLAINTIFF/PETITIONER: LENNY D. LANDLORD DEFENDANT/RESPONDENT: TERRENCE D. TENNANT, ET AL	CASE NUMBER: A-12345-B

4. **Legal document assistant or unlawful detainer assistant (Bus. & Prof. Code, § 6400 et seq.).** A legal document assistant or unlawful detainer assistant ☐ did ☒ did **not**   for compensation give advice or assistance with this form. *(If declarant has received **any** help or advice for pay from a legal document assistant or unlawful detainer assistant, state):*

   a. Assistant's name: c. Telephone no.:
   b. Street address, city, and zip code: d. County of registration:
                                              e. Registration no.:
                                              f. Expires on *(date):*

5. ☒ **Declaration under Code of Civil Procedure Section 585.5** *(required for entry of default under Code Civ. Proc., § 585(a)).* This action

   a. ☐ is ☒ is not   on a contract or installment sale for goods or services subject to Civ. Code, § 1801 et seq. (Unruh Act).
   b. ☐ is ☒ is not   on a conditional sales contract subject to Civ. Code, § 2981 et seq. (Rees-Levering Motor Vehicle Sales and Finance Act).
   c. ☐ is ☒ is not   on an obligation for goods, services, loans, or extensions of credit subject to Code Civ. Proc., § 395(b).

6. **Declaration of mailing (Code Civ. Proc., § 587).** A copy of this *Request for Entry of Default* was

   a. ☐ **not mailed** to the following defendants, whose addresses are **unknown** to plaintiff or plaintiff's attorney *(names):*

   b. ☒ **mailed** first-class, postage prepaid, in a sealed envelope addressed to each defendant's attorney of record or, if none, to each defendant's last known address as follows:

     (1) Mailed on *(date):*   (2) To *(specify names and addresses shown on the envelopes):*

     August 16, 20xx   Terrence D. Tenant, 6789 Angel Street, Apt. 10, Los Angeles, CA 90012
     August 16, 20xx   Tillie D. Tenant, 6789 Angel Street, Apt. 10, Los Angeles, CA 90012

I declare under penalty of perjury under the laws of the State of California that the foregoing items 4, 5, and 6 are true and correct.

Date: August 16, 20xx

Lenny D. Landlord	*Lenny D. Landlord*
(TYPE OR PRINT NAME)	(SIGNATURE OF DECLARANT)

7. **Memorandum of costs** *(required if money judgment requested).* Costs and disbursements are as follows (Code Civ. Proc., § 1033.5):

   a. Clerk's filing fees .... $
   b. Process server's fees .... $
   c. Other *(specify):* .... $
   d. .... $
   e. **TOTAL** .... $ _____
   f. ☐ Costs and disbursements are waived.

   g. I am the attorney, agent, or party who claims these costs. To the best of my knowledge and belief this memorandum of costs is correct and these costs were necessarily incurred in this case.

I declare under penalty of perjury under the laws of the State of California that the foregoing is true and correct.

Date:

(TYPE OR PRINT NAME)	(SIGNATURE OF DECLARANT)

8. ☒ **Declaration of nonmilitary status** *(required for a judgment).* No defendant named in item 1c of the application is in the military service so as to be entitled to the benefits of the Servicemembers Civil Relief Act (50 U.S.C. App. § 501 et seq.).

I declare under penalty of perjury under the laws of the State of California that the foregoing is true and correct.

Date: August 16, 20xx

Lenny D. Landlord	*Lenny D. Landlord*
(TYPE OR PRINT NAME)	(SIGNATURE OF DECLARANT)

Civ-100 [Rev. January 1, 2007]	**REQUEST FOR ENTRY OF DEFAULT** (Application to Enter Default)	Page 2 of 2

Item 3: We have preprinted an "X" in this box to indicate the case is an unlawful detainer proceeding.

Enter the date you'll be filing the default papers with the court and type in your name opposite the place for signature. Now turn the form over.

CAPTION: Type the names of the plaintiff and defendant, just as you did on the second page of the proof of service of summons. (See "Filing Your Complaint and Getting Summonses Issued" in Chapter 6.)

Item 4: As we saw when preparing the Complaint ("Preparing the Complaint," Item 18, in Chapter 6), you must indicate if an "unlawful detainer assistant" or a "legal document preparer" (a bonded paralegal) advised or assisted you. Assuming you are using this book on your own, put an "X" in the "did not" box. Do not complete the rest of Item 4.

Item 5: Put an X next to Item 5 and check the boxes next to the words "is not" in Items a, b, and c. (This is a general-purpose form, and none of these items applies to unlawful detainer lawsuits. Even so, many clerks insist that these items be checked, and doing so is easier than arguing.)

Item 6: Check box 6b. (You don't check box 6a because obviously you know the tenant's most recent address—at your property.) Then, type the date you'll mail the defendants their copies, and their mailing address, under headings (1) and (2). Below that, again type in the date you'll be filing the papers, and your name opposite the place for signature.

Item 7: Leave this entire item blank. You'll list your court costs when you file for your money judgment after the tenant is evicted.

Item 8: If none of the defendants against whom you're taking a default judgment is on active duty in the U.S. armed forces (Army, Navy, Marines, Air Force, and Coast Guard), or is a member of the Public Health Service or National Oceanic and Atmospheric Administration, or is in the National Guard and called to active service for more than a month, put an X in box b. Then, simply enter the date you'll file the papers and type your name opposite the place for you to sign.

If any of the defendants is in the military, no default can be taken against him until a judge appoints an attorney for him. That procedure is fairly complicated and beyond the scope of this chapter. See an attorney if a person you're suing is in the military and refuses to leave after you've served him with the Summons and Complaint. (Servicemembers' Civil Relief Act of 1940, 50 U.S.C. App. § 521 et seq.) Some landlords take the expedient shortcut of complaining to their military tenant's commanding officer about nonpayment of rent or other problems. This often works a lot faster than the legal process.

Make two copies of the completed (but unsigned) form. Don't sign the Request for Entry of Default until you actually go down to the courthouse to file the papers and have mailed a copy to the defendant. (See below.)

Preparing the Judgment Issued by the Clerk for Possession of the Premises

The judgment form provides the legal basis for issuance of a Writ of Possession, the document authorizing the sheriff or marshal to evict the tenant. You will present it to the clerk with the Request for Entry of Default.

A blank, tear-out version of the Judgment—Unlawful Detainer is in Appendix 3. The CD-ROM also includes this form. Instructions for using the CD are in Appendix 2.

As with the Summons, Complaint, and Request for Entry of Judgment, there is a statewide form for a judgment in an unlawful detainer case. This Judgment—Unlawful Detainer form can be used in various situations. In the instructions below, we show you how to fill it out as a default judgment issued by the clerk, for possession of the property. (As we'll see below, this form is filled out in a different way to obtain a default judgment for monetary sums, after the tenant has vacated the property. This form can also be used in contested cases; see "Responding to the Answer" and "Preparing for Trial" in Chapter 8.)

This form is not difficult to fill out. Enter the names and addresses of the landlord and tenant, the court name and address, and the case number as you have done on previous forms (again, we suggest omitting your email address). In the box containing the words "JUDGMENT—UNLAWFUL DETAINER," put an X in the boxes next to the words "By Clerk," "By Default," and "Possession Only."

UD-110

ATTORNEY OR PARTY WITHOUT ATTORNEY *(Name, state bar number, and address)*:	FOR COURT USE ONLY
LENNY D. LANDLORD 1234 Angeleno Street Los Angeles, CA 90010 TELEPHONE NO.: 213-555-6789 FAX NO. *(Optional)*: 213-555-5678 E-MAIL ADDRESS *(Optional)*: ATTORNEY FOR *(Name)*: Plaintiff in Pro Per	

SUPERIOR COURT OF CALIFORNIA, COUNTY OF LOS ANGELES
STREET ADDRESS: 110 North Grand Avenue
MAILING ADDRESS: Same
CITY AND ZIP CODE: Los Angeles, CA 90012
BRANCH NAME: CENTRAL DISTRICT, DOWNTOWN BRANCH

PLAINTIFF: LENNY D. LANDLORD

DEFENDANT: TERRENCE D. TENANT, TILLIE D. TENANT

JUDGMENT—UNLAWFUL DETAINER	CASE NUMBER:
[X] **By Clerk** [X] **By Default** [ ] **After Court Trial** [ ] **By Court** [X] **Possession Only** [ ] **Defendant Did Not Appear at Trial**	A-12345-B

JUDGMENT

1. [X] **BY DEFAULT**
    a. Defendant was properly served with a copy of the summons and complaint.
    b. Defendant failed to answer the complaint or appear and defend the action within the time allowed by law.
    c. Defendant's default was entered by the clerk upon plaintiff's application.
    d. [X] **Clerk's Judgment** (Code Civ. Proc., § 1169). For possession only of the premises described on page 2 (item 4).
    e. [ ] **Court Judgment** (Code Civ. Proc., § 585(b)). The court considered
        (1) [ ] plaintiff's testimony and other evidence.
        (2) [ ] plaintiff's or others' written declaration and evidence (Code Civ. Proc., § 585(d)).

2. [ ] **AFTER COURT TRIAL.** The jury was waived. The court considered the evidence.
    a. The case was tried on *(date and time)*:

       before *(name of judicial officer)*:

    b. Appearances by:
       [ ] Plaintiff *(name each)*:   [ ] Plaintiff's attorney *(name each)*:
                                        (1)
                                        (2)

       [ ] Continued on *Attachment* 2b (form MC-025).

       [ ] Defendant *(name each)*:   [ ] Defendant's attorney *(name each)*:
                                          (1)
                                        (2)

       [ ] Continued on *Attachment* 2b (form MC-025).

    c. [ ] Defendant did not appear at trial. Defendant was properly served with notice of trial.

    d. [ ] A statement of decision (Code Civ. Proc., § 632) [ ] was not [ ] was requested.

Form Approved for Optional Use
Judicial Council of California
UD-110 [New January 1, 2003]

JUDGMENT—UNLAWFUL DETAINER

Code of Civil Procedure, §§ 415.46,
585(d), 664.6, 1169

PLAINTIFF: LENNY LANDLORD	CASE NUMBER:
DEFENDANT: TERRENCE D. TENANT ET AL	A-12345-B

JUDGMENT IS ENTERED AS FOLLOWS BY: ☐ **THE COURT** ☒ **THE CLERK**

3. **Parties.** Judgment is

a. ☒ for plaintiff *(name each):*   Lenny Landlord

and against defendant *(name each):*   Terrence D. Tenant, Tillie D. Tenant

☐ Continued on *Attachment* 3a (form MC-025).

b. ☐ for defendant *(name each):*

4. ☒ Plaintiff ☐ Defendant   is entitled to possession of the premises located at *(street address, apartment, city, and county):*

   6789 Angel Street, Apt. 10, Los Angeles, CA 90010

5. ☐ Judgment applies to all occupants of the premises including tenants, subtenants if any, and named claimants if any (Code Civ. Proc., §§ 715.010, 1169, and 1174.3).

> check box 5 only if you had a Prejudgment Claim of Right of Possession served; otherwise, ignore it

6. **Amount and terms of judgment**

a. ☐ Defendant named in item 3a above must pay plaintiff on the complaint:

b. ☐ Plaintiff is to receive nothing from defendant named in item 3b.

☐ Defendant named in item 3b is to recover costs: $

☐ and attorney fees: $.

(1) ☐ Past-due rent	$	
(2) ☐ Holdover damages	$	
(3) ☐ Attorney fees	$	
(4) ☐ Costs	$	
(5) ☐ Other *(specify):*	$	
(6) **TOTAL JUDGMENT**	$	

c. ☐ The rental agreement is canceled. ☐ The lease is forfeited.

7. ☐ **Conditional judgment.** Plaintiff has breached the agreement to provide habitable premises to defendant as stated in *Judgment—Unlawful Detainer Attachment* (form UD–110S), which is attached.

8. ☐ **Other** *(specify):*

☐ Continued on *Attachment* 8 (form MC-025).

Date: ☐ _____
                 JUDICIAL OFFICER

Date: _____
☐ Clerk, by _____ , Deputy

(SEAL)

CLERK'S CERTIFICATE *(Optional)*

I certify that this is a true copy of the original judgment on file in the court.

Date:

Clerk, by _____ , Deputy

UD-110 [New January 1, 2003]   **JUDGMENT—UNLAWFUL DETAINER**   Page 2 of 2

Item 1: Put an X in Item 1 next to the words "BY DEFAULT," and also in box 1d next to the words "Clerk's Judgment."

Item 2: Leave this part blank and proceed to the other side (page 2) of the form. At the top of page 2, fill in the names, in capitals, of the plaintiff (you), the first-named defendant (followed by "ET AL" if there is more than one defendant), and the court case number. After the words "JUDGMENT IS ENTERED AS FOLLOWS BY:" put an X in the box following the words "THE CLERK."

Item 3: Put an X in box 3a and type, in upper and lower case, the names of the plaintiff(s) and the names of all defendants against whom you're obtaining the clerk's default judgment for possession. Leave box 3b blank.

Item 4: Put an X in the box next to the word "Plaintiff" (leave the box next to "Defendant" blank) and list the address of the property including street address, any apartment number, city, and county.

Item 5: If you used the optional procedure in Chapter 6 to have Prejudgment Claim of Right to Possession served on unnamed occupants by a sheriff, marshal, or registered process server, check this box. Otherwise, leave it blank.

Items 6–8: Leave all these boxes blank.

After you fill out the form, make one copy for your records.

Preparing the Writ of Possession

The final form you need to evict is the Writ of Possession. (The name of the preprinted form you'll use is a Writ of Execution. It's a multipurpose one for use as a writ of "possession," ordering the sheriff or marshal to put you in possession of real property, or as a writ of "execution" that requests enforcement of a money judgment.) Like the Summons, the Writ of Possession is "issued" by the court clerk, but you have to fill it out and give it to the clerk with the other default forms. (See below.) The clerk will issue the writ as soon as court files contain the Judgment for Possession. The original and copies of the Writ of Possession are given to the sheriff or marshal, who then "executes" the judgment by evicting the tenants against whom you obtained the judgment.

A blank, tear-out version of the Writ of Execution for possession is in Appendix 3. The CD-ROM also includes this form. Instructions for using the CD are in Appendix 2. A form for use in Los Angeles County is also included.

The usual information goes in the big boxes at the top of the writ form—your name, address, and phone number; the name and address of the court; the names of plaintiffs and defendants; and the case number. (There's also an optional line where you can enter your email address. We advise that you not do so. The court will not communicate with you via email, and since this document is a public record, anyone who looks at it will have your address.) Also put Xs in the box next to the words "Judgment Creditor" in the top large box and in the boxes next to the words "POSSESSION OF" and "Real Property" as shown. Fill out the rest of the writ according to these instructions.

Item 1: Type the name of the county in which the property is located. The sheriff or marshal (or constable in justice court districts) of that county will perform the eviction.

Item 2: Nothing need be filled in here.

Item 3: Put an X in the box next to the words "judgment creditor" and type your name and the names of any other plaintiffs. You are "judgment creditors" because you won the judgment.

Item 4: Type in the names of up to two defendants and list the residence address. If you got a judgment against more than two persons, check the box next to the words "additional judgment debtors on reverse." List the other names and address in the space provided in Item 4 on the back of the form.

Item 5: Fill in the date the judgment will be entered. If nothing goes wrong, this should be the date you take the papers down to the courthouse.

Item 6: Nothing need be filled in here.

Item 7: Only box a, next to the words "has not been requested," should be checked.

Item 8: Leave box 8 blank—it does not apply here.

Item 9: Put an X in box 9. On the back side of the form, at Item 24, check boxes 24 and 24a and enter the date the Complaint was filed. Then, if you used the optional procedure in Chapter 6 ("Service on Unknown Occupants"), by which a sheriff, marshal, or registered process server served a Prejudgment Claim of Right to

EJ-130

ATTORNEY OR PARTY WITHOUT ATTORNEY *(Name, State Bar number and address):*

LENNY D. LANDLORD
1234 Angeleno Street
Los Angeles, CA 90010

TELEPHONE NO.: 213-555-6789   FAX NO. *(Optional):* 213-555-5678

E-MAIL ADDRESS *(Optional):*

ATTORNEY FOR *(Name):* Plaintiff in Pro Per

[ ] ATTORNEY FOR   [X] JUDGMENT CREDITOR   [ ] ASSIGNEE OF RECORD

SUPERIOR COURT OF CALIFORNIA, COUNTY OF   Los Angeles

STREET ADDRESS:

MAILING ADDRESS:

CITY AND ZIP CODE:

BRANCH NAME:

PLAINTIFF:

DEFENDANT:

WRIT OF [ ] EXECUTION (Money Judgment) [X] POSSESSION OF [ ] Personal Property [X] Real Property [ ] SALE	CASE NUMBER: A-12345-B

1. **To the Sheriff or Marshal of the County of:**   Los Angeles

   You are directed to enforce the judgment described below with daily interest and your costs as provided by law.

2. **To any registered process server:** You are authorized to serve this writ only in accord with CCP 699.080 or CCP 715.040.

3. *(Name):* Lenny D. Landlord
   is the [X] judgment creditor [ ] assignee of record   whose address is shown on this form above the court's name.

4. **Judgment debtor** *(name and last known address):*

   Terrence D. Tenant
   6789 Angel Street, Apt. 10
   Los Angeles, CA 90012

   Tillie D. Tenant
   6789 Angel Street, Apt. 10
   Los Angeles, CA 90012

   [ ] Additional judgment debtors on next page

5. **Judgment entered** on *(date):*
   Aug. 16, 20xx

6. [ ] **Judgment renewed** on *(dates):*

7. **Notice of sale** under this writ
   a. [X] has not been requested.
   b. [ ] has been requested *(see next page).*

8. [ ] Joint debtor information on next page.

[SEAL]

9. [X] See next page for information on real or personal property to be delivered under a writ of possession or sold under a writ of sale.

10. [ ] This writ is issued on a sister-state judgment.

11. Total judgment . . . . $

12. Costs after judgment (per filed order or memo CCP 685.090) . . . . $

13. Subtotal *(add 11 and 12)* . . . . $

14. Credits . . . . $

15. Subtotal *(subtract 14 from 13)* . . . . $

16. Interest after judgment (per filed affidavit CCP 685.050) (not on GC 6103.5 fees). . . $

17. Fee for issuance of writ . . . . $

18. **Total** *(add 15, 16, and 17)* . . . . $

19. Levying officer:
    (a) Add daily interest from date of writ *(at the legal rate on 15)* (not on GC 6103.5 fees) of. . . . . . $
    (b) Pay directly to court costs included in 11 and 17 (GC 6103.5, 68511.3; CCP 699.520(i)) . . . . $

20. [ ] The amounts called for in items 11–19 are different for each debtor. These amounts are stated for each debtor on Attachment 20.

Issued on *(date):*   Clerk, by _____ , Deputy

NOTICE TO PERSON SERVED: SEE NEXT PAGE FOR IMPORTANT INFORMATION.

Page 1 of 2

EJ-130

PLAINTIFF: LENNY D. LANDLORD	CASE NUMBER:
DEFENDANT: TERRENCE D. TENANT, TILLIE D. TENANT	A-12345-B

— **Items continued from page 1**—

21. ☐ **Additional judgment debtor** *(name and last known address):*

22. ☐ **Notice of sale** has been requested by *(name and address):*

23. ☐ **Joint debtor** was declared bound by the judgment (CCP 989–994)
   a. on *(date):*   a. on *(date):*
   b. name and address of joint debtor: b. name and address of joint debtor:

   c. ☐ additional costs against certain joint debtors *(itemize):*

24. ☒ *(Writ of Possession* or *Writ of Sale)* **Judgment** was entered for the following:
   a. ☒ Possession of real property: The complaint was filed on *(date):*   August 10, 20xx
      (Check (1) or (2)):
      (1) ☐ The Prejudgment Claim of Right to Possession was served in compliance with CCP 415.46.
         The judgment includes all tenants, subtenants, named claimants, and other occupants of the premises.
      (2) ☒ The Prejudgment Claim of Right to Possession was NOT served in compliance with CCP 415.46.
         (a) $30.00   was the daily rental value on the date the complaint was filed.
         (b) The court will hear objections to enforcement of the judgment under CCP 1174.3 on the following
            dates *(specify):* September 18, 20xx   **Check with court for dates and any special wording**
   b. ☐ Possession of personal property.
      ☐ If delivery cannot be had, then for the value *(itemize in 9e)* specified in the judgment or supplemental order.
   c. ☐ Sale of personal property.
   d. ☐ Sale of real property.
   e. Description of property:

   6789 Angel Street, Apt. 10
   Los Angeles, CA 90012

NOTICE TO PERSON SERVED

WRIT OF EXECUTION OR SALE. Your rights and duties are indicated on the accompanying *Notice of Levy* (Form EJ-150).
WRIT OF POSSESSION OF PERSONAL PROPERTY. If the levying officer is not able to take custody of the property, the levying officer will make a demand upon you for the property. If custody is not obtained following demand, the judgment may be enforced as a money judgment for the value of the property specified in the judgment or in a supplemental order.
WRIT OF POSSESSION OF REAL PROPERTY. If the premises are not vacated within five days after the date of service on the occupant or, if service is by posting, within five days after service on you, the levying officer will remove the occupants from the real property and place the judgment creditor in possession of the property. Except for a mobile home, personal property remaining on the premises will be sold or otherwise disposed of in accordance with CCP 1174 unless you or the owner of the property pays the judgment creditor the reasonable cost of storage and takes possession of the personal property not later than 15 days after the time the judgment creditor takes possession of the premises.
▶ *A Claim of Right to Possession form accompanies this writ (unless the Summons was served in compliance with CCP 415.46).*

EJ-130 [Rev. January 1, 2006]	**WRIT OF EXECUTION**	Page 2 of 2

Possession on unnamed occupants, put an X in box (1). Otherwise, put an X in box (2) and list the daily rental value of the property in Item 24a(2)(a)—the same as in Item 10 of the Complaint. For Item 24a(2)(b), call the court clerk for a future date (two to three weeks away), in case a person not named in the writ filed a post-judgment Claim of Right to Possession, and list that date in the space provided. Under e, list the complete street address, including apartment number if any, city, and county of the property.

Items 10–20: These items apply only when you get a money judgment, and should not be filled in on this writ, which reflects only a Judgment for Possession of the property. (Later, after you have a default hearing before a judge and get a money judgment, you will fill out another writ (of execution) and fill in Items 10–20—see "Getting a Money Judgment for Rent and Costs," below.) Instead, simply type the words "POSSESSION ONLY" next to Item 11. Type "0.00" (zero) next to items 18 and 19a. (We have preprinted "0.00" in Item 19b because it always applies, even when collecting the money part of the judgment, which we discuss in Chapter 9.)

You should make one copy of the Writ of Possession for your own records and three copies per defendant to give to the sheriff or marshal.

Filing the Forms and Getting the Writ of Possession Issued

On the day after the response period ends, after you have made sure no answer was filed (see the first section in this chapter), mail a copy of the Request for Entry of Default to the tenant(s) at the property's street address. Then sign your name on the three places on the original. (Technically, if you sign this form before you mail the copy to the tenant(s), you will be committing perjury, because in one of the places on the form you state under penalty of perjury that a copy was mailed—before you signed.)

Then take the following forms to the courthouse:

- the original Summons for each defendant, stapled to the Proof of Service of Summons completed and signed by the process server (see Chapter 6)
- the original plus at least two copies of the Request for Entry of Default
- the original plus at least one copy of the Judgment for Possession, and
- the original plus three copies per defendant of the Writ of Possession.

Give the court clerk the originals and copies of all the forms you've prepared. Tell the clerk that you're returning completed Summonses in an unlawful detainer case and that you want him to:

1. enter a default Judgment for Possession of the premises, and
2. issue a Writ of Possession.

He will file the originals of the Summonses, the Proofs of Service of the Summons, the Request for Entry of Default, and the Judgment, but will hand you back the original writ, stamped. The clerk should also file-stamp and hand back to you any copies you give him. You will have to pay a $7.00 fee for issuance of the writ.

In Los Angeles and Orange Counties, you must fill out a special "local" form before the clerk will issue you a Writ of Possession. The Los Angeles form is called an Application for Writ of Possession for ... Real Property, and is filled out as shown below; a blank copy is included in Appendix 3 and on the CD-ROM. The Orange County form (Application for Writ of Possession—Unlawful Detainer, number L-1051) is simple and needs no instructions from us. You can download the form from the Orange County website at www.occourts.org/locforms. Other counties may also require you to use their own, similar forms—be sure to call the clerk and check it out before heading to the courthouse.

Some readers have told us that in Los Angeles County, clerks won't enter default judgments over the counter. Instead, you must either come back several days later for your default judgment and writ, or leave a self-addressed, stamped envelope with your papers and the $7.00 fee so the clerk can send it to you.

NAME, ADDRESS, AND TELEPHONE NUMBER OF ATTORNEY OR PARTY WITHOUT ATTORNEY	STATE BAR NUMBER	Reserved for Clerk's File Stamp
LENNY D. LANDLORD 1234 Angeleno Street Los Angeles, CA 90010 213-555-6789 ATTORNEY FOR (Name): In Pro Per		

SUPERIOR COURT OF CALIFORNIA, COUNTY OF LOS ANGELES

COURTHOUSE ADDRESS:
110 North Grand Avenue, Los Angeles, CA 90012

PLAINTIFF:
LENNY LANDLORD

DEFENDANT:
TERRENCE D. TENANT, TILLIE D. TENANT

APPLICATION FOR ISSUANCE OF WRIT OF EXECUTION, POSSESSION OR SALE	CASE NUMBER: A-12345-B

I, Lenny D. Landlord _____ declare under penalty of perjury under the laws of the State of California:

1. I am the judgment creditor _____ in the above-entitled action.

2. The following ☒Judgment / ☐Order was made and entered on ___August 16, 20xx___ .
   ☐Judgment was renewed on _____ .

3. Judgment/Order as entered/renewed provides as follows:

   Judgment Creditor: (name and address)

   Lenny D. Landlord
   1234 Angeleno Street
   Los Angeles, CA 90010

   Judgment Debtor: (name and address)

   Terrence D. Tenant   Tillie D. Tenant
   6789 Angel Street   6789 Angel Street
   Los Angeles, CA 90012   Los Angeles, CA 90012

   Amount of Order and/or Description of Property:

   POSSESSION ONLY; RESIDENTIAL RENTAL PROPERTY

4. ☒ (Unlawful Detainer Proceedings Only) The daily rental value of the property as of the date the complaint was filed is $ 30.00 .

5. ☐ This is an unlawful detainer judgment, and a Prejudgment Claim of Right to Possession was served on the occupant(s) pursuant to Code of Civil Procedure section 415.46. Pursuant to Code of Civil Procedure sections 715.010 and 1174.3, this writ applies to all tenants; subtenants, if any; named claimants, if any; and any other occupants of the premises.

6. ☐ This is a Family Law Judgment/Order entitled to priority under Code of Civil Procedure section 699.510.

7. This writ is to be issued to: ☒ Los Angeles County   ☐ Other (Specify):_____

APPLICATION FOR ISSUANCE OF WRIT OF EXECUTION, POSSESSION OR SALE

CIV 096 09-04
LASC Approved

Code Civ. Proc., § 712.010
Page 1 of 2

Case Title: LANDLORD V. TENANT	Case Number: A-12345-B

INSTRUCTIONS

Fill in date below showing total of amount ordered (do not show separate amounts for principal, fees and pre-judgment costs and interest), amount actually paid, date paid and whether applied to order and/or to accrued interest if accrued interest is claimed, and balance due. Due date of costs of enforcement is the date they were added to the judgment pursuant to a cost bill after judgment, not date incurred.

Failure to claim interest shall be deemed a waiver thereof for the purpose of this writ only.

ON INSTALLMENT ORDERS: EACH PAYMENT ORDERED AND DUE DATE MUST BE STATED SEPARATELY.
PERSON TO WHOM AMOUNT IS ORDERED PAID MUST SIGN DECLARATION.

TOTAL ORDERED PAID		ACTUALLY PAID			BALANCE DUE	
DUE DATE	AMOUNT	DATE PAID	ON ORDER	ON ACCRUED INTEREST	ON ORDER	ON ACCRUED INTEREST
N/A		N/A			N/A	

There is actually remaining due on said order the sum of $_____ plus $_____ accrued costs plus
$_____ accrued interest plus $_____ interest per day accruing from date of this application to date of writ, for which sum it is prayed that a writ of possession/sale/execution issue in favor of

_____Lenny D. Landlord_____
(Judgment Creditor)

and against ___Terrence D. Tenant and Tillie D. Tenant_____
(Judgment Debtor)

to the County of ___Los Angeles_____

I declare under penalty of perjury under the laws of the State of California that the foregoing is true and correct.

Executed on ___August 16, 20xx_____

_____*Lenny Landlord*_____
(Signature)

APPLICATION FOR ISSUANCE OF WRIT OF EXECUTION, POSSESSION OR SALE

Having the Marshal or Sheriff Evict

Once the court clerk issues the Writ of Possession and gives you the original (plus stamped copies), you are responsible for taking it to the sheriff or marshal, who will carry out the actual eviction. You can get the marshal's or sheriff's location from the court clerk.

Take the original of the Writ of Possession, plus three copies for each defendant you're having evicted, to the office of the marshal or civil division of the sheriff's office (whichever your county has). You will be required to pay a $75 fee, which is recoverable from the tenant. You must also fill out a set of instructions telling the sheriff or marshal to evict the defendants. Usually the sheriff or marshal has a particular form of instructions, but you can prepare the instructions in the form of a signed letter. A sample letter is shown below.

Sample Letter of Instructions for Sheriff or Marshal

August 18, 20xx
12345 Angeleno Street
Los Angeles, CA 90010

Los Angeles County Marshal
Civil Division
210 W. Temple
Los Angeles, CA 90012

Re: Landlord v. Tenant
    Los Angeles County Superior Court
    Los Angeles District, Case No. A-12345-B

Please serve the writ of execution for possession of the premises in the above-referenced action on Terrence D. Tenant and Tillie D. Tenant and place the plaintiff in possession of the premises at 6789 Angel Street, Apartment 10, Los Angeles, California. You may call me at 213-555-6789 to schedule the final posting/eviction date.

Sincerely,
Lenny D. Landlord
Lenny D. Landlord

Within a few days (or weeks, in large urban areas) a deputy sheriff or marshal will go to the property and serve the occupants (either personally or by posting and mailing) with a five-day eviction notice that says, in effect, "If you're not out in five days, a deputy will be back to throw you out." (Many sheriffs and marshals will specify the next business day if the fifth day falls on a weekend or holiday.) In most cases, tenants leave before the deadline. If the property is still occupied after five days, call the marshal's or sheriff's office to ask that the defendants be physically evicted. Most sheriff's or marshal's offices don't automatically go back to perform the eviction, so it's up to you to call them if they don't call you.

You should meet the sheriff or marshal at the property to change the locks. If you think the ex-tenant will try to move back into the premises, you may wish to supervise, to make sure he really moves his things out. If he tries to stay there against your wishes or to re-enter the premises, he is a criminal trespasser, and you should call the police.

If you did not have the Prejudgment Claim of Right to Possession forms served (as discussed in Chapter 6), the sheriff or marshal will not physically remove a person who:

- was not named as a defendant in your suit, and
- has filed—before the final eviction date—a written claim that he was in possession of the premises when you filed your suit, or had a right to be in possession before you filed your suit.

For example, if you rented to a husband and wife, sued and served them both with Summonses and Complaint, and got judgments against them both, the sheriff or marshal will refuse to evict the wife's brother who files a claim stating that he moved in months ago at her invitation, even though the rental agreement had a provision prohibiting this. (The optional procedure in Chapter 6 is a sort of preventive medicine to make sure that such unknown occupants can't wait to do this until the sheriff comes, and must do it early in the proceeding.)

If an unknown occupant does file a claim with the sheriff or marshal before the final eviction date, the eviction will be delayed until a later hearing where the person must show why he should not be evicted, too. This involves procedures that are beyond the scope of this book. See an attorney if you encounter this problem.

(We discuss hiring and working with lawyers in *The California Landlord's Law Book: Rights & Responsibilities*, Chapter 8.)

As for the tenant's belongings, the deputy who carries out the eviction will not allow the tenants to spend hours moving their belongings out, nor will their possessions be placed on the street. Rather, the tenant will be allowed to carry out one or perhaps a few armloads of possessions. The remainder will be locked in the unit. Of course, you should change the locks or the tenant may just go right back in. This does not mean you have a right to hold the tenant's possessions for ransom until the back rent is paid. Doing that is illegal and could subject you to a lawsuit. You only have the right to insist on "reasonable storage charges" equal to 1/30th of the monthly rent for each day, starting with the day the deputy sheriff or marshal performs the eviction, as a condition of releasing the property.

Don't be too insistent on this, though. You don't want to have to store a bunch of secondhand possessions on the property and be unable to rent the premises to a rent-paying tenant, nor do you particularly want to front moving and storage charges to have the belongings hauled off to a storage facility. (See *The California Landlord's Law Book: Rights & Responsibilities*, Chapter 21, for a detailed discussion of what you can legally do with a tenant's abandoned property.) Given this reality, it's amazing how many landlords and tenants who've been at each other's throats can suddenly be very reasonable and accommodating when it comes to arranging for the tenant to get his locked-up belongings back.

Getting a Money Judgment for Rent and Costs

Once the tenants have moved out of the premises, you should seek a judgment for the money they owe you. Although a court clerk can give you a Judgment for Possession of the premises, a money judgment for the rent and court costs (including filing, process server, writ, and sheriff's fees) has to be approved by a judge at a "default hearing." You must also prepare a Request for Entry of Default (the same form you used earlier, filled out differently) and a Judgment form.

Unlawful detainer money judgments against tenants are notoriously difficult to collect. (We discuss collection procedures, as well as the likelihood of success, in Chapter 9.) So why bother getting a judgment? First, you've done most of the work already, and there isn't much more involved. Second, the law gives you ten years to collect (and another ten years if you renew your judgment), and you may someday find the tenant with some money; having a judgment ready will make it easier to collect if and when that happens.

Determining Rent, Damages, and Costs

The first step is figuring out how much money you're entitled to. You won't know for sure how much this is until the tenant leaves. Use the following guidelines and worksheets.

 Nonpayment of rent cases. You are entitled to:

- **Overdue rent.** This is the amount of rent you demanded in the three-day notice.

   EXAMPLE: You served your three-day notice on August 3 for $900 rent due on the 1st and covering August 1 to 31. You got a default Judgment for Possession on the 16th, and your default hearing is scheduled for August 23. You are entitled to judgment for the entire $900 rent for August, even if the tenant leaves before the end of the month.

Get What You're Due

Some judges believe that you're not entitled to the rent for the entire month if you get your judgment before the month is up. This is wrong; rent payable in advance accrues and is due in its entirety for the whole period, without proration on a daily basis. See *Friedman v. Isenbruck* (1952) 111 Cal. App. 2d 326, 335, 224 P.2d 718; and *Rez v. Summers* (1917) 34 Cal. App. 527, 168 P. 156.

- **Leases.** A tenant who was evicted while renting under a fixed-term lease is legally liable to you for the balance of the rent on the lease, less what you can get from a replacement tenant. (See *The California Landlord's Law Book: Rights & Responsibilities*, Chapter 2.) However, you have to bring a separate lawsuit to recover this amount. The judgment in an unlawful detainer is limited to the rent the tenant owed when served with a three-day notice, plus prorated daily rent up until the date of judgment.

- **Damages.** If, after you obtained a default Judgment for Possession, the tenant stayed past the end of the period for which rent was due, you are entitled to an additional award of "damages at the rate of reasonable rental value" for each day the tenant stayed beyond the initial rental period. You specified the reasonable daily rental value (1/30th of one month's rent) in Item 10 of the Complaint.

   EXAMPLE: You were a little too patient and didn't serve your three-day notice until the 17th of August. You got a default Judgment for Possession on the 28th, and your tenant was evicted on September 4. You are entitled to a judgment for the $900 rent for August. In addition, you're entitled to prorated daily damages for each of the four days in September the tenant stayed, at the rate of 1/30th of $900 or $30 for each, or $120. The total is $1,020.

- **Your court costs.** This does not include things like copy fees or postage, but does include fees you had to pay court clerks, the process server, and the sheriff or marshal.

You cannot get a judgment in this proceeding for the costs of repairing or cleaning the premises, but you can deduct them from the security deposit. (If you collected "last month's rent," you cannot use that money toward cleaning and damages; see *The California Landlord's Law Book: Rights & Responsibilities*, Chapter 5.) If the deposit won't cover cleaning and repair costs, you'll have to go after the difference in a separate suit in small claims court, or superior court if the costs are high enough to justify it.

You do not need to credit the security deposit when you seek your money judgment. If there is anything left over after you pay for cleaning and repairs, the balance is credited against the judgment after you obtain it, not

before. (For more information on how to itemize and return security deposits, see *The California Landlord's Law Book: Rights & Responsibilities*, Chapter 20.)

EXAMPLE: Lola obtained a judgment for $680, including rent, prorated damages, and court costs. She holds her tenant's $400 security deposit. The cost of cleaning and repairing is $200, and Lola subtracts this from the deposit; the remaining $200 of the deposit is applied against the $680 judgment, so that the tenant owes Lola $480 on the judgment.

Worksheet #1

**Calculating Amount of Judgment:
Eviction Based on Nonpayment of Rent**

Overdue Rent:

(amount demanded in three-day notice) $ _____

Damages:

_____ days x $ _____ (daily rental value) = $ _____

Court Costs:

$ _____ filing fee

$ _____ process server

$ _____ writ fee

$ _____ sheriff's or marshal's fee $ _____

                                          TOTAL $ _____

Notice **30-day or 60-day notice cases.**

You are entitled to:

- Prorated daily "damages" at the daily rental value for each day the tenant stayed beyond the 30-day (or 60-day) notice period. You are not entitled to judgment for any rent or damages that accrued before the 30 days (or 60 days) passed. You can, however, deduct this amount from the security deposit; see Chapter 9. The daily rental value is listed in Item 10 of the Complaint.

- Court costs, including your filing, service of process, writ, and sheriff's or marshal's fees.

EXAMPLE: You served Jackson, whose $900 rent is due on May 15th of each month, with a 60-day termination notice on April 1. This means he is required to leave on May 31. He pays the rent for the period of April 15 through May 14, but refuses to leave on the 31st and refuses to pay the $480 prorated rent, due on May 15th, for the period of May 15 through 31 (1/30th of the $900 monthly rent, or $30/day, for 16 days). On June 1, you sue on the 60-day notice, and finally get Jackson out on June 25. In this kind of unlawful detainer suit, you are entitled to judgment for prorated daily "damages" only for the period of June 1 (the day after he should have left under the 60-day notice) through June 25 (the day he left), for a total of $750 (25 x $30/day), and your court costs. To be paid for the earlier period of May 15 through 31st, you'll have to either sue him in small claims court (usually not worth the trouble) or deduct it from any security deposit he paid.

Lease violation cases.

You are entitled to:

- "damages," prorated at the rate of 1/30th the monthly rent (you listed this figure in Item 10 of the Complaint) for each day beyond the expiration of the three-day notice period that the tenant stayed and for which you haven't already been paid in the form of rent, and
- court costs—filing, service, and writ fees.

The amount of your money judgment may be quite small, and you may get a judgment only for your court costs, particularly if you accepted the regular monthly rent in advance for the month during which you served the three-day notice.

EXAMPLE: Say you accepted the regular monthly rent of $1,000 from Ron when it was due the first of the month. Two weeks later, Ron begins having loud parties. You give Ron a written warning, but it continues. On the 16th, at the urging of all your other tenants who threaten to move, you give Ron an unconditional three-day notice to quit.

Ron doesn't move, and you file suit on the 20th and take a default Judgment for Possession on the 26th. The marshal posts a five-day eviction notice on the 28th, giving Ron until the 3rd of the next month before he gets the boot. Ron leaves on the 2nd, so you're out only two days' prorated rent or "damages" at the reasonable rental value of $33.33 per day (1/30th x $1,000 per month), for a grand total of $66.66 plus court costs.

If Ron had misbehaved earlier, and you had served the three-day notice only a few days after that, having collected rent on the first of the month, you might even have gotten Ron out before the end of the month. In that case, your judgment would have been for court costs only. Ron isn't entitled to a prorated refund for the last few days of the month for which he paid but didn't get to stay, since he "forfeited" his rights under the rental agreement or lease—including any right to stay for days prepaid.

No-notice cases.

You are entitled to:

- prorated daily "damages" at the daily rental value (you listed this figure in Item 10 of the Complaint) for each day beyond the date of termination of tenancy (either the date the lease expired or the termination date of the 30-day notice the tenant gave you), and
- court costs, including filing, service, and writ fees.

EXAMPLE: Hilda sued Sally, whose six-month lease expired June 30. Even if Sally hadn't paid all the $900 rent for June, Hilda would be entitled only to prorated daily damages (rental value per day) of $30 ($900/30) per day for each day beyond June 30 that Sally stayed in possession of the premises. So, if Hilda got Sally out by July 25, Hilda would be entitled to damages of 25 x $30, or $750, plus costs.

Past due rent. You cannot seek past-due rent unless the three-day notice was based on nonpayment of rent. So, if Sally hadn't paid all her rent when it was due in early June, Hilda should have used a three-day notice and the eviction procedure in Chapter 2.

Worksheet #2

Calculating Amount of Judgment:
Eviction Based on 30-Day or 60-Day Notice,
Violation of Lease or No Notice

Overdue Rent:

(amount demanded in three-day notice) $ _____

Damages:

_____ days x $ _____ (daily rental value) = $ _____

Court Costs:

$ _____ filing fee

$ _____ process server

$ _____ writ fee

$ _____ sheriff's or marshal's fee $ _____

TOTAL $ _____

Preparing the Request for Entry of Default (Money Judgment)

You must complete a second Request for Entry of Default to get your money judgment. A sample is shown above.

Fill in the caption boxes the same way you did for the first Request for Entry of Default form. (See above.) This time, though, put an X only in the box next to the words "COURT JUDGMENT." Do not put an X in any other box, not even the "Entry of Default" box, since the defendant's default has already been entered. Then fill in the numbered items as follows.

Item 1a: Enter the date you filed the Complaint and your name, just as you did in the first Request for Entry of Default.

Item 1b: Type your name.

Item 1c: Leave this box blank. The clerk already entered the defaults of the defendants when you filed your first Request for Entry of Default.

Item 1d: Put an X in this box. This asks the clerk to schedule a "default hearing" in front of a judge. (Some courts instead accept a written declaration that says what you'd say in front of the judge. See below.) Type the defendants' names.

Item 1e: Leave these boxes blank. This is only for a clerk's judgment, and the clerk can't enter a money judgment in an unlawful detainer case.

Items 2a-f: In the line entitled "a. Demand of Complaint," list in the "Amount" column the total of rent plus prorated daily damages for any days the tenant stayed beyond the end of the rental period, as calculated above in "Determining Rent, Damages, and Costs."

For example, in the rent nonpayment example above, where the tenant didn't pay the August rent and stayed until September 4, the past-due rent (for August) is $900, and the damages are $120 (four September days at $30—1/30th of $900), for a total of $1,020. This sum goes in the "Amount" column.

Don't list anything next to lines b, b(1), or b(2) entitled "Statement of damages." This does not apply to unlawful detainer cases.

Next to "c. Interest" and "e. Attorney fees," enter "0.00." Next to "d. Costs," enter the total of the filing fee, the process server's fee for serving all the defendants, and other court costs tallied in Item 5. (See below.) Total these amounts at Item 2f. Under the "Credits Acknowledged" column, list all amounts and the total as "0.00," since the defendant has not paid you anything. Don't include the security deposit. Finally, under "Balance," list the same amounts as under the "Amount" column.

Item 2g: List the same prorated daily rent amount and the same date from which you are asking for prorated daily damages that you did in the original Request for Entry of Default. Then, fill in the date you'll be filing the default papers with the court, type your name opposite the place for signature, and sign the form.

Item 3: We have preprinted an "X" in this box, to indicate the case is an unlawful detainer proceeding.

CAPTION, Second page: Type the names of the plaintiff and defendant, just as you did on the second page of the Proof of Service of Summons.

Items 4 and 5: Fill in these items exactly the same as you did in the original Request for Entry of Default.

Item 6: Fill in this item exactly as you did in the first Request for Entry of Default, checking box b and entering the date of mailing of this second one to the defendant's address. (Even though the defendant has moved now, after eviction, that's still his address as last known to you, and it could be forwarded.) Mail copies to the tenants and put "ADDRESS CORRECTION AND FORWARDING REQUESTED" on the envelopes. This will help you locate them when you go to collect your money judgment. (See Chapter 9.)

CIV-100

ATTORNEY OR PARTY WITHOUT ATTORNEY *(Name, State Bar number, and address):* LENNY D. LANDLORD 12345 ANGELENO STREET LOS ANGELES, CA 90010 TELEPHONE NO.: 213-555-6789 FAX NO. *(Optional):* 213-555-5678 E-MAIL ADDRESS *(Optional):* ATTORNEY FOR *(Name):* Plaintiff in Pro Per	**FOR COURT USE ONLY**

SUPERIOR COURT OF CALIFORNIA, COUNTY OF   LOS ANGELES
STREET ADDRESS: 110 North Grand Avenue
MAILING ADDRESS: Same
CITY AND ZIP CODE: Los Angeles, CA 90012
BRANCH NAME: CENTRAL DISTRICT/DOWNDOWN BRANCH

PLAINTIFF/PETITIONER:

DEFENDANT/RESPONDENT:

REQUEST FOR (Application)	☐ **Entry of Default** ☒ **Court Judgment**	☐ **Clerk's Judgment**	CASE NUMBER: A-12345-B

1. **TO THE CLERK:** On the complaint or cross-complaint filed
   a. on *(date):*   August 10, 20xx
   b. by *(name):*   Lenny D. Landlord
   c. ☒ Enter default of defendant *(names):*
      Terrence D. Tenant, Tillie D. Tenant
   d. ☐ I request a court judgment under Code of Civil Procedure sections 585(b), 585(c), 989, etc., against defendant *(names):*

      (Testimony required. Apply to the clerk for a hearing date, unless the court will enter a judgment on an affidavit under Code Civ. Proc., § 585(d).)
   e. ☐ Enter clerk's judgment
      (1) ☐ for restitution of the premises only and issue a writ of execution on the judgment. Code of Civil Procedure section 1174(c) does not apply. (Code Civ. Proc., § 1169.)
         ☐ Include in the judgment all tenants, subtenants, named claimants, and other occupants of the premises. The *Prejudgment Claim of Right to Possession* was served in compliance with Code of Civil Procedure section 415.46.
      (2) ☐ under Code of Civil Procedure section 585(a). *(Complete the declaration under Code Civ. Proc., § 585.5 on the reverse (item 5).)*
      (3) ☐ for default previously entered on *(date):*

2. **Judgment to be entered.**

		Amount		Credits acknowledged		Balance
a. Demand of complaint	$	1,260.00	$	0.00	$	1,260.00
b. Statement of damages *						
(1) Special	$		$		$	
(2) General	$		$		$	
c. Interest	$	0.00	$	0.00	$	0.00
d. Costs *(see reverse)*	$	192.00	$	0.00	$	192.00
e. Attorney fees	$	0.00	$	0.00	$	0.00
f. **TOTALS**	$	1,452.00	$	0.00	$	0.00

   g. **Daily damages** were demanded in complaint at the rate of: $ 30.00   per day beginning *(date):* Sept. 1, 20xx
   (* *Personal injury or wrongful death actions; Code Civ. Proc., § 425.11.*)

3. ☒ *(Check if filed in an unlawful detainer case)* **Legal document assistant or unlawful detainer assistant** information is on the reverse *(complete item 4).*

Date: September 12, 20xx

Lenny D. Landlord   ▶ *Lenny D. Landlord*
_____   _____
(TYPE OR PRINT NAME)   (SIGNATURE OF PLAINTIFF OR ATTORNEY FOR PLAINTIFF)

FOR COURT USE ONLY	(1) ☐ Default entered as requested on *(date):* (2) ☐ Default NOT entered as requested *(state reason):* Clerk, by _____, Deputy

Page 1 of 2

REQUEST FOR ENTRY OF DEFAULT
(Application to Enter Default)

Code of Civil Procedure,
§§ 585–587, 1169
www.courtinfo.ca.gov

PLAINTIFF/PETITIONER: LENNY D. LANDLORD	CASE NUMBER:
DEFENDANT/RESPONDENT: TERRENCE D. TENANT, ET AL	A-12345-B

4. **Legal document assistant or unlawful detainer assistant (Bus. & Prof. Code, § 6400 et seq.).** A legal document assistant or unlawful detainer assistant ☐ did ☒ did **not** for compensation give advice or assistance with this form. *(If declarant has received **any** help or advice for pay from a legal document assistant or unlawful detainer assistant, state):*

   a. Assistant's name: c. Telephone no.:
   b. Street address, city, and zip code: d. County of registration:
                                            e. Registration no.:
                                            f. Expires on *(date)*:

5. ☒ **Declaration under Code of Civil Procedure Section 585.5** *(required for entry of default under Code Civ. Proc., § 585(a)).* This action

   a. ☐ is ☒ is not   on a contract or installment sale for goods or services subject to Civ. Code, § 1801 et seq. (Unruh Act).
   b. ☐ is ☒ is not   on a conditional sales contract subject to Civ. Code, § 2981 et seq. (Rees-Levering Motor Vehicle Sales and Finance Act).
   c. ☐ is ☒ is not   on an obligation for goods, services, loans, or extensions of credit subject to Code Civ. Proc., § 395(b).

6. **Declaration of mailing (Code Civ. Proc., § 587).** A copy of this *Request for Entry of Default* was

   a. ☐ **not mailed** to the following defendants, whose addresses are **unknown** to plaintiff or plaintiff's attorney *(names)*:

   b. ☒ **mailed** first-class, postage prepaid, in a sealed envelope addressed to each defendant's attorney of record or, if none, to each defendant's last known address as follows:

      (1) Mailed on *(date)*:   (2) To *(specify names and addresses shown on the envelopes)*:

      September 12, 20xx   Terrence D. Tenant, 6789 Angeleno Street, Apt. 10, Los Angeles, CA 90012

      September 12, 20xx   Tillie D. Tenant, 6789 Angeleno Street, Apt. 10, Los Angeles, CA 90012

I declare under penalty of perjury under the laws of the State of California that the foregoing items 4, 5, and 6 are true and correct.

Date: September 12, 20xx

Lenny D. Landlord	▶ *Lenny D. Landlord*
(TYPE OR PRINT NAME)	(SIGNATURE OF DECLARANT)

7. **Memorandum of costs** *(required if money judgment requested)*. Costs and disbursements are as follows (Code Civ. Proc., § 1033.5):

   a. Clerk's filing fees . . . . $ 80.00
   b. Process server's fees . . . . $ 30.00
   c. Other *(specify)*:   writ fee . . . . $ 7.00
   d.   sheriff's eviction fee $ 75.00
   e. **TOTAL** . . . . $ 192.00

   f. ☐ Costs and disbursements are waived.

   g. I am the attorney, agent, or party who claims these costs. To the best of my knowledge and belief this memorandum of costs is correct and these costs were necessarily incurred in this case.

I declare under penalty of perjury under the laws of the State of California that the foregoing is true and correct.

Date: September 12, 20xx

Lenny D. Landlord	▶ *Lenny D. Landlord*
(TYPE OR PRINT NAME)	(SIGNATURE OF DECLARANT)

8. ☒ **Declaration of nonmilitary status** *(required for a judgment)*. No defendant named in item 1c of the application is in the military service so as to be entitled to the benefits of the Servicemembers Civil Relief Act (50 U.S.C. App. § 501 et seq.).

I declare under penalty of perjury under the laws of the State of California that the foregoing is true and correct.

Date: September 12, 20xx

Lenny D. Landlord	▶ *Lenny D. Landlord*
(TYPE OR PRINT NAME)	(SIGNATURE OF DECLARANT)

Civ-100 [Rev. January 1, 2007]   **REQUEST FOR ENTRY OF DEFAULT**   Page 2 of 2
                                   (Application to Enter Default)

Item 7: This is where you total your court costs. List the clerk's filing fee and your process server's fee in Items 7a and b. In Item 7c, "Other," type in "writ fee" and add the cost of the Writ of Possession. Below that, in Item d, add the sheriff's eviction fee. Total these items at Item 7e. This total should also be listed on Item 2d on the front.

Item 8: Date and sign the Declaration of Nonmilitary Status the same way you did on the original Request for Entry of Default.

Preparing a Declaration as to Rent, Damages, and Costs

Most courts allow you, and many require you, to prepare a written declaration under penalty of perjury in lieu of testifying before a judge at a default hearing. The judge simply reads the declaration's statements about rent, damages, and court costs, and awards you a judgment without a hearing. In the Central Division of Los Angeles County, you must use a declaration; default hearings are not held. If you want to get your money judgment this way rather than attending a default hearing, call the court and ask whether or not it accepts declarations in lieu of testimony in unlawful detainer default cases. If you'd rather testify in person, or if the court doesn't allow declarations, proceed to "Preparing the Proposed Judgment," below.

In January 2003, the Judicial Council wrote an optional, statewide form for this type of declaration. In our opinion it is unnecessarily complex, lengthy, and legally incorrect. Contrary to our opinion of what the law is, this form implies that you must attach originals of certain documents, such as rental agreements and proofs of services of notices (you might not even have these). Worse, it requires you to needlessly fill out even more forms (and perhaps pay additional filing fees) to get permission from a judge to use copies of original documents—that you might not have! Fortunately, this form is optional, so you don't have to use it. If you find this form unworkable or difficult, we recommend instead that you try to use either the typewritten Declaration in Support of Default Judgment form, or improvise your own form, based on the following examples. Landlords using this book have done so since 1986, and courts have accepted the forms without requiring the use of original rental agreements or a complete history of rent increases.

In the event you want to use this statewide Declaration for Default Judgment by Court form, we include it in the appendix and on the CD-ROM, and give you the following instructions for filling it out.

First, enter the information (name, address, court location, case number, names of plaintiff and defendant) that you listed in the big boxes at the top of the Complaint, Request for Entry of Default, and Writ of Possession forms.

Item 1: Check box 1a. Check box 1b(1) if you own the property and the facts of the rental are better known to you than anyone else. If, instead, a property manager or other agent is better informed than you, and is therefore signing this declaration, check box 1b(2) or 1b(3) as appropriate.

Item 2: List the complete address of the property.

Item 4a: This item asks for the same information you supplied in Items 6a and 6b in the Complaint. Fill in the same information about whether the rental agreement was written or oral, the names(s) of the defendant(s) who signed it, the term of the tenancy, and the initial rent amount and due date.

Item 4b: If you have the original rental agreement, or attached it to the Complaint (which we didn't recommend, because you may need the original at trial if the case is contested), check this box. If you attached a copy of the rental agreement to the Complaint and are now going to attach the original to this declaration, check the box next to the words "to this declaration, labeled Exhibit 4b," and attach the original, labeling it "Exhibit 4b" at the bottom.

Item 4c: If you do not have an original rental agreement, and did not attach one to the Complaint, you are supposed to check this box and the one next to the words "to this declaration, labeled Exhibit 4c," and attach your copy as "Exhibit 4c." However, if you do this, you are also required, according to this form, to include "a declaration and order to admit the copy." We think this is legally unnecessary and needlessly cumbersome; it's one of the reasons you may choose not to use this badly designed form and use instead the typewritten one. But if you use this form and did not have the original rental agreement or lease, and did not attach a copy of it to the Complaint, then you should prepare a separate page explaining why you do not have the original, followed by the words, "I declare under penalty of perjury under the law of the State of California that the foregoing is true and correct," and by the date and your signature. Follow this with a short paragraph stating "IT IS HEREBY ORDERED that the copy of the lease or rental agreement submitted herewith as Exhibit 4c may be admitted," followed by a signature line labeled "JUDGE OF THE SUPERIOR COURT." Be prepared to pay the Clerk $26 for the privilege of using this form and doing it this way.

Item 5: If the rental agreement has not changed since its inception (for example, you have not increased the rent, changed the rent due date, or changed any other term of the tenancy), skip this box and go to the second page. Otherwise, check the box and any box for Items 5a through 5f that apply.

If you have increased the rent more than once during the tenancy, you should check box 5a and add a separate Attachment 5a listing a complete history of rent increase, including rent amounts and effective dates, *except for the most recent increase.* As to the most recent increase, check and fill out Item 5b, indicating the rent before and after the increase, and the effective date; you also should check box 5b(1) (tenant paid the increased rent) or box 5b(2) (tenant was served a notice of change of terms of tenancy) as appropriate.

In the rare case of an increase by written agreement, check box 5b(3). If you have the original of such a document, check box 5e and the box next to "to this declaration, labeled Exhibit 5e," and attach that Agreement, labeled "Exhibit 5e." If you have only a copy, attach a separate statement under penalty of perjury and a proposed judge's order to admit the copy. (See similar example for rental agreement copies in instructions for Item 4c, above.) Check box 5f instead of 5e, check the words next to "to this declaration, labeled Exhibit 5f," and attach the copy labeled "Exhibit 5f." Again, we think this requirement is unnecessary and cumbersome, and is another reason you might prefer to use the typewritten form.

On the second page, list, in capitals, the plaintiff and defendants' names and the case number.

Item 6a: Fill out Item 6a, referring to the type of notice served on the tenant, the same way you filled out Item 7a of the Complaint.

Item 6b: If the notice served was a three-day notice to pay rent or quit, check this box to indicate the rent demanded in the notice (the same dollar figure as in Item 10 in the Complaint) and the dates of the rental period (this information should be listed on the three-day notice to pay or quit).

Item 6c: If the rent demanded in a three-day notice to pay rent or quit is different from the monthly rent, explain why. For example, you might type in: "Monthly rent was $1,000.00, three-day notice demanded only $800 due to earlier partial payment on March 4, 20xx."

Item 6d: Check this box and the box next to the words "The original Complaint."

Item 7a: List the name(s) of defendant(s) who were served a three-day, 30-day, or other notice, and the date of service, in the same way you did in Item 8a in the Complaint.

Item 7b: Check this box only if you used the optional procedure in Chapter 6 to have a Prejudgment Claim of Right to Possession served on unnamed occupants by a sheriff, marshal, or registered process server. Otherwise, leave this box blank.

Item 8: If the three-day notice you attached to the complaint included a filled out Proof of Service at the bottom, check the box next to the words, "the original Complaint." If not, type a proof of service, using our sample three-day notice's Proof of Service as a guide, have the person who served the notice sign it, and attach that original as "Exhibit 8b."

Item 9: List the date the three-day, 30-day, or other notice expired. This should be the same date listed in Item 7b of your Complaint.

Item 10: List the same daily fair rental value of the property that you listed in Complaint Item 11, and check box b.

Item 11: Since you should have waited until after the tenant vacated to fill out this form, check box 11a only, and list the date the tenant vacated.

Item 12: Check this box. In Item 12a, list the date you listed in Complaint Item 17f. In Item 12b, again list the date the tenant vacated. In Item 12c, list the number of days between the date in Item 12a and 12b, *including* both those dates. (For example, if the day in 12a is January 10 and the day in 12b is January 15, the number of days is 6, not 5.) In Item 12d, multiply this number of days by the daily fair-rental-value damages amount in Item 10. This amount is called the "holdover damages" figure that goes in Item 15a(2) on the next page.

Item 13: Leave this item blank.

1
2
3
4
5
6
7
8
9
10
11
12
13
14
15
16
17
18
19
20
21
22
23
24
25
26
27
28

Name: LENNY D. LANDLORD
Address: 12345 ANGELENO STREET
LOS ANGELES, CA 90010
Phone: 213-555-1234

Plaintiff in Pro Per

Sample Declaration for Nonpayment of Rent

SUPERIOR COURT OF CALIFORNIA, COUNTY OF _____LOS ANGELES_____

_____LOS ANGELES_____ DIVISION

LENNY D. LANDLORD
          Plaintiff,

     v.

TERRENCE D. TENANT, et al
          Defendant(s).

Case No. _____A-12345-B_____

DECLARATION IN SUPPORT OF DEFAULT
JUDGMENT FOR RENT, DAMAGES, AND COSTS

(C.C.P. SECS. 585(d), 1169)

I, the undersigned, declare:

1. I am the plaintiff in the above-entitled action and the owner of the premises at _____6789 Angel

Street, Apartment 10_____, City of

_____Los Angeles_____, County of _____Los Angeles_____, California.

2. On _____August 1_____, 20 xx_____, defendant(s) rented the premises from me pursuant

to a written/~~oral~~ [cross out one] agreement under which the monthly rent was $_____900.00_____ payable

in advance on the _____first_____ day of each month.

3. The terms of the tenancy [check one]:

☒ were not changed; or

☐ were changed, effective _____, _____, in that monthly rent was

validly and lawfully increased to $_____ by ☐ agreement of the parties and subsequent payment

of such rent; or

☐ [month-to-month tenancy only] service on defendant(s) of a written notice of at least 30 days, setting forth

1   the increase in rent.

2   4. The reasonable rental value of the premises per day, that is, the current monthly rent divided by 30, is

3    $_____30.00_____.

4   5. Pursuant to the agreement, defendant(s) went into possession of the premises.

5   6. On _____August 3_____, __20xx__, defendant(s) were in default in the payment of rent in

6   the amount of $_____900.00_____, and I caused defendant(s) to be served with a written notice demanding that

7   defendant(s) pay that amount or surrender possession of the premises within three days after service of the notice.

8   7. Defendant(s) failed to pay the rent or surrender possession of the premises within three days after service of

9   the notice, whereupon I commenced this action, complying with any local rent control or eviction protection

10   ordinance applicable, and caused Summons and Complaint to be served on each defendant. Defendant(s) have

11   failed to answer or otherwise respond to the Complaint within the time allowed by law.

12   8. Defendant(s) surrendered possession of the premises on _____September 9_____,__20xx__,

13   after entry of a clerk's Judgment for Possession and issuance of a Writ of Execution thereon.

14   9. The rent was due for the rental period of _____August 1_____, __20xx__,

15   through _____August 31_____, __20xx__. After this latter date, and until defendant(s) vacated the

16   premises, I sustained damages at the daily reasonable rental value of $_____30.00_____, for total damages of

17   $_____270.00_____.

18   10. I have incurred filing, service, and writ fees in the total amount of $_____192.00_____ in this action.

19   11. If sworn as a witness, I could testify competently to the facts stated herein.

20   I declare under penalty of perjury under the laws of the State of California that the foregoing is true and

21   correct.

22

23   DATED:_____September_____, __20xx__

24   _____*Lenny D. Landlord*_____
        Plaintiff in Pro Per

25

26

27

28

1

Name: LORNA D. LANDLADY
Address: 3865 Oak Street
          Anaheim, CA 92801
Phone: 818-555-1234

Sample Declaration for Violation of Lease

2

3

4

Plaintiff in Pro Per

5

6

7

8

9

SUPERIOR COURT OF CALIFORNIA, COUNTY OF ORANGE

10

CENTRAL ORANGE COUNTY JUDICIAL DIVISION

LORNA D. LANDLADY_____) Case No. 5-0368

11

       Plaintiff,   )

) DECLARATION IN SUPPORT OF DEFAULT

12

   v.   ) JUDGMENT FOR DAMAGES AND COSTS

)

13

TERESA A. TENANT , et al   )

       Defendant(s).   ) (C.C.P. SECS. 585(d), 1169)

14

_____)

15

16

I, the undersigned, declare:

17

1. I am the plaintiff in the above-entitled action and the owner of the premises at 15905 Lafayette

18

Street, Apartment 202, City of Anaheim, County of Orange, California.

19

2. On September 1, 20xx, defendant(s) rented the premises from me pursuant to a written one-year

20

lease under which the monthly rent was $900.00 payable in advance on the first day of each month.

21

The terms of the agreement have not been changed.

22

3. Pursuant to the agreement, defendants went into possession of the premises.

23

4. Defendants last paid rent on March 1, 20xx, for March.

24

5. On March 14, 20xx, Teresa began having loud parties that would begin around noon and last

25

until about 4 a.m. On the 14th, my other tenants began to complain and threaten to move. I went to

26

the apartment above, and the floor was vibrating from all the noise. I knocked at Teresa's door, but

27

apparently no one could hear the knocking, with the music as loud as it was. Finally, I just walked in,

28

found Teresa, and asked her to turn down the music. She did, but she turned it back up when I left. The

Declaration in Support of Default Judgment for Damages and Costs   Page 1 of 2 same thing happened the next two days.

6. On March 16, 20xx, I caused defendant to be served with a three-day notice to perform covenant or quit. She had another party on the 18th and didn't leave on the 19th, so I filed suit on the 20th.

7. I obtained a default Judgment for Possession on March 28, 20xx.

8. Defendant moved out on the second day of April.

9. The damages for the period I didn't receive rent were equal to the prorated daily reasonable rental value of $20.00 per day, which for two days is $40.00. My court costs have been $80.00 for the filing fee, $30.00 process server's fees, $3.50 for issuance of the Writ of Possession, and $75.00 to have the sheriff evict, for a total of $188.50

10. If sworn as a witness, I could testify competently to the facts stated herein.

I declare under penalty of perjury under the laws of the State of California that the foregoing is true and correct.

DATED: ___April 15, 20xx___   _Lorna D. Landlady_____
                                    Plaintiff in Pro Per

```
 1   Name:     LINDA D. LANDLADY
     Address:  459 ROSE STREET                    ┌─────────────────────────────────────────┐
 2             BERKELEY, CA 94710                 │  Sample Declaration: 30-, 60-, or 90-Day Notice │
     Phone:    510-555-1234                       └─────────────────────────────────────────┘
 3
     Plaintiff in Pro Per
 4

 5

 6

 7

 8            SUPERIOR COURT OF CALIFORNIA, COUNTY OF _____ALAMEDA_____

 9                   ___OAKLAND-PIEDMONT-EMERYVILLE___ DIVISION

10

11     _LINDA D. LANDLADY_____   )   Case No. ____5-0258_____
                Plaintiff,                 )
12                                         )   DECLARATION IN SUPPORT OF DEFAULT
       v.                                  )   JUDGMENT FOR DAMAGES AND COSTS
13                                         )
       _THAD TENANT, et al_____   )
14         Defendant(s).                   )   (C.C.P. SECS. 585(d), 1169)
                                           )
15     _____)

16     I, the undersigned, declare:

17         1. I am the plaintiff in the above-entitled action and the owner of the premises at _____950 Parker Street_

18     _____, City of

19     _Oakland_____, County of _____Alameda_____, California.

20         2. On ___February 1_____, __20xx__, defendant(s) rented the premises from me pursuant to

21     a written/oral [cross out one] agreement under which the monthly rent was $_____400.00_____ payable in

22     advance on the _____1st_____ day of each month.

23         3. The terms of the tenancy [check one]:

24         [X] were not changed; or

25         [ ] were changed, effective _____, _____, in that monthly rent was

26     validly and lawfully increased to $_____ by

27         [ ] agreement of the parties and subsequent payment of such rent; or

28         [ ] [month-to-month tenancy only] service on defendant(s) of a written notice of at least 30 days, setting forth
```

1   the increase in rent.

2   4. The reasonable rental value of the premises per day, that is, the current monthly rent divided by 30, is

3   $___13.33___.

4   5. Pursuant to the agreement, defendant(s) went into possession of the premises.

5   6. On ___August 30___, 20xx___, I served defendant with a written 30-day/ ~~60-day~~

6   [cross out one] termination notice.

7   7. Defendant(s) was still in possession of the property after the period of the notice expired on

8   ___September 30___, 20xx___, and stayed until ___October 20___, 20xx___,

9   when the sheriff evicted him/her/them pursuant to a clerk's Judgment for Possession and issuance of a Writ of

10   Execution.

11   8. I sustained damages at the daily reasonable rental value of $___13.33___ for ___21___ days

12   between ___September 30___, 20xx___ and ___October 20___, 20xx___

13   for a total of $___279.93___.

14   9. I have incurred filing, service, and writ fees in the total amount of $___188.50___in this action.

15   10. If sworn as a witness, I could testify competently to the facts stated herein.

16   I declare under penalty of perjury under the laws of the State of California that the foregoing is true and

17   correct.

18

19   DATED:___October 31___, 20xx___

20   *Linda D. Landlady*
        Plaintiff in Pro Per

21

22

23

24

25

26

27

28

Item 14: Check this box and list your total court costs, consisting of filing fee, cost indicated on returned Summons for service of process, fee for issuance of Writ of Possession, and sheriff's or marshal's eviction fee. This item goes in Item 15a(3), "Costs."

On the top of page 3, again list names of plaintiff, defendant(s), and case number.

Item 15: Check Item 15a and list past-due rent from Item 6b, "holdout damages" from Item 12d, and costs from Item 14. Add them for a "total judgment" amount. Leave box 15b blank. If the eviction is based on rent nonpayment or other breach, check the box in Item 15c as applicable—either the one next to "cancellation of the rental agreement" for a month-to-month rental agreement, or "forfeiture of the lease" in the case of a fixed term lease.

Finally, date and sign the document and check any of Items 16 through 23 to indicate what exhibits you've added.

We also include a Los Angeles County form that some courts there require you to use. (Some samples are shown above for a Declaration in Support of Default Judgment form.) If you do your own declaration using our template, prepare it on typed, double-spaced 8½" x 11" legal (pleading) paper with the numbers down the left-hand side.

Blank, tear-out versions of a Declaration in Support of Default Judgment for Rent, Damages, and Costs, and Declaration in Support of Default Judgment for Damages and Costs, are in Appendix 3. The Judicial Council form is also in that appendix. The CD-ROM also includes these forms. Instructions for using the CD are in Appendix 2.

Evictions based on violation of a lease provision or causing a nuisance. Such an eviction results in the tenant's "forfeiture" of the right to stay for a period for which he already paid rent. In cases like this, judges are more reluctant to find in your favor, even in a default situation, so you have to be very specific and detailed in your testimony. You must explain how the tenant committed a "material" (serious) breach of the lease, illegally sublet, or committed a nuisance. Otherwise, a judge could rule that the eviction was unfounded, even though you got the tenant out with a Clerk's Judgment and Writ of Possession.

Preparing the Proposed Judgment

You should prepare a proposed judgment for the judge to sign. That way, you'll be able to simply hand the form to the judge to sign right after the hearing, instead of going home to prepare the judgment and going back to court to leave it for his signature.

A blank, tear-out version of the Judgment—Unlawful Detainer form is in Appendix 3. The CD-ROM includes this form. Instructions for using the CD are in Appendix 2.

The usual information goes in the big boxes at the top of this Judgment form. It's the same information you used on the form for a clerk's judgment for possession.

In the box containing the words "JUDGMENT— UNLAWFUL DETAINER," put an X in the boxes next to the words "By Court Only" and "By Default."

Item 1: Put an X in Item 1 next to the words "BY DEFAULT," and also in box 1e next to the words "Court Judgment." Then check box 1e(1) if you will be attending a live default hearing, or box 1e(2) if you will be submitting a written declaration.

Item 2: Leave this part blank and proceed to the other side (page 2) of the form. At the top of page 2, fill in the names, in capitals, of the plaintiff (you), the first named defendant (followed by "ET AL" if there is more than one defendant), and the court case number. Also, put an X in the box following the words, "THE COURT," which itself follows the words "JUDGMENT IS ENTERED AS FOLLOWS BY:"

Item 3: Put an X in Box 3a and type, in upper and lower case, the name(s) of the plaintiff(s) and the names of all defendants against whom you're obtaining this default judgment for the money owed you. Leave box 3b blank.

Items 4 and 5: Leave these items blank, since you already have a judgment for possession of the property from the clerk.

Item 6: All the items here are exactly the same as in Item 15 of the statewide Declaration for Default Judgment by Court form. Check boxes 6 and 6a and, in Item 6a(1), (2), and (4), check and list, as applicable, the rent, holdover damages, and costs, and add these for a "total judgment" amount in Item 6a(6). If the eviction is based on rent nonpayment or other breach, check, in Item 6c, either "The rental agreement is canceled" or "The lease is forfeited," as appropriate.

Items 7 and 8: Leave these blank.

Submitting Your Papers and/or Going to the Default Hearing

Make one copy of the proposed money judgment for your records, and one copy of the Request for Entry of Default for yourself plus one for each defendant. Mail a copy of the Request for Entry of Default to each tenant, and sign the proof of mailing on the back of the original. If you are submitting a declaration, also make a copy of it. You need to mail each defendant only a copy of the Request for Entry of Default, not a copy of any declaration or proposed judgment.

If you're submitting a declaration, give the original and copies of the Request for Entry of Default and the declaration to the court clerk, who should file the originals and rubber-stamp the copies and return them to you. Also give her the original and copy of the proposed judgment, which she will hold on to for submission to the judge. After a few days, the judge should sign the original, and the clerk will file it and return your copy to you. (To avoid another trip to the courthouse, give the clerk a self-addressed, stamped envelope in which to mail your copy of the judgment.) Once you get the judgment, you will be ready to proceed to Chapter 9 to have the sheriff or marshal collect it.

If you are going to appear before a judge at a default hearing, file only the Request for Entry of Default and ask the court clerk to set a hearing date. In most counties, hearings are held on certain days and times during the week. The defendant is not allowed to participate in the hearing, and therefore is not given any notice of it—she missed the chance to fight by not answering the Complaint within the time allowed.

On the day of the default hearing, take the original and copy of the proposed judgment and go to court a few minutes early. If you're lucky, you may see another landlord testifying before your case is called. When the clerk or judge calls your case, go forward and say to the judge something like, "Good morning, Your Honor, I'm Lenny D. Landlord appearing in pro per." The clerk will swear you in as your own witness. Some judges prefer that you take the witness stand, but others will allow you to present your case from the "counsel table" in front of the judge's bench.

You should be prepared to testify to the same kinds of facts that go into written declarations. (See above.) Lenny Landlord's testimony should go something like this:

"My name is Lenny D. Landlord. On January 1, 20xx, I rented my premises at 6789 Angel Street, Apartment 10, to Terrence and Tillie Tenant, the defendants in this proceeding. They signed a rental agreement for a month-to-month tenancy. I have a copy of the rental agreement, which I wish to introduce into evidence as Exhibit No. 1. The rent agreed on was $850 per month, but on May 31, 20xx, I gave the defendants a 30-day notice that the rent would be increased to $900 per month effective July 1, 20xx. This amount of rent was paid in July 20xx, but on August 1 the defendants failed to pay the rent for August. On August 3 I served Tillie Tenant with a three-day notice to pay rent or quit. I have a copy of the three-day notice which I wish to introduce into evidence as Exhibit No. 2. They didn't pay the rent and were still in possession on August 8, and I filed this lawsuit on August 9. They left the premises on August 25, but I believe I'm entitled to the rent for all of August."

If Lenny's tenants hadn't been evicted until, say, September 9, Lenny's last sentence would instead be something like:

"They left the premises on September 9, so I sustained damages at the daily reasonable rental value rate of $30 for nine days, for damages of $270, in addition to the $900 contract rent, for total rent and damages of $1,170."

Finally, Lenny might want to add the following testimony about his court costs:

"My court costs have been $90 for the filing fee, $30 process server's fee for serving both defendants, $7.00 for issuance of the original Writ of Possession, and $75 to have the marshal post the eviction notice, for a total of $202."

If you need to call another witness such as an agent who entered into the rental agreement on your behalf or a person who served the three-day notice, tell this to the judge and have that person testify.

The judge may ask you a question or two, but probably won't if you've been thorough. He will then

UD-110

ATTORNEY OR PARTY WITHOUT ATTORNEY *(Name, state bar number, and address):*	FOR COURT USE ONLY

LENNY D. LANDLORD
12345 Angeleno Street
Los Angeles CA 90010

TELEPHONE NO.: 213-555-6789   FAX NO. *(Optional):* 213-555-5678

E-MAIL ADDRESS *(Optional):*

ATTORNEY FOR *(Name):* Plaintiff in Pro Per

SUPERIOR COURT OF CALIFORNIA, COUNTY OF Los Angeles

STREET ADDRESS: 110 North Grand Avenue

MAILING ADDRESS: Same

CITY AND ZIP CODE: Los Angeles, CA 90012

BRANCH NAME: Central District/Downtown Branch

PLAINTIFF: LENNY D. LANDLORD

DEFENDANT: TERRENCE D. TENANT, TILLIE D. TENANT

JUDGMENT—UNLAWFUL DETAINER	CASE NUMBER:
☐ **By Clerk** ☒ **By Default** ☐ **After Court Trial**	A-12345-B
☒ **By Court** ☐ **Possession Only** ☐ **Defendant Did Not Appear at Trial**	

JUDGMENT

1. ☐ **BY DEFAULT**
   a. Defendant was properly served with a copy of the summons and complaint.
   b. Defendant failed to answer the complaint or appear and defend the action within the time allowed by law.
   c. Defendant's default was entered by the clerk upon plaintiff's application.
   d. ☐ **Clerk's Judgment** (Code Civ. Proc., § 1169). For possession only of the premises described on page 2 (item 4).
   e. ☒ **Court Judgment** (Code Civ. Proc., § 585(b)). The court considered
      (1) ☐ plaintiff's testimony and other evidence.
      (2) ☐ plaintiff's or others' written declaration and evidence (Code Civ. Proc., § 585(d)).

2. ☐ **AFTER COURT TRIAL.** The jury was waived. The court considered the evidence.
   a. The case was tried on *(date and time):*

      before *(name of judicial officer):*

   b. Appearances by:

      ☐ Plaintiff *(name each):*   ☐ Plaintiff's attorney *(name each):*

                                                      (1)

                                                      (2)

      ☐ Continued on *Attachment* 2b (form MC-025).

      ☐ Defendant *(name each):*   ☐ Defendant's attorney *(name each):*

                                                      (1)

                                                      (2)

      ☐ Continued on *Attachment* 2b (form MC-025).

   c. ☐ Defendant did not appear at trial. Defendant was properly served with notice of trial.

   d. ☐ A statement of decision (Code Civ. Proc., § 632) ☐ was not ☐ was requested.

Page 1 of 2

Form Approved for Optional Use Judicial Council of California UD-110 [New January 1, 2003]	**JUDGMENT—UNLAWFUL DETAINER**	Code of Civil Procedure, §§ 415.46, 585(d), 664.6, 1169

| PLAINTIFF: LENNY D. LANDLORD | CASE NUMBER: |
| DEFENDANT: TERRENCE D. TENANT, ET AL | A-12345-B |

JUDGMENT IS ENTERED AS FOLLOWS BY: ☐ **THE COURT** ☐ **THE CLERK**

3. **Parties.** Judgment is

a. ☒ for plaintiff *(name each):* Lenny D. Landlord

and against defendant *(name each):* Terrence D. Tenant, Tillie D. Tenant

☐ Continued on *Attachment* 3a (form MC-025).

b. ☐ for defendant *(name each):*

4. ☐ Plaintiff ☐ Defendant is entitled to possession of the premises located at *(street address, apartment, city, and county):*

5. ☐ Judgment applies to all occupants of the premises including tenants, subtenants if any, and named claimants if any (Code Civ. Proc., §§ 715.010, 1169, and 1174.3).

6. **Amount and terms of judgment**

a. ☒ Defendant named in item 3a above must pay plaintiff on the complaint:

    b. ☐ Plaintiff is to receive nothing from defendant named in item 3b.

☐ Defendant named in item 3b is to recover costs: $

(1)	☐	Past-due rent	$	list rent demanded in any three-day notice
(2)	☐	Holdover damages	$	list prorated damages
(3)	☐	Attorney fees	$	
(4)	☐	Costs	$	list court costs—filing, service, sheriff fees
(5)	☐	Other *(specify):*	$	
(6)	**TOTAL JUDGMENT**		$ Total	

☐ and attorney fees: $.

c. ☐ The rental agreement is canceled. ☐ The lease is forfeited.

7. ☐ **Conditional judgment.** Plaintiff has breached the agreement to provide habitable premises to defendant as stated in *Judgment—Unlawful Detainer Attachment* (form UD–110S), which is attached.

8. ☐ **Other** *(specify):*

☐ Continued on *Attachment* 8 (form MC-025).

Date: _____ ☐ _____
JUDICIAL OFFICER

Date: _____ ☐ Clerk, by _____ , Deputy

(SEAL)

CLERK'S CERTIFICATE *(Optional)*

I certify that this is a true copy of the original judgment on file in the court.

Date: _____

Clerk, by _____ , Deputy

UD-110 [New January 1, 2003] **JUDGMENT—UNLAWFUL DETAINER** Page 2 of 2

announce the judgment that you should get possession of the property (in effect repeating the part of the judgment you got from the clerk) plus a specified amount of rent/damages, plus costs. Don't be afraid to ask the judge to specify the dollar amount of the court costs. (That way you'll have judgment for them without having to file another form called a Memorandum of Costs.) Also, don't be afraid to politely differ with the judge ("Excuse me, Your Honor, but ...") as to the dollar amount of the rent/damages if you're sure you

calculated the amount correctly—especially if the judge awarded only part of the rent for the first month the tenant didn't pay. You're entitled to the entire amount of unpaid rent that came due at the beginning of the month even if the tenant left before the month's end.

Once the judge gives judgment in your favor, hand the judgment form with the correct amounts filled in to the courtroom clerk, and ask him to file-stamp and return a copy to you. We discuss how to collect the money part of the judgment in Chapter 9. ■

Contested Cases

Read this chapter only if the tenant has filed a response to your unlawful detainer Complaint. This chapter outlines how a contested unlawful detainer suit is resolved, either by settlement between the parties or at a trial. The purpose is to give you a solid idea of how a typical case is likely to proceed. We do not, and cannot, provide you with the full guidance necessary to handle all contested unlawful detainer cases to a successful conclusion. But we believe that an overview of the process is necessary whether you hire a lawyer or decide that your particular situation is simple enough that you can do it yourself.

➡ If the tenant has not filed a response to your unlawful detainer Complaint, and you have waited at least five days, you are entitled to seek a default judgment. That procedure is described in detail in Chapter 7.

What Is Involved in a Contested Eviction Case

Your tenant can complicate your life enormously simply by filing one or two pieces of paper with the court and mailing copies to you. If the tenant files a written response to your unlawful detainer Complaint (whether it is in the form of a motion, demurrer, or answer), you will have to fill out some additional documents and probably appear in court one or more times. All of this will require that you be very much on your toes. As a general rule, judges will not evict a tenant unless every legal "t" and "i" has been scrupulously crossed and dotted. In a contested case, some or all of the following may occur:

- If you or your process server erred in some particular of service, you may have to start from scratch by serving the tenant with a new notice to quit and/or a new Summons and Complaint.
- If the tenant convinces the judge that the Complaint you filed is deficient in some particular, you may have to redraft your Complaint one or more times, without any guidance from the judge.
- If your tenant accuses you, you may have to defend against such charges as:
  - You illegally discriminated against the tenant (for example, the tenant is gay, the tenant is Latino).

- The premises were legally uninhabitable.
- Your eviction is in retaliation against the tenant for complaining to the health authorities or organizing other tenants.
- Your eviction is in violation of the local rent control ordinance.
- You may have to disclose large amounts of business and sometimes personal information to the tenant by answering written questions under oath (interrogatories), producing documents, and allowing the tenant to inspect the premises.
- You may have to appear before a judge (or jury) to argue your case.
- Even if you win, your tenant may be entitled to remain on the premises because of a hardship.
- Even if you win, if you have evicted your tenant for the wrong reasons, you may be setting yourself up for a lawsuit for wrongful eviction.
- If you lose, you're back to the drawing board and will owe the tenant court costs (and perhaps attorney's fees, if the tenant was represented by an attorney) and maybe some damages as well.

Should You Hire an Attorney?

Clearly, you may be in for a good deal of trouble if your tenant contests your suit. Does this mean you should simply give up and hire a lawyer? At the very least, once you become aware of the tenant's response (and assuming you have not already filed for a default judgment), you should seriously consider locating and hiring an attorney experienced in landlord/tenant matters. Without knowing the particulars of a given contested case, it is impossible to predict whether or not you can safely handle it on your own.

Unless you are extremely experienced in these matters, you should always turn the case over to a lawyer if the tenant:
- is represented by a lawyer
- makes a motion or files a demurrer (these terms are explained below)
- demands a jury trial, or
- alleges any of the following defenses in his answer (discussed in "Preparing for Trial," below):
  - violation of a rent control ordinance
  - discriminatory eviction

- retaliatory eviction, or
- requests extensive pretrial disclosure of information that you feel would be harmful to disclose.

Understandably, you may be reluctant to turn the case over to a lawyer when you've taken it this far on your own. We're reluctant to recommend lawyers, too. The whole point of this book, after all, is to equip you to handle your unlawful detainer suit yourself. Unfortunately, we can't anticipate and prepare you to deal with every possible defense a tenant's lawyer may throw at you, or for that matter even predict what the tenant will raise in a motion. In short, once you find yourself facing a contested unlawful detainer suit, getting experienced help may be your best, and in the long run most cost-efficient, bet.

How to Settle a Case

You may negotiate a settlement with a tenant before or even during trial. Although it may not seem true in the heat of battle, it is our experience that considering the usually unpalatable alternative of a trial, it is very often in your economic interest to reach a settlement short of trial. That's why most unlawful detainer cases are settled without a trial.

Why Settle?

Why is a reasonable—or sometimes even a somewhat unreasonable—settlement better than fighting it out in court? Aside from the possibility that your tenant might win the lawsuit (as well as a judgment against you for court costs and attorney's fees), the time and trouble entailed in going to court often mean you are better off compromising. Even landlords who plow forward to trial and ultimately "win" a court judgment commonly suffer a larger out-of-pocket loss than if they had have compromised earlier. For example, a tenant who refuses to pay the $1,000 rent on the first of the month will be able to stay anywhere from four to six weeks before having to leave if he properly contests an unlawful detainer case. This means that if the tenant loses the case and is evicted after six weeks, the landlord loses $1,500 rent in the meantime, plus court costs approaching $200. If the landlord hires a lawyer, he'll be out at least another several hundred dollars, and probably a good deal more if a full-scale trial develops.

Although these amounts will be added to the judgment against the tenant, the truth is that a great many such judgments are uncollectable. (See Chapter 9.)

Given this unhappy reality, the landlord is usually ahead of the game by accepting a reasonable compromise, even if the tenant gets an unfairly favorable result. Depending on the situation, this may mean that a tenant who has violated a lease or rental agreement provision is allowed to stay on if all past-due rent is paid. Or if the tenant is simply impossible to have around over the long term, the landlord may want to enter into a written settlement agreement under which the tenant agrees to leave within a few weeks in exchange for the forgiveness of some or even all the rent that will have accrued through that time.

No matter what sort of deal you make, if it involves the tenant moving out, it should be in writing, and should provide you with an immediate eviction remedy should the tenant refuse to keep his part of the bargain.

> **EXAMPLE:** When Dmitri fails to pay his rent of $1,000 on May 1, Ivan serves him with a three-day notice. When that runs out without Dmitri paying the rent, Ivan sues Dmitri for an eviction order and the $1,000. Dmitri contests the suit with an answer that alleges Ivan breached the implied warranty of habitability by not getting rid of cockroaches. Ivan believes this is nonsense because he maintains the building very well, but does concede that the building is old and that tenants have had occasional problems with bugs and rodents. At trial, Ivan will attempt to prove that Dmitri's poor housekeeping caused the cockroaches and that Dmitri never complained about them before filing his Answer. Both Ivan and Dmitri think they will win at trial, but each is sensible enough to know he might lose and that a trial will certainly take up a lot of time, money, and energy. So they (or their lawyers) get together and hammer out a settlement agreement. Dmitri agrees to give Ivan a Judgment for Possession of the property, effective July 1, and Ivan agrees to drop his claim for back rent.

What Kind of Agreement Should You Make?

There are two ways in which you and the tenant can settle the unlawful detainer lawsuit. You can agree to either of the following:

- You'll file an unconditional entry of a judgment awarding you certain things, like possession of the property and rent, without your having to go back to court again (we'll call this the "unconditional judgment" option).
- You will be entitled to a judgment if the tenant fails to do certain things (such as leave or pay by a certain date), and that a tenant who complies as promised will be entitled to a dismissal of the lawsuit. We'll refer to this second option as the "deferred judgment" option.

Here's the difference between these two approaches: With an unconditional entry of judgment, the tenant agrees that the landlord is entitled to file an unlawful detainer judgment that can be enforced on a certain date. With the deferred judgment option—an agreement that judgment will be entered if the tenant fails to comply as promised (and to dismiss the case if the tenant does comply)—the landlord does not initially have a judgment and must take additional steps to get one if he needs it.

Clearly, the unconditional entry of judgment favors the landlord, because if things go awry, the landlord won't have to go back to court. And an agreement that judgment will be entered only if the tenant fails to comply favors the tenant, because if the tenant does not live up to the conditions, the landlord will have to revive the lawsuit that has been put on hold. Of course, the tenant will also prefer the second route because he'll undoubtedly expect to perform as he promises (to move or pay), and would like to have the lawsuit dismissed, rather than suffer the consequences of having a judgment on file against him.

No matter which route you choose, you'll need to fill out a form called a Stipulation for Entry of Judgment. You'll fill it out differently, however, depending on your choice. Instructions for both ways of completing the form are below.

In previous editions of this book, we called the first type of agreement for an unconditional entry of judgment a Stipulation for Judgment, because under a "stipulation," or agreement, you were automatically entitled to a judgment. We referred to the second kind of agreement as a Settlement Agreement. Effective January 2003, a new Judicial Council form called a Stipulation for Entry of Judgment can be used to reflect either of these types of agreements. Because of the potential for confusion between the Stipulation for Entry of Judgment form and the term "Stipulation for Judgment," we no longer use this latter term.

How to Negotiate With a Tenant

Here are some thoughts on negotiating with a tenant you are trying to get out:

- Be courteous, but don't be weak. If you have a good case, let the tenant know you have the resources and evidence to fight and win if you can't reach a reasonable settlement.
- Don't get too upset about how the tenant is using the system to get undeserved concessions out of you, and don't be so blinded by moral outrage that you reject workable compromises. At this point you want to balance the costs of a settlement against the costs of fighting it out and choose the less expensive alternative. If this sometimes means that a rotten tenant gets a good deal, so be it. The alternative, your getting an even worse deal from California's court system, is even less desirable.

For advice on negotiating techniques, see *Getting to Yes: Negotiating Agreements Without Giving In*, by Fisher and Ury, of the Harvard Negotiation Project (Penguin).

Designing an Agreement for the Deferred Judgment Option

For the reasons just explained, we do not recommend that you choose the second, deferred judgment option unless there are some very solid reasons why you think the tenant will deliver on his promises. If you go that route, however, keep in mind that you're offering a substantial benefit to the tenant: the opportunity to avoid the negative mark of an eviction judgment on his credit record, which will haunt him for years. In exchange for your agreement to dismiss the lawsuit if he performs, be sure that there is a fair trade-off, such as your getting an immediate, substantial payment of cash. If he doesn't come through and you're forced to file for a judgment, you'll have just that—a mere judgment for money can be hard to collect.

UD–115

ATTORNEY OR PARTY WITHOUT ATTORNEY (Name and state bar number, and address):	FOR COURT USE ONLY
LENNY D. LANDLORD 1234 ANGELENO STREET LOS ANGELES, CA 90010 TELEPHONE NO.: 213-555-6789 FAX NO. (Optional): E-MAIL ADDRESS (Optional): ATTORNEY FOR (Name): Plaintiff in Pro Per	

SUPERIOR COURT OF CALIFORNIA, COUNTY OF   LOS ANGELES
STREET ADDRESS: 110 North Grand Avenue
MAILING ADDRESS: Same
CITY AND ZIP CODE: Los Angeles, CA 90012
BRANCH NAME: CENTRAL/DOWNTOWN

PLAINTIFF: LENNY D. LANDLORD

DEFENDANT: TERRENCE D. TENANT, ET AL

STIPULATION FOR ENTRY OF JUDGMENT (Unlawful Detainer)	CASE NUMBER: A-12345-B

1. IT IS STIPULATED by plaintiff (name each):   Lenny D. Landlord   and
   defendant (name each):   Terrence D., Tenant, Tillie D. Tenant

2. [X] Plaintiff [ ] Defendant (specify name):   Lenny D. Landlord   is awarded
   a. [X] possession of the premises located at (street address, apartment number, city, and county):

      6789 Angeleno St., Apt. 10, Los Angeles, Los Angeles County

   b. [X] cancellation of the rental agreement.   [ ] forfeiture of the lease.
   c. [X] past due rent $ 900.00
   d. [X] total holdover damages $ 300.00
   e. [ ] attorney fees $
   f. [X] costs $ 123.00
   g. [ ] deposit of $ [ ] See item 3.
   h. [ ] other (specify):
   i. Total $ 1,232.00 to be paid by [X] (date): Nov. 1, 20xx   [ ] installment payments (see item 5)

3. [X] Deposit. If not awarded under item 2g, then plaintiff must
   a. [ ] return deposit of $ to defendant by (date):
   b. [X] give an itemized deposit statement to defendant within three weeks after defendant vacates the premises
      (Civ. Code, § 1950.5).
   c. [X] mail the [X] deposit [X] itemized statement   to the defendant at (mailing address):
      P.O. Box 1234, Los Angeles, CA 90010-1234

4. [X] A writ of possession will issue immediately, but there will be no lockout before (date): Sept. 30, 20xx

5. [ ] AGREEMENT FOR INSTALLMENT PAYMENTS
   a. Defendant agrees to pay $ on the (specify day)   day of each month beginning
      on (specify date)   until paid in full.

   b. If any payment is more than (specify)   days late, the entire amount in item 2i will become immediately due and
      payable plus interest at the legal rate.

6. a. [X] Judgment will be entered now.
   b. [ ] Judgment will be entered only upon default of payment of the amount in item 2i or the payment arrangement in item 5a.
      The case is calendared for dismissal on (date and time)   in
      department (specify)   unless plaintiff or defendant otherwise notifies the court.
   c. [ ] Judgment will be entered as stated in Judgment —Unlawful Detainer Attachment (form UD-110S), which is attached.
   d. [ ] Judgment will be entered as stated in item 7.

Page 1 of 2

Form Approved for Optional Use Judicial Council of California UD-115 [New January 1, 2003]	STIPULATION FOR ENTRY OF JUDGMENT (Unlawful Detainer)	Code of Civil Procedure, § 664.6

PLAINTIFF: LENNY D. LANDLORD	CASE NUMBER:
DEFENDANT: TERRENCE D. TENANT, ET AL	A-12345-B

7. ☐ Plaintiff and defendant further stipulate as follows *(specify):*

8. a. **The parties named in item 1 understand that they have the right to (1) have an attorney present and (2) receive notice of and have a court hearing about any default in the terms of this stipulation.**

   b. Date: Sept. 8, 20xx

   LENNY D. LANDLORD
   _____
   (TYPE OR PRINT NAME)

   _____
   (TYPE OR PRINT NAME)

   ▶ _____
   (SIGNATURE OF PLAINTIFF OR ATTORNEY)

   ▶ _____
   (SIGNATURE OF PLAINTIFF OR ATTORNEY)

   ☐ Continued on *Attachment* 8b (form MC-025).

   c. Date: Sept. 8, 20xx

   TERRENCE D. TENANT
   _____
   (TYPE OR PRINT NAME)

   TILLIE D. TENANT
   _____
   (TYPE OR PRINT NAME)

   _____
   (TYPE OR PRINT NAME)

   ▶ _____
   (SIGNATURE OF DEFENDANT OR ATTORNEY)

   ▶ _____
   (SIGNATURE OF DEFENDANT OR ATTORNEY)

   ▶ _____
   (SIGNATURE OF DEFENDANT OR ATTORNEY)

   ☐ Continued on *Attachment* 8c (form MC-025).

9. IT IS SO ORDERED.

Date:

_____
JUDICIAL OFFICER

STIPULATION FOR ENTRY OF JUDGMENT
(Unlawful Detainer)

You should also avoid agreements under which the tenant promises to pay a past-due rent in future installments. Even if the agreement says you get a judgment for possession if the tenant fails to pay the installments, you'll still have to file papers and go back to court to get a judgment for the amount of the unpaid installments.

Completing the Stipulation for Entry of Judgment Form

Whether you and the tenant agree that you can file a judgment right now, or decide that you will file one only if the tenant fails to perform as promised, you'll need to complete and file a form. Here are instructions for both routes. On the preceding pages is a filled-out sample Stipulation for Entry of Judgment form.

 A blank Stipulation for Entry of Judgment is included in Appendix 3, together with a Judgment—Unlawful Detainer Attachment (Form UD-110S), which you might use as an attachment to this form in certain situations (see Item 6c instructions, below). If you pursue an unconditional judgment or a deferred judgment, you will not need a separate Judgment Pursuant to Stipulation (the stipulation becomes the judgment when the judge signs it).

By now, you're familiar with the beginning parts of these forms. As with all Judicial Council forms, in the boxes at the top of the form list your name, address, and telephone number; the words "Plaintiff in Pro Per"; the court, county, court address, and branch, if applicable; and names of the plaintiff and defendants, as well as the case number.

Item 1: List your name and the names of the defendants who will be signing this stipulation.

Item 2: If the tenant will be vacating the property, put an X in the box next to the word "Plaintiff." Do not put an X in the box next to the word "Defendant," unless the tenant will be staying in possession of the premises, presumably after having come up to date on the rent that will accrue through the current month or other rental period, plus your court costs, paid immediately in cash or by cashier's or certified check or money order.

Item 2a: List the complete address of the property, including street address; unit number, if any; city; and county.

Item 2b: If the tenant will be vacating the property, put an X in the box next to either the words "cancellation of the rental agreement" or "forfeiture of the lease," as applicable.

Items 2c–2: If the tenant will be paying past-due rent, and/or prorated daily damages, put Xs where appropriate and indicate the dollar amount(s) in these items.

Item 2f: If the tenant will also be paying your court costs, put an X in this box and indicate the amount.

Item 2g: If you are stating in Item 2 that you, the plaintiff, are awarded the things listed, and you agree that you will not have to return the tenant's security deposit to him or her, put an X in this box and indicate the dollar amount of the deposit. (Avoid agreeing to this, if possible, because it will leave you without any funds to claim or repair the premises, after the tenant has vacated.)

Item 2i: Add up the dollar amounts in Items 2c, 2d, 2f, and 2g.

Item 3: If you have declined to agree (as we suggest in the instructions for Item 2g, above) to apply the tenant's security deposit before he or she moves out, then you should check box 3a or 3b, indicating the deposit will be subject to proper deductions (for cleaning and damages) in the normal fashion. We recommend negotiating for a promise to return and/or itemizing the tenant's security deposit within three weeks after he or she vacates the premises, since that allows you a fund from which to deduct the costs of any necessary cleaning or repairs in excess of ordinary wear and tear, and allows you the time ordinarily allowed by law to do this. If, on the other hand, all you can negotiate for is to return a certain dollar amount of the deposit to the tenant by a certain date, then check box 3a and indicate the dollar amount of the deposit and date. In either case, if box 3a or 3b is checked, you should check the items in box 3c to indicate the tenant's mailing address, to which you will be mailing the deposit and/or itemization.

Item 4: Check the box that gives you an immediate writ of possession. If the tenant will not be moving prior to a certain agreed date, you should still put an X in this box, and indicate that date. This allows you to agree that the tenant may stay in the premises until a certain date, and to have him or her evicted the next day if the tenant fails to move. For example, if the tenant agrees to vacate by June 15, with that date specified in Item 4, you can have the clerk issue a Writ of Possession and give it to the sheriff on June 5, with appropriate instructions "to conduct final lockout and delivery of possession of premises to me on or after June 15, 20xx." This is important because, otherwise, there will be a delay of at least one week between the time you give the sheriff the Writ of Possession, and the time the tenant will have to leave.

Item 5: If you agree the tenant will pay a certain sum in monthly installments, this is the place to indicate that the tenant will pay a certain dollar amount each month, on a certain day of the month, until the amount listed in Item 2i has been paid. You can also specify that if any payment is more than a certain number of days later, the entire amount listed in Item 2i becomes due.

Items 6a and 6b: Whether you check box 6a or 6b is one of the most important aspects of this stipulation. Check box 6a if you have been able to negotiate an unconditional judgment, hopefully one that says that you will be entitled to possession of the premises, whether by a certain date or immediately. If, on the other hand, you are merely entering into an agreement for judgment entered in the future, if the tenant fails to comply with certain conditions (such as failure to pay rent installments as promised in Item 5), then box 6b should be checked. In that case, you will also have to fill out a date, time, and court department, approved by the judge, for the case to be dismissed, in the event the tenant complies with all the provisions of this type of agreement.

Item 6c: Sometimes an actual judgment, which has certain conditions, can be entered. We've characterized this as a hybrid; you enter the judgment now, but it doesn't take effect until later, and only if the court finds that the conditions have been met. This type of judgment, however, is about as cumbersome to the landlord as is the agreement for entry of judgment in the future if certain conditions have not been met by the tenant. You can probably see why: It involves another trip to the courthouse. With this type of judgment, you'll need to set a future date for a court hearing, to determine whether the conditions have or have not been met. If you want this kind of conditional judgment, check box 6c, fill out another form called a Judgment—Unlawful Detainer Attachment (Form UD-110S), and attach it to the Stipulation for Entry of Judgment form. We include a blank form of this type in Appendix 3 and on the CD-ROM, but because we

do not recommend this path, we have not included instructions on completing it.

Items 6d and 7: If you and the tenant agree on additional terms, which are not easily adapted to this form, you should check both these boxes, and indicate those terms in Item 7 on the reverse side (page 2) of the form.

Item 8: In Items 8b and 8c, enter the date the stipulation is signed, together with the printed names and signatures of all plaintiffs and all defendants.

Once the form is filled out and signed by all parties, submit it to the judge, who should sign, date, and file it. If box 6a is checked, this document will be the equivalent of an unconditional judgment. However, if box 6b or 6c is checked, you might need to schedule further court hearings, or to file declarations under penalty of perjury, in order to proceed further. If box 6b is checked and you end up back in court, you also will need to submit a separate judgment along with a written declaration under penalty of perjury, to the effect that the tenant has not complied with the agreement.

Appearing in Court

Regardless of which type of stipulation you are able to negotiate with the tenant, the law recognizes only two ways that stipulations can become binding. Either the terms must be recited in "open court" in front of a judge, or they must be in writing. In many ways, a written agreement is preferable, because it leaves no doubt as to what was agreed to. But most tenants will not seriously negotiate until they're at the courthouse, face to face with you, about to start trial in a few minutes if there's a failure to agree. If you're facing someone who won't even talk to you, it's often impossible to prepare a completed written stipulation beforehand.

You may, however, be able to begin negotiations and even come to a partial agreement with the tenant before going to court. If so, it's a good idea to at least fill in the boxes at the top of the form, including the names of the parties in Items 1, 2, and 8, and the address of the premises in Item 2. Finish as much of the remainder as you can, to reflect the extent of the settlement that's been agreed to. Bring an original and several copies to court with you on the day of trial. If you finalize your settlement at the courthouse and can complete the form neatly in ink as the terms are negotiated, you may be able to present it to the judge for signature and get it filed (some judges insist on typed forms). If the judge

	Stipulations for Entry of Judgment		
Type	**When judgment is entered in court**	**What happens if tenant doesn't move?**	**Filling out the form**
Unconditional Judgment	As soon as the judge signs the form, in Item 9 ("IT IS SO ORDERED"), the form becomes an unconditional judgment.	Landlord can ask sheriff to evict (see instructions to Item 4)	Check box 6a.
Deferred Judgment	When the landlord establishes in court that the tenant hasn't complied with the agreement, the judge will sign the order.	The landlord will have to appear in court at a later date, or file a declaration under penalty of perjury, stating how the tenant has failed to live up to the agreement, and will have to submit a separate proposed judgment.	Check box 6b.
Conditional Judgment	The judgment will be entered after a court hearing in which the landlord convinces the judge that the tenant did not comply.	The landlord initiates the hearing.	Check box 6c, but this method is not recommended.

won't accept it, you must recite its terms in court, in front of a judge, while the proceedings are tape-recorded or a court reporter takes everything down.

Those of you who are dealing with tenants who won't negotiate prior to trial may find that the stomach-churning prospect of starting trial will convince a tenant to negotiate and settle. It won't hurt to be prepared— fill out parts of the stipulation form as directed above and hope for the best. If you reach an agreement and the court will accept a neatly hand-filled form, great. If the court refuses your form, recite the terms in court, before a court reporter or in the presence of a tape recorder.

⚠️ Unless the tenant(s) and the judge have accepted and signed a written Stipulation for Entry of Judgment, or you at least have the terms of the settlement "on the record," taken down by a court reporter or tape recorded, do not tell the judge you have settled the case. Do not agree to "drop" the matter or take it "off calendar."

The Tenant's Written Response to an Unlawful Detainer Complaint

Sooner or later you will receive a copy of the tenant's written response to your unlawful detainer Complaint. This response can take several forms. Let's discuss these in the order of their likelihood, assuming the tenant has a lawyer or is well-informed about responding to unlawful detainer Complaints.

Motions as Responses to an Unlawful Detainer Complaint

A tenant can object to something in your Summons or Complaint by filing a response which, rather than answering the Complaint allegations, simply asserts that the Complaint isn't technically up to snuff. It is common for tenants to bring these types of issues to the attention of the court (and thus obtain delay) in the form of a request called a motion. A motion is a written request that a judge make a ruling on a particular issue, before any trial occurs. Once a motion (or motions) are filed with the court, the case will automatically be delayed by several weeks because the tenant doesn't have to respond to the substance of your Complaint until the procedural questions raised in the motion (or motions) are cleared up.

For example, a tenant (or her attorney) could file a motion to "quash service of Summons," in which the judge is asked to state that the Summons wasn't properly served, and to require the landlord to serve it again, properly. A court hearing to consider the merits of the motion will normally be held between one and two weeks after filing.

Or a tenant who believes a landlord's request for extra "statutory damages" due to the tenant's malicious conduct isn't backed up by enough allegations of ill-will on the tenant's part can make a motion to have the judge "strike" (consider as deleted) the request for statutory damages from the unlawful detainer Complaint.

To have any motion heard by a judge, a tenant files a set of typewritten papers. The first paper is a notice of motion, which notifies you of the date and time the motion will be heard and summarizes the basis ("grounds") for the motion. The second paper is a short legal essay called a memorandum of points and authorities, stating why the tenant should win the motion. Motions sometimes also include a "declaration" in which the tenant states, under penalty of perjury, any relevant facts—for example, that the tenant wasn't properly served with the Summons.

From the landlord's point of view, the worst thing about a tenant's motion is not that the judge might grant it, but that it can delay the eviction for at least several weeks, during which the tenant will not be paying rent. This is true even if the tenant loses the motion. Motions generally can be heard no sooner than 26 days after the tenant files the motion papers and mails copies of them to the landlord. (C.C.P. §§ 1177 and 1005.) One exception is motions to quash, which under C.C.P. § 1167.4(a) must be heard no later than seven days after filing.

Before the hearing, the landlord should file a written response arguing that the tenant's motion should be denied. The judge will read both sides' papers in advance and will allow limited discussion by each side at the hearing, perhaps asking a few questions. The judge then rules on the motion. If the motion is denied, the judge will require the tenant to file an Answer to the Complaint within five days.

Here is a brief discussion of the kinds of motions commonly filed in unlawful detainer cases.

The Motion to Quash

Officially called a "motion to quash Summons or service of Summons," this motion alleges some defect in the Summons or the way it was served. (If the defect is in the way it was served on one tenant, only that tenant may make this kind of motion.) If the judge agrees, the case is delayed until you have a new Summons served on the tenant. Typical grounds for a tenant's motion to quash, based on defective service include any of the following:

- The Summons was served on one defendant but not the other.
- The wrong person was served.
- No one was served.
- The process server didn't personally serve the Summons as claimed in the Proof of Service (and instead mailed it, laid it on the doorstep, or served it in some other unauthorized manner).
- You, the plaintiff, served the Summons.

Grounds based on a defect in the Summons itself include either of the following:

- The wrong court or judicial district is listed.
- The Complaint requests sums not awardable in an unlawful detainer action, such as pretermination rent in a 30-day or 60-day notice case, utility charges, or late security deposit installments; this makes the case a regular civil action in which a different Summons giving more than five days to respond is necessary. (*Greene v. Municipal Court* (1975) 51 Cal. App. 3d 446; *Castle Park No. 5 v. Katherine* (1979) 91 Cal. App. 3d Supp. 6; *Saberi v. Bakhtiari* (1985) 169 Cal. App. 3d 509.)

If the motion to quash is based on allegations that can logically be responded to by your process server, he will have to appear at the hearing on the motion to testify to when, where, and how the papers were served. For instance, if the tenant's motion to quash states that the Summons and Complaint were served solely by first-class mail (which is not permitted), you would need your process server to testify as to how the papers were, in fact, served. Before the hearing, you should file with the court clerk the Proof of Service (on the back of the original Summons) that the process server filled out.

If you encounter a motion to quash, you will need the assistance of an attorney unless, of course, you are able to interpret and contest the tenant's motion papers and know how to file and serve your response papers and argue the motion in a court hearing.

Motion to Strike

A motion to strike asks the judge to strike (delete) all or part of a Complaint. For example, if your unlawful detainer Complaint asks for additional statutory damages based on the tenant's "malice," but without alleging any specific facts that tend to show the tenant's malicious intent, the tenant may make a motion to strike the statutory damages request from the Complaint. If the judge grants the motion, it doesn't mean that the judge or clerk goes through your Complaint and crosses out the part objected to, but the case is treated as if that had been done.

Motions to strike are heard no sooner than 21 days after the tenant files the motion, which means that, win or lose on the motion, you lose three weeks.

Other defects in the Complaint that might subject it to a tenant's motion to strike include:

- a request for attorneys' fees, if you don't allege a written rental agreement or lease that contains an attorneys' fees clause

- a request for prorated daily damages at the reasonable rental value without an allegation of the daily rental value

- a request for something not awardable in an unlawful detainer action (see motions to quash, above), or

- your failure to "verify" (sign under penalty of perjury) the Complaint (this could result in a successful motion to strike the entire Complaint).

How you should respond to a motion to strike depends on the part of your Complaint objected to, but in most cases you can shorten the delay caused by the motion by simply filing and serving an "amended Complaint" that corrects your errors. After that, you must make a motion to be allowed to file another amended Complaint. (C.C.P. § 472.) Telling you how and when to file an amended Complaint is beyond the scope of this book. However, you can only amend the Complaint once without special permission from the judge. If you do this, you render the motion to strike moot and should be able to proceed with your unlawful detainer without waiting for a hearing.

Assuming there is a hearing on the motion to strike, the judge will decide whether or not to strike the material the tenant objects to. Once this is done, the tenant has to file an Answer within the time allowed by the judge, usually five days.

You may get a default judgment if the Answer isn't filed by that time. (See Chapter 7.)

Demurrers

A "demurrer" is a written response to an unlawful detainer Complaint that claims that the Complaint (or the copy of the three-day, 30-day, or 60-day notice attached to it) is deficient in some way. When a tenant files a demurrer, he is really saying, "Assuming only for the purpose of argument that everything the landlord says in the Complaint is true, it still doesn't provide legal justification to order me evicted." When this is the case, it's usually because the Complaint (including attachments) itself shows that the landlord has not complied with the strict requirements for preparation and service of the three-day, 30-day, or 60-day notice. For example, if the attached three-day notice doesn't demand that the tenant pay a specific dollar amount of rent or leave within three days, it's obvious from the Complaint alone that the tenancy has not been properly terminated, and that the tenant therefore should win.

Typical objections directed to the attached three-day, 30-day, or 60-day notice by a demurrer include any of the following:

- not stating the premises' address, or stating an address different from that alleged elsewhere in the Complaint

- stating an amount of rent more than that alleged elsewhere in the Complaint as past due

- including in the termination notice charges other than rent, such as late fee charges, or

- alleging that the notice was served before the rent became past due.

Objections directed at the unlawful detainer Complaint itself include:

- failure to check boxes containing essential allegations, such as compliance with rent control or just cause eviction ordinances, or

- allegation of contradictory statements.

Demurrers can often be more technical than motions to quash or strike. If a successful demurrer is based on a defect in the notice attached to the Complaint, you could wind up not only having the eviction delayed, but also with a judgment against you for court costs and attorney's fees. It is for this reason (and because we simply can't predict the content of any particular demurrer) that we tell you to consult an attorney if you are faced with one.

The Tenant's Answer

Sooner or later, if you adequately respond to any motions or demurrer filed by the tenant, the tenant will be required to respond to the substance of your Complaint. This response is called the Answer. It will finally let you know what aspects of your case the tenant plans to contest and what other arguments, if any, the tenant plans to advance as to why she thinks you should lose (called "affirmative defenses").

Like your unlawful detainer Complaint, the tenant's Answer is usually submitted on a standard fill-in-the-boxes form. (It can also be typed from scratch on 8½" x 11" paper with numbers in the left margin, but this is increasingly rare.) A typical Answer is shown below.

Here is what you need to pay attention to in the tenant's Answer.

The Tenant's Denial of Statements in the Complaint

The first part of the Answer with which you must concern yourself is Item 2. Here, the defendant denies one or more of the allegations of your Complaint. If box 2a is checked, this means that the tenant denies everything you alleged.

At trial, you will have to testify to everything you alleged in the Complaint: ownership, lease or rental agreement existence, rent amount, rent overdue, service of three-day notice, refusal to pay rent, and so on.

If box 2b is checked, the space immediately below should indicate which, if any, of your allegations is denied, either by specific reference to the numbered allegation paragraphs in your Complaint or in a concise statement. At trial, you will be required to offer testimony or other evidence as to any of your allegations the tenant denies.

For example, in the sample Answer, Terrence and Tillie Tenant deny the allegations of paragraphs "6d, 7a(1), 7b(1), 8a(1), 10, and 11" of Lenny Landlord's Complaint. This means Lenny has to go back and look at his Complaint to see exactly what Terrence and Tillie are denying. He would find that the allegations denied are:

- that Lenny changed the rental agreement by increasing the rent (Complaint Item 6d)
- that a three-day notice to pay rent or quit was served (Item 7a(1))
- that the notice expired on August 8 (Item 7b(1))

- that any such notice was served on the date Lenny indicated (Item 8a(1))
- that the rent due was $900 (Item 10), and
- that the fair rental value is $30 per day (Item 11).

This means that Lenny will, at the very least, have to have the person who served the three-day notice testify in court that she in fact served it. Lenny, himself, will have to testify about when he last received the rent and how much the tenants owed when the notice was served.

The Tenant's Affirmative Defenses

→ If none of the boxes in Item 3 of the Answer are checked, skip this discussion and go directly to "Other Things in the Answer," below.

In addition to responding to the landlord's statements in the Complaint, the tenant is entitled to use the Answer to make some of his own. These statements (in Item 3 of the Answer) are called "affirmative defenses." The tenant checks the boxes next to any applicable defenses and explains the relevant facts in some detail in Item 3j (on the reverse).

If an affirmative defense is proved by the tenant to the satisfaction of a judge, the tenant wins, even if everything you said in the unlawful detainer Complaint is true. The duties imposed on you by law, the breach of which can give rise to these defenses, are discussed in detail in *Volume 1*. Below, we discuss when you may need an attorney to help you handle a defense, and, if you decide to go it alone, how you will need to respond at trial.

If you are still representing yourself, but upon inspecting the Answer (Item 3) discover that an affirmative defense is being raised, now is the time to start looking for help. You should at least consult an attorney to assess the probable strength of the tenant's case—even if you think the affirmative defense is untrue or just a bluff. We are reluctant to advise a consultation with a lawyer solely because an affirmative defense is raised by the tenant. However, please understand that by making such a response, the tenant is warning you that he has something in mind that may torpedo your case. If you proceed on your own and later are unable to handle the defense, all your hard work up to this point may go down the drain.

ATTORNEY OR PARTY WITHOUT ATTORNEY *(Name and Address)*:	TELEPHONE NO.:	FOR COURT USE ONLY
TERRENCE D. TENANT, TILLIE D. TENANT P.O. Box 12345 Los Angeles, CA 90010 ATTORNEY FOR *(Name)*: Defendants in Pro Per	213-555-6789	

NAME OF COURT: SUPERIOR COURT OF CALIFORNIA, COUNTY
STREET ADDRESS: OF LOS ANGELES
MAILING ADDRESS: 100 North Grand Avenue
CITY AND ZIP CODE: Los Angeles, CA 90012
BRANCH NAME: CENTRAL/DOWNTOWN

PLAINTIFF: LENNY D. LANDLORD

DEFENDANT: TERRENCE D. TENANT, TILLIE D. TENANT

ANSWER—Unlawful Detainer	CASE NUMBER: A-12345-B

1. Defendant *(names)*: Terrence D. Tenant, Tillie D. Tenant

   answers the complaint as follows:

2. ***Check ONLY ONE of the next two boxes:***
   a. ☐ Defendant generally denies each statement of the complaint. *(Do not check this box if the complaint demands more than $1,000).*
   b. ☒ Defendant admits that all of the statements of the complaint are true EXCEPT
      (1) Defendant claims the following statements of the complaint are false *(use paragraph numbers from the complaint or explain)*:

      6d, 7a(1), 7b(1), 8a(1), 10, 11

      ☐ Continued on Attachment 2b(1).
      (2) Defendant has no information or belief that the following statements of the complaint are true, so defendant denies them *(use paragraph numbers from the complaint or explain)*:

      ☐ Continued on Attachment 2b(2).

3. AFFIRMATIVE DEFENSES   *(**NOTE:** For each box checked, you must state brief facts to support it in the space provided at the top of page two (item 3j).)*
   a. ☒ *(nonpayment of rent only)* Plaintiff has breached the warranty to provide habitable premises.
   b. ☐ *(nonpayment of rent only)* Defendant made needed repairs and properly deducted the cost from the rent, and plaintiff did not give proper credit.
   c. ☐ *(nonpayment of rent only)* On *(date)*:   , before the notice to pay or quit expired, defendant offered the rent due but plaintiff would not accept it.
   d. ☐ Plaintiff waived, changed, or canceled the notice to quit.
   e. ☐ Plaintiff served defendant with the notice to quit or filed the complaint to retaliate against defendant.
   f. ☐ By serving defendant with the notice to quit or filing the complaint, plaintiff is arbitrarily discriminating against the defendant in violation of the Constitution or laws of the United States or California.
   g. ☐ Plaintiff's demand for possession violates the local rent control or eviction control ordinance of *(city or county, title of ordinance, and date of passage)*:

      (Also, briefly state the facts showing violation of the ordinance in item 3j.)
   h. ☐ Plaintiff accepted rent from defendant to cover a period of time after the date the notice to quit expired.
   i. ☐ Other affirmative defenses are stated in item 3j.

(Continued on reverse)

Form Approved by the Judicial Council of California 982.1(95) [Rev. January 1, 1997]	**ANSWER—Unlawful Detainer**	Civil Code, § 1940 et seq.; Code of Civil Procedure, § 425.12

PLAINTIFF *(Name)*: LENNY D. LANDLORD	CASE NUMBER:
DEFENDANT *(Name)*: TERRENCE D. TENANT, et al	A-12345-B

3. AFFIRMATIVE DEFENSES *(cont'd)*

   j. Facts supporting affirmative defenses checked above *(identify each item separately by its letter from page one)*:

     Plaintiff failed, after repeated demands, to repair a defective heater, a bathroom toilet that will not flush, a leaky roof, and a severe cockroach infestation.

    (1) ☐ All the facts are stated in Attachment 3j.   (2) ☐ Facts are continued in Attachment 3j.

4. OTHER STATEMENTS

   a. ☐ Defendant vacated the premises on *(date)*:

   b. ☒ The fair rental value of the premises alleged in the complaint is excessive *(explain)*: For reasons set forth
        in Item 3j above, the reasonable rental value is only $300.00 per month.

   c. ☐ Other *(specify)*:

5. DEFENDANT REQUESTS

   a. that plaintiff take nothing requested in the complaint.

   b. costs incurred in this proceeding.

   c. ☐ reasonable attorney fees.

   d. ☒ that plaintiff be ordered to (1) make repairs and correct the conditions that constitute a breach of the warranty to provide habitable premises and (2) reduce the monthly rent to a reasonable rental value until the conditions are corrected.

   e. ☐ other *(specify)*:

6. ☐ Number of pages attached *(specify)*:

UNLAWFUL DETAINER ASSISTANT (Business and Professions Code sections 6400-6415)

7. *(Must be completed in all cases)* An **unlawful detainer assistant** ☐ did **not** ☐ did for compensation give advice or assistance with this form. *(If defendant has received **any** help or advice for pay from an unlawful detainer assistant, state)*:

   a. Assistant's name: b. Telephone No.:

   c. Street address, city, and ZIP:

   d. County of registration: e. Registration No.:   f. Expires on *(date)*:

Terrence D. Tenant	▶ *Terrence D. Tenant*
(TYPE OR PRINT NAME)	(SIGNATURE OF DEFENDANT OR ATTORNEY)

Tillie D. Tenant	▶ *Tillie D. Tenant*
(TYPE OR PRINT NAME)	(SIGNATURE OF DEFENDANT OR ATTORNEY)

*(Each defendant for whom this answer is filed must be named in item 1 **and** must sign this answer unless his or her attorney signs.)*

VERIFICATION

(Use a different verification form if the verification is by an attorney or for a corporation or partnership.)

I am the defendant in this proceeding and have read this answer. I declare under penalty of perjury under the laws of the State of California that the foregoing is true and correct.

Date: August 15, 20xx

Tillie D. Tenant	▶ *Tillie D. Tenant*
(TYPE OR PRINT NAME)	(SIGNATURE OF DEFENDANT)

982.1(95) [Rev. January 1, 1997]   **ANSWER—Unlawful Detainer**   Page two

Here is a brief description of each affirmative defense that may be raised in the Answer.

Item 3a: Breach of Warranty of Habitability

In suits based on nonpayment of rent, this defense asserts that the tenant should be excused from paying all the rent because of your failure to keep the place in good repair. (See *The California Landlord's Law Book: Rights & Responsibilities*, Chapter 11.) Technically, the habitability defense should not be raised in suits based on reasons other than nonpayment of rent. If a tenant does assert it improperly, you should object at trial.

Item 3b: Repair-and-Deduct Defense

As discussed in *The California Landlord's Law Book: Rights & Responsibilities*, Chapter 11, state statute forbids an eviction within six months after the exercise of the tenant's "repair-and-deduct" rights unless the notice to quit states a valid reason for the eviction and the landlord proves the reason in court if the tenant contests it. Even if you think the tenant's deduction was improper, be prepared to prove a valid reason (under the repair-and-deduct statute) for the eviction.

Item 3c: Refusal of Rent

If you gave the tenant a Three-Day Notice to Pay Rent or Quit, you must accept rent offered during the three-day notice period. This defense is occasionally used when a tenant's offer of a check is rejected by the landlord during the three-day period because of a requirement that payment be made by cash or money order—usually, after a few bounced checks. As long as you insisted on being paid by cash or money order well before the time that the tenant insists on using the check (and can document this), you should be able to beat this defense. (See *The California Landlord's Law Book: Rights & Responsibilities*, Chapter 3.)

This point is often mistakenly raised by tenants when landlords properly refuse rent after the applicable notice period expired. Once the judge understands that the rent was offered only after the three-day period, and not before, you should prevail.

Item 3d: Waiver or Cancellation of Notice to Quit

If the landlord acted in a way that was somehow inconsistent with the three-, 30-, or 60-day notice, the notice may effectively be cancelled. For example, if your three-day notice complained about the rent not being paid on the first of the month, but you'd accepted it on the fifth every month for the past year, you might have given up or "waived" the right to complain. Another example would be your acquiescing for several months to the tenant's breach of the no-pets lease clause and then serving the tenant with a Three-Day Notice to Perform Covenant or Quit that says the tenant must get rid of the pet or leave within three days. Item 3d might also be checked if the tenant claims you accepted or agreed to accept rent later than the notice deadline. (See Chapter 2 for a discussion of the consequences of accepting rent after serving a three-day notice, and Chapter 3 regarding acceptance of rent following service of a 30-day notice terminating a month-to-month tenancy.)

Item 3e: Retaliation

This alleges that your true reason for serving a notice—usually a 30- or 60-day notice terminating a month-to-month tenancy—was to retaliate for the tenant's exercise of a specified legal right. Retaliation is often claimed by tenants who have complained to local government authorities about housing conditions, or who have attempted to organize your other tenants. (See *The California Landlord's Law Book: Rights & Responsibilities*, Chapter 15.)

Item 3f: Discrimination

This defense refers to discrimination prohibited under state and federal law. (See *The California Landlord's Law Book: Rights & Responsibilities*, Chapter 9, for a discussion of this complex topic.)

Item 3g: Violation of Rent Control Ordinance

Many rent control ordinances not only limit the amount of rent you may charge, but also have "just cause eviction" provisions that limit your freedom to terminate a month-to-month tenancy. Your tenant can defend the lawsuit based on your failure to comply with any aspect of the ordinance, including:

- property registration requirements
- rent limits, or
- special requirements for three-day, 30-day, or 60-day eviction notices.

Cities that require registration of rents (Berkeley, Santa Monica, East Palo Alto, Los Angeles, Palm Springs, Thousand Oaks, and West Hollywood) must limit the sanctions against landlords who are in "substantial compliance" with a rent control law and made only a good-faith mistake in calculating rent or registering property with the local rent control agency. (Civ. Code § 1947.7.) The statute appears to apply only to sanctions imposed by local rent control agencies, however. You should still expect to have your Complaint dismissed if it is based on a three-day notice that demanded an amount of rent that was illegal under a rent control ordinance.

Item 3h: Acceptance of Rent

If you accepted rent for a period beyond the termination date in a termination notice, you may have revoked that notice. For example, if rent is due in advance on the first of each month, and you gave your tenant a 30-day notice on June 15, the tenancy terminates on July 15. By accepting a full month's rent on July 1, however, you accepted rent for the period through July 31, well beyond the termination date of the 15th, and you implicitly revoked the 30-day notice.

In many instances, this defense is identical to the "waiver and cancellation" defense (Item 3d, above), and the tenant can check either or both defenses.

Item 3i: Other Affirmative Defenses

Although Items 3a through 3h list the most common defenses, an imaginative tenant's attorney may use Item 3i to describe additional defenses. (This ability of tenants' attorneys to introduce strange theories into the most mundane case is a large part of the reason we advise you to consider hiring an attorney if one appears for the tenant.) As with the listed defenses, the facts specific to any defense checked here must be listed in Item 3j, below.

Item 3j: Specific Facts Relating to the Defenses

Under Item 3j on the reverse of the Answer, the tenant is supposed to explain the affirmative defense boxes checked. No special language or format is necessary, and almost any brief, factual statement will do. These statements are supposed to give you an idea of what the defendant is going to try to prove at trial. At trial, the defendant may testify only to subjects he brought up in the Answer.

Other Things in the Answer

Item 4 on the back of the Answer form has spaces for miscellaneous "other statements." If the tenant has given up possession of the property before filing

his Answer (Item 4a), for instance, the case will be treated as a regular civil lawsuit. You and the tenant can then ask for things not allowed in an unlawful detainer action, but the case won't get to trial as fast as an unlawful detainer suit normally would. (Civ. Code § 1952.3.) An unlawful detainer suit is a special "summary" (expedited) procedure with shorter response times, and more restrictions on the issues that may be raised, than regular suits.

In Item 4b, the tenant can state that the prorated daily "fair rental value" you alleged is too high (usually because of a habitability defense).

Defendant's Requests

In Item 5, the tenant says what he or she wants. Item 5a allows the tenant to request attorney's fees. This is proper only if the written rental agreement or lease has an attorney's fees clause. Because of the restrictions on unlawful detainer suits, there is really nothing else the tenant can properly ask for here.

Finally, Item 5b allows the tenant to ask the court to order the landlord to make repairs and order the rent reduced, if the tenant claims breach of the warranty of habitability as a defense in Item 3a.

Responding to the Answer

If the tenant has simply denied your allegations, not raised any defenses of his own, and is not represented by an attorney, you are still on pretty firm ground as far as going ahead on your own is concerned. The next step is getting a trial date.

The Request to Set Case for Trial—Unlawful Detainer

Like almost everything else in the legal system, the trial on your now-contested unlawful detainer Complaint will not happen automatically. You have to ask for it in a form known as a Request to Set Case for Trial.

If the tenant has moved out. If the tenant who has filed an Answer moves out before you file your Request to Set Case for Trial, you can still ask the court to set the case for trial. You would normally do this if you want to get a judgment against the tenant for rent and court costs. However, the case becomes a "regular civil action" without "preference" (Civ. Code § 1952.3), and you should not state your case has preference for trial setting. The court will then set it for trial much more slowly.

To complete this form, type in the information in the boxes at the top of the form, which ask for your name and address, the court and its location, the names of the parties, and the case number, just as you did when preparing the Complaint.

In the large box below the case-identification queries, put an X next to the word "REQUEST," unless the tenant has already filed a Request to Set Case for Trial. (If the tenant has requested a jury trial, which happens rarely, you'll need to contact an attorney.) If the tenant has already filed this form, put an X in the box next to the words "COUNTER-REQUEST."

Item 1: Put an X in this box. If there is more than one defendant, and at least one of them has filed an Answer, but at least one other defendant has not, you should obtain a default against all defendants who have not filed an Answer. You'll be requesting only entry of a default, not a clerk's judgment for possession. (Later, after winning at trial against the defendants who have filed an Answer, you can ask the judge to order that the judgment also be against those "defaulted" defendants.) See Chapter 7 on filling out the Request for Entry of Default, but don't check the boxes relevant to obtaining a Clerk's Judgment for Possession.

Item 2: List the rental's address, including the county. If the tenant is still in possession of the property (that is, the tenant has not turned over the key or otherwise unequivocally demonstrated that he's turned over possession of the property to you), check box (a). This should result in your having a trial within 20 days of filing your Request to Set Case for Trial. On the other hand, if the tenant has turned over possession of the property to you, and you still seek a money judgment, check box (b). In this situation, as we have noted above, the court will likely set the case for trial much more slowly than if the tenant were still in possession of the property.

Item 3: Check the box next to the words "a nonjury trial." Do not request a jury trial. Jury trials are procedurally much more complex than trials before judges, and it is easy to get in way over your head. Also, the party requesting a jury trial has to deposit jury fees (about $200/day) with the court in advance. All you want is a

simple trial, lasting no more than a few hours at most, in front of a judge.

Item 4: The purpose of this item is to give the court a fair estimate of how long the trial will take. Unless the tenant has demanded a jury trial (in which case you should probably see an attorney), check box (b) and indicate either 1 or 2 hours as an estimate for the trial length. Your estimated time for trial should be anywhere from one hour, for a simple case where the tenant has failed to assert any affirmative defenses, to two hours in cases involving fairly complicated issues like alleged rent control violations, discriminatory or retaliatory evictions, or breach of the warranty to provide habitable premises.

Item 5: Indicate any dates that you will not be available for trial. Remember that the court is required by law to set a trial date no later than 20 days from the date you file your Request to Set Case for Trial. If you list dates when you are unavailable (note that you must give a reason), the court may have to schedule trial for more than 20 days from the date you file the Request. If you are content with this latter prospect, add the sentence, "Plaintiff waives the requirement under CCP 1170.5(a) for trial within 20 days of filing of this document."

Item 6: In this item, you simply indicate, as you did in the Complaint and Summons, that an unlawful detainer assistant "did not" assist you. Then, print your name and the date, and sign the document.

On the second page, in the box at the top, list your name after "PLAINTIFF" and the name of the first-named defendant, followed by "ET AL" if there is more than one defendant. Do this just as you did the top of the second and third pages of the Complaint. Also list the case number.

This second page is a Proof of Service by Mail, which shows that a person other than you mailed copies of the form to the tenant who filed the Answer. List the residence or business address of the person who will mail the form for you, in Item 2 of this side of the form. Also, put an X in box 3a. In box 3c (1) and (2), list the date the copy of your Request to Set Case for Trial will be mailed, and the name of the city in which it will be mailed. Just below the words "I declare under penalty of perjury ... ," list the date that person will be signing the proof of service (after he or she mails it). Type that person's name in the space at the left below the place for that date.

UD-150

ATTORNEY OR PARTY WITHOUT ATTORNEY *(Name, State Bar number, and address):*	FOR COURT USE ONLY
LENNY D. LANDLORD 12345 Angeleno Street Los Angeles, CA 90010 TELEPHONE NO.: 213-555-6789 FAX No. *(Optional):* 213-555-6789 E-MAIL ADDRESS *(Optional):* ATTORNEY FOR *(Name):* Plaintiff in Pro Per	

SUPERIOR COURT OF CALIFORNIA, COUNTY OF LOS ANGELES

STREET ADDRESS: 110 N. Grand Street
MAILING ADDRESS: Same
CITY AND ZIP CODE: Los Angeles, Ca 90012
BRANCH NAME: CENTRAL DISTRICT/DOWNTOWN BRANCH

PLAINTIFF: LENNY D. LANDLORD

DEFENDANT: TERRENCE D. TENANT, TILLIE D. TENANT

[X] **REQUEST** [ ] **COUNTER-REQUEST** **TO SET CASE FOR TRIAL—UNLAWFUL DETAINER** [ ] **Plaintiff** [ ] **Defendant**	CASE NUMBER: A-12345-B

1. [X] **Plaintiff's request.** I represent to the court that all parties have been served with process and have appeared or have had a default or dismissal entered against them. I request that this case be set for trial.

2. **Trial preference.** The premises concerning this case are located at *(street address, apartment number, city, zip code, and county):*
   6789 Angeleno Street, Apt. 10, Los Angeles, 90012, Los Angeles County

   a. [X] To the best of my knowledge, the right to possession of the premises is still in issue. This case is entitled to legal preference under Code of Civil Procedure section 1179a.

   b. [ ] To the best of my knowledge, the right to possession of the premises is no longer in issue. No defendant or other person is in possession of the premises.

3. **Jury or nonjury trial.** I request [ ] a jury trial [X] a nonjury trial.

4. **Estimated length of trial.** I estimate that the trial will take *(check one):*

   a. [ ] days *(specify number):*   b. [X] hours *(specify if estimated trial is less than one day):* 1

5. **Trial date.** I am not available on the following dates *(specify dates and reasons for unavailability):*

UNLAWFUL DETAINER ASSISTANT (Bus. & Prof. Code, §§ 6400–6415)

6. *(Complete in all cases.)* An unlawful detainer assistant [X] did **not** [ ] did   for compensation give advice or assistance with this form. *(If declarant has received **any** help or advice for pay from an unlawful detainer assistant, complete a–f.)*

   a. Assistant's name: c. Telephone no.:
   b. Street address, city, and zip code: d. County of registration:
                                                e. Registration no.:
                                                f. Expires on *(date):*

I declare under penalty of perjury under the laws of the State of California that the foregoing is true and correct.

Date: September 18, 20xx

Lenny D. Landlord	*Lenny D. Landlord*
(TYPE OR PRINT NAME)	(SIGNATURE OF PARTY OR ATTORNEY FOR PARTY)

NOTICE

- An unlawful detainer case must be set for trial on a date not later than **20 days after the first request** to set the case for trial is made (Code Civ. Proc., § 1170.5(a)).
- If a jury is requested, $150 must be deposited with the court 5 days before trial (Code Civ. Proc., § 631).
- Court reporter and interpreter services vary. Check with the court for availability of services and fees charged.
- If you cannot pay the court fees and costs, you may apply for a fee waiver. Ask the court clerk for a fee waiver form.

Page 1 of 2

PLAINTIFF: LENNY D. LANDLORD	CASE NUMBER:
DEFENDANT: TERRENCE D. TENANT, ET AL	A-12345-B

PROOF OF SERVICE BY MAIL

Instructions: *After having the parties served by mail with the* Request/Counter-Request to Set Case for Trial—Unlawful Detainer, *(form UD-150), have the person who mailed the form UD-150 complete this* Proof of Service by Mail. *An **unsigned** copy of the* Proof of Service by Mail *should be completed and served with form UD-150. Give the* Request/Counter-Request to Set Case for Trial —Unlawful Detainer *(form UD-150) and the completed* Proof of Service by Mail *to the clerk for filing. If you are representing yourself, someone else must mail these papers and sign the* Proof of Service by Mail.

1. I am over the age of 18 and **not a party to this case.** I am a resident of or employed in the county where the mailing took place.
2. My residence or business address is *(specify):*
   100 A Street, Los Angeles, CA 90010

3. I served the *Request/Counter-Request to Set Case for Trial—Unlawful Detainer* (form UD-150) by enclosing a copy in an envelope addressed to each person whose name and address are shown below AND

   a. [X] **depositing** the sealed envelope in the United States mail on the date and at the place shown in item 3c with the postage fully prepaid.

   b. [ ] **placing** the envelope for collection and mailing on the date and at the place shown in item 3c following ordinary business practices. I am readily familiar with this business's practice for collecting and processing correspondence for mailing. On the same day that correspondence is placed for collection and mailing, it is deposited in the ordinary course of business with the United States Postal Service in a sealed envelope with postage fully prepaid.

   c. (1) Date mailed: September 18, 20xx

   (2) Place mailed *(city and state):* Los Angeles, CA

I declare under penalty of perjury under the laws of the State of California that the foregoing is true and correct:

Date: September 18, 20xx

Sam D. Server	Sam D. Server
(TYPE OR PRINT NAME)	(SIGNATURE OF PERSON WHO MAILED *FORM UD-150*)

NAME AND ADDRESS OF EACH PERSON TO WHOM NOTICE WAS MAILED

	Name	Address *(number, street, city, and zip code)*
4.	Terrence D. Tenant	6789 Angeleno Street, Apt. 10 Los Angeles, CA 90012
5.	Tillie D. Tenant	6789 Angeleno Street, Apt. 10 Los Angeles, CA 90012
6.		
7.		
8.		
9.		

[ ] List of names and addresses continued on a separate attachment or form MC-025, titled Attachment to Proof of Service by Mail.

UD-150 [New January 1, 2005]	**REQUEST/COUNTER-REQUEST TO SET CASE FOR TRIAL—UNLAWFUL DETAINER**	Page 2 of 2

Finally, under the heading of "NAME AND ADDRESS OF EACH PERSON TO WHOM NOTICE WAS MAILED," type the names and addresses of each defendant who has filed an Answer to the Complaint. Use a separate set of boxes for each defendant, even if more than one defendant has filed the same Answer. Also, use the mailing address the tenant (or his attorney) indicated in the upper left box in the Answer. Do this even if the address is different from the tenant's residence address. (You do not have to list any defendants who have not answered, and against whom you will be taking a default.)

Make two photocopies and have a friend mail one to the tenant (or his attorney) at the mailing addresses in the boxes at the end of the form. Have the friend sign the Proof of Service by Mail, indicating that he mailed the copy, and take the original and one copy to the courthouse. The court clerk will file the original and stamp the copy for your records.

The court will hold on to your Request to Set Case for Trial for up to five days to give the tenant a chance to file a Counter-Request to Set. This gives the tenant the opportunity to also list unavailable dates and dispute any of the information you listed. Then the clerk will set the case for trial on a date no more than 20 days after the date you filed your Memorandum, and will notify you by mail of the date, time, and place of the trial.

Summary Judgment

As soon as you've served and filed the Memorandum to Set Case for Trial, you may want to make a pretrial motion of your own to request a Summary Judgment— a judgment without an actual trial. To be eligible for a Summary Judgment, you must convince a judge that there is no real dispute about the facts in the case—that is, you and the tenant are only really arguing over the legal issues. If the judge agrees, she can issue a judgment on the spot. (C.C.P. § 1170.7.) Not only do you save the effort of preparing for trial, but it also allows you to significantly shorten the time you have to wait to get a judgment and get your tenant out.

This section shows you how to make a Summary Judgment motion in a rent nonpayment case (Chapter 2), using the form provided in the forms section in the back of the book. If your eviction is on any ground other than for nonpayment of rent, you will need the assistance of an attorney to pursue this remedy. The potential variation in the facts makes it impossible to accurately show you how to draft your papers without producing what would amount to another book.

You must pay a $100 filing fee to the court clerk when you file this kind of motion. (This is in addition to the $85 to $95 fee you paid to file the case.) This may well be worth the price, because if you file this motion quickly after the tenant files her Answer, you could get the tenant evicted one to two weeks sooner than if you waited for the court to set the case for trial. Also, this motion will save you the time and effort involved in a trial. Finally, the $100 filing fee for this motion will be added to the money judgment you will get against the tenant.

Here is an overview of how a Summary Judgment proceeding works.

The first step is to obtain a motion hearing date at least five days away. Then type the motion papers, which include a Notice of Motion for Summary Judgment, your declaration under penalty of perjury stating the basic facts of the case from your perspective, and a brief legal essay stating why the motion should be granted. Copies of these papers must be served on the tenant at least five days before the hearing, the originals filed with the court, and a motion fee paid to the clerk. At the hearing, you or your lawyer appear. You don't bring witnesses to testify at this stage because you are only dealing with questions of law, not questions of fact. The important things have already been done, including the written declarations and argument you filed earlier. In most cases, if the tenant doesn't respond to your motion with his own written declaration contradicting yours, the judge is required to grant the motion, so that you win your case without trial—and sooner. If you lose the motion, you have not really lost anything but some time and $100. You will still be able to present your full case at the trial.

EXAMPLE: Your declaration says that you rented your property to Terrence and Tillie Tenant, that the rent was $900 per month due on the first, and that they didn't pay on the first of August. It also states that on August 5, you served them with a three-day notice and they still didn't pay or leave. Tillie and Terrence can defeat your motion by filing their own declaration saying that the rent wasn't $900, that they paid the rent, that they never received the notice, or that you failed to repair serious defects in the property after they notified you of them.

If you decide you want to try to speed up your case by requesting a Summary Judgment, carefully read the following instructions.

➡️ If you believe that you and your tenant disagree significantly over the facts, or you are not sure that a Summary Judgment will work and therefore want to wait for the trial rather than engage in yet another procedure, skip to "Other Pretrial Complications," below.

💼 Our instructions assume that the tenant is not represented by an attorney. If she is, you will probably want to consult one and may want to arrange to be represented. Our instructions do not cover how you should proceed if an attorney has appeared for the tenant.

Step 1: Select a Date for the Hearing on Your Motion

First, find out when the court hears motions. Some of the larger courts hear them on several different days of the week, while smaller courts have their "law and motion" day once a week. Call or visit the court clerk and tell her you're a plaintiff in an unlawful detainer case and wish to have a Summary Judgment motion heard. (You may have to remind the clerk that, unlike motions in regular cases, Summary Judgment motions in unlawful detainer cases are heard on just five days' notice, according to C.C.P. § 1170.7.) Ask what dates and times are available.

In some counties you can choose a date over the phone. In others, the clerk won't schedule your motion hearing on the court calendar until you file your Notice of Motion. (See Step 2, below.)

Pick the earliest date that is at least five days after the day you'll be able to have the motion papers personally served on the tenant. If the court has a policy that only a certain number of cases can be heard at each session, remind the clerk that the case is an unlawful detainer case entitled to priority.

Step 2: Prepare the Papers

If you think you've already been run through the mill on the paperwork required to do a "simple" eviction,

it's time to grit your teeth and prepare for some more. Even the most simple request to a court, including your Summary Judgment motion papers, must be submitted on typed, double-spaced, 8½" x 11" legal pleading paper with the numbers down the left-hand side. You can copy the blank sheet of pleading paper in Appendix 3. The papers consist of three parts, which can be combined into one document. These are:

1. Notice of Motion, which tells the tenant where, when, and on what legal grounds you're making the motion
2. Declaration, in which you and/or someone else states the pertinent facts under penalty of perjury, and
3. Memorandum of Points and Authorities (usually referred to simply as "points and authorities"), a short legalistic statement that explains why the facts stated in the declaration legally entitle you to judgment.

Below are provided instructions and sample completed forms demonstrating how to draft each of these documents.

 A blank, tear-out version of a Notice of Motion for Summary Judgment; Plaintiff's Declaration; and Points and Authorities are in Appendix 3. The CD-ROM also includes these items. Instructions for using the CD are in Appendix 2.

Step 3: Photocopy the Papers

Once you've prepared and signed your Summary Judgment motion papers, make a set of photocopies for each tenant who has answered the Complaint, plus one for your files. For instance, if three tenants have answered the Complaint, you will need at least four photocopies.

Step 4: Have the Papers Served

Because of the short (five-day) notice given the tenant, you must have the papers personally served on each tenant or on another person over 18 at the tenant's home. Unlike service of the Summons, service on an adult at the tenant's residence—or on an employee in the office of the tenant's attorney, if the tenant is represented—is sufficient, and the time for the tenant to respond is not extended by the fact that he did not receive them personally. (C.C.P. § 1011.)

1	Name: list your mailing address and phone number
	Address:
2	
	Phone:
3	
	Plaintiff in Pro Per
4	

SUPERIOR COURT OF CALIFORNIA, COUNTY OF _____ list county _____

list division here

_____ DIVISION

your name

_____) Case No. case number _____

Plaintiff,)

)

v.) NOTICE OF MOTION FOR SUMMARY JUDGMENT;

) PLAINTIFF'S DECLARATION; POINTS AND AUTHORITIES

defendants' names) (C.C.P. 437C, 1170.7)

_____)

Defendant(s).) Hearing Date: _____ list hearing date, time,

) Time: _____ and courtroom number

_____) Courtroom: _____

TO DEFENDANTS defendants' names _____

AND THEIR ATTORNEY OF RECORD:

PLEASE TAKE NOTICE that on _____, _____, at _____ ___.M in the above-

entitled Court, at list court address and city _____,

City of _____, California, the above-named plaintiff

will move the Court for an Order granting summary judgment for possession of the subject premises herein, rent,

damages, and costs in the above-entitled action.

This motion is made on the ground that defendants' defense has no merit and there exists no triable issue of

fact as to plaintiff's cause of action, plaintiff having established that defendants are guilty of unlawfully detaining

the subject premises following nonpayment of the rent due, service of a three-day notice to pay rent or quit, and

failure to pay the rent or vacate the premises within the time given in the said notice.

This motion is based on this notice, the declaration of plaintiff attached hereto, the points and authorities

1   attached hereto, the pleadings, records, and files herein, and on such argument as may be presented at the

2   hearing on the motion.

3   DATED:_____[date]_____, _____

4   _____[your signature]_____
                                              Plaintiff in Pro Per

5

6   DECLARATION OF PLAINTIFF

7   I, the undersigned, declare:

8   1. I am the plaintiff in the within action and the owner of the subject premises located at _____

9   _____[list premises' address, city, and county]_____, City of

10   _____, County of _____, California.

11   2. On _____[date premises rented]_____, _____, defendant(s) rented the premises from me pursuant to

12   a written/oral agreement. The monthly rent was $_____[monthly rent]_____payable in advance on the _____
     • • [cross one out]

13   day of each month, the reasonable rental value of the premises per day being $_____.

14   3. Pursuant to the agreement, defendant(s) went into possession of the premises.

15   4. On _____[date defendants served with 3-day notice]_____, _____, defendant(s) were in default in the payment of rent in

16   the amount of $___[rent due when 3-day notice served]___ and I served defendant(s) _____[list of names of defendants]_____

17   _____ with a written notice demanding

18   that defendant(s) pay that amount or surrender possession of the premises within three days of service of the said

19   notice. A true copy of that notice is attached to the Complaint herein as Exhibit "B" thereto.

20   5. Prior to my service of the said three-day notice, defendant(s) had not notified me of any substantial defect

21   in the premises relating to the tenantability or habitability thereof.

22   6. Defendant(s) failed to pay the said rent or surrender possession of the said premises within three days of

23   service of the said notice, whereupon I commenced the instant action, complying with all applicable rent

24   control and/or eviction protection ordinances. Defendant(s) still remain in possession of the premises.

25   7. This rent was due for the rental period of _____[list period covered by rent demanded in 3-day notice]_____, _____, through

26   _____, _____. After this latter date and to the present, I sustained

27   [if applicable, list total prorated rent after period; if none, list zero (0)] asonable rental value indicated above in paragraph 2, for total damages in the amount of

28   $_____, and total rent and damages in the amount of $___[total unpaid rent in 3-day notice plus prorated rent]___

1   8. I have incurred service and filing fees in the total amount of $ _____ in the within action. **list court costs amount**

2   9. If sworn as a witness, I could testify competently to the facts stated herein.

3   I declare under penalty of perjury under the laws of the State of California that the foregoing is true and

4   correct.

5

6   DATED:_____, _____   **date and sign**

7   _____
     Plaintiff in Pro Per

8

9

10

11

12

13

14

15

16

17

18

19

20

21

22

23

24

25

26

27

28

POINTS AND AUTHORITIES

you don't have to fill in anything on this page

I. PLAINTIFF'S MOTION FOR SUMMARY JUDGMENT IS PROPERLY BEFORE THE COURT.

In an unlawful detainer action a motion for summary judgment may be made on five days' notice. C.C.P. Sec. 1170.7. The time limits imposed by subdivision (a) of section 437c, as well as the requirement in subdivision (b) of a separate statement of material facts not in dispute, are not applicable to summary judgment motions in unlawful detainer actions. C.C.P. Sec. 437c(r).

The "separate statement" requirement for summary judgment motions does not apply to unlawful detainer actions. C.C.P. Section 437c, subdivision (q), states: "Subdivisions (a) and (b) shall not apply to actions brought pursuant to Chapter 4 (commencing with section 1159) of Title 3 of Part 3." The latter refers to the unlawful detainer statutes, and the requirement for a separate statement of facts is in section 437c(b). Thus, C.C.P. Section 437c(q) expressly states, though by an obscure reference to its own subdivision (b) and to C.C.P. Sections 1159 et seq., that unlawful detainer summary judgment motions do not require a separate statement of facts contended to be undisputed. While Rule 342, California Rules of Court, is silent on this issue, to construe such silence as requiring a separate statement of undisputed facts in unlawful detainer summary judgment motions, notwithstanding C.C.P. Section 437c(q), would allow a rule of court to supersede a statute, which is not permitted.

In all other respects, the motion is required to be granted on the same terms and conditions as a summary judgment motion under C.C.P. Sec. 437c, and such a motion must be decided solely on the affidavits or declarations filed. Ibid, subd. (c).

II. PLAINTIFF HAS ESTABLISHED THE PRIMA FACIE ELEMENTS OF AN UNLAWFUL DETAINER ACTION FOR NONPAYMENT OF RENT.

Under section 1162(2) of the Code of Civil Procedure, a tenant or subtenant is guilty of unlawful detainer

> When he continues in possession … after default in the payment of rent … and three days' notice, in writing requiring its payment, stating the amount which is due, or possession of the property, shall have been served on him ….

Elements other than default in rent, service of the notice, the expiration of three days without payment, and the continuance in possession include the existence of a landlord-tenant relationship (Fredricksen v. McCosker (1956) 143 Cal. App. 2d 114) and proper contents of the notice (Wilson v. Sadleir (1915) 26 Cal. App. 357, 359).

1 Plaintiff's declaration establishes all these elements, so that plaintiff is entitled to summary judgment.

2 III. DEFENDANT(S) CANNOT PREVAIL UNDER A DEFENSE OF BREACH OF
   THE IMPLIED WARRANTY OF HABITABILITY.
3

4 Under the rule of Green v. Superior Court (1974) 10 Cal. 3d 616, the California Supreme Court held that in

5 an unlawful detainer action founded on nonpayment of rent, the tenant could assert as a defense that the

6 landlord breached an implied warranty to keep the premises habitable. The Court cited with approval the case of

7 Hinson v. Delis (1972) 26 Cal. App. 3d 62 in this regard. In Hinson, the tenant sued the landlord in a regular

8 civil action for breach of this implied warranty. After the trial court ruled in favor of the landlord, the Court of

9 Appeal reversed, holding that there existed such a warranty in the law, as to which, "The tenant must also give

10 notice of alleged defects to the landlord and allow a reasonable time for repairs to be made." Hinson at p. 70.

11 When the Green court held that the warranty of habitability established by the Hinson court could be asserted

12 by the tenant as a defense to an unlawful detainer action, as well as a basis for suit by the tenant, it did not

13 modify or remove this requirement of notice by the tenant to the landlord of the alleged defects by which the

14 tenant seeks to withhold rent. Therefore, the notice requirement also applies where the defense is asserted by the

15 tenant in an unlawful detainer action.

16 Plaintiff's declaration establishes that defendant(s) failed to give plaintiff notice of the alleged defects in the

17 premises. Unless a triable issue of fact exists in this regard, defendant(s) cannot assert this defense, as a matter of

18 law.

19 DATED:_____ _____ | **date and sign** |

20

21   _____
                                                    Plaintiff in Pro Per

22

23

24

25

26

27

28

1

2   PROOF OF PERSONAL SERVICE
                                         (C.C.P.§ 1011 (b))

3   I the undersigned, declare:

4   I am over the age of 18 years and not a party to the within action.

5   On ___September 5_____, ___20xx___, I served the within Notice of Motion for Summary

6   Judgment, Declaration of Plaintiff, and Points and Authorities on defendant(s) by delivering true copies thereof to

7   each such defendant, or other person not less than 18 years of age, at defendants' residence address of

8   ___6789 Angel Street, Apt. 10_____, City of

9   ___Los Angeles_____, California, between 8:00 A.M. and 6:00 P.M.

10   I declare under penalty of perjury under the laws of the State of California that the foregoing is true and

11   correct.

12

13   DATED:___September 5_____, __20xx__   _Fred Friend_____
                                                   Signature

14

15

16

17

18

19

20

21

22

23

24

25

26

27

28

As with a Summons, you can't serve the papers yourself, but must have a friend or other disinterested person over 18 do it for you. Since service can be made on any adult who answers the door at the tenant's residence, all the tenants named as defendants can be served at the same time this way, provided one copy for each defendant is given to the person answering. The person serving the papers then fills out the Proof of Service on the originals, before they are filed with the court.

The C.C.P. § 1011 Proof of Service deliberately does not include a place for you to insert the time of service, because noting time of service when serving a Motion for Summary Judgment is not necessary. Many people, however, inappropriately use the Service of Summons Proof of Service form when serving this motion—and the Service of Summons form *does* require you to note the time of service. Perhaps this explains why some clerks have come to believe that a Proof of Service must always include the time of service. If you want to be extra careful, add the time of service (such as "at 4:56 PM") right after the date on our form.

Step 5: File the Papers

Finally, you must file the original motion papers, including Proof of Service, with the court clerk as soon as possible after the copies are served on the tenant. The clerk should file the originals and file-stamp and return any copies to you. She will also place the motion hearing "on calendar" (if that wasn't done when you called earlier), and ask you to pay a motion fee of $200.

Step 6: Prepare the Proposed Order and Judgment

While you're waiting the five or more days until the hearing, you should prepare a proposed order granting your motion and a proposed judgment for the judge to sign. This allows you to hand the judge the necessary papers to sign right at the hearing if he grants your motion. If you don't have the judgment ready for the judge to sign, a delay of several days might result from your having to run home, type the papers, bring them back to court, and get them to the judge for signature. Once signed, you can take them to the clerk and get the actual eviction rolling, using the procedures in "The Writ of Execution and Having the Sheriff or Marshall Evict," below.

Instructions and samples for your proposed order granting the motion and the resulting judgment are shown below. We show you instructions for both a typewritten judgment, and a judgment on the optional statewide Judgment—Unlawful Detainer form. (We suggest using the typewritten form because the statewide form doesn't seem to be intended for use where the landlord prevails by Summary Judgment motion.)

Step 7: Prepare the Writ of Execution

Chapter 7 shows how to prepare a Writ of Execution for possession of the property after getting a default Judgment for Possession. Chapter 9 shows how to fill out another Writ of Execution for the money part of the judgment after the tenant leaves. If you win a Summary Judgment motion, however, you get both parts of the judgment—money and possession of property—at the same time. You need only one Writ of Execution. Refer to both sets of instructions in Chapters 7 and 9 to fill in the appropriate information on the Writ of Execution. A sample is shown below.

Step 8: Argue Your Motion in Court

The evening before the hearing, you should sit down, try to relax, and review the points stated in your motion papers. On the day of the hearing, try to get to the courtroom a little early. At the entrance, there may be a bulletin board with a list of the cases to be heard that morning. If your case isn't listed, check with the clerk.

Try to find out whether or not the tenant has filed a written response to your motion. The fact that you didn't receive a copy of any response in the mail doesn't prove anything, because the law seems to allow the tenant to file a response at any time before the hearing. If the tenant appears at the hearing, it won't hurt to walk up and ask if he filed a response to your papers. If the answer is "Yes," ask for a copy. Also, if you can fight your way through all the attorneys clustered around the courtroom clerk, ask her to check the file to see if there's a response. If there is, ask to see it. Assuming the judge doesn't have the file in her chambers, the clerk will hand it to you. If the tenant has filed a response to your motion, the papers should be at the top of the papers in the file, just above your motion papers. Look for any declaration or affidavit that contradicts your declaration. If there isn't one, you will

Name:

list your mailing address and phone number

Address:

Phone:

Plaintiff in Pro Per

SUPERIOR COURT OF CALIFORNIA, COUNTY OF _____

list county

_____ DIVISION

list division here

your name	**case number**
_____)	Case No. _____
Plaintiff,)	
v.)	ORDER GRANTING MOTION
defendants' names)	FOR SUMMARY JUDGMENT
_____)	
Defendant(s).)	
_____)	**list date and courtroom in which your hearing will be held**

Plaintiff's motion for summary judgment came on for hearing in Department _____ of

the above-entitled Court on _____, _____, said plaintiff appearing in pro per

if defendants didn't appear, insert "not"

insert defendants' attorney's name; if no attorney, type "in pro per" and cross out "by"

and defendant(s) _____ appearing by _____

The matter having been argued and submitted,

IT IS HEREBY ORDERED that plaintiff's motion for summary judgment for restitution of the premises the

fill in amount

subject of this action, rent and damages in the sum of $ _____, and costs of suit be, and the

same is, granted.

leave date and signature lines blank for judge to fill in

DATED:_____, _____

_____
Judge of the Superior Court

1

Name: LENNY D. LANDLORD
Address: 12345 Angeleno Street

2

Los Angeles, CA 90010

Phone: 213-555-6789

3

4

Plaintiff in Pro Per

5

6

7

8

SUPERIOR COURT OF CALIFORNIA, COUNTY OF _____ LOS ANGELES _____

9

_____ LOS ANGELES _____ DIVISION

10

11

LENNY D. LANDLORD _____   )   Case No. __A-12345-B_____

Plaintiff,   )

12

)   ORDER GRANTING MOTION

v.   )   FOR SUMMARY JUDGMENT

13

)

TERRENCE D. TENANT, TILLIE D. TENANT)

14

Defendant(s).   )

15

)

16

Plaintiff's motion for summary judgment came on for hearing in Department _____ 12 _____ of

17

the above-entitled Court on _____ September 9 _____, _____ 20xx _____, said plaintiff appearing in pro per

18

and defendant(s) __not__ appearing by _____ in pro per _____.

19

The matter having been argued and submitted,

20

IT IS HEREBY ORDERED that plaintiff's motion for summary judgment for restitution of the premises the

21

subject of this action, rent and damages in the sum of $ _____ 1,120.00 _____, and costs of suit be, and the

22

same is, granted.

23

DATED:_____, _____

24

25

_____

Judge of the Superior Court

26

27

28

1 Name: [list your mailing address and phone number]
   Address:

2

   Phone:

3

   Plaintiff in Pro Per

4

5

6

7

8   SUPERIOR COURT OF CALIFORNIA, COUNTY OF _____ [list county] _____

9   _____ [list division here] _____ DIVISION

10

11   _____ [your name] _____   ) Case No. _____ [case number] _____
)
                Plaintiff,   )
12   ) JUDGMENT FOLLOWING GRANTING
        v.   ) OF MOTION FOR SUMMARY JUDGMENT
13   _____ [defendants' names] _____)
)
14   Defendant(s).   )
)
15   _____)

16   The motion of plaintiff for summary judgment having been granted,

17   IT IS HEREBY ORDERED AND ADJUDGED that plaintiff have and recover from defendant(s) _____

18   _____ [list names of defendants] _____

19   possession and restitution of the real property located at _____ [list address, city, and county of property] _____

20   _____ , City of _____ ,

21   County of _____ , California, rent and damages in the sum of

22      $ _____ , plus costs of suit in the sum of $ _____ , for the total sum of $ ___ [fill in rent/damages amount and total amount after adding costs]

23

24   DATED: _____ , _____

25   _____
                                        Judge of the Superior Court
26

27

28

1

Name: LENNY D. LANDLORD
Address: 12345 Angeleno Street
            Los Angeles, CA 90010

2

Phone: 213-555-6789

3

Plaintiff in Pro Per

4

5

6

7

8   SUPERIOR COURT OF CALIFORNIA, COUNTY OF _____LOS ANGELES_____

9   _____LOS ANGELES_____ DIVISION

10

11   LENNY D. LANDLORD   )   Case No. ___A-12345-B___
                Plaintiff,   )
12   )   JUDGMENT FOLLOWING GRANTING
     v.   )   OF MOTION FOR SUMMARY JUDGMENT
13   )
     TERRENCE D. TENANT, TILLIE D. TENANT)
14   Defendant(s).   )
)
15   )

16   The motion of plaintiff for summary judgment having been granted,

17   IT IS HEREBY ORDERED AND ADJUDGED that plaintiff have and recover from defendant(s) _____

18   Terrence D. Tenant and Tillie D. Tenant

19   possession and restitution of the real property located at _____6789 Angeleno Street, Apt. 10_____

20   _____, City of _____Los Angeles_____,

21   County of _____Los Angeles_____, California, rent and damages in the sum of

22   $ ___1,120.00___, plus costs of suit in the sum of $ ___110.00___, for the total sum of $ ___1,230.00___.

23

24   DATED:_____, _____

25

26   _____
                                         Judge of the Superior Court

27

28

UD-110

ATTORNEY OR PARTY WITHOUT ATTORNEY *(Name, state bar number, and address):*	FOR COURT USE ONLY
list your name, address, and phone number	

TELEPHONE NO.:   FAX NO. *(Optional):*

E-MAIL ADDRESS *(Optional):*

ATTORNEY FOR *(Name):* Plaintiff in Pro Per

SUPERIOR COURT OF CALIFORNIA, COUNTY OF

STREET ADDRESS:

MAILING ADDRESS: court, county, address, and branch

CITY AND ZIP CODE:

BRANCH NAME:

PLAINTIFF: plaintiff's and defendants' names

DEFENDANT:

JUDGMENT—UNLAWFUL DETAINER	CASE NUMBER:
☐ By Clerk ☐ By Default ☐ After Court Trial	case number
☒ By Court ☐ Possession Only ☐ Defendant Did Not Appear at Trial	

JUDGMENT

1. ☐ **BY DEFAULT**

    a. Defendant was properly served with a copy of the summons and complaint.

    b. Defendant failed to answer the complaint or appear and defend the action within the time allowed by law.

    c. Defendant's default was entered by the clerk upon plaintiff's application.

    d. ☐ **Clerk's Judgment** (Code Civ. Proc., § 1169). For possession only of the premises described on page 2 (item 4).

    e. ☐ **Court Judgment** (Code Civ. Proc., § 585(b)). The court considered

       (1) ☐ plaintiff's testimony and other evidence.

       (2) ☐ plaintiff's or others' written declaration and evidence (Code Civ. Proc., § 585(d)).

2. ☐ **AFTER COURT TRIAL.** The jury was waived. The court considered the evidence.

    a. The case was tried on *(date and time):*

       before *(name of judicial officer):*   leave Items 1 and 2 blank everywhere

    b. Appearances by:

       ☐ Plaintiff *(name each):*   ☐ Plaintiff's attorney *(name each):*

                                                          (1)

                                                          (2)

       ☐ Continued on *Attachment* 2b (form MC-025).

       ☐ Defendant *(name each):*   ☐ Defendant's attorney *(name each):*

                                                          (1)

                                                          (2)

       ☐ Continued on *Attachment* 2b (form MC-025).

    c. ☐ Defendant did not appear at trial. Defendant was properly served with notice of trial.

    d. ☐ A statement of decision (Code Civ. Proc., § 632) ☐ was not ☐ was requested.

Page 1 of 2

Form Approved for Optional Use
Judicial Council of California
UD-110 [New January 1, 2003]

JUDGMENT—UNLAWFUL DETAINER

Code of Civil Procedure, §§ 415.46,
585(d), 664.6, 1169

PLAINTIFF:		CASE NUMBER:
	plaintiff's and defendants' name(s)	**case number**
DEFENDANT:		

JUDGMENT IS ENTERED AS FOLLOWS BY: [X] THE COURT   [ ] THE CLERK

3. **Parties.** Judgment is

  a. [X] for plaintiff *(name each):* **plaintiff's name**

     and against defendant *(name each):* **defendants' name(s)**

     [ ] Continued on *Attachment* 3a (form MC-025).

  b. [ ] for defendant *(name each):*

4. [X] Plaintiff [ ] Defendant is entitled to possession of the premises located at *(street address, apartment, city, and county):*

    list complete address of property

5. [ ] Judgment applies to all occupants of the premises including tenants, subtenants if any, and named claimants if any (Code Civ. Proc., §§ 715.010, 1169, and 1174.3). **check only if you used Prejudgment Claim of Right to Possession procedure. Ch. 6, Sec. 12**

6. **Amount and terms of judgment**

  a. [X] Defendant named in item 3a above must pay plaintiff on the complaint: b. [ ] Plaintiff is to receive nothing from defendant named in item 3b.

(1) [ ]	Past-due rent	$	**list amounts of past-due rent demanded in 3-day notice and/or holdover (daily pro-rated) damages, and total court costs, and total them**
(2) [ ]	Holdover damages	$	
(3) [ ]	Attorney fees	$	
(4) [ ]	Costs	$	
(5) [ ]	Other *(specify):*	$	
(6)	**TOTAL JUDGMENT**	$	

    [ ] Defendant named in item 3b is to recover costs: $

    [ ] and attorney fees: $.

  c. [ ] The rental agreement is canceled. [ ] The lease is forfeited.

    check as appropriate

7. [ ] **Conditional judgment.** Plaintiff has breached the agreement to provide habitable premises to defendant as stated in *Judgment—Unlawful Detainer Attachment* (form UD–110S), which is attached.

8. [X] **Other** *(specify):* Judgment granted pursuant to separate Order Granting Motion for Summary Judgment

    [ ] Continued on *Attachment* 8 (form MC-025).

Date: [ ] _____
                                 JUDICIAL OFFICER

Date: [ ] Clerk, by _____ , Deputy

(SEAL)

    CLERK'S CERTIFICATE *(Optional)*

    I certify that this is a true copy of the original judgment on file in the court.

    Date:

    Clerk, by _____ , Deputy

UD-110

ATTORNEY OR PARTY WITHOUT ATTORNEY *(Name, state bar number, and address):*
   LENNY D. LANDLORD
   1234 ANGELENO STREET
   LOS ANGELES, CA 90010
   TELEPHONE NO.:   213-555-6789   FAX NO. *(Optional):*
 E-MAIL ADDRESS *(Optional):*
 ATTORNEY FOR *(Name):*   Plaintiff in Pro Per
	FOR COURT USE ONLY

SUPERIOR COURT OF CALIFORNIA, COUNTY OF   LOS ANGELES
STREET ADDRESS: 110 N. Grand Avenue
MAILING ADDRESS: Same
CITY AND ZIP CODE: Los Angeles, CA 90012
BRANCH NAME: CENTRAL DISTRICT/DOWNTOWN BRANCH

PLAINTIFF: LENNY D. LANDLORD

DEFENDANT: TERRENCE D. TENANT, TILLIE D. TENANT

JUDGMENT—UNLAWFUL DETAINER	CASE NUMBER:
☐ **By Clerk** ☐ **By Default** ☐ **After Court Trial** ☒ **By Court** ☐ **Possession Only** ☐ **Defendant Did Not Appear at Trial**	A-12345-B

JUDGMENT

1. ☐ **BY DEFAULT**
   a. Defendant was properly served with a copy of the summons and complaint.
   b. Defendant failed to answer the complaint or appear and defend the action within the time allowed by law.
   c. Defendant's default was entered by the clerk upon plaintiff's application.
   d. ☐ **Clerk's Judgment** (Code Civ. Proc., § 1169). For possession only of the premises described on page 2 (item 4).
   e. ☐ **Court Judgment** (Code Civ. Proc., § 585(b)). The court considered
      (1) ☐ plaintiff's testimony and other evidence.
      (2) ☐ plaintiff's or others' written declaration and evidence (Code Civ. Proc., § 585(d)).

2. ☐ **AFTER COURT TRIAL.** The jury was waived. The court considered the evidence.
   a. The case was tried on *(date and time):*

     before *(name of judicial officer):*

   b. Appearances by:
     ☐ Plaintiff *(name each):*   ☐ Plaintiff's attorney *(name each):*
                                        (1)
                                        (2)

     ☐ Continued on *Attachment* 2b (form MC-025).

     ☐ Defendant *(name each):*   ☐ Defendant's attorney *(name each):*
                                        (1)
                                        (2)

     ☐ Continued on *Attachment* 2b (form MC-025).

   c. ☐ Defendant did not appear at trial. Defendant was properly served with notice of trial.

   d. ☐ A statement of decision (Code Civ. Proc., § 632) ☐ was not ☐ was   requested.

Page 1 of 2

PLAINTIFF: LENNY D., LANDLORD	CASE NUMBER:
DEFENDANT: TERRENCE D. TENANT, ET AL	A-12345-B

JUDGMENT IS ENTERED AS FOLLOWS BY: ☒ **THE COURT** ☐ **THE CLERK**

3. **Parties.** Judgment is

    a. ☒ for plaintiff *(name each):* Lenny D. Landlord

        and against defendant *(name each):* Terrence D. Tenant, Tillie D. Tenant

        ☐ Continued on *Attachment* 3a (form MC-025).

    b. ☐ for defendant *(name each):*

4. ☒ Plaintiff ☐ Defendant is entitled to possession of the premises located at *(street address, apartment, city, and county):*

    6789 Angel Street, Apt. 10, Los Angeles, Los Angeles County

5. ☐ Judgment applies to all occupants of the premises including tenants, subtenants if any, and named claimants if any (Code Civ. Proc., §§ 715.010, 1169, and 1174.3).

6. **Amount and terms of judgment**

    a. ☒ Defendant named in item 3a above must pay plaintiff on the complaint:

(1)	☒	Past-due rent	$ 900.00
(2)	☒	Holdover damages	$ 220.00
(3)	☐	Attorney fees	$
(4)	☒	Costs	$ 243.00
(5)	☐	Other *(specify):*	$
(6)		**TOTAL JUDGMENT**	$ 1,363.00

    b. ☐ Plaintiff is to receive nothing from defendant named in item 3b.

        ☐ Defendant named in item 3b is to recover costs: $

        ☐ and attorney fees: $.

    c. ☐ The rental agreement is canceled. ☐ The lease is forfeited.

7. ☐ **Conditional judgment.** Plaintiff has breached the agreement to provide habitable premises to defendant as stated in *Judgment—Unlawful Detainer Attachment* (form UD–110S), which is attached.

8. ☐ **Other** *(specify):*

    ☒ Continued on *Attachment* 8 (form MC-025). Judgment granted pursuant to separate Order Granting Motion for Summary Judgment.

Date: ☐ _____

                          JUDICIAL OFFICER

Date: ☐ Clerk, by _____ , Deputy

(SEAL)

CLERK'S CERTIFICATE *(Optional)*

I certify that this is a true copy of the original judgment on file in the court.

Date:

Clerk, by _____ , Deputy

UD-110 [New January 1, 2003] | **JUDGMENT—UNLAWFUL DETAINER** | Page 2 of 2

EJ-130

ATTORNEY OR PARTY WITHOUT ATTORNEY *(Name, state bar number and address):*	FOR COURT USE ONLY
LENNY D. LANDLORD 1234 ANGELENO STREET LOS ANGELES, CA 90010 TELEPHONE NO.: 213-555-6789 FAX NO. *(Optional):* E-MAIL ADDRESS *(Optional):* ATTORNEY FOR *(Name):* ☐ ATTORNEY FOR ☒ JUDGMENT CREDITOR ☐ ASSIGNEE OF RECORD	

SUPERIOR COURT OF CALIFORNIA, COUNTY OF   LOS ANGELES
STREET ADDRESS: 110 N. Grand Avenue
MAILING ADDRESS: Same
CITY AND ZIP CODE: Los Angeles, CA 90012
BRANCH NAME: LOS ANGELES DIVISION

PLAINTIFF: LENNY D. LANDLORD

DEFENDANT: TERRENCE D. TENANT, TILLIE D. TENANT

WRIT OF	☒ **EXECUTION (Money Judgment)** ☒ **POSSESSION OF** ☐ **Personal Property** ☒ **Real Property** ☐ **SALE**	CASE NUMBER: A-12345-B

1. **To the Sheriff or any Marshal or Constable of the County of:** Los Angeles

You are directed to enforce the judgment described below with daily interest and your costs as provided by law.

2. **To any registered process server:** You are authorized to serve this writ only in accord with CCP 699.080 or CCP 715.040.

3. *(Name):* Lenny D. Landlord
   is the ☒ judgment creditor ☐ assignee of record   whose address is shown on this form above the court's name.

4. **Judgment debtor** *(name and last known address):*

   ┌─────────────────────┐
   │ Tillie D. Tenant
   │ 6879 Angeleno Street, Apt. 10
   │ Los Angeles, CA 90012
   └─────────────────────┘

   ┌─────────────────────┐
   │ Terrence D. Tenant
   │ 6879 Angeleno Street, Apt. 10
   │ Los Angeles, CA 90012
   └─────────────────────┘

   ☐ additional judgment debtors on next page

5. **Judgment entered** on *(date):* Sept. 9, 20xx
6. ☐ **Judgment renewed** on *(dates):*

7. **Notice of sale** under this writ
   a. ☐ has not been requested.
   b. ☒ has been requested *(see next page).*
8. ☐ Joint debtor information on next page.

   [SEAL]

9. ☐ See next page for information on real or personal property to be delivered under a writ of possession or sold under a writ of sale.
10. ☐ This writ is issued on a sister-state judgment.
11. Total judgment . . . . $ 1,120.00
12. Costs after judgment (per filed order or memo CCP 685.090) . . . . $ .00
13. Subtotal *(add 11 and 12)* . . . . $ 1,120.00
14. Credits . . . . $
15. Subtotal *(subtract 14 from 13)* . . . $ 1,120.00
16. Interest after judgment (per filed affidavit CCP 685.050) . . . . $ 0.00
17. Fee for issuance of writ . . . . $ 7.00
18. **Total** *(add 15, 16, and 17)* . . . . . . $ 1,127.00
19. Levying officer:
   (a) Add daily interest from date of writ *(at the legal rate on 15)* of. . . . . $ 0.17
   (b) Pay directly to court costs included in 11 and 17 (GC 6103.5, 68511.3; CCP 699.520(i)) . . . . $ 0.00
20. ☐ The amounts called for in items 11-19 are different for each debtor. These amounts are stated for each debtor on Attachment 20.

Issued on *(date):*	Clerk, by _____, Deputy

NOTICE TO PERSON SERVED: SEE NEXT PAGE FOR IMPORTANT INFORMATION.

Page 1 of 2

Form Approved for Optional Use
Judicial Council of California
EJ-130 [Rev. January 1, 2003]

WRIT OF EXECUTION

Code of Civil Procedure, §§ 699.520, 712.010, 715.010

SHORT TITLE:	CASE NUMBER:
LANDLORD V. TENANT	A-12345-B

— Items continued from the first page —

4. ☐ **Additional judgment debtor** *(name and last known address):*

7. ☐ **Notice of sale** has been requested by *(name and address):*

8. ☐ **Joint debtor** was declared bound by the judgment (CCP 989-994)
    a. on *(date):*   a. on *(date):*
    b. name and address of joint debtor: b. name and address of joint debtor:

    c. ☐ additional costs against certain joint debtors *(itemize):*

9. ☒ *(Writ of Possession or Writ of Sale)* **Judgment** was entered for the following: August 10, 20xx
    a. ☒ Possession of real property: The complaint was filed on *(date):*   **(Check (1) or (2)):**
        (1) ☒ The Prejudgment Claim of Right to Possession was served in compliance with CCP 415.46.
               The judgment includes all tenants, subtenants, named claimants, and other occupants of the premises.
        (2) ☐ The Prejudgment Claim of Right to Possession was NOT served in compliance with CCP 415.46.
            (a) $ was the daily rental value on the date the complaint was filed.
            (b) The court will hear objections to enforcement of the judgment under CCP 1174.3 on the following
                dates *(specify):*
    b. ☐ Possession of personal property
        ☐ If delivery cannot be had, then for the value *(itemize in 9e)* specified in the judgment or supplemental order.
    c. ☐ Sale of personal property
    d. ☐ Sale of real property
    e. Description of property:

       6789 Angel Street, Apt. 10
       Los Angeles, CA 90012

— NOTICE TO PERSON SERVED —

WRIT OF EXECUTION OR SALE. Your rights and duties are indicated on the accompanying Notice of Levy.
WRIT OF POSSESSION OF PERSONAL PROPERTY. If the levying officer is not able to take custody of the property, the levying officer will make a demand upon you for the property. If custody is not obtained following demand, the judgment may be enforced as a money judgment for the value of the property specified in the judgment or in a supplemental order.
WRIT OF POSSESSION OF REAL PROPERTY. If the premises are not vacated within five days after the date of service on the occupant or, if service is by posting, within five days after service on you, the levying officer will remove the occupants from the real property and place the judgment creditor in possession of the property. Except for a mobile home, personal property remaining on the premises will be sold or otherwise disposed of in accordance with CCP 1174 unless you or the owner of the property pays the judgment creditor the reasonable cost of storage and takes possession of the personal property not later than 15 days after the time the judgment creditor takes possession of the premises.
► *A Claim of Right to Possession form accompanies this writ (unless the Summons was served in compliance with CCP 415.46).*

probably win the motion by default. On the other hand, if the tenant has submitted a declaration, the judge will most likely have to rule that there is a "triable issue of fact" presented by the tenant's papers and that Summary Judgment is therefore improper. The judge will not attempt to decide at this time which side's statements are true—that's the trial's function. The fact that there is a contradiction is enough to defeat your motion and necessitate a trial.

When your case is called, step forward. Some judges prefer to ask questions, but others prefer that the person bringing the motion (you) start talking first. If the tenant has not filed a declaration, you should politely point out to the judge all of the following:

- C.C.P. § 1170.7 requires the judge to grant a Summary Judgment motion in an unlawful detainer case on the same basis as in regular civil cases under § 437c.

- There is no requirement for a "separate statement" of disputed or undisputed facts, as required in Summary Judgment motions in regular civil cases. Subdivision "(r)" of C.C.P. § 437c says this.

- C.C.P. § 437c requires the judge to rule based only on what the declarations or affidavits of the parties say, not what the tenant says at the hearing.

- Therefore, if the tenant hasn't filed a declaration, your motion should be granted, regardless of what arguments the tenant advances. The tenant cannot rely on the statements in his or her Answer, even if signed under penalty of perjury. (C.C.P. § 437c(o)(1).)

Say this in your own words, and don't be nervous. If the tenant has filed papers in response to your motion, be prepared to point out that the tenant's declaration doesn't contradict yours (if this is so), or perhaps even that the tenant's papers aren't in the proper legal form of a declaration under penalty of perjury (if that's correct). If the tenant tries to file the papers right there at the hearing, and you haven't received copies, you should let the judge know and ask to see what the tenant is filing. You may want to ask the judge to pass your case for a few minutes while you review the response.

After the tenant or his lawyer has had a chance to argue his side, the judge will either rule on the motion or take the matter "under submission." (In some cases, the judge will grant a one-week continuance or postponement to a tenant who states a credible defense but

hasn't come up with a written declaration.) If the judge denies the motion, you will have to wait until trial to get a judgment. If the judge grants the motion, present your proposed order and judgment for him to sign. Once that's done, you can have the clerk issue a Writ of Execution, which is then forwarded to the sheriff to begin the eviction. (See Chapter 7.)

Other Pretrial Complications

Between the time you file a Memorandum to Set Case for Trial and the date set for trial, the tenant may file legal documents requiring action on your part. They can include the following.

Countermemo to Set/Jury Demand

Many tenants think it is in their interest to demand a jury trial. They are often right. Not only does this delay scheduling of the case, but (in certain areas) it sometimes guarantees an audience more receptive to the tenant's arguments and less skeptical than a case-worn judge.

The tenant can ask for a jury trial with a document called a "jury demand" or in a "counter-memorandum," a response to your Memorandum to Set. There is normally nothing you can do to avoid a jury trial if the tenant demands it and pays the jury fees in advance.

If a jury trial is demanded, it is wise for you to seek legal representation. In a jury trial, a complex set of rules governs what evidence the jury may hear. It's very difficult for a nonlawyer to competently deal with these rules. In a trial before a judge without a jury, things are much simpler because judges, who know the rules themselves, just disregard evidence that it is improper for them to consider.

Discovery Requests

One of the biggest surprises to many nonlawyers about the legal system is that in all civil cases, including eviction lawsuits, each side has the right to force the other side to disclose, before trial, any relevant information it has about the case. Discovery is most often initiated by lawyers, not by tenants representing themselves, and if your tenant is represented by a lawyer, you may want to be, too. This following brief discussion of discovery techniques is just to give you an overview.

Depositions

In very rare instances, a tenant's lawyer may mail you a document that instructs you to show up at the lawyer's office and answer questions under oath about the case at a "deposition." The tenant's lawyer's questions and your responses to them are taken down by a court reporter. Any of your answers can be used against you later at trial. You must pay the court reporter a fairly hefty fee for a copy of the transcript, typically about a dollar for each double-spaced page; if you win the lawsuit, this sum is recoverable in the judgment as a court cost.

The rules on the types of questions the lawyer is allowed to ask are fairly complicated. The basic rule is that you must answer any question that might lead the tenant's lawyer to the discovery of relevant evidence. Your refusal to answer a proper question or to attend a deposition after proper notification can be punished by a court-ordered fine, if the other side requests it, or, in extreme cases, by dismissal of your case.

Interrogatories and Requests for Admissions

Another far more common way the tenant may obtain relevant information is to mail you questions called "interrogatories." They may be typed or may be entered on a standard form provided by the court clerk. You are required to answer all interrogatories within ten days if they're mailed to you (five days if they are personally served). As with depositions, the rules about the type of questions you have to answer are fairly technical, but basically you have to respond to all questions that might lead the other side to relevant information.

Requests for Admissions are something like interrogatories, but instead of having to make a possibly detailed response to a particular question, you have only to admit or deny statements put to you by the other side.

Because admission or denial of a key statement can be used against your position in court, you must be very careful in answering each request. Your failure to answer (or to answer on time) is equivalent to admitting that all the statements are true. This can be extremely damaging, if not fatal, to your case.

Requests to Produce and/or Inspect

A third discovery device is the Request to Produce and/or Inspect. This is a written request that you produce specified documents, books, or other records for inspection and copying by the other party, on a certain date and time. The party receiving the notice usually makes photocopies and mails them, rather than waiting for the other party or attorney to show up to inspect the records.

You must respond within five days, and produce the documents for actual inspection within ten days. Again, the rules on the type of material that can be requested this way are technical, but generally any records that can lead to relevant information can be sought.

 If the tenant seeks to have you produce sensitive or confidential business records that you do not believe are directly relevant to the proceeding, see a lawyer.

So far we have assumed that the discovery was initiated by the tenant. However, you can also use discovery to obtain information relating to the tenant's defense of the case. While this is not normally necessary, there are always exceptional cases. For example, you might want the tenant claiming a bogus habitability defense to admit she didn't complain to you or anyone else about the condition of the property until after you insisted on receiving the rent. Unfortunately, the special skills involved in properly drafting interrogatories and requests for admissions and in conducting depositions are beyond the scope of this book.

If you think you need to utilize discovery to find out more about the tenant's defense, consult an attorney.

Preparing for Trial

Preparing a case for trial and handling the trial itself are both very difficult subjects to handle in a self-help law book. Few eviction cases go to trial, but each case has its own unpredictable twists and turns that can greatly affect trial preparation and tactics. Simply put, there is no way for us to guide you step by step through this process. For this reason, we believe you will probably elect to bring a lawyer into the case, assuming you are still doing it yourself, to assist with the preparation for and conduct of the trial.

Here we provide you with a basic overview of what needs to be done for and at the trial so that you will know what to expect and better be able to assist your lawyer.

If the tenant filed an Answer to your Complaint, and the court has set the case for trial but you think the tenant has moved out and might not show up for trial, prepare for trial anyway. First, the tenant might not have actually moved out, and you're safer waiting to get a judgment before retaking possession (unless, of course, you've settled the case and the tenant has returned the keys). Second, unless you and the tenant have settled the case, you'll still want to get the money part of the judgment. Third, if you don't show up for trial—and the tenant does—the tenant will win and be entitled to move back in and to collect costs from you.

What You Have to Prove at Trial

What you must prove at trial obviously depends on the issues raised in your Complaint and the tenant's Answer. For example, the testimony in a case based on nonpayment of rent where the tenant's defense is that you failed to keep the premises habitable will be very different from that in a case based on termination of a month-to-month tenancy by 30-day notice where the tenant denies receiving the notice.

All contested evictions are similar, however, in that you, the plaintiff, have to do two things in order to win: First, you have to establish the basic elements of your case; this means you have to present hard evidence (usually through documents or live testimony) of the basic facts that would cause the judge to rule in your favor if the tenant didn't present a defense. If you don't produce evidence on every essential factual issue contested by the tenant in his Answer, the tenant can win the case by pointing this out to the judge right after you "rest" your case. This is done by the tenant making a "motion for judgment" after you have presented your evidence and closed your case.

The second thing you have to do is provide an adequate response to any rebuttal or defense the tenant presents. For example, the tenant may say he didn't have to pay the rent because you didn't fix the leaky roof, overflowing toilet, or defective water heater. You should counter with whatever facts relieve you of this responsibility. This might be that you kept the premises habitable or that the tenant didn't tell you about the defects until well after you began to ask about the late rent. (See *The California Landlord's Law Book: Rights & Responsibilities*, Chapter 11, on the landlord's duty to keep the property habitable.)

Elements of Your Case

If the tenant has denied everything in your Complaint, you will have to prove your case. To give you some idea of what is required, we set out the legal elements that must be proved for various types of eviction below. Also remember that if the tenant has admitted an element, you don't have to prove it. For example, if the tenant's Answer admits that your allegations in paragraph 9 of the Complaint are true, and you alleged in that paragraph that the tenant was served with a three-day notice on a certain date, you don't have to present testimony to prove it.

Okay, now find the symbol representing your type of eviction and review the elements that you will have to prove.

 Eviction for Nonpayment of Rent.
- You, your agent, or the person from whom you purchased the property (or her agent) rented the property to the tenant pursuant to an oral or written agreement.
- The monthly rent was a certain amount.
- The tenant got behind in the rent, so that she owed a certain amount.
- The tenant was properly served with a Three-Day Notice to Pay Rent or Quit.
- The notice demanded that the tenant pay the exact amount of rent due or leave within three days.
- The tenant neither paid the amount demanded in the notice nor left within three days (plus any extensions allowed if the third day fell on a weekend or holiday).
- The tenant is still in possession of the property.
- You have complied with any applicable rent control or just cause eviction ordinances and regulations.

 Eviction for Termination of Month-to-Month Tenancy.
- You, your agent, and so on, rented the property to the tenant.
- The tenancy is month to month, having either started out that way or having become month to month after a fixed-term lease expired.
- If a local rent control or eviction ordinance requires "just cause" for terminating a month-to-month tenancy, the reason you give for termination is

true and you've complied with all aspects of the ordinance and any applicable regulations.

- The tenant was served with a written notice requiring that he leave and giving him at least 30 days to do so if his tenancy lasted less than a year, and at least 60 days if a year or more.
- The 30-day (or longer) period has expired and the tenant is still in possession of the property.

 Eviction for Violation of Lease/Nuisance/Waste.

- You, your agent, and so on, rented the property to the tenant.
- The lease or rental agreement contains a valid clause requiring the tenant to do something (for example, pay a security deposit installment by a certain date) or to refrain from doing something (like having pets or subletting the property), and the tenant has violated the clause, or the tenant seriously damaged the property, used it unlawfully, or created a legal nuisance.
- The tenant was served with a three-day notice demanding that she vacate the property within that time, or, if the violation was correctable, that the tenant correct it within that time.
- The tenant neither vacated the property nor corrected the problem (if correctable) after the three days, plus any extensions.
- The tenant is still in possession of the property.
- You have complied with applicable rent control or just cause eviction ordinances or regulations.

Assessing and Countering the Tenant's Defenses

If the tenant raised any affirmative defenses in his answer, you must be ready to counter them at trial.

As we have emphasized, trying to assess and counter these defenses can be extremely risky unless you are experienced in doing so. Even if you otherwise feel competent to conduct your own trial, you should bring in a lawyer to help you with this aspect of the case. (See "Should You Hire an Attorney?" above.)

Habitability Defense

The "habitability defense" is commonly raised in evictions for nonpayment of rent. If the tenant's Answer states that his rent payment was partly or entirely excused because you kept the property in poor repair, you should first read Chapter 11 in *The California Landlord's Law Book: Rights & Responsibilities*, on landlords' duties to keep rental property in good repair. If in fact you haven't properly maintained the property, the tenant may win the lawsuit. To win, the tenant must prove to the judge that you "breached" (violated) a "warranty," which is implied by law, to provide the tenant with "habitable" (reasonably livable) premises in exchange for the rent. You don't have to prove that you properly maintained the property; rather, the tenant has to prove to the judge's satisfaction that you didn't make needed repairs.

To establish that you breached the implied warranty of habitability, the tenant must prove all of the following:

- You failed to provide one or more of the minimum "tenantability" requirements, including waterproofing, a working toilet, adequate heating and electricity, and hot and cold running water. (Civ. Code § 1941.1.)
- The defects were serious and substantial.
- The tenant or some other person (such as a health department inspector) notified you (or your manager) about the defect before you served the three-day notice to pay rent.
- You failed to make repairs within a reasonable time.

Once the tenant makes the showing described above, you must show a valid excuse for allowing the deficiency to continue. If you can convince the judge that the problems the tenant is complaining about are either non-habitability-related (such as old interior paint, carpets, or drapes) or minor (dripping but working faucets, cracked windows, and so on.), or that the tenant didn't complain until receiving the three-day notice, you will have knocked one or more holes in the tenant's habitability defense.

If the tenant produces evidence showing that you failed to make required repairs within 60 days after receiving written notice to do so from a health department or other official following an inspection of the property by that person, the burden shifts to you to show that you had a good reason for not making the repair. (See *The California Landlord's Law Book: Rights & Responsibilities*, Chapter 11.) (Civ. Code § 1941.3.)

Other Defenses

Other defenses tenants often raise include:

- discrimination on the basis of race, sex, or children (see *The California Landlord's Law Book: Rights & Responsibilities*, Chapter 9)

- retaliation for the tenant's exercise of a legal right such as complaining to the building inspector or organizing other tenants (see *The California Landlord's Law Book: Rights & Responsibilities*, Chapter 15)

- the landlord's breach of an express promise to make repairs, or other misconduct, or

- failure to comply with the requirements of a local rent control ordinance (see *The California Landlord's Law Book: Rights & Responsibilities*, Chapter 4, and your "home" chapter—either Chapter 2, 3, 4, or 5—in this volume).

Preparing the Judgment Form

When you go to trial you should have a judgment form ready for the judge to sign if she rules in your favor. Below are instructions for filling out a judgment after trial, on the statewide Judgment—Unlawful Detainer form, together with a sample. Fill out the items in the heading and caption boxes, so as to include your name, address, and telephone number; the court's name and location; the names of the parties; and the case number, as you've done many times.

In the box containing the words "JUDGMENT— UNLAWFUL DETAINER," put an X in the boxes next to the words "By Court" and "After Court Trial." If no defendant appeared at trial, also put an X in the box next to the words "Defendant Did Not Appear at Trial."

Item 1: Leave this item blank.

Item 2: Put an X in this box. In 2a, list the date and time that trial occurred, together with the judge's name. In Item 2b, put an X next to the word "Plaintiff" and list your name. If any defendants showed up for trial, put an X next to "Defendant" and list the name of each defendant who appeared at trial. If any defendant appeared with an attorney, check the box next to "Defendant's attorney" and list his or her name on the right. If no defendant appeared at trial, put an X in Item 2c next to the words "defendant did not appear at trial."

Do not check box 2d unless anyone requested that the judge give a "statement of decision" before the judge pronounced judgment. (This is extremely rare.)

Turn the form over and list your and the defendants' names, and the case number, in the spaces at the top of the reverse side of the form.

Item 3: Put an X here and list your name and the names of all defendants.

Item 4: Put an X next to Plaintiff and list the complete rental property address.

Item 5: Do not put an X in this box unless you previously served a Prejudgment Claim of Right to Possession.

Items 6 and 6a: Put Xs in boxes 6 and 6a. In nonpayment or rent cases, put an X in box 6a(1) and list the past-due rent demanded in the three-day notice and in Item 10 and 17c of the Complaint. In cases not involving failure to pay rent, such as a termination of month-to-month tenancy based on a 30-day or 60-day notice, do not check box 6a(1) or fill in an amount. In all cases, put an X in box 6a(2) "holdover damages" and list the amount obtained by multiplying the daily rental value (requested in Complaint Item 11) by the number of days between the date indicated in Complaint Item 17f and the date to and including the trial. Leave box 6a(3) blank. Check box 6a(4) and indicate the amount of court costs. Do not fill in anything in (5)—we don't think any sums other than those in (1) through (4) can be awarded in an unlawful detainer action. (For the same reason, leave Item 8 blank.) Finally, add up the amounts and put that total in Item 6a(6).

Item 6c: Put an X next to the "rental agreement is canceled" box if the tenancy was month to month. Put an X next to the "lease is forfeited" box if the tenant had a fixed-term lease and he or she breached it by nonpayment of rent or another violation of the rental agreement.

UD-110

ATTORNEY OR PARTY WITHOUT ATTORNEY (Name, state bar number, and address):

list your mailing address and phone number

TELEPHONE NO.:   FAX NO. (Optional):

E-MAIL ADDRESS (Optional):

ATTORNEY FOR (Name):

FOR COURT USE ONLY

SUPERIOR COURT OF CALIFORNIA, COUNTY OF

STREET ADDRESS:

MAILING ADDRESS:

CITY AND ZIP CODE: **court, county, address, branch name**

BRANCH NAME:

PLAINTIFF: **plaintiff's and defendants' names**

DEFENDANT:

JUDGMENT—UNLAWFUL DETAINER

☐ **By Clerk**   ☐ **By Default**   ☒ **After Court Trial**
☒ **By Court**   ☐ **Possession Only**   ⬤ **Defendant Did Not Appear at Trial**

CASE NUMBER:

case number

to be checked by hand, if defendant doesn't appear

JUDGMENT

1. ☐ **BY DEFAULT**
   a. Defendant was properly served with a copy of the summons and complaint.
   b. Defendant failed to answer the complaint or appear and defend the action within the time allowed by law.
   c. Defendant's default was entered by the clerk upon plaintiff's application.
   d. ☐ **Clerk's Judgment** (Code Civ. Proc., § 1169). For possession only of the premises described on page 2 (item 4).
   e. ☐ **Court Judgment** (Code Civ. Proc., § 585(b)). The court considered
      (1) ☐ plaintiff's testimony and other evidence.
      (2) ☐ plaintiff's or others' written declaration and evidence (Code Civ. Proc., § 585(d)).

2. ☒ **AFTER COURT TRIAL.** The jury was waived. The court considered the evidence.
   a. The case was tried on (date and time):   **list date and time of trial**

      before (name of judicial officer):   **list name of judge or commissioner who heard case**

   b. Appearances by:
      ☒ Plaintiff (name each):   **list your name**   ☐ Plaintiff's attorney (name each):
                                                                    (1)
                                                                    (2)

      ☐ Continued on Attachment 2b (form MC-025).

      ⬤ Defendant (name each):   **list name(s) of defendant(s) who appear at trial**   ⬤ Defendant's attorney (name each):
                                                                                                      (1) **check and list name(s) of any attorney(s) representing**
                                                                                                      (2) **any defendant**

   to be checked by hand, if defendants do appear at trial

      ☐ Continued on Attachment 2b (form MC-025).

   c. ⬤ Defendant did not appear at trial. Defendant was properly served with notice of trial.

   d. ☐ A statement of decision (Code Civ. Proc., § 632) ☐ was not ☐ was requested.

   to be checked by hand, if defendant doesn't appear

Page 1 of 2

Form Approved for Optional Use
Judicial Council of California
UD-110 [New January 1, 2003]

JUDGMENT—UNLAWFUL DETAINER

Code of Civil Procedure, §§ 415.46, 585(d), 664.6, 1169

PLAINTIFF:		CASE NUMBER:
DEFENDANT:	plaintiff's and defendants' names	case number

JUDGMENT IS ENTERED AS FOLLOWS BY: [X] **THE COURT**   [ ] **THE CLERK**

3. **Parties.** Judgment is

   a.   [X] for plaintiff *(name each):*   list plaintiffs' names(s)

      and against defendant *(name each):*   list all defendants' names, even those, if any, who defaulted

         [ ] Continued on *Attachment* 3a (form MC-025).

   b.   [ ] for defendant *(name each):*

4.   [X] Plaintiff   [ ] Defendant   is entitled to possession of the premises located at   *(street address, apartment, city, and county):*

         list complete address of the property

5.   [ ] Judgment applies to all occupants of the premises including tenants, subtenants if any, and named claimants if any (Code Civ. Proc., §§ 715.010, 1169, and 1174.3).   check only if you used the optional prejudgment claim procedure in Ch. 6

6.   **Amount and terms of judgment**

   a.   [X] Defendant named in item 3a above must pay plaintiff on the complaint: b.   [ ] Plaintiff is to receive nothing from defendant named in item 3b.

(1) [ ]	Past-due rent	$	
(2) [ ]	Holdover damages	$	
(3) [ ]	Attorney fees	$	
(4) [ ]	Costs	$	
(5) [ ]	Other *(specify):*	$	
(6)	**TOTAL JUDGMENT**	$	

list and check applicable past-due rent demanded in three-day notice and/or holdover (prorated daily) damages, and court costs, and total them

[ ] Defendant named in item 3b is to recover costs: $

   [ ] and attorney fees: $.

   c.   [ ] The rental agreement is canceled.   [ ] The lease is forfeited.

         check as applicable for eviction based on nonpayment or other breach

7.   [ ] **Conditional judgment.** Plaintiff has breached the agreement to provide habitable premises to defendant as stated in *Judgment—Unlawful Detainer Attachment* (form UD–110S), which is attached.

8.   [ ] **Other** *(specify):*

         [ ] Continued on *Attachment* 8 (form MC-025).

Date: [ ] _____

                       JUDICIAL OFFICER

Date: [ ] Clerk, by _____, Deputy

(SEAL)

CLERK'S CERTIFICATE *(Optional)*

I certify that this is a true copy of the original judgment on file in the court.

Date:

         Clerk, by   _____, Deputy

UD-110

ATTORNEY OR PARTY WITHOUT ATTORNEY *(Name, state bar number, and address):*	FOR COURT USE ONLY
LENNY D. LANDLORD 1234 ANGELENO STREET LOS ANGELES, CA 90010 TELEPHONE NO.: 213-555-6789 FAX NO. *(Optional):* E-MAIL ADDRESS *(Optional):* ATTORNEY FOR *(Name):* Plaintiff in Pro Per	

SUPERIOR COURT OF CALIFORNIA, COUNTY OF   LOS ANGELES
STREET ADDRESS: 110 N. Grand Avenue
MAILING ADDRESS: Same
CITY AND ZIP CODE: Los Angeles, CA 90012
BRANCH NAME: LOS ANGELES DIVISION

PLAINTIFF: LENNY D. LANDLORD

DEFENDANT: TERRENCE D. TENANT, ET AL

JUDGMENT—UNLAWFUL DETAINER	CASE NUMBER:
[ ] **By Clerk** [ ] **By Default** [X] **After Court Trial** [X] **By Court** [ ] **Possession Only** [ ] **Defendant Did Not Appear at Trial**	A-12345-B

JUDGMENT

1. [ ]   **BY DEFAULT**
    a. Defendant was properly served with a copy of the summons and complaint.
    b. Defendant failed to answer the complaint or appear and defend the action within the time allowed by law.
    c. Defendant's default was entered by the clerk upon plaintiff's application.
    d. [ ]   **Clerk's Judgment** (Code Civ. Proc., § 1169). For possession only of the premises described on page 2 (item 4).
    e. [ ]   **Court Judgment** (Code Civ. Proc., § 585(b)). The court considered
        (1) [ ]   plaintiff's testimony and other evidence.
        (2) [ ]   plaintiff's or others' written declaration and evidence (Code Civ. Proc., § 585(d)).

2. [X]   **AFTER COURT TRIAL.** The jury was waived. The court considered the evidence.
    a. The case was tried on *(date and time):* September 20, 20xx
      before *(name of judicial officer):* Julia Judge

    b. Appearances by:
      [X] Plaintiff *(name each):*   [ ] Plaintiff's attorney *(name each):*
        Lenny D. Landlord   (1)
                                  (2)

      [ ] Continued on *Attachment* 2b (form MC-025).

      [X] Defendant *(name each):*   [ ] Defendant's attorney *(name each):*
        Terrence D. Tenant,   (1)
        Tillie D. Tenant   (2)

      [ ] Continued on *Attachment* 2b (form MC-025).

    c. [ ]   Defendant did not appear at trial. Defendant was properly served with notice of trial.

    d. [ ]   A statement of decision (Code Civ. Proc., § 632)   [ ] was not   [ ] was   requested.

Form Approved for Optional Use
Judicial Council of California
UD-110 [New January 1, 2003]

JUDGMENT—UNLAWFUL DETAINER

Code of Civil Procedure, §§ 415.46,
585(d), 664.6, 1169

| PLAINTIFF: LENNY D., LANDLORD | CASE NUMBER: |
| DEFENDANT: TERRENCE D. TENANT, ET AL | A-12345-B |

JUDGMENT IS ENTERED AS FOLLOWS BY: [X] **THE COURT** ☐ **THE CLERK**

3. **Parties.** Judgment is

a. [X] for plaintiff (name each): Lenny D. Landlord

    and against defendant (name each): Terrence D. Tenant, Tillie D. Tenant

    ☐ Continued on Attachment 3a (form MC-025).

b. ☐ for defendant (name each):

4. [X] Plaintiff ☐ Defendant is entitled to possession of the premises located at (street address, apartment, city, and county):

    6789 Angel Street, Apt. 10, Los Angeles, Los Angeles County

5. ☐ Judgment applies to all occupants of the premises including tenants, subtenants if any, and named claimants if any (Code Civ. Proc., §§ 715.010, 1169, and 1174.3).

6. **Amount and terms of judgment**

a. [X] Defendant named in item 3a above must pay plaintiff on the complaint:

(1)	[X]	Past-due rent	$	900.00
(2)	[X]	Holdover damages	$	220.00
(3)	☐	Attorney fees	$	
(4)	[X]	Costs	$	110.00
(5)	☐	Other (specify):	$	
(6)	**TOTAL JUDGMENT**		$	1,230.00

b. ☐ Plaintiff is to receive nothing from defendant named in item 3b.
    ☐ Defendant named in item 3b is to recover costs: $
    ☐ and attorney fees: $.

c. [X] The rental agreement is canceled. ☐ The lease is forfeited.

7. ☐ **Conditional judgment.** Plaintiff has breached the agreement to provide habitable premises to defendant as stated in Judgment—Unlawful Detainer Attachment (form UD–110S), which is attached.

8. ☐ **Other** (specify):

    ☐ Continued on Attachment 8 (form MC-025).

Date: _____   ☐ _____
                                          JUDICIAL OFFICER

Date: _____   ☐ Clerk, by _____ , Deputy

(SEAL)

CLERK'S CERTIFICATE (Optional)

I certify that this is a true copy of the original judgment on file in the court.

Date:

Clerk, by _____ , Deputy

UD-110 [New January 1, 2003]   **JUDGMENT—UNLAWFUL DETAINER**   Page 2 of 2

Preparing the Judgment When You've Partially Won—Or Lost

Customarily, the party who wins prepares the judgment. The instructions above are based on the assumption that you, the landlord, will win the case after trial—something that happens in the great majority of contested cases. But if the judge allows the tenant to stay and pay reduced rent because you breached the warranty of habitability, even though you're not a clear victor, you'll still need to fill out the judgment form. And if, heaven forbid, you lose outright, you may still be asked by the judge to prepare the judgment. In either event, here are a few pointers:

Partial victory for the tenant on the issue of breach of warranty of habitability. Suppose the tenant claimed he owed none of the $1,000 monthly rent because of a leaky roof, but the judge said he owed $500 and could stay if he pays that reduced amount within five days. Fill out the form as instructed above, but check Item 7 ("Conditional Judgment"). You'll have to fill out another form, Judgment—Unlawful Detainer Attachment, and attach it to the Judgment form. We include a blank form of this type in Appendix 3, but we hope you won't have to use it.

Total victory for the tenant. If the tenant prevails, check Item 3d, and in Item 4, check the box next to "defendant." Leave Item 6a blank, and check Item 6b ("plaintiff is to recover nothing from defendant ....").

A blank, tear-out version of the Judgment After Trial is in Appendix 3. The CD-ROM also includes this form. Instructions for using the CD are in Appendix 2.

The Trial

As the plaintiff, you have the burden of proving to the judge (or jury if it's a jury trial) that you are entitled to the relief requested in your Complaint. You present your case first.

Much of your case will consist of two types of evidence: your testimony, and documents that you offer to prove one or more of your points. In addition, you may want to bring in witnesses.

Once you have met your "burden of proof," it is the tenant's turn. To defeat your case the tenant must offer testimony and/or documents to:

- convince the judge (the jury, if it's a jury trial) that your proof on one or more issues was wrong or deficient, or
- prove that one of her affirmative defenses is valid.

After the tenant has put on her case, you will have an opportunity to rebut the tenant's case. After your rebuttal, both you and the tenant can summarize your cases. The case is then submitted to the judge or jury for its verdict. If you win, you will be entitled to evict the tenant unless the tenant appeals the verdict and obtains a stay of the eviction pending the appeal. Also, it is possible for the tenant to request a new trial and an order barring the eviction because of hardship.

Now let's take a minute to go into a little more detail on the procedures outlined above.

Don't Send Your Manager to Court

If you handle your case yourself, without an attorney, don't make the mistake of sending your manager or other agent to court when your case is heard. Although a manager or agent can appear in court to testify, the plaintiff (the property owner) who represents himself *must* appear at trial to present the case. If the owner who represents himself does not appear at trial, and sends a manager or other agent instead, the judge may refuse to proceed further.

If you have an attorney, the attorney may appear on your behalf, although a judge has the authority to demand your presence.

The Clerk Calls the Case

The trial begins when the clerk calls your case by name, usually by calling out the last name of the parties (for example, in the case of *Lenny D. Landlord v. Terrence and Tillie Tenant*, "*Landlord v. Tenant*"). As mentioned, since you're the plaintiff, you present your case first, when the judge asks you to begin.

Last-Minute Motions

Before you begin your case, the tenant may make a last-minute motion, perhaps for a continuance or postponement of the trial, or to disqualify the judge. A party to a lawsuit is allowed to disqualify one judge—sometimes even at the last minute—simply by filing a declaration under penalty of perjury that states a belief that the judge is prejudiced. (C.C.P. § 170.6.) Unlawful detainer defendants frequently use this procedure to disqualify judges notoriously unsympathetic to tenants' defenses or sometimes just to delay things. Landlords rarely use this procedure, even against somewhat pro-tenant judges, due to their desire to get the trial moving.

It isn't too likely that the judge will agree to postpone the trial. If the tenant disqualifies the judge, however, the case must be transferred to another judge or postponed if no other judge is available.

Another frequent last-minute motion is one to "exclude witnesses." If you or the tenant so requests, witnesses (but not parties) will be required to leave the courtroom until it's their turn to testify. This prevents witnesses from patterning their testimony after other witnesses on their side they see testify. If you are your only witness and the tenant comes in with a string of friends to testify to what a slumlord you are, you can at least minimize the damage by insisting that each be kept out while the others testify. Remember, however, that a motion to exclude works both ways. If you ask the judge to exclude the tenant's witnesses, your witnesses must also wait in the corridor.

Opening Statements

Both you and the tenant have a right to make an opening statement at the start of the trial. Chances are that the judge has heard many cases like yours, so that an opening statement would be a fruitless exercise. If you do make a statement, keep it very brief. Say what you're going to prove, but don't start proving it, and above all, don't argue all the points. Here's what an opening statement in a nonpayment of rent case might sound like:

The Courtroom

Unlawful detainer trials are conducted in courtrooms that look much like those on television. In addition to the judge, a clerk and bailiff are normally present. They sit at tables immediately in front of the judge's elevated bench, or slightly off to the side. The clerk's job is to keep the judge supplied with the necessary files and papers and to make sure that the proceedings flow smoothly. A clerk is not the same as a court reporter, who keeps a word-by-word record of the proceedings. In courtrooms where eviction cases are heard, a reporter is not present unless either party insists on (and pays for) one. The bailiff, usually a uniformed deputy sheriff or marshal, is present to keep order.

Courtrooms are divided about two-thirds of the way toward the front by a sort of fence known as "the bar." The judge, court personnel, and lawyers use the area on one side of the bar, and the public, including parties and witnesses waiting to be called, sits on the other side. You're invited to cross the bar only when your case is called by the clerk, and any witnesses you have may do so only when you call them to testify. You then come forward and sit at the long table (the one closest to the empty jury box) known as the "counsel table," facing the judge.

"Your Honor, this is an unlawful detainer action based on nonpayment of rent. Mr. Tenant's Answer admits the fact of the lease, and that the monthly rent is $550, due on the first of the month, but denies everything else. I will testify to my receipt of previous rents, so that the balance due the day the three-day notice was served was $550. I will also testify that I served the three-day notice to pay rent or quit on Mr. Tenant, who was never home or at work when I went there, by posting a copy of it on the door and mailing a second copy to his home, and that later when I called him he admitted having received it. Finally, I will testify that he didn't pay the rent within three days after that, and, of course, is still in possession."

Presenting Your Case

There are two ways you can offer testimony to prove the disputed elements of your case. The most common is to testify yourself.

As you may know from old Perry Mason episodes, parties to lawsuits usually testify in response to questions posed by their own lawyer. This is called "direct examination" (as opposed to "cross-examination," when the other side asks you questions). If you represent yourself this is done by simply recounting the relevant facts.

Your testimony should be very much like that you would give at a default hearing. (See Chapter 7.) If the tenant's Answer admits certain of your allegations, such as the basic terms of the tenancy or service of the three-day or other termination notice, you can leave that part out, having noted in your opening remarks that it's not disputed.

After you've finished testifying, the tenant or her lawyer may cross-examine you. The general rule is that you, like any other witness, can be cross-examined on anything relating to your testimony on direct examination. You should respond courteously, truthfully, and as briefly as possible. Contrary to popular myth, you don't have to give a "yes" or "no" answer to any question for which it would be inappropriate. You have a right to explain and expand on your answer in detail if you feel it's necessary. For example, the question, "Have you stopped pocketing security deposits?" is best answered by, "I have never 'pocketed' a deposit," rather than by "yes" or "no."

Don't appear hostile toward the person doing the cross-examining; it could hurt your case. If you have a lawyer, he has the right to object to any question that is abusive or irrelevant. If you are representing yourself and consider a question to be particularly awful, ask the judge if you have to answer it.

> **EXAMPLE:** After you've finished testifying, the tenant begins cross-examining you with, "Ms. Landlord, didn't you remember my telling you I couldn't pay the rent because I lost my job?" Since the issue of the tenant's hardship isn't a legal defense to failure to pay rent, it's legally irrelevant, and your lawyer should say, "Your Honor, I object to this question as irrelevant." The judge should "sustain" this objection, meaning you don't have to answer.

If the case is tried by a judge, objections on the ground of relevancy are often overruled by the judge, who figures her training equips her to sort out the wheat from the chaff when decision time comes around. This discrepancy between legal rules and the real world is one example among thousands of why doing your own trial is not advised.

Another way to prove part or all of the disputed elements of your case is by questioning the tenant at the start. The law allows you to call the defendant as a witness before you or any of your own witnesses testify. (Evid. Code § 776.)

Handled properly, the tenant will testify truthfully, if reluctantly, so as to establish most or all of the basic elements of your lawsuit, even if he denied these elements in the answer. Here's an example of such an exchange:

Landlord: *Mr. Tenant, you rented the premises at 123 State Street, Los Angeles, from me, didn't you?*

Tenant: *Yes.*

Landlord: *And that was in March 20xx, correct?*

Tenant: *Yes.*

Landlord: *I'd like to show you a copy of this document entitled "Rental Agreement," attached as Exhibit "A" to the Complaint. This is your signature here at the bottom, isn't it?*

Tenant: *Well … ah.*

Landlord: *You paid the monthly rent of $550 until August 20xx, didn't you?*

Tenant: *Well, yeah, but in July I got laid off, and …*

Landlord: *Please just answer the question, Mr. Tenant.*

Tenant: *Yeah.*

Landlord: *And you didn't pay the $550 rent in August 20xx, did you?*

Tenant: *Well, no.*

Landlord: *And I'd like to show you a copy of this document entitled "Three-Day Notice to Pay Rent or Quit" attached as Exhibit "B" to the Complaint. You told me on August 5 when I phoned you that you received the notice, didn't you?*

Tenant: *Yeah.*

Landlord: *And you, in fact, did receive it, correct?*

Tenant: *Yes.*

Landlord: *And you're still living in the premises, aren't you?*

Tenant: *Yes.*

Landlord: *I have no further questions, Your Honor.*

You should also call other witnesses to testify about basic elements of your case that you were unable to cover, or that will likely be disputed by the tenant (such as service of a three-day notice served by a person other than yourself). After the clerk swears your witness in, he may only answer questions asked by you, unless the judge allows narrative testimony and the tenant doesn't object.

The Tenant's Case

After you and your witnesses have testified and been cross-examined, it's the tenant's turn to present evidence to contradict you on any of the elements of your case or to present defenses. He can testify himself and/or call other persons (even you) to testify.

After the tenant and any of his witnesses have testified, you or your lawyer may cross-examine them on any issue raised in their testimony.

Your Rebuttal

You now have a second chance to testify and to have any witnesses testify, to respond to denials or points raised by the tenant in his defense. This is called the "rebuttal" phase of the trial. The rules are the same as those for your earlier testimony, with one important difference: The only subjects you may go into on rebuttal are those addressed by the tenant or his witnesses. The purpose is to rebut what they said, not to raise other issues. For example, this is the time to testify that the problems the tenant complains about are fairly minor or that he never asked you to make repairs until after you served a three-day notice. Again, the tenant may cross-examine you and your witnesses.

Closing Arguments

After both sides have presented their testimony, each is allowed to make a brief closing argument to the judge. The plaintiff goes first.

The Judge's Decision

After the closing statements, the judge decides the case. Some judges do not announce their decision in court, but rather take the case "under submission" or "under advisement." This may mean that the judge wants to think the matter over before deciding. If this happens, you will be notified of the result by mail.

If the judge announces a decision in your favor, you should produce your prepared judgment form for the judge to sign, fill in the dollar amount awarded, and hand it to the clerk.

The Writ of Execution and Having the Sheriff or Marshal Evict

To have the clerk issue a Writ of Execution after trial, simply hand the original writ form to the court clerk after the judgment is signed and pay a writ issuance fee. (See Chapter 7 for instructions on how to fill out the writ form and what happens before and during the eviction.) The writ will be for both the money and possession parts of the judgment. A sample writ for both the possession and money parts of the judgment (following a Summary Judgment) is shown in Chapter 7. A writ to enforce a judgment obtained after trial is filled out the same way. Take the original and copies of the writ to the sheriff or marshal, along with appropriate instructions for evicting. (See Chapter 7.) We discuss collecting the money part of the judgment in the next chapter.

After the sheriff or marshal has evicted the tenant and turned possession of your property back over to you, you may find yourself stuck with property the tenant has left behind. You should not simply throw away or otherwise dispose of the property, nor should you refuse to return it because the tenant won't pay what he owes you. You do have the right to insist the tenant pay reasonable storage charges, and to hold onto the property if the tenant won't pay that. However, most of the time doing so isn't worth the trouble, and you'll be happier just to get rid of the stuff by turning it over to the tenant, no strings attached. If you wind up with property the tenant won't reclaim, you will have to hold onto it for at least 18 days, notify the tenant by mail that she can pick up the property, and auction it off if it's worth more than $300. (C.C.P. § 1174.) We discuss this at length in *The California Landlord's Law Book: Rights & Responsibilities*, Chapter 21.

Appeals

The losing party has a right of appeal, which must be filed with the clerk of the correct court within 30 days of the date of judgment. The loser appeals to the Superior Court Appellate Division.

On appeal, you or the tenant may argue only issues of law, not fact. For example, the tenant may argue that the trial court erred in refusing to hear evidence on the tenant's retaliation defense, since he was behind in the rent. This is a legal issue. But the tenant may not argue that the judge or jury was wrong in believing that you didn't retaliate against the tenant for calling the health department. This is an issue of fact. Similarly, you could argue on appeal that the judge erred in ruling your three-day notice was invalid because it didn't list all the tenants' names—an issue of law. But you couldn't argue that the judge shouldn't have believed the tenant who claimed never to have received the three-day notice—an issue of fact.

Appeals are very technical and time-consuming. You should contact a lawyer before undertaking an appeal.

Appeals by the Landlord

It very seldom makes sense for a landlord to appeal a tenant's victory. Landlords who lose unlawful detainer cases generally do so because of rulings on factual issues, for example, the judge rules that the landlord didn't properly maintain the premises or had illegal retaliation in mind when he gave the tenant a 30-day notice. As we saw above, an appeals court will not reconsider the factual rulings made by the trial judge, and an appeal of this sort of ruling is a waste of time. When landlords do lose cases on legal issues that might be argued on appeal, it is usually for technical reasons, such as the three-day notice not being in the correct form. In these cases, it usually makes more sense for the landlord, instead of filing an appeal that will likely take at least three months, to go back and correct the mistake. For example, the landlord would prepare and serve a new, proper three-day notice and begin a new unlawful detainer lawsuit.

Appeals by the Tenant

Most appeals of unlawful detainer judgments are by tenants, and many of these appeals seem designed to prolong the tenant's stay as long as possible. Filing an appeal, however, does not automatically "stay" (delay) enforcement of your Judgment for Possession of the property and rent. However, a tenant who files an appeal can ask the court for a stay pending the appeal if he is willing to pay the rent during the period of the stay.

The appeal is initiated when the tenant files a Notice of Appeal in the trial court. This is a simple one-page document that says nothing more than that the tenant appeals the judgment. After the tenant files the Notice of Appeal, he can obtain a stay only by filing a motion, which must be heard by the same judge who ruled against him. Trial judges routinely deny requests for stays and will grant them only if the tenant appears to be basing the appeal on a genuine legal issue, rather than simply stalling for time. If a tenant files a motion for a stay, you should receive written notice to appear in court to oppose the motion. In any event, a judge who grants a stay is required to condition the stay on the tenant's paying the monthly rent to the court. (C.C.P. § 1176(a).)

Whether or not a stay is granted, the tenant must prepare more documents. First, she must pay a court reporter to prepare a transcript of the trial proceedings, or file a narrative "proposed statement" of what occurred at trial. After that, the case is transferred to the appellate court, and the tenant files a "brief," her argument about why the trial judge erred. At each stage, you will be notified by mail and required to file papers of your own in response.

Tenant's Possible "Relief From Forfeiture"

Under C.C.P. § 1179, a tenant found by a court to be in breach of his or her lease can sometimes still avoid eviction by having a judge grant the tenant's "petition for relief from forfeiture." In plain English, this means that if a tenant failed to pay rent, or otherwise violated the rental agreement (say, by having a dog in violation of a no-pets clause), she could offer to pay all the back rent (or otherwise cure the violation), and pay the landlord's court costs, in exchange for being allowed to remain as a tenant—despite losing the case following a trial or even a default judgment. A judge has very wide discretion to grant or deny relief from forfeiture, and will be more inclined to do so if the tenant is facing serious hardship. This relief can apparently be done during trial or immediately after judgment in your favor against the tenant—the judgment will be nullified if the tenant pays the rent or otherwise cures the violation.

This relief from forfeiture remedy does not apply to evictions based on a 30-day or 60-day termination notice, or on expiration of a fixed-term lease. It applies only where a tenant is said to have "forfeited" his or her remaining lease term by breaching the lease, most commonly by failing to pay rent.

Up to now, tenant petitions for relief from forfeiture have been very rare, because the tenant not only had to pay the rent he or she was unable to pay earlier, but also had to prepare a rather complicated set of legal forms—none of them the fill-in-the-blanks variety you see in this book. However, effective January 2003, a tenant representing himself may make this type of request verbally, in court, if you are present—which you of course will be, in a trial of a contested case.

In addition, the law also allows the judge to suggest granting relief from forfeiture, and then to grant his or her own suggestion! (This is called granting relief "on the court's own motion.")

Because of this change in the law, there are several ways a tenant can stave off eviction: by filing a written petition for relief from forfeiture, after judgment has been entered against him by default or otherwise, or by simply asking the judge to allow him to remain in your property if he pays you the rent.

Should you receive legal papers called anything like a petition for relief from forfeiture, see a lawyer quickly—unless you don't mind the tenant staying if the tenant brings the rent up to date and pays your court costs. If the tenant or the judge brings this subject up in court during a trial in a contested case, you might not have much time to deal with the prospect, unless you ask the judge to let the case proceed to judgment, then postpone the matter for a few days to allow you to contact an attorney.

Unfortunately, we can't offer much more in the way of specific advice, since the law on this subject is fairly vague and judges have a lot of discretion in this area. In particular, the ability of judges and tenants to raise this issue verbally, and without any advance notice, is a new wrinkle whose effects on eviction lawsuits is yet to be known. ■

Collecting Your Money Judgment

After you obtain a judgment for possession of property in your unlawful detainer action, you also are awarded at least some amount of money (if only for court costs). Unfortunately, having a judgment for the payment of money is not the same as having the money itself. It is unlikely that the ex-tenant you have just evicted will be both able and willing to pay you just because you converted your legal right to be paid into a formal court order.

Nothing will happen—that is, you won't get paid—unless you pursue your claim. In fact, a judgment for money is really little more than a sort of court-sanctioned hunting license, good for ten years (and renewable for subsequent ten-year periods), that allows you to use certain techniques to collect the debt. This chapter shows you a few of those techniques.

For a much more thorough guide to finding assets, devising a collection plan, and collecting your judgment, see *How to Collect When You Win a Lawsuit in California*, by Robin Leonard (Nolo).

Collecting From Cotenants. For convenience, we talk about judgments in this chapter as if they were against only one person. Many times, though, a landlord will get a money judgment against two or more people, usually cotenants under the same rental agreement. You have the right to pursue all the debtors or just the one(s) who have assets to seize until you collect the entire amount. This is because all the debtors are said to be "jointly and severally" liable to you.

> **EXAMPLE:** Because the two tenants you sued for nonpayment of rent, Larry and Moe, were cotenants under the same written lease, you obtained a judgment against both of them. Since Larry is unemployed, you garnished Moe's wages and eventually collected the entire amount from him. This is okay; the fact that Moe wound up paying it all is between him and Larry.

Collection Strategy

Before you start trying to collect the money the tenant owes you, take a minute to assess your chances of success and devise a strategy for proceeding.

Your Chances of Collecting

Some assets are easier to grab than others. Generally, you should try to go after assets in this order:

- the tenant's security deposit
- the tenant's paycheck, then
- the tenant's bank or other deposit accounts.

In general, if you can't collect from the tenant's pay or bank account, you're probably out of luck. Most of the tenant's personal possessions are either exempt, by law, from being seized to pay a court judgment or not enough to bother.

Even if the asset is valuable, the sale of personal property, including vehicles, will often net you less than the expenses you'll have to front the sheriff for storage and auction costs. In other words, you'll wind up losing money.

Using a Collection Agency

You may have many better things to do—like running your rental business—than tracking down nonpaying tenants you've managed to evict. If you feel debt collection isn't worth the time it takes, or if your attempts at attaching wages or bank accounts are unsuccessful, you might consider turning the judgment over to a collection agency.

Generally, collection agencies take as their fee between 33% and 50% of what they collect. They do, however, typically pay fees for sheriffs or marshals, so you're not out money if you don't collect. The fee you pay a collection agency is not recoverable from the debtor. For example, if a collection agency collects a $1,000 judgment for you, pocketing $400, you get $600, but you have to give the judgment debtor full credit for the $1,000 that was collected.

Professional collection agencies would like to have you believe that only they have recourse to secret sources of information that will lead to the whereabouts or assets of a person who owes you money. This isn't true; anyone with a little ingenuity and energy can become a "skip tracer." In fact, once you learn the tricks, you will most likely tackle the task with more dedication and commitment and may well do a better job than any professional skip tracer.

Using the Tenant's Security Deposit

As mentioned, your best chance to collect the judgment lies in the security deposit the tenant put up when he moved in. If there's anything of the deposit left over after making legitimate deductions for repairs and cleaning (see *The California Landlord's Law Book: Rights & Responsibilities*, Chapter 20), you can apply it to the judgment. If the judgment is fully covered by the deposit, you're home free.

> **EXAMPLE:** You collected an $800 security deposit from Maurice when he moved in in January. When he didn't pay his $500 rent in September, you moved quickly, got a judgment for possession, and had him evicted before the end of the month. Your court costs were $180. Maurice left a broken window that cost you $30 to repair and left the carpet very dirty, necessitating professional cleaning at a cost of $75. You got a judgment of $680 (unpaid rent plus costs). You're entitled to deduct $105 for repairs and cleaning from the deposit. This leaves $695 to apply to a judgment of $680, so you will be fully compensated. The money left over after that must be promptly returned to Maurice, using the procedures outlined in *The California Landlord's Law Book: Rights & Responsibilities*, Chapter 20.

> **EXAMPLE:** In January, Francesca paid you a security deposit of $900, an amount equal to one month's rent. Because of her repeated loud parties, you gave Francesca a 30-day notice on April 5, terminating her tenancy effective May 5. Francesca refused to pay the rent for the five days in May and also refused to leave. You brought an unlawful detainer action, finally getting her evicted on May 30. You got a judgment for $750 prorated "damages" for the days she stayed after the 5th (25 days at $30/day), plus $140 court costs, for a total of $890. After deductions for cleaning and damages ($200 for carpet cleaning and furniture repair), and the ten days' rent not reflected in the judgment (10 x $30, or $300), only $400 of Francesca's security deposit remains to apply toward the judgment. You can try to have the sheriff or marshal collect the remaining $490 of the judgment as explained in the rest of this chapter.

Remember that you must still send the tenant an itemized statement showing what you did with the security deposit, even if there's nothing left of it to return to him. If you use all or part of the security deposit to satisfy your judgment, you must include this fact in your accounting to the tenant. (See *The California Landlord's Law Book: Rights & Responsibilities*, Chapter 20.) In the likely event the tenant leaves without telling you where she can be found, you will be relieved of liability if you mail the statement to the address at the property you just evicted her out of. If the tenant left a forwarding address at the post office, the mail will be forwarded.

Finding the Tenant

 Skip this section if you know where the ex-tenant works, lives, or banks.

If you can't find where your ex-tenant banks, works, or lives, you'll have to start the collection process by finding the tenant. This involves doing a little investigation before you prepare any more paperwork.

Internet

Ask any regular Internet surfer how to find a long-lost friend and he'll spout off several Internet sites that search for people. Admittedly, many of these records are out of date or incomplete, but they provide a starting place. Professional debt collectors use them all, with varying degrees of success. Here are several free Internet sites that might prove helpful as you search for your missing tenant:

- www.allonesearch.com—searches the data contained in over 400 search engines, databases, indexes, and directories
- www.merlindata.com—searches 30 million public records
- www.555-1212.com—searches phone directories
- www.databaseamerica.com—searches the national change of address registry
- www.whowhere.lycos.com—searches for phone numbers, addresses, and websites
- www.bigbook.com—searches Yellow Page directories

- www.infospace.com—searches white page directories, Yellow Page directories, and reverse directories
- www.switchboard.com—searches directory assistance listings for addresses, phone numbers, and email addresses
- www.bop.gov—search the federal Bureau of Prisons to see if your missing debtor is an inmate in a federal penitentiary
- www.ss.ca.gov—search corporation records of the California Secretary of State.

If the free sites prove fruitless, you can try searching on one or more of the Internet sites that charge for their services:

- www.informus.com—this employment screening company searches driving records, criminal records, and credit reports
- www.cdb.com—searches public records
- http://1800ussearch.com—searches public records.

Telephone Directories

If you haven't already done so, call directory assistance (area code plus 555-1212) for all areas the tenant might possibly live and ask if there is a listing.

If you get the tenant's phone number but not the address, call the number from outside the calling area so it appears on your phone bill as a long distance call. Once the bill arrives, contact your phone company. Explain that you don't recognize the number and want to find out to whom the call was made. The representative will trace the call. Usually, you will be told the name of the person the number is listed to and the person's address, unless it is an unlisted number.

Directories of Unlisted Phone Numbers

It's possible the tenant now has an unlisted phone number. Calling it "unlisted" may be a misnomer, however. Unlisted numbers don't appear in the official phone company directories. But they often show up in directories of unlisted numbers, which are compiled surreptitiously and circulate among bill collectors. You may be able to gain access to one through an auto repossessor or other person who works in the collections industry. You'll be charged as much as $100 for a copy of a directory or for the information you need. If the information is good enough, it may be worth it.

Crisscross Directories

The idea behind crisscross directories is that if you know only certain information about the tenant, you can fill in the missing pieces. For example, if you know the street on which the tenant lives, you can locate the exact address. If you know the address, you can get the phone number. If you know just the phone number, you can find the address. Some crisscross directories include a person's occupation and business name. You can also obtain the names, addresses, and phone numbers of neighbors (or former neighbors); you can then ask them for information about the tenant.

Crisscross directories are available for most major metropolitan areas. You can find them in public libraries, title companies or the county tax assessor's or recorder's office. Also, most Internet search services include a crisscross directory feature.

Voter Registration Records

Contact the registrar of voters for the city in which you suspect the tenant lives. If the tenant has registered to vote, the listing will include her name, address, phone number, birthdate, party affiliation, and date of registration. If the tenant has moved within the same county, the registrar will have the new address.

U.S. Postal Service

If the tenant has left a forwarding address with the Postal Service, you can find out what it is. Send a first-class letter to the tenant's last known address, include your own return address on the envelope's top left corner, and write "Return Service Requested" in clear, legible script directly below your address. The Postal Service will send the letter back to you, at no charge, with a sticker indicating the ex-tenant's forwarding address. (If the ex-tenant left no forwarding address, the Postal Service will stamp the letter with this information and return the letter to you.)

If you have a post office box number for the tenant, the post office will release the street address and phone number of the box holder only if the box is listed in the name of a business. Some post offices will give you this information over the phone, but often you must request it in writing. You do not have to explain why you want the information.

The post office usually won't give out an individual box holder's address unless you provide a statement that the name, address, and telephone number are needed to serve legal papers in a pending proceeding. Whether this will work depends on the post office branch, and possibly whether the person making the request is a registered process server. You may even need a court order.

Credit Reports

A credit report includes a tenant's name, address, phone number, Social Security number, and date of birth, as well as credit history and possibly employment information. A credit bureau might provide a copy of the tenant's credit report if you state that you need the information for a legitimate business purpose, such as collecting a debt. (Civ. Code § 1785.11(a)(3)(F).)

Credit bureaus typically provide credit reports to banks, credit card issuers, finance companies, mortgage lenders, landlords, and other businesses that subscribe to their credit reporting services. Credit bureaus often are unwilling to provide information to nonsubscribers; however, it can't hurt you to ask. Check your local phone book for the phone numbers of the "big three" bureaus—Experian, Equifax, or TransUnion. If you can't find a listing, check their Internet sites (www. experian.com, www.equifax.com, or www.tuc.com). Most of the information on the site is about ordering your own file or becoming a subscriber. But the bureaus constantly update their pages, and you can email their customer service departments with your inquiry.

If a bureau will provide you with a copy of the tenant's credit report, you will probably have to provide a copy of your judgment or other documents showing that you're entitled to the report. You will probably have to pay a fee of $50-$60.

Business Records

If the tenant owns a business that sells taxable goods (the sale of most goods in California is taxed), the statistics unit of the Board of Equalization (916-445-0840 or www.boe.ca.gov) will probably have information on the business.

If the tenant is one of the many of millions of Californians licensed by the Department of Consumer Affairs or another agency, location information may be easily available. Start with the Department of Consumer Affairs (800-952-5210 or www.dca.ca.gov). If another agency licenses the tenant, the Department of Consumer Affairs can provide a referral to the correct agency. Business addresses are usually listed in these records, and sometimes you'll get a home address.

If the tenant is a sole proprietor, California partnership, or member of a California partnership, you can search the fictitious name records at the clerk's office in the county in which the principal place of business is located. This lists the business's owners and their addresses.

If the tenant is a California corporation, or is the owner of a California corporation, a foreign corporation authorized to do business in California, a California limited liability company, a limited partnership, or a foreign general partnership authorized to do business in California, she must register with the Secretary of State. You can request information about the business by writing to the Secretary of State, and enclosing the complete name of the business and paying a small fee.

- **Corporations**—California Secretary of State, IRC Unit, 1500 11th Street, Sacramento, CA 95814; 916-653-7315.
- **LLCs**—California Secretary of State, LLC Unit, 1500 11th Street, Sacramento, CA 95814; 916-653-3795.
- **Partnerships**—California Secretary of State, Partnership Unit, 1500 11th Street, Sacramento, CA 95814; 916-653-3365.

You can also get this information, online and at no cost, at www.ss.ca.gov/business/business.htm.

Locating the Tenant's Assets

 If you already know where the tenant banks or works, skip to "Garnishing Wages and Bank Accounts," below.

It doesn't make much sense to prepare papers and pay filing fees for papers to collect the money part of the judgment until you locate property of the tenant that can be legally taken ("levied on") by the sheriff or marshal to apply to the judgment. The first sources of funds you should try to locate are the tenant's bank accounts and his paycheck.

The Rental Application

If you used a good rental application (like the one in the appendix of *The California Landlord's Law Book: Rights & Responsibilities*), the tenant's bank accounts and employer should be listed on it. Of course, one or both may have changed since the application was prepared. If you keep copies of your tenant's rent checks (or you have the original of a bounced check), you may have more recent information. You may also be able to get that information from your bank, although you may be charged a search fee.

The Judgment Debtor Examination

Suppose you know your ex-tenant has money in a checking account, but you don't know which bank or branch. Or perhaps you know where she lives, but not where she works and has a paycheck to garnish. Wouldn't it be nice if you could get her to sit down and answer all your questions? Happily, you can, if you know where your former tenant lives or works. You do this by going to court to conduct a "judgment debtor's examination."

The judgment debtor's examination is a proceeding in which a person against whom an unpaid judgment is entered (a "judgment debtor") is ordered to show up in court at a certain date and time to answer, under oath, your questions about income and assets. The only requirements for using this procedure are that the debtor lives or works no more than 150 miles from the courthouse, and that you not have taken a debtor's examination in the past four months. There are exceptions to these requirements. If the debtor lives more than 150 miles from the courthouse, you may schedule an examination at a closer court. If you've conducted a debtor's exam within the last 120 days, you can submit an affidavit explaining why you need to hold another exam so soon. If the tenant fails to show or refuses to answer legitimate questions about his financial affairs, he can be fined or even (rarely) jailed for a few days.

Getting a Court Date

In order to have the court issue the Order of Examination (the court order that tells the tenant to come to court for the examination), fill out a form called "Application and Order for Appearance and Examination." Once the judge has approved and signed it, the form serves as the order itself. A copy of the form is included in the forms section of the book. You can use it or a photocopy.

 A blank, tear-out version of an Application and Order for Appearance and Examination is in Appendix 3. The CD-ROM also includes this form. Instructions for using the CD are in Appendix 2.

Before you begin filling out the form, call the clerk of the court where you obtained a judgment. Find out in what courtroom or department debtor's examinations are held and ask the clerk to set a date and time for the debtor's examination. Many courts schedule debtor examinations on a particular day of the week. Some allow you to pick a convenient date yourself. Ask for a date at least four weeks away, to allow you some time to have the debtor served with the order. The debtor must be served personally at least ten days before the debtor's examination. Once you've obtained a date and time, fill out the form in the following manner.

Caption Boxes: List your name, address, phone number, court name and location, and case title and number in the boxes at the top of the form, in the same way as on the Complaint and other court forms. Just below the spaces for the names of the parties, put Xs in the boxes next to "ENFORCEMENT OF JUDGMENT" and "Judgment Debtor."

The Order: The first portion of the form below the caption boxes is the "Order to Appear for Examination," the part addressed to the debtor. List the debtor's name in Item 1. In Item 2, put an X in box "a" only. Below that, list the date and time for the examination, as well as the courtroom (or "department") number you got from the court clerk. If the address of the court is the same as that in the caption box (it usually is), check the box next to the words "shown above." If for some reason the court at which the examination is to take place has an address different from that on the caption, list that address instead.

Leave Item 3 blank unless you want someone besides the sheriff or a registered process server to serve the order on the ex-tenant. If you want someone else to serve the order (this must be an adult who isn't a party in the case), put that person's name in Item 3. Leave the date and signature blank; the judge will complete them.

AT-138, EJ-125

ATTORNEY OR PARTY WITHOUT ATTORNEY *(Name, state bar number, and address)*:	FOR COURT USE ONLY
Lenny D. Landlord 12345 Angeleno Street Los Angeles, CA 90010	

TELEPHONE NO.: 213-555-6789   FAX NO.:

ATTORNEY FOR *(Name)*: Plaintiff in Pro Per

NAME OF COURT: SUPERIOR COURT OF CALIFORNIA, COUNTY OF LOS ANGELES
STREET ADDRESS: 110 North Grand Avenue
MAILING ADDRESS: Same
CITY AND ZIP CODE: Los Angeles, CA 90012
BRANCH NAME: CENTRAL DISTRICT/DOWNTOWN BRANCH

PLAINTIFF: LENNY D. LANDLORD

DEFENDANT: TERRENCE D. TENANT, TILLIE D. TENANT

APPLICATION AND ORDER FOR APPEARANCE AND EXAMINATION	CASE NUMBER:
[X] **ENFORCEMENT OF JUDGMENT** [ ] **ATTACHMENT (Third Person)** [X] **Judgment Debtor** [ ] **Third Person**	A-12345-B

ORDER TO APPEAR FOR EXAMINATION

1. TO *(name)*: Terrence D. Tenant, Tillie D. Tenant
2. YOU ARE ORDERED TO APPEAR personally before this court, or before a referee appointed by the court, to
   a. [X] furnish information to aid in enforcement of a money judgment against you.
   b. [ ] answer concerning property of the judgment debtor in your possession or control or concerning a debt you owe the judgment debtor.
   c. [ ] answer concerning property of the defendant in your possession or control or concerning a debt you owe the defendant that is subject to attachment.

Date: November 1, 20xx   Time: 9:00 A.M.   Dept. or Div.: 3   Rm.:
Address of court [X] shown above   [ ] is:

3. This order may be served by a sheriff, marshal, registered process server, **or** the following specially appointed person *(name)*:

Date: _____

_____
JUDGE OR REFEREE

This order must be served not less than 10 days before the date set for the examination.
IMPORTANT NOTICES ON REVERSE

APPLICATION FOR ORDER TO APPEAR FOR EXAMINATION

4. [X] Judgment creditor   [ ] Assignee of record   [ ] Plaintiff who has a right to attach order
   applies for an order requiring *(name)*: Terrence D. Tenant, Tillie D. Tenant   to appear and furnish information
   to aid in enforcement of the money judgment or to answer concerning property or debt.
5. The person to be examined is
   a. [X] the judgment debtor.
   b. [ ] a third person (1) who has possession or control of property belonging to the judgment debtor or the defendant or (2) who owes the judgment debtor or the defendant more than $250. An affidavit supporting this application under Code of Civil Procedure section 491.110 or 708.120 is attached.
6. The person to be examined resides or has a place of business in this county or within 150 miles of the place of examination.
7. [ ] This court is **not** the court in which the money judgment is entered or *(attachment only)* the court that issued the writ of attachment. An affidavit supporting an application under Code of Civil Procedure section 491.150 or 708.160 is attached.
8. [ ] The judgment debtor has been examined within the past 120 days. An affidavit showing good cause for another examination is attached.

I declare under penalty of perjury under the laws of the State of California that the foregoing is true and correct.

Date: October 10, 20xx

Lenny D. Landlord
_____
(TYPE OR PRINT NAME)

▶ *Lenny D. Landlord*
_____
(SIGNATURE OF DECLARANT)

(Continued on reverse)

Form Adopted for Mandatory Use Judicial Council of California AT-138, EJ-125 [Rev. July 1, 2000]	**APPLICATION AND ORDER FOR APPEARANCE AND EXAMINATION** (Attachment—Enforcement of Judgment)	Code of Civil Procedure, §§ 491.110, 708.110, 708.120

The Application: The second part of the form, below the order, is the application for issuance of the order. In Item 1, put an X in the box next to the words "Judgment creditor" (you), and fill in the ex-tenant's name in the blank. In Item 2, put an X in the first box, before the words "judgment debtor" (tenant) only. Fill in the date and your name and sign the application.

Make at least three copies of the form, being sure to copy both sides. (The reverse contains important warnings to the debtor about failure to appear as ordered, and the order is void without this information.) Take the original and the copies to the court clerk, who will have the original signed by the judge and file it. You can either pick up the file-stamped copies later or give the clerk a self-addressed, stamped envelope to mail the copies to you. One of these copies must be personally served on the debtor.

Having a Copy Served on the Debtor

You must make arrangements to have the Order of Examination served on the debtor. Unlike most other legal documents, an Order of Examination must be served by a sheriff, marshal, or registered private process server unless you listed someone else's name in Item 3 of the Order. As a general rule, private process servers are faster and more aggressive—but also more expensive—than using a sheriff or marshall. Give the process server the debtor's home or business address as well as the best time to serve him. Make sure the process server understands that service must be completed at least ten days before the date of the examination.

About two weeks before the hearing, call the process server to see if the Order of Examination has been served. If it has, make sure the process server has filed a Proof of Service with the court. (Most process servers have their own form for this.) Or, have the process server give you the filled-out form, and file it with the court yourself. The Proof of Service should be filed at least five days before the date of the examination. Some courts cancel the debtor's examination if you don't file the Proof of Service on time; check with your court if you're running late. If the process server has been unable to serve the paper at least ten days before the hearing, you'll have to call the court clerk to ask that the examination be taken "off calendar" and to get a new date at least two to three weeks off. Unless the court will let you change the date, you'll have to prepare and submit a new application form, with the new date, and try again.

What to Ask at the Examination

Our form Questionnaire for Judgment-Debtor Examination gives some sample questions to ask the debtor. Go through them carefully before the hearing and ask only those that apply. Use a photocopy of the form to list the answers to the questions. Don't feel intimidated by the length of this questionnaire; many questions will not apply.

A blank, tear-out version of Questionnaire for Judgment-Debtor Examination is in Appendix 3. The CD-ROM also includes this form. Instructions for using the CD are in Appendix 2.

On the day of the examination, appear in court prepared to meet the debtor. If she doesn't show, the judge may reschedule the examination or issue a "bench warrant" for her arrest. To have a bench warrant issued, you will have to complete a form and return it to the court with a fee of $20 to have the sheriff or marshal serve it.

When your case is called, you and the debtor should come forward. The debtor will be ordered to take an oath and answer your questions about her income or assets. The two of you will probably be directed to a spare room or some part of the courthouse, perhaps just the benches down the hall (or seats right in the courtroom if it isn't being used for something else). Should the debtor refuse to give you straight answers, tell her you're going back to the courtroom to ask the judge to order her to answer. If she refuses to come back to the courtroom for this, or simply wanders off, you can ask the judge to order the bailiff to bring her back— or issue an arrest warrant if she skips out altogether.

Important. There is one question you don't want to overlook: "Do you have any money with you today?" If the answer is "no," you have the right to insist that the debtor show you his empty wallet to make sure. If the debtor has money, you can ask the judge to order that it be turned over to you on the spot. The judge has the power to order the debtor to do this, but may allow the debtor to keep some of it for essentials. Ask also if the debtor has his checkbook with him. If he does and knows the balance in

EJ-130

ATTORNEY OR PARTY WITHOUT ATTORNEY *(Name, state bar number and address):*	FOR COURT USE ONLY

ATTORNEY OR PARTY WITHOUT ATTORNEY *(Name, state bar number and address):*

Lenny D. Landlord
12345 Angeleno Street
Los Angeles, CA 90010

TELEPHONE NO. : (213) 555-6789   FAX NO. *(Optional):*

E-MAIL ADDRESS *(Optional):*

ATTORNEY FOR *(Name):* Plaintiff in Pro Per

[ ] ATTORNEY FOR [X] JUDGMENT CREDITOR [ ] ASSIGNEE OF RECORD

SUPERIOR COURT OF CALIFORNIA, COUNTY OF LOS ANGELES

STREET ADDRESS:

MAILING ADDRESS: 110 North Grand Avenue

CITY AND ZIP CODE: Los Angeles, CA 90012

BRANCH NAME: CENTRAL DISTRICT/DOWNTOWN BRANCH

PLAINTIFF: LENNY D. LANDLORD

DEFENDANT: TERRENCE D. TENANT
TILLIE D. TENANT

WRIT OF

[X] **EXECUTION (Money Judgment)**
[ ] **POSSESSION OF** [ ] **Personal Property**
        [ ] **Real Property**
[ ] **SALE**

CASE NUMBER:

A-12345-B

1. **To the Sheriff or any Marshal or Constable of the County of:** Los Angeles

You are directed to enforce the judgment described below with daily interest and your costs as provided by law.

2. **To any registered process server:** You are authorized to serve this writ only in accord with CCP 699.080 or CCP 715.040.

3. *(Name):* Lenny D. Landlord
is the [X] judgment creditor [ ] assignee of record   whose address is shown on this form above the court's name.

4. **Judgment debtor** *(name and last known address):*

Tillie D. Tenant
6789 Angel Street, Apt. 10
Los Angeles, CA 90010

Terrence D. Tenant
6789 Angel Street, Apt. 10
Los Angeles, CA 90010

[ ] additional judgment debtors on next page

5. **Judgment entered** on *(date):*
6. [X] **Judgment renewed** on *(dates):*
    Sept. 9, 20xx
7. **Notice of sale** under this writ
  a. [ ] has not been requested.
  b. [X] has been requested *(see next page).*
8. [ ] Joint debtor information on next page.

[SEAL]

9. [ ] See next page for information on real or personal property to be delivered under a writ of possession or sold under a writ of sale.
10. [ ] This writ is issued on a sister-state judgment.
11. Total judgment . . . . $ 1,120.00
12. Costs after judgment (per filed order or memo CCP 685.090) . . . . $ 0.00
13. Subtotal *(add 11 and 12)* . . . . $ 1,120.00
14. Credits . . . . $
15. Subtotal *(subtract 14 from 13)* . . . . . $ 1,120.00
16. Interest after judgment (per filed affidavit CCP 685.050) . . . . $
17. Fee for issuance of writ . . . . $ 0.00
18. **Total** *(add 15, 16, and 17)* . . . . . . $ 7.00
    1,127.00
19. Levying officer:
  (a) Add daily interest from date of writ *(at the legal rate on 15)* of. . . . . $ 0.31
  (b) Pay directly to court costs included in 11 and 17 (GC 6103.5, 68511.3; CCP 699.520(i)) . . . . $ 0.00
20. [ ] The amounts called for in items 11-19 are different for each debtor. These amounts are stated for each debtor on Attachment 20.

Issued on *(date):*   Clerk, by   , Deputy

NOTICE TO PERSON SERVED: SEE NEXT PAGE FOR IMPORTANT INFORMATION.

Page 1 of 2

Form Approved for Optional Use
Judicial Council of California
EJ-130 [Rev. January 1, 2003]

WRIT OF EXECUTION

Code of Civil Procedure, §§ 699.520, 712.010, 715.010

the account, you may be able to get the judge to order him to write you a check—which you should cash at his bank immediately after the hearing. If you put it in your account, chances are the debtor's account will be closed before the check can be presented for collection. You can even ask the judge to order the debtor to turn over to you any jewelry, cell phone, laptop computer, or other goods the tenant unthinkingly brings to the exam.

Once you've found out where the former tenant banks or works, you're ready to go after his bank account or paycheck. See the discussion just below.

Garnishing Wages and Bank Accounts

This section describes your next step: how to prepare the proper documents to give to the sheriff or marshal. These are:

- a Writ of Execution, and
- written instructions to the sheriff or marshal (or, if you're going after wages, an Application for Earnings Withholding Order).

Once you start emptying a tenant's bank account or garnishing his wages, you may have only to wait a few weeks before the money from the marshal or sheriff comes in the mail.

Preparing the Writ of Execution

The Writ of Execution for the money part of the judgment allows the sheriff or marshal to take all the money out of the tenant's bank savings or checking account (up to the amount of the judgment, of course) or to order an employer to take up to 25% out of the tenant's paycheck.

Once issued by the court, the Writ of Execution remains valid for 180 days.

You prepare the Writ of Execution for a money judgment in the same manner as the Writ of Possession of the premises (see Chapter 7), with the following exceptions.

Check the "EXECUTION (Money Judgment)" box, rather than the "POSSESSION OF" and "Real Property" boxes in the top part of the form.

In Item 1, fill in the county in which the levy will take place, regardless of what county the judgment was entered in.

Leave all of Item 9 blank.

In Item 11, list the total judgment that was awarded as rent, damages, and costs.

Item 12 is filled in as zero ("0.00"), since it refers to certain costs incurred to collect a judgment. You must file special papers to be entitled to receive postjudgment costs.

In Item 13, fill in the same amount that you listed for Item 11.

In Item 14, credit should be given for any payments made by the tenant toward the judgment. Be sure to apply any amount of the security deposit left over after deducting for cleaning, damages, and any rent not reflected in the judgment. (See *The California Landlord's Law Book: Rights & Responsibilities*, Chapter 20.)

After subtracting any partial payments and other credits, fill in the balance in Item 15.

Fill in "0.00" in Item 16. Again, you must file special papers with the court before you're entitled to receive postjudgment interest.

In item 17, enter $7.00, the fee for issuance of this writ of execution (the fee for the issuance of the first writ, for possession, should be included in the judge's award of costs).

Add the amounts in Items 15–17 together, putting the sum in Item 18.

Finally, calculate the daily interest on the judgment at the rate of 10%. (This can add up, since it may take a long time to collect the judgment.) Multiply the amount in Item 15 by 0.10 to get the yearly interest, then divide this amount by 365 to get the daily interest amount. List this amount in Item 19a. List 0.00 in Item 19b. Item 19b tells the sheriff or marshal to collect for the county any court fees that were waived for the plaintiff on account of indigency. Since you as a rental property owner almost certainly cannot claim you're indigent, this figure should be zero.

A sample money judgment Writ of Execution is shown above.

When your writ is filled out, make four copies (remember to copy the back side) and ask the court clerk to open the file, check the judgment, and issue the Writ of Execution. After collecting the $7.00 writ-issuance fee from you, the clerk will stamp the original writ with the date and a court seal, stamp the copies with the date (but not the court seal), and hand you back both the original and copies. The original and three copies are given to the sheriff or marshal. Keep one copy for your records.

Bank Accounts

Before you waste the fees you'll have to pay the sheriff, call the ex-tenant's bank and ask if there's money in the account.

Although banks are forbidden to tell you specifically how much money an individual has in her checking account, virtually all banks will respond to a telephone request as to whether a particular check is good. For example, if you call the bank and ask whether your "$100 check from Skelly Jones, Account No. 123-45678, is good," a bank employee will normally answer "Yes" or "No." Some banks give this type of information over an atutomated telephone answering system.

To get cash in a bank account, start by calling the sheriff or marshal in the county in which the account is located. Make sure that the office serves bank levies; in a few counties, you must hire a registered process server. Give the original and three copies of the Writ of Execution to the sheriff, marshal or registered process server, along with the necessary fee (about $40 as of this writing, but call ahead to get the exact amount) and a letter or filled-out "instructions" form. Most sheriff's or marshal's departments have their own form, which they like you to use. If you use a simple letter, it should look like the one below.

After the sheriff, marshal, or process server serves the necessary papers on the bank, the bank will hold the money for ten days, then pay it over to the county sheriff or marshal. After a few more weeks, the sheriff or marshal will forward the money to you, provided the tenant hasn't filed a "Claim of Exemption." (See "If the Debtor Files a Claim of Exemption," below.)

Sample Instructions to Sheriff for Writ of Execution

September 15, 20xx

Lenny Landlord
12345 Angeleno Street
Los Angeles, CA 90010

Los Angeles County Sheriff
111 N. Hill Street
Los Angeles, California 90012

Re: Lenny Landlord v. Terrence D. Tenant and Tillie D. Tenant
     Los Angeles County Superior Court No. A-12345-B

Enclosed are the original and three copies of a Writ of Execution issued by the municipal court, and a check in the amount of $40. Please levy on all monies of the judgment debtors Terrence D. Tenant and Tillie D. Tenant at the West Los Angeles branch of First National Bank, 123 First Street, Los Angeles, California.

Sincerely,

Lenny D. Landlord

Lenny D. Landlord

Wages

The law allows you to have the sheriff or marshal order the judgment debtor's employer to withhold up to 25% of her wages each pay period to satisfy a judgment. (If the person has a very low income, the amount you can recover can be considerably less than 25%.) Also, you may have to wait in line if other creditors got to the employer first. So if you know where your ex-tenant works (and he doesn't quit or declare bankruptcy when you start garnishing his paycheck), you may be able to collect the entire judgment, though it may take a while before all the money dribbles in.

ATTORNEY OR PARTY WITHOUT ATTORNEY *(Name and Address)*:	TELEPHONE NO.:	LEVYING OFFICER *(Name and Address)*:

Lenny D. Landlord   (213) 555-6789
12345 Angeleno Street
Los Angeles, CA 90010

ATTORNEY FOR *(Name)*:   Plaintiff in Pro Per

NAME OF COURT, JUDICIAL DISTRICT OR BRANCH COURT, IF ANY:
Superior Court of California, County of Los
Angeles, Los Angeles Division

PLAINTIFF: Lenny D. Landlord

DEFENDANT: Terrence D. Tenant, Tillie D. Tenant

APPLICATION FOR EARNINGS WITHHOLDING ORDER (Wage Garnishment)	LEVYING OFFICER FILE NO.:	COURT CASE NO.: A-12345-B

TO THE SHERIFF OR ANY MARSHAL OR CONSTABLE OF THE COUNTY OF Los Angeles
OR ANY REGISTERED PROCESS SERVER

1. The judgment creditor *(name)*: Lenny D. Landlord

requests issuance of an Earnings Withholding Order directing the employer to withhold the earnings of the judgment debtor (employee).

Name and address of employer

Ernie Employer
123 Business Lane
Los Angeles, CA

Name and address of employee

Terrence D. Tenant
6789 Angel Street, Apt. 10
Los Angeles, CA 90010

Social Security Number *(if known)*:   555-12-3456

2. The amounts withheld are to be paid to
  a. [X] The attorney (or party without an attorney)   b. [ ] Other *(name, address, and telephone)*:
      named at the top of this page.

3. a. Judgment was entered on *(date)*: September 6, 20xx
  b. Collect the amount directed by the Writ of Execution unless a lesser amount is specified here:
    $

4. [ ] The Writ of Execution was issued to collect delinquent amounts payable for the **support** of a child, former spouse, or spouse of the employee.

5. [ ] Special instructions *(specify)*:

6. *(Check a or b)*
  a. [X] I have not previously obtained an order directing this employer to withhold the earnings of this employee.
     —OR—
  b. [ ] I have previously obtained such an order, but that order *(check one)*:
     [ ] was terminated by a court order, but I am entitled to apply for another Earnings Withholding Order under the provisions of Code of Civil Procedure section 706.105(h).
     [ ] was ineffective.

Lenny D. Landlord   ▶ *Lenny D. Landlord*
....   _____
(TYPE OR PRINT NAME)   *(SIGNATURE OF ATTORNEY OR PARTY WITHOUT ATTORNEY)*

I declare under penalty of perjury under the laws of the State of California that the foregoing is true and correct.
Date: October 10, 20xx
.......Lenny D. Landlord....................   ▶ *Lenny D. Landlord*
....   _____
(TYPE OR PRINT NAME)   *(SIGNATURE OF DECLARANT)*

Form Adopted by the
Judicial Council of California
982.5(1) [Rev. January 1, 1993]

APPLICATION FOR EARNINGS WITHHOLDING ORDER
(Wage Garnishment)

CCP 706.121

Like double checking on bank accounts, it's a good idea to check to see if the debtor is still employed before paying fees to the sheriff or marshal. You can easily check on whether a tenant is employed at a particular business. Call the personnel department and simply state that you'd like to "verify the employment of Emmett Employee." If the tenant no longer works there, ask to speak to his former supervisor or someone in that person's department, who may have been contacted by a more recent employer following through on a reference. Also, people who once worked together sometimes keep in touch for years afterwards. You'll get the most information if you assume a polite, friendly approach. If you're asked why you need the information, you can truthfully say that you're the ex-tenant's former landlord and that you need his new address so you can send him an accounting of his security deposit.

To initiate a wage garnishment, start by completing an Application for Earnings Withholding Order.

A blank, tear-out version of an Application for Earnings Withholding Order is in Appendix 3. The CD-ROM also includes this form. Instructions for using the CD are in Appendix 2.

List your name and the usual information about the court name and address, the names of the parties, and the case number in the boxes at the top of the form. In the box at the upper right-hand corner, list the name and address of the office of the sheriff or marshal. Be sure also to enter the name of the county where the debtor is employed below these boxes, just before Item 1.

List your name in Item 1, and the names and addresses of the debtor and his employer in the boxes below that. You must provide the employer's street address; a mailing address isn't enough. Below the box at the right for the employee/debtor's name and address is a space for her Social Security number, if known.

Put an X in box 2a to indicate that the funds are to be paid to you. In Item 3a, list the date the judgment was entered. Leave Item 3b blank unless for some reason you aren't owed the full amount listed in the Writ of Execution. Check Item 6a if this is your first wage garnishment. Or check the appropriate boxes in Item 6b to reflect previous wage garnishment attempts you have made. Finally, type your name and sign twice at the bottom, listing the date as well.

Call the sheriff or marshal for the county in which the judgment debtor works and find out if they serve wage garnishments, or whether you must use a registered process server. Also, find out the fee for a wage garnishment. Forward the original and three copies of the Writ of Execution, a check for the required fee, a letter of instructions, and the completed Application for Earnings Withholding Order.

Sample Instructions to Marshal for Application for Earnings Withholding Order

October 10, 20xx

Lenny Landlord
12345 Angeleno Street
Los Angeles, CA 90010

Office of the Marshal
Los Angeles Division, Los Angeles County
110 N. Hill Street
Los Angeles, CA 90012

Re: Landlord v. Tenant
     Los Angeles Superior Court Case No. A-12345-B

Enclosed is an Application for Earnings Withholding Order, an original and three copies of a Writ of Execution from the Superior Court for the Los Angeles Division, and a check for $XX.00. Please levy on the wages of Terrence D. Tenant, who is employed at Ernie Employer, 123 Business Lane, Los Angeles, California.

Sincerely,
Lenny D. Landlord
Lenny D. Landlord

The original goes to the sheriff or marshal of the county in which the employer is located or to a registered process server, if required by county policies. Send along the original and three copies of the Writ of Execution and the appropriate fee. The fee varies from county to county, so call the marshal or sheriff's civil division to find out the amount.

The debtor's wages should be levied on until you are paid in full unless:

- the debtor successfully claims an exemption (see below)

- someone else already has effected a wage garnishment
- your garnishment is supplanted by a support order (for example, for child support)
- the debtor stops working at that place of employment, or
- the debtor declares bankruptcy. (See Chapter 10 for your options if the tenant declares bankruptcy.)

Seizing Other Property

Although it's not likely to be worth the time and trouble, you may want to try to seize property of the debtor if you haven't gotten the whole judgment paid yet.

Motor Vehicles

To find out whether it is worth the time and trouble to have the tenant's vehicle seized and sold at an auction to pay off the judgment, first find out its market value. Go to your local library and check the most recent edition of the *Kelly Blue Book* (published monthly), check online (www.kbb.com), or check newspaper want ads for the price of similar vehicles. If the value isn't at least $2,500, forget it. Even if the vehicle is paid off, the owner/debtor is legally entitled to the first $2,300 of the proceeds. Sheriff's storage and sales charges, which you'll have to pay for up front, will run at least $300, and likely more.

If the "legal owner" of the vehicle is the bank or finance company that loaned the money to buy the vehicle, the situation is even worse. If you have the car sold, the legal owner (who normally has the right to repossess if payments aren't made) is entitled to be paid what it is owed out of the proceeds of the sale. This amount is called the "payoff figure"; it may well equal, or even exceed, the sale value of the vehicle. If it does, a levy and sale of a debtor's vehicle will net you no money and you'll be out substantial costs. Here are a few examples.

> **EXAMPLE:** You have a judgment against your former tenant Skip, the owner of a three-year-old Chevrolet with a book value of $5,000. The DMV informs you, in its response to your Vehicle Registration Information Request, that the legal owner is General Motors Acceptance Corp. in San

Jose. You call GMAC, giving the owner's name, license plate number, and V.I.N. (serial) number (if you have it), and ask for a "payoff figure." They tell you it's $3,500. This means that even if the vehicle is sold for $4,500 at a sheriff's auction, GMAC will get the first $3,500. Since Skip is entitled to the $2,300 exemption, the remaining $1,000 will go to him, and you'll get nothing. Moreover, you'll be out the $300 you fronted to the sheriff for service, storage, and sales costs.

> **EXAMPLE:** The legal owner of Darlene's four-year-old Honda is Household Finance. Household Finance tells you the payoff figure is $3,000. The book value of the vehicle is $7,000, but at a sheriff's auction it might not net more than $5,000, leaving only $2,000 after the legal owner is paid off. Subtract the $2,300 exemption that goes to Darlene, and that leaves you with $100—less any storage and sale costs you've paid. Of course, if your auction sale price of $5,000 was overly optimistic—and the car only netted $4,000—you would get nothing and be out the costs of storage and sale.

As the above examples show, levying on a vehicle can actually cost you money. Most owners of new autos owe more on them than they could sell them for at an auction. By the time the loan is paid off, the auction value of the vehicle is fairly low, and might not be enough over $2,300 to be profitable for you. As a general rule, you should forget about having the debtor's vehicle seized and sold unless its fair market value is at least $2,500 to $3,000 above what the debtor still owes on it.

If you decide it's worthwhile, give the original and at least two copies of the Writ of Execution to the sheriff or marshal, along with your letter or other written instructions requesting a levy on defendant's automobile. Be sure to give the description and license number of the vehicle and say where and when it can be found on a street or other public place (the sheriff cannot go into a private garage or warehouse). You will also need to give the sheriff or marshal a check for the total amount of the fees and deposit for towing and storage; check to find out how much this will be.

Instructions to Sheriff for Levying on a Vehicle

November 1, 20xx

Cruz Creditor
123 Market Street
Monterey, California

Monterey County Sheriff
P.O. Box 809
Salinas, CA 93902

Re: Creditor v. Debtor
Monterey County Superior Court
Case No. 2468-C

As instructed yesterday by a member of your office staff, I am enclosing a deposit check for $300 and an original and three copies of a writ of execution in the above-entitled case.

Please levy on the automobile of judgment debtor Dale Debtor; the vehicle is a 1992 Cadillac El Dorado sedan, license number 1SAM123. It is normally parked in front of the debtor's residence address of 12345 East Main Street, Salinas, California. Please call me at 408-555-5678 if you have any questions.

Sincerely,

Cruz Creditor

Cruz Creditor

Be patient, because the whole process could easily take several months. First, it may take up to several weeks for the sheriff or marshal to arrange for a tow truck to be present when the vehicle is available and not locked in a garage. Second, once it's picked up, it will take at least a month to auction it off (unless the debtor redeems the vehicle by paying off the judgment, which sometimes happens). Finally, once the sheriff gets the money from the auction, he will hold it for about another month after paying off the towing and storage charges and any loan.

Identifying the Legal Owner of a Vehicle

You may be able to identify the legal owner of your ex-tenant's vehicle by filing a Vehicle Registration Information Request with the DMV. But before the DMV releases that information, it allows the ex-tenant the opportunity to object to having the information released. Since most debtors won't let the DMV release information to you, a debtor's examination may be a better bet. (See above.)

Other Personal Property

As mentioned, most of your tenant's personal property is probably protected from creditors. Here is a list of statutorily exempt property (these limits change every three years, with the next change scheduled for 2007). (All references are to the California Code of Civil Procedure.)

- motor vehicles, up to a net equity (market value less payoff) of $2,300 (§ 704.010)
- household items, including furniture, appliances, and clothing that are "ordinarily and reasonably necessary" (§ 704.020)
- materials to be used for repair or maintenance of a residence, up to a net equity of $2,425 (§ 704.030)
- jewelry, heirlooms, and artworks, up to a net value of $6,075 (§ 704.040)
- health aids (§ 704.050)
- tools used in a trade or business, up to a net value of $6,075 for each spouse in business (§ 704.060)
- 75% of wages or up to 30 times the federal minimum wage, whichever is greater (§ 704.070)
- Bank deposits from the Social Security Administration to $2,425 ($3,650 for husband and wife); unlimited if SS funds are not commingled with other funds. Bank deposits of other public benefits to $1,225 ($1,825 for husband and wife) (§ 704.080)
- jail or prison inmate's trust account, up to $1,225 (§ 704.090)

EJ-100

ATTORNEY OR PARTY WITHOUT ATTORNEY *(Name, State Bar number, and address):*

After recording return to:

> **fill in caption boxes and case number**

TELEPHONE NO.:

FAX NO. *(Optional)*:

E-MAIL ADDRESS *(Optional)*:

ATTORNEY FOR *(Name):*   Plaintiff in Pro Per

SUPERIOR COURT OF CALIFORNIA, COUNTY OF

STREET ADDRESS:

MAILING ADDRESS:

CITY AND ZIP CODE:

BRANCH NAME:

FOR RECORDER'S OR SECRETARY OF STATE'S USE ONLY

PLAINTIFF:

DEFENDANT: **indicate whether judgment completely or partially paid**

CASE NUMBER:

FOR COURT USE ONLY

ACKNOWLEDGMENT OF SATISFACTION OF JUDGMENT

☐ FULL   ☐ PARTIAL   ☐ MATURED INSTALLMENT

> **check box a and box (1) if judgment is paid in full**

Satisfaction of the judgment is acknowledged as follows:

☐ Full satisfaction

   (1) ☐ Judgment is satisfied in full.

   (2) ☐ The judgment creditor has accepted payment or performance other than that specified in the judgment in full satisfaction of the judgment.

> **check box b if judgment is partially paid**

☐ Partial satisfaction

   The amount received in partial satisfaction of the judgment is $

☐ Matured installment

   All matured installments under the installment judgment have been satisfied as of *(date):*

2. Full name and address of judgment creditor:*

> **type your name and address**

3. Full name and address of assignee of record, if any:

> **type "N/A"**

4. Full name and address of judgment debtor being fully or partially released:*

> **type tenant's name and address**

5. a. Judgment entered on *(date):*   **fill in date of judgment**

   b. ☐ Renewal entered on *(date):*

6. ☐ An ☐ abstract of judgment ☐ certified copy of the judgment has been recorded as follows *(complete all information for each county where recorded):*

     COUNTY   DATE OF RECORDING   INSTRUMENT NUMBER

> **leave items 6 and 7 blank**

7. ☐ A notice of judgment lien has been filed in the office of the Secretary of State as file number *(specify):*

NOTICE TO JUDGMENT DEBTOR: If this is an acknowledgment of full satisfaction of judgment, it will have to be recorded in each county shown in item 6 above, if any, in order to release the judgment lien, and will have to be filed in the office of the Secretary of State to terminate any judgment lien on personal property.

Date: **sign and date form**

▸ _____

*(SIGNATURE OF JUDGMENT CREDITOR OR ASSIGNEE OF CREDITOR OR ATTORNEY**)*

Page 1 of 1

*The names of the judgment creditor and judgment debtor must be stated as shown in any Abstract of Judgment which was recorded and is being released by this satisfaction. ** A separate notary acknowledgment must be attached for each signature.

Form Approved for Optional Use
Judicial Council of California
EJ-100 [Rev. January 1, 2005]

ACKNOWLEDGMENT OF SATISFACTION OF JUDGMENT

Code of Civil Procedure, §§ 724.060, 724.120, 724.250

- matured life insurance benefits needed for support; unmatured life insurance policy cash surrender value completely exempt; loan value exempt to $9,700 (§ 704.100)
- retirement benefits paid by a public entity (§ 704.110)
- vacation credits payable to a public employee; if receiving installments, at least 75% (§ 704.113)
- private retirement benefits, including IRAs and Keoghs (§ 704.115)
- unemployment, disability, and strike benefits (§ 704.120)
- health or disability insurance benefits (§ 704.130)
- personal injury or wrongful death damages (§§ 704.140, 704.150)
- workers' compensation benefits (§ 704.160)
- welfare benefits and aid from charitable organizations (§ 704.170)
- relocation benefits paid by government entity (§ 704.180)
- student financial aid (§ 704.190)
- burial plots (§ 704.200)
- bank account and cash traceable to an exempt asset (§ 703.080)
- business licenses, except liquor licenses (§§ 695.060, 708.630).

Real Estate

Don't overlook the possibility that the ex-tenant owns or might purchase real estate. Putting a lien on real estate is simple and inexpensive, and it will likely get you results if the debtor wants to sell or refinance the property. The process is explained in *How to Collect When You Win a Lawsuit in California*, by Robin Leonard (Nolo).

If the Debtor Files a Claim of Exemption

There are several legal maneuvers a debtor can use to delay or even stop the collection process. The most common is the filing, with the sheriff or marshal, of a simple form known as a Claim of Exemption. In it, a debtor claims that the bank account, paycheck, or property being subjected to garnishment is legally exempt from execution to satisfy a judgment or that she needs her wages to support her and her family.

For example, an ex-tenant whose bank account is attached might claim that the funds in the account consist entirely of funds that are exempt by law, such as welfare or Social Security payments. Another exemption commonly claimed is that the debtor has insufficient funds to provide for "ordinary necessities" of life. A judgment debtor may not claim this type of exemption if the debt was itself incurred to pay for necessities of life—like rent. What this means in practice is that it's improper for your ex-tenant to claim a hardship exemption to avoid paying a judgment for rent. However, if the tenant attempts to claim this exemption anyway (easy to do on the standard fill-in-the-blanks exemption forms), you have the burden of pointing out to a judge that the debtor can't claim a "necessities of life" exemption if the money you're seeking was for nonpayment of rent. If you do nothing, the tenant will be able to claim the exemption and get back any seized property or prevent a wage garnishment.

If the sheriff or marshal notifies you that the debtor has filed a Claim of Exemption, you will have to respond with a few forms of your own. If you do nothing in the face of a Claim of Exemption filed by a debtor, the sheriff or marshal will automatically treat the wages or bank account attached as legally exempt. Your response depends on what the tenant's Claim of Exemption states. A good general discussion of exemption law is contained in *Money Troubles: Legal Strategies to Cope With Your Debts,* by Robin Leonard and John Lamb (Nolo).

Once the Judgment Is Paid Off

You may be pleasantly surprised to find that through deposit credits, wage garnishments, bank account seizures, or a combination of these, your judgment is in fact paid off entirely, including interest and costs. This may take a long time, but after that, the judgment is said to be "satisfied" (even if you aren't). When this happens, you are legally required to fill out a form called an Acknowledgment of Satisfaction of Judgment and file it with the court, so that the court records no longer reflect an unpaid judgment against your ex-tenant. A sample filled-out form is shown above. Note that the form must be notarized before you file it with the court.

 A blank, tear-out version of an Acknowledgment of Satisfaction of Judgment is in Appendix 3. The CD-ROM also includes this form. Instructions for using the CD are in Appendix 2. ■

When a Tenant Files for Bankruptcy

If a tenant files for bankruptcy, all ongoing legal proceedings against him—including an eviction lawsuit—must cease until the bankruptcy court says otherwise. (11 U.S.C. § 362.) This is required under something called the "automatic stay." Any creditor who violates the stay—that is, attempts to collect from the person who declared bankruptcy ("debtor," in legalese) or pursues a legal proceeding such as eviction—can, and probably will, be fined by the bankruptcy court. The bankruptcy court might agree to remove ("lift") the automatic stay for a creditor who can show that the stay is not serving its intended purpose of freezing the debtor's assets. Getting the court to lift the stay takes time and is fairly complicated.

Because filing for bankruptcy stops dead an eviction, some tenants, attorneys, and typing services (especially in the Los Angeles area) file bankruptcies to delay eviction, rather than to erase unmanageable debt burdens or set up repayment plans. Because a debtor can begin a bankruptcy case by filing just three or four pages of documents (a legitimate bankruptcy filer must file the rest of the forms within 15 days), filing a bankruptcy petition simply to stave off an eviction is extremely easy.

Kinds of Bankruptcy

A tenant can file for different kinds of bankruptcy. The most common are Chapter 7, which erases debts completely, and Chapter 13, which lets a debtor repay a portion of his debts over three to five years. Most tenants who file bankruptcy just to delay an eviction file Chapter 7 bankruptcies, and most of this chapter's discussion assumes your tenant has filed a Chapter 7. Also possible, though very rare for residential tenants, are Chapter 11 bankruptcies (repayment plans for individuals with debts over $1 million) or Chapter 12 bankruptcies (repayment plans for family farmers). The word "chapter" refers to a particular chapter of the Bankruptcy Code, Title 11 of the U.S. Code, the federal laws that govern bankruptcy.

When a Tenant Can File for Bankruptcy

A tenant can file for bankruptcy at any time—before the tenancy begins, during the tenancy, after you've served a three-day notice, after you've filed an eviction lawsuit, or even after you've won and obtained a judgment of possession. As noted above, most commonly a tenant will file in hopes of delaying an eviction. And, as expected, these tenants wait until the last possible moment—sometimes just a day before the sheriff shows up—before filing.

If a tenant has filed for Chapter 13 bankruptcy—which can last as long as five years—the tenant's bankruptcy may have started long before you rented to her. The tenant may inform you, the court where you file the unlawful detainer action, or the sheriff or marshal of the bankruptcy only as the eviction date approaches. In this event, you may not continue until you obtain permission from the bankruptcy court.

The Automatic Stay

The Bankruptcy Abuse Prevention and Consumer Protection Act of 2005 affects the procedures landlords must follow when dealing with a tenant who has filed for bankruptcy. Generally, if a tenant has filed for either Chapter 7 or Chapter 13 bankruptcy and is behind in the rent, becomes unable to pay the rent, or violates another term of the tenancy that would justify a termination, a landlord cannot deliver a termination notice or proceed with an eviction. This prohibition is known as the "automatic stay," and it means that landlords must go to the federal bankruptcy court and ask the judge to "lift" (remove) the stay. (11 U.S.C. § 365(e).) In most cases, the judge will lift the stay within a matter of days and the landlord can proceed with a termination and eviction. (Landlords don't have to go to court if a tenant is using illegal drugs or endangering the property, as explained below in "Exceptions to Stay: Drugs or Damage to Property.")

Prebankruptcy Actions

The automatic stay does not apply, however, if the eviction lawsuit is over and the landlord obtained a judgment for possession before the tenant filed for bankruptcy. In this situation, under the Bankruptcy Abuse Prevention and Consumer Protection Act of 2005, landlords can generally proceed with the eviction without having to go to court and ask for the stay to be lifted.

In very narrow circumstances, and only for evictions based on rent nonpayment, a tenant can stop the eviction even if the landlord got a judgment before the tenant filed for bankruptcy. A tenant has only 30 days after filing for bankruptcy to try this—and must complete all three of the following steps:

- **Step One.** The tenant must file a paper with the court certifying that state law allows the tenant to avoid eviction by paying the unpaid rent, even after the landlord has won a judgment for possession. California extends this option to tenants. The certification must be served on the landlord.
- **Step Two.** The tenant must deposit with the clerk of the bankruptcy court any rent that would be due 30 days from the date the petition was filed.
- **Step Three.** The tenant must certify to the bankruptcy court (and serve the landlord with this certification) that he has paid the back rent.

At any point during the 30-day period, the landlord can file an objection to the tenant's certification. The court will hold a hearing within ten days. If the landlord convinces the judge that the tenant's certifications are not true, the court will lift the stay and the landlord can proceed to recover possession of the property.

Exceptions to Stay: Drugs or Damage to Property

Landlords sometimes need to evict a tenant who is using illegal drugs or endangering the property. If the tenant files for bankruptcy before the landlord wins a judgment for possession, the landlord can proceed with the eviction without asking the bankruptcy judge to lift the stay. Here are the specifics:

- **When the landlord has begun an eviction case but doesn't have a judgment.** Landlords must prepare a certification, or sworn statement, that they have begun an unlawful detainer case based on the tenant's endangerment of the property or use of illegal drugs (or such use by the tenant's guests).
- **When the landlord hasn't yet filed an eviction lawsuit.** Landlords must prepare a certification, or sworn statement, that the activity described above has happened within the past 30 days.

The landlord must file the certification with the bankruptcy court and serve the tenant as they would serve any legal notice. If the tenant does not file an objection within 15 days of being served, the landlord can proceed with the eviction without asking the court for relief from the stay.

A tenant who objects must file with the court, and serve on the landlord a certification challenging the truth of the landlord's certification. The bankruptcy court will hold a hearing within ten days, at which the tenant must convince the court that the situation the landlord describes did not exist or has been remedied. If the court rules for the landlord, the landlord may proceed with the eviction without asking that the stay be lifted; but if the tenant wins, the landlord may not proceed.

Finding the Right Bankruptcy Court

To file a motion in bankruptcy court to have the automatic stay lifted, you must first find out which bankruptcy court the tenant filed in. Look for the court's address and phone number on any bankruptcy paper you receive from the court, the tenant, or the tenant's bankruptcy lawyer. If you can't find the information on the papers, look for the district and branch names on the bankruptcy papers and use the chart shown here.

Once you have the phone number of the bankruptcy court, call the court clerk and ask to be sent a copy

Federal Bankruptcy Courts in California	
Central District	**Northern District**
Federal Building 300 North Los Angeles St. Los Angeles, CA 90012 213-894-3118	P.O. Box 7341 235 Pine Street, 19th Floor San Francisco, CA 94120 415-268-2300
506 Federal Building 411 West Fourth Street Santa Ana, CA 92701 714-338-5300	P.O. Box 2070 1300 Clay Street Oakland, CA 94604 510-879-3600
1415 State Street Santa Barbara, CA 93101 805-884-4800	280 South First Street Room 3035 San Jose, CA 95113 408-535-5118
3420 12th Street Riverside, CA 92501 951-774-1000	99 South E Street Santa Rosa, CA 95404 707-525-8539
Eastern District	**Southern District**
501 I Street, Suite 3-200 Sacramento, CA 95814 916-930-4400	325 West F Street San Diego, CA 92101 619-557-5620
5301 U.S. Courthouse 1130 O Street, Suite 2656 Fresno, CA 93721 559-498-7217	
P.O. Box 5276 1130-12th Street Modesto, CA 95352 209-521-5160	

of the local court rules, together with a "Relief From Stay Cover Sheet." Once you have the rules, read the section entitled "Motion Practice," "Notice," or something similar. It will tell you how the court wants motions to be filed. It's very important to follow all local court rules scrupulously; if you don't, your papers could get thrown out.

Call the clerk back and ask to "calendar" (set a date for) a court hearing on a motion for relief from the automatic stay. The clerk should give you a court date over the phone. Be sure it is enough days ahead so you have time to prepare the papers and give the tenant the number of days' written notice of your motion required by your local rules (usually ten days). Also ask the clerk for the time and location of the hearing.

Preparing the Papers

Before your court date, you must prepare these documents:

- Relief From Stay Cover Sheet
- Notice of Motion for Relief From Automatic Stay and Proof of Service
- Motion for Relief From Automatic Stay
- Declaration in Support of Motion for Relief From Automatic Stay
- Order Granting Relief From Automatic Stay.

Samples are shown below for all these forms except the Relief From Stay Cover Sheet, a preprinted form which you should get from your local court clerk. You will need to use pleading paper (the 8½" x 11" paper with the numbers down the left side) for all forms. Make copies of the blank sheet in Appendix 3.

Have the following papers in front of you when you get ready to start preparing your own documents; they contain much of the information you need:

- the tenant's bankruptcy papers that were sent to you
- the papers you filed in court for the eviction, and
- any papers the tenant filed in court to oppose the eviction.

Fill out the top of the forms accurately. Be sure the caption on the top of all the papers accurately states the bankruptcy district, the case name as indicated on the tenant's bankruptcy papers, the bankruptcy case number, and the type of bankruptcy (Chapter 7 or 13) the tenant is filing, as well as the court date, time, place

LENNY D. LANDLORD
12345 Angeleno Street
Los Angeles, CA 90010
Tel: 213-555-1234

Creditor and Moving Party in Pro Per

UNITED STATES BANKRUPTCY COURT
CENTRAL DISTRICT OF CALIFORNIA

In re:	) Case No. 292-12345-ABCDE
	)
TERRENCE D. TENANT,	) CHAPTER 7
TILLIE D. TENANT	)
	) R.S. No. _____
	)
Debtors.	) Hearing Date: 9/15/xx
	) Time: 10:00 AM

NOTICE OF MOTION FOR RELIEF FROM AUTOMATIC STAY

TO TERRENCE D. TENANT AND TILLIE D. TENANT, DEBTORS,
AND TO THEIR ATTORNEY OF RECORD:

PLEASE TAKE NOTICE that on September 15, 20xx, at 10:00 AM, in the above-entitled Court,

at 312 North Spring Street, Los Angeles, California, Creditor LENNY D. LANDLORD will move for

relief from the automatic stay herein, with regard to obtaining a judgment in state court that includes

possession of the real property at 6789 Angel Street, Apartment 10, Los Angeles, California. The

grounds for the motion are set forth in the accompanying motion and declaration.

You, and the trustee in this case, are advised that no written response is required to oppose this

motion, and that no oral testimony will normally be permitted in opposition to the motion. You and/or

your attorney, or other party including the trustee, however, must appear to oppose the motion or the

relief requested may be granted. Applicable law is 11 U.S.C. § 362, Bankruptcy Rules 4001 and 9014,

and In re Smith (C.D. Cal 1989) 105 B.R. 50, or C.C.P. § 715.050.

DATED: _August 30, 20xx_   *Lenny D. Landlord*
                                 Lenny D. Landlord
                                 Creditor in Pro Per

LENNY D. LANDLORD
12345 Angeleno Street
Los Angeles, CA 90010
Tel: 213-555-1234

Creditor and Moving Party in Pro Per

UNITED STATES BANKRUPTCY COURT
CENTRAL DISTRICT OF CALIFORNIA

, In re:	) Case No. 292-12345-ABCDE
	)
TERRENCE D. TENANT,	) CHAPTER 7
TILLIE D. TENANT	)
	) R.S. No. _____
	)
Debtors.	) Hearing Date: 9/15/xx
_____	) Time: 10:00 AM

MOTION FOR RELIEF FROM AUTOMATIC STAY

Creditor LENNY D. LANDLORD moves this Court for an Order granting relief from the automatic

stay, on the following grounds:

On September 1, 20xx, Debtors filed a petition under Chapter 7 of the U.S. Bankruptcy Code.

Debtors occupy the real property at 6789 Angel Street, Apartment 10, Los Angeles, California,

pursuant to a tenancy from month to month. Debtors failed to pay the rent of $900 for the period of

August 1, 20xx, to August 31, 20xx, and have paid no rent for any period subsequent. As a result, on

August 5, 20xx, Creditor served Debtors with a three-day notice to pay rent or quit, to which Debtors

failed to respond. Creditor filed an unlawful detainer action entitled Landlord v. Tenant, Case No.

A-12345-B, in the Superior Court of California for the County of Los Angeles, on August 9, 20xx.

Creditor obtained against Debtors a judgment for possession of the premises on August 15, 20xx.

Creditor is informed and believes that Debtors filed the petition in bankruptcy solely to avoid

execution of any judgment for possession of real property in the state court proceeding, and without

intending to seek the fresh start provided under Title 11 of the U.S. Code. In addition, as evidence of

1 bad faith in their bankruptcy filing, Debtors filed only a "skeleton petition" and listed this Creditor as

2 the only substantial creditor in the case. Creditor attaches his declaration under penalty of perjury,

3 which includes true copies of all litigation documents in the state court unlawful detainer proceeding.

4

5 DATED: __August 30, 20xx__   *Lenny D. Landlord*

6   Lenny D. Landlord
                                       Creditor in Pro Per

7

8

9

10

11

12

13

14

15

16

17

18

19

20

21

22

23

24

25

26

27

28

1 LENNY D. LANDLORD
   12345 Angeleno Street
2 Los Angeles, CA 90010
   Tel: 213-555-1234
3
4 Creditor and Moving Party in Pro Per

5

6

7

8   UNITED STATES BANKRUPTCY COURT
                         CENTRAL DISTRICT OF CALIFORNIA
9

10 In re:) Case No. 292-12345-ABCDE
)
11   TERRENCE D. TENANT,   ) CHAPTER 7
      TILLIE D. TENANT   )
12   ) R.S. No. _____
)
13   Debtors.   ) Hearing Date: 9/15/xx
   _____) Time: 10:00 AM

14

15   DECLARATION IN SUPPORT OF MOTION FOR RELIEF FROM AUTOMATIC STAY

16

17   I, LENNY D. LANDLORD, declare:

       I am over the age of 18 years. I am the moving party in the above-entitled action. If called as a
18
   witness, I could testify competently to the following:
19
       On August 9, 20xx, I caused to be filed in the Superior Court of the State of California, for the
20
   County of Los Angeles, Los Angeles Judicial District, a verified complaint in unlawful detainer, a copy
21
   of which is attached hereto as Exhibit "A." The case number is A-12345-B. All the allegations stated
22
   therein are true to my knowledge.
23
       I obtained a judgment for possession of the real property at 6789 Angel Street, Apartment 10, Los
24
   Angeles, California, in the state-court action against Debtors, on August 15, 20xx.
25
       As is indicated in the unlawful detainer complaint, the tenancy is a residential month-to-month
26
   tenancy. I am the owner of the premises. In my opinion, the rent that Debtors agreed to pay as alleged
27
   in the unlawful detainer complaint is the reasonable rental value of the premises.
28
       Debtors remain in possession of the premises. I will suffer irreparable harm if the automatic stay

1 is not vacated as to enforcement of any judgment for possession of the real property, because each

2 day I incur additional costs as the result of Debtors' nonpayment of rent and their failure to vacate

3 the premises, in that I must make mortgage payments on the property while I am unable to rent it to

4 prospective tenants, other than Debtors, who would pay rent that I could use to defray the mortgage.

5 I am informed and believe that the tenancy is not a sellable asset of the bankruptcy estate, so that

6 continued possession of the real property by Debtors is not necessary to freeze their assets for sale to

7 benefit their creditors or to effect any reorganization by Debtors.

8 I declare under penalty of perjury under the laws of the United States that the foregoing is true and

9 correct.

10

DATED: August 30, 20xx   *Lenny D. Landlord*

11   Lenny D. Landlord
                                                         Creditor in Pro Per

12

13

14

15

16

17

18

19

20

21

22

23

24

25

26

27

28

LENNY D. LANDLORD
12345 Angeleno Street
Los Angeles, CA 90010
Tel: 213-555-1234

Creditor and Moving Party in Pro Per

UNITED STATES BANKRUPTCY COURT
CENTRAL DISTRICT OF CALIFORNIA

In re:	) Case No. 292-12345-ABCDE
	)
TERRENCE D. TENANT,	) CHAPTER 7
TILLIE D. TENANT	)
	) R.S. No. _____
	)
Debtors.	) Hearing Date: 9/15/xx
	) Time: 10:00 AM

ORDER GRANTING RELIEF FROM AUTOMATIC STAY

The motion of Creditor LENNY D. LANDLORD for relief from the automatic stay under 11 U.S.C. § 362 came on for hearing in the above-entitled Court on September 15, 20xx, at 10:00 AM; the Creditor appearing in pro per. The Court having taken the matter under submission following argument,

It is hereby ordered that Creditor LENNY D. LANDLORD have relief from the automatic stay provided by Debtors' filing of the petition in this case, in that Creditor may proceed with the prosecution of the state court unlawful detainer action of Landlord v. Tenant, et al., Case No. A-12345-B, in the Superior Court of California for the County of Los Angeles, Los Angeles Division, and that Creditor may execute on any judgment for possession or restitution of the premises at 6789 Angel Street, Apartment 10, Los Angeles, California, notwithstanding the pendency of the within-entitled action.

DATED: _____, 20_____

_____
United States Bankruptcy Judge

1

PROOF OF SERVICE BY MAIL

2   My address is _____ 123 Main Street _____

3   Los Angeles _____, California.

4   On _____ August 15 _____, 20 __ xx __, I served the within: _____ Notice of Motion for _____

5   Relief From Automatic Stay, Motion for Relief From Automatic Stay, Declaration in Support of Mo-

6   tion for Relief From Automatic Stay, and Proposed Order Granting Relief from Automatic Stay

7   _____

8   _____

9   by depositing true copies thereof, enclosed in separate, sealed envelopes, with the postage thereon fully prepaid, in the

10   United States Postal Service mail in _____ Los Angeles _____ County, addressed as follows:

11   Terrence D. Tenant

     Tillie D. Tenant

12   6789 Angel Street, Apt. 10

13   Los Angeles, CA 90010

14   (Debtors)

15   Thomas T. Trustee

16   12345 Business Boulevard

     Los Angeles, CA 90010

17   (Trustee)

18

19   Lana L. Lawyer

     246 Litigation Lane

20   Los Angeles, CA 90010

21   (Debtors' Attorney)

22   I am, and was at the time herein-mentioned mailing took place, a resident of or employed in the County where

23   the mailing occurred, over the age of eighteen years old, and not a party to the within cause.

24   I declare under penalty of perjury under the laws of California and of the United States of America that the

25   foregoing is true and correct.

26   DATED: _____ August 15, 20xx _____, _____

27   *Samuel D. Server*
                                     Samuel D. Server
28

of hearing, and other information the bankruptcy court clerk has given to you. The clerk will fill in the item "R.S. No." when you file each form.

Tell the truth. The facts you state in the Motion for Relief From Automatic Stay and the Declaration in Support of Motion for Relief From Automatic Stay must be true. Remember that you are signing these documents under penalty of perjury and that it is a federal crime to lie.

You may properly state that you believe the tenant is using bankruptcy merely to avoid eviction, based simply on the timing of the bankruptcy filing while your eviction lawsuit is pending—unless you know that the tenant is honestly filing to discharge many other debts. In the Motion and Declaration, state that the tenant has filed a "skeleton petition" (the bare minimum of forms in bankruptcy court without a detailed list of assets and debts, which must be filed later) only if that is true. (You can find this out from the bankruptcy court or the tenant's bankruptcy attorney.) The same is true with respect to a bankruptcy petition that lists only a few creditors, including you. Don't state this as fact in your Motion unless you have confirmed it with the bankruptcy court.

If the tenant's bankruptcy is a Chapter 13 case, be sure to include, if true, that the tenant has not paid or offered any rent for any month after filing bankruptcy.

Filing the Papers

File the original documents, including a Proof of Service by Mail (see the next section), with the bankruptcy court. Be sure to attach relevant eviction documents to the Declaration in Support of Motion for Relief From Automatic Stay, including copies of the complaint you filed in the eviction lawsuit; the tenant's answer, if any; and any judgment. Label each attachment (on the bottom of the form) as "Exhibit A," "Exhibit B," and so on.

You can mail the documents to the bankruptcy court, but you are better off taking them in person in case you have mistakes you need to correct. In fact, if you live a great distance from the bankruptcy court, you may want to take along extra copies of pleading paper and a portable typewriter so you can fix the papers on the spot. Also, take your checkbook. You must pay a $75 filing fee, and if you have to retype any papers, the clerk will charge you 75 cents or more a page to make copies.

When making copies of your motion papers, be sure to make a set for yourself, the tenant, and anyone else who must receive copies (see the next section) and an extra few copies for the court clerk.

Mailing the Motion Papers and Preparing a Proof of Service

Someone over age 18 who isn't a party to the eviction case must mail copies of your motion papers to tenants who have filed bankruptcy; their bankruptcy attorney, if any; the "trustee" (a person appointed by the bankruptcy court to oversee the bankruptcy); and all the creditors listed on the debtor's bankruptcy papers. The trustee's and creditors' names and addresses should be listed on the tenant's bankruptcy papers; you can also get this information from the court clerk.

The person who mails the motion papers must complete and sign a Proof of Service by Mail, which you will attach to the original Notice of Motion for Relief From Automatic Stay you file with the court.

A blank, tear-out version of a Proof of Service by Mail is in Appendix 3. The CD-ROM also includes this form. Instructions for using the CD are in Appendix 2.

Prepare your forms carefully. Your documents should look something like the samples shown below. However, it is crucial that you adapt the documents according to your own particular circumstances, based on the facts you know to be true.

If You Want to Hire an Attorney

If you don't want to represent yourself in filing a motion for relief from the automatic stay, you need to hire an attorney. But be careful—not just any attorney will do. You will want to hire an attorney with experience representing creditors in bankruptcy. If you know other landlords who have used bankruptcy attorneys, call for a referral. Otherwise, look in the Yellow Pages under attorneys, subheading Bankruptcy.

Call one and ask if she handles motions for relief from automatic stays for landlords. If she says "yes," explain that a tenant filed bankruptcy to delay your eviction and that you'd like to hire the lawyer to file a motion for relief from the automatic stay. Ask her what the fee is, assuming one court appearance. Anything much above $750 is excessive. If the attorney bills by the hour, ask for an estimate of how many hours the job should take—and get it in writing before you agree.

Preparing for the Hearing

If the debtor files and sends you an opposition paper, be sure to study it before the hearing. Go through your records and jot down some notes in response to each argument the debtor raises. Get statements from appraisers stating that the tenant's rent is not below market rate to show that the lease is not a valuable asset. Make copies of your monthly mortgage payment bills to show that you are suffering a hardship because the tenant is delaying eviction with bankruptcy.

The Hearing

On the day of the hearing, arrive at the bankruptcy courtroom about a half-hour early. If there are several courtrooms, and you don't know where your motion will be heard, check the calendar that is usually posted outside each courtroom. Typically, bankruptcy courts hear many cases, and many different types of motions, on a given day and time. If a calendar is not posted, or if you can't find your case on the list, check with the court clerk.

Once you find the correct courtroom, pay attention to the cases that are called before yours—even if the motions are not similar to yours—to get a feel for how the judge conducts hearings.

When your case is called, walk up to the podium, state your name, and say that you are appearing "in pro per." If the tenants and their attorney show up, they should identify themselves, too. Since you are the party making the motion, the judge may ask you questions or ask you to speak first. Very briefly summarize the points you made in your papers and be sure you can back up your assertions. For example, you may want to say:

- The bankruptcy was filed only after you filed the unlawful detainer lawsuit in court or just before the eviction was to take place.
- The tenancy is from month to month.
- The tenancy is not a valuable asset of the bankruptcy estate because the rent you're charging is not significantly less than the fair-market rental.
- The tenant filed only a "skeleton petition," without detailed schedules of assets and liabilities.
- The tenant listed only a few creditors, including you.
- The tenant hasn't paid any rent that came due after he or she filed bankruptcy.

Whether or not the tenant shows up (many don't), the hearing will probably be very brief. The judge may ask you some questions, but hearings are not like trials. The facts supporting your motion should have been included in your declaration.

The judge will probably decide on the spot whether or not to grant the motion. If he does, ask him to use the proposed Order Granting Relief From Automatic Stay. If he won't sign this Order, ask him if he wants you to prepare one with different language, or whether he will have his own order typed up and, if so, when that will be ready.

Once the judge signs the order, give a copy of it to the court clerk or the sheriff or marshal performing the eviction. They might require a certified copy of the order. If so, you will have to pay the bankruptcy court clerk's office a small fee for a certified copy. You're now ready to proceed with your eviction. ■

Rent Control Chart

Reading Your Rent Control Ordinance

The following chart contains most of the information about how your rent control ordinance affects evictions, but we recommend that you check the ordinance itself and always make sure that it hasn't changed since this was printed. In case you are (understandably) intimidated at the prospect of deciphering your city's ordinance, here are a few hints about reading and understanding rent control ordinances.

Almost all rent control ordinances begin with a statement of purpose, followed by definitions of terms used in the ordinance. If such terms as "rental unit" and "landlord" aren't defined specifically enough to tell you who and what is covered by the ordinance, another section dealing with applicability of the ordinance usually follows. After that, the ordinance usually sets out the structure and rules of the rent board and will say whether landlords must register their properties with the board. Your ordinance probably then has a section entitled something like "Annual Increases" or "General Rent Ceiling."

Following the rent sections should be a section on "Individual Adjustments" or "Hardship Adjustments." This section tells you how to get an increase over and above any general across the board increase. Finally, any requirement that you show "just cause" for eviction should be found under a section entitled "Just (or Good) Cause for Eviction." It will contain a list of the permissible reasons for eviction, along with any extra requirements for eviction notices, and prohibit evictions for any other reason.

To see if you've complied with your city's rent control ordinance before you begin an eviction, check the ordinance for:

- **Registration requirements.** If you're required to register your unit with the rent board but didn't, your tenant may be able to win an eviction lawsuit.
- **Rent increase restrictions.** Read the individual adjustment section to see if the landlord must apply to the rent board for increases over a certain amount. If so, make sure any rent increases were properly applied for and legal. This is especially important if you're planning to evict for nonpayment of rent, because you must list the rent that's legally due on the three-day notice.
- **Special notice requirements.** Check both the general and individual rent adjustment sections, as well as any regulations adopted by the rent board, for special notice requirements for rent increase notices. Again, if you're evicting for nonpayment of rent, you want to be sure that all previous increases were given with a valid notice.
- **Just cause requirements.** This is crucial; you can evict only for one of the permissible reasons, and you must comply with any additional notice requirements. If you want to evict tenants so you can demolish the building or simply go out of business, you may do so under the Ellis Act (Govt. Code §§ 7060–7060.7), even if this reason isn't listed in the ordinance. However, you definitely should have a lawyer handle the eviction.

If you're evicting to move a relative or manager into the unit or to remodel, demolish, or convert the unit, any just cause requirement will have numerous technical notice and compensation requirements. You should consult a lawyer.

Finding Municipal Codes and Rent Control Ordinances Online

If you own rental property in a city that has rent control, you should have a current copy of the city's rent control law. You can usually obtain a paper copy from the administrative agency that oversees the workings of the ordinance. It's quicker, however, to read the material online. Most cities have posted their ordinances, as you will see from the list below. Use the Rent Control Chart, which provides detailed, city-by-city analyses, as a guide to your own reading of the law. Keep in mind that ordinances often change and their meaning evolves as rent boards issue regulations and make decisions.

Berkeley

www.ci.berkeley.ca.us

Click "Municipal Codes & Zoning Ordinance" to get to the Municipal Code. For rent control provisions, see Municipal Code Chapter 13.76. The Rent Stabilization Board itself is at www.ci.berkeley.ca.us/rent.

Beverly Hills

www.ci.beverly-hills.ca.us or www.beverlyhills.org

Go to the "shortcuts" pull-down menu and choose "Municipal Code" on the next page. For rent control provisions, see Title 4, Chapters 5 and 6, of the Municipal Code.

Campbell

www.ci.campbell.ca.us

Click "City Clerk," and choose "Municipal Code" on the next page. For rent control provisions, see Title 6, Chapter 6.09, of the Municipal Code.

East Palo Alto

www.ci.east-palo-alto.ca.us

Go to the "Browse by Topic" pull-down menu and choose Municipal Code under "City Hall and Government." Then press the "Go" button.

Fremont

www.ci.fremont.ca.us

In the "Departments" and "List of Departments" pull-down menu, click "City Clerk's Office." On the next page, click "Fremont Municipal Code."

Hayward

www.ci.hayward.ca.us

For Municipal Code, click "Municipal Code-Fees." Then click "Hayward Municipal Code." However, the Rent Control Ordinance is not part of Municipal Code and not available online.

Los Angeles

www.ci.la.ca.us or www.lacity.org

To get to the Los Angeles Municipal Code from the official city website, click on the "City Charter, Rules & Codes" box at the left. On the next page, click on "Municipal Codes." On the next page, choose "Municipal Code." Rent control provisions are in Chapter XV.

Los Gatos

www.town.los-gatos.ca.us

Move your cursor to "Government" at left, and then move the cursor to "Town Codes," and click that. Rent control provisions are in Chapter 14, Article VIII.

Oakland

www.ci.oakland.ca.us

Click the "Municipal Code" pull-down menu and then click "Rent Ordinance." Click "Go." Rent control provisions are in Title 8, Chapter 8.22.

Palm Springs

www.ci.palm-springs.ca.us

Under "Departments," click "City Clerk." Scroll down to Municipal/Zoning Ordinance Code. Rent control provisions are in title 4, Chapter 4.02 and following.

San Francisco

www.ci.sf.ca.us/rentbd or

www.sfgov.org/site/rentboard_index.asp

This is the best place online to get rent control ordinance provisions and regulations, maintained by the rent board (click "Ordinances and Rules"). For the entire collection of city codes, go to the City's main website at www.ci.sf.ca.us. Click on "Municipal Codes" under "City Resources," which is below an "Explore" heading. This page also includes the Administrative Code, including the Chapter 37 rent control provisions.

San Jose

www.ci.san-jose.ca.us or www.sanjose.ca.gov

Click "Municipal Code" (under "Local Government") at right.

Santa Monica

www.ci.santa-monica.ca.us/rentcontrol

This city's rent control laws are in the City Charter, not in the Municipal Code. Click "Charter Amendment and Regulations." The Rent Control Board maintains the site listed here. If you want to see the Municipal Code as well, go to the official city site at www.ci.santa-monica.ca.us or santa-monica.org/home/index.asp, and choose Municipal Code under the Quick Index pull-down menu.

Thousand Oaks

www.ci.thousand-oaks.ca.us

This city's rent control ordinances (755-NS [7/1980], 956-NS [3/1987], and 1284-NS [5/1997]) were never made a part of the Municipal Code, and thus cannot be found in the online Municipal Code. If you'd like to look at the Municipal Code anyway, go to the official city site above. Then click "Common Questions," then up to "City Hall," then choose "Municipal Code" from the pull-down menu.

West Hollywood

www.ci.west-hollywood.ca.us or www.weho.org

To get to the Municipal Code from this city's official site, click "Municipal Code" under "City Hall."

California Imposes Statewide Limitations on Cities' Rent Control Ordinances

State law significantly limits local rent control laws in the 14 California cities that have them. (Civ. Code §§ 1954.50-53.) The law has three major components.

1. No rent control for single-family residences.

As of January 1, 1999, tenancies that began on or after January 1, 1996 in single-family residences and condominiums will no longer be subject to rent control. Only tenants who have continuously occupied the premises since before January 1, 1996 may enjoy the benefits of rent control past January 1, 1999. This includes not only tenants with leases signed before January 1, 1996, but also those tenants who have rented the same unit on a month-to-month basis, starting prior to January 1, 1996. (Civ. Code §§ 1954.52 (a) (3).)

2. No rent control for new residences.

This law also prohibits any rent control on new residences, defined as those that have certificates of occupancy issued after January 31, 1995.

For more details on this state law, contact the local agency that administers rent control in your area. (Civ. Code §§ 1954.52 (a)(1),(2).)

3. "Vacancy decontrol" for apartments.

This change affects Berkeley, East Palo Alto, Santa Monica, and West Hollywood, the only cities that formerly did not let landlords raise the rent when a tenant moves out and another comes in.

Effective January 1, 1999, landlords may raise the rent on multifamily housing units in any rent-controlled city if the prior tenant left voluntarily or was evicted for nonpayment of rent. Once rerented at this new rent, however, the property is still subject to local rent control ordinances at the higher rent.

Landlords may not, however, raise rents after a voluntary vacancy if the landlord has been cited for serious health, safety, fire, or building code violations that have continued unabated for six months preceding the vacancy. (Civ. Code §§ 1954.53.)

BERKELEY

Name of Ordinance

Rent Stabilization and Eviction for Good Cause Ordinance, City Charter Art. XII, §§ 120-124, Berkeley Municipal Code Ch. 13.76.

Adoption Date

6/3/80. Last amended 11/2005, by initiative.

Exceptions

Units constructed after 6/3/80, owner-occupied single-family residences, and duplexes. (§ 13.76.050.)

Rental units owned (or leased) by nonprofit organizations that (1) receive governmental funding and rent such units to low-income tenants, or (2) provide such units as part of substance abuse treatment.

Administration

Rent Stabilization Board
2125 Milvia Street
Berkeley, CA 94704
510-644-6128
FAX: 510-644-7723
email: rent@ci.berkeley.ca.us
Websites: www.ci.berkeley.ca.us. (This is the general city site. Click on "Municipal Codes & Zoning Ord." to get to Municipal Code. For the rent board add /rent. The rent board's site, at "Laws and Regs" icon, is the best way to get to rent control and eviction rules).

Registration

Required or landlords cannot raise rent. (The provision that a tenant can withhold rents if the landlord fails to register was ruled unconstitutional in *Floystrup v. Berkeley Rent Stablization Board* (1990) 219 Cal. App. 3d 1309.) Stiff penalties for noncooperation. (§ 13.76.080.)

Vacancy Decontrol

State law (Civ. Code § 1954.53) supersedes the ordinance. Upon voluntary vacancy or eviction for nonpayment of rent, rents may be increased to any level following such vacancies. Once property is rerented, it is subject to rent control based on the higher rent.

Just Cause

Required. (§ 13.76.130.) This requirement applies even if the property is exempt from other rent control requirements because it qualifies as new construction or government-owned/operated housing. Specific good cause to evict must be stated in both the notice and in any unlawful detainer complaint.

Other Features

The landlord's unlawful detainer complaint must allege compliance with both the implied warranty of habitability and the rent control ordinance, except for evictions for remodeling or demolition. If the remodeling, demolition, or moving in of the landlord or a relative on which the eviction was based doesn't occur within two months of the tenant's leaving, the tenant can sue the landlord to regain possession of property and recover actual damages (treble damages or $750 if the landlord's reason for the delay was willfully false). (§ 13.76.150.) Also, government-subsidized "Section 8" landlords must register their units and are subject to the yearly annual general adjustment if they raise rents above that set by the Housing Authority.

Reasons Allowed for Just Cause Evictions	Additional Local Notice Requirements and Limitations
Nonpayment of rent.	Ordinary Three-Day Notice to Pay Rent or Quit is used.
Breach of lease provision.	Three-Day Notice to Perform Covenant or Quit is used. Provision must be "reasonable and legal and … been accepted by the tenant or made part of the rental agreement." If the provision was added after tenant moved in, landlord can evict for breach only if tenant was told in writing that she did not have to accept the new term. Tenant must be given "written notice to cease," which precludes an unconditional Three-Day Notice to Quit even if the breach is considered uncorrectable.
Willful causing or allowing of substantial damage to premises and refusal to both pay the reasonable cost of repair and cease causing damage, following written notice.	Even though damage is involved, an unconditional Three-Day Notice to Quit is not allowed. Only a three-day notice that gives the tenant the option of ceasing to cause damage and pay for repair is allowed.
Tenant refuses to agree to rental agreement or lease on expiration of prior one, where new proposed agreement contains no new or unlawful terms.	This applies only if a lease or rental agreement expires of its own terms. No notice is required. However, tenant must have refused to sign a new one containing the same provisions; an improvised notice giving the tenant several days to sign the new agreement or leave is a good idea, even though not required by ordinance or state law.
Tenant continued to be so disorderly as to disturb other tenants, following written notice to cease, or is otherwise subject to eviction under C.C.P. § 1161(4), for committing a nuisance, very seriously damaging the property, or subletting contrary to the lease or rental agreement, unless the landlord has unreasonably withheld consent to sublet where original tenant remains, property is not illegally overcrowded as a result of the subletting, and other requirements are met—see ordinance for details.	Although a warning notice should precede three-day notice based on disturbing neighbors, the three-day notice, according to C.C.P. § 1161(4), may be an unconditional Three-Day Notice to Quit.
Tenant, after written notice to cease, continues to refuse landlord access to the property as required by Civ. Code § 1954.	If provision is in lease, use three-day notice giving tenant option of letting you in or moving. If not, and tenancy is month to month, use 30-day notice specifying reason, following written demand for access.
Landlord wants to make substantial repairs to bring property into compliance with health codes, and repairs not possible while tenant remains.	Under state law, eviction for this reason is allowed only if rental agreement is month to month, not for a fixed term. Landlord must first obtain all permits required for the remodeling, must provide alternative housing for the tenant (at the same rent) if he owns other vacant units in city, and must give evicted tenant right of first refusal to rerent after remodeling is finished. (Tenant given alternate temporary housing may be evicted from it if he refuses to move into old unit after work is completed.)
Landlord wants to demolish property.	Landlord must first obtain city "removal permit." (Although ordinance requires "good faith" to demolish, a euphemism for not doing it because of rent control, the state Ellis Act severely limits cities from refusing demolition permits on this basis.)

Reasons Allowed for Just Cause Evictions	Additional Local Notice Requirements and Limitations
Landlord wants to move self, spouse, parent, or child into property, and no comparable vacant unit exists in the property.	30-day notice terminating month-to-month tenancy for this reason must specify name and relationship of person moving in. (Month-to-month tenancies only.)
Tenant, after written notice to cease, continues to conduct illegal activity on the premises.	Although a warning notice should precede a three-day notice based on illegal activity, the three-day notice, according to C.C.P. § 1161(4), may be an unconditional Three-Day Notice to Quit.
Landlord wants to move in herself, lived there previously, and lease or rental agreement specifically allows for this.	Termination procedure must be in accordance with lease provision. Thirty days' written notice is required to terminate month-to-month tenancy unless agreement provides for lesser period as short as seven days.
Landlord wants to go out of rental business under state Ellis Act.	The requirement that the landlord must give the tenant six months' notice and pay $4,500 in relocation fees to tenants of each unit was ruled illegal, as preempted by the state Ellis Act, in *Channing Properties v. City of Berkeley* (1992) 11 Cal. App. 4th 88, 14 Cal. Rptr. 2d 32.

BEVERLY HILLS

Name of Ordinance
Rent Stabilization Ordinance, Beverly Hills Municipal Code, Title 4, Chapters 5 and 6, §§ 4-5.101 to 4-6.08.

Adoption Date
4/27/79. Last amended 3/30/2001.

Exceptions
Units constructed after 10/20/78, units that rented for more than $600 on 5/31/78, single-family residences, rented condominium units. (§ 4-5.102.)

Administration
Rent Information Office
455 N. Rexford Drive
Beverly Hills, CA 90210
310-285-1031
Website: www.ci.beverly-hills.ca.us or www. beverlyhills.org. (General city site. No site for the rent control ordinance.)

Registration
Not required.

Vacancy Decontrol
Rents may be increased to any level on rerenting following eviction for nonpayment of rent, as well as for voluntary vacancies.

Once property is rerented, it is subject to rent control based on the higher rent.

Just Cause
Required for units other than those that rented for more than $600 on 5/31/78; for these units, a month-to-month tenancy may be terminated only on 60 days' notice, however. (§§ 4-5.501 to 4-5.513.)

Other Features
Though not required by the ordinance, termination notice should state specific reason for termination; this indicates compliance with ordinance, as alleged (item 13) in your unlawful detainer Complaint. Landlord is required to pay tenant substantial relocation fee if evicting to move in self or relative, or to substantially remodel, demolish, or convert to condominiums. Tenant may sue landlord who uses moving-in of self or relative as a "pretext" for eviction, for three times the rent that would have been due for the period the tenant was out of possession.

Reasons Allowed for Just Cause Evictions	Additional Local Notice Requirements and Limitations
Nonpayment of rent.	Ordinary Three-Day Notice to Pay Rent or Quit is used.
Breach of lease provision, following written notice to correct problem.	Three-Day Notice to Cure Covenant or Quit is used. The tenant must be given "written notice to cease," which precludes an unconditional Three-Day Notice to Quit even if the breach is uncorrectable.
Commission of a legal nuisance (disturbing other residents) or damaging the property.	Unconditional Three-Day Notice to Quit may be used.
Tenant is using the property for illegal purpose. This specifically includes overcrowding as defined in ordinance based on number of bedrooms and square footage.	Unconditional Three-Day Notice to Quit may be used.
Tenant refuses, after written demand by landlord, to agree to new rental agreement or lease on expiration of prior one, where proposed agreement contains no new or unlawful terms.	This applies when a lease or rental agreement expires of its own terms. The ordinance requires the landlord to have made a written request for renewal or extension at least 30 days before the old one expired.
Tenant has refused the landlord reasonable access to the property as required by Civ. Code § 1954.	If access provision is in lease, use three-day notice giving tenant option of letting you in or moving. If not, and tenancy is month to month, use 30-day notice specifying reason, following written demand for access to property.

Reasons Allowed for Just Cause Evictions	Additional Local Notice Requirements and Limitations
Fixed-term lease has expired, and person occupying property is subtenant not approved by landlord.	Eviction is allowed on this basis only if person living there is not original tenant or approved subtenant. If lease has not expired and contains no-subletting clause, use Three-Day Notice to Quit to evict for breach of lease.
Landlord wants to move self, parent, or child into property, and no comparable vacant unit exists in the property. In multiple-unit dwelling, landlord can evict only the most recently moved-in tenant for this reason.	Landlord must give tenant 90-day notice that states the name, relationship, and address of person to be moved in, and a copy of the notice must be sent to the City Clerk. Landlord must also pay tenant(s) a "relocation fee" of up to $2,500, depending on the length of tenancy and the size of unit. The fee must be paid when the tenant leaves, or tenant can sue landlord for three times the fee plus attorney's fees. (§ 11-7.05.) Landlord does not have to pay fee if tenant fails to leave at end of 90-day period or pays to relocate tenant to comparable housing elsewhere.
Employment of resident manager has been terminated and the property is needed for occupancy by the new manager.	This type of eviction is not covered in this book because the question of what notice is required is extremely complicated, depending in part on the nature of the management agreement. You should seek legal advice.
Landlord wants to demolish property or convert to condominiums, or otherwise remove property from rental market.	Landlord must first obtain removal permit from city. For substantial remodeling, tenant gets right of first refusal when work done. Landlord must give tenant one year's notice. Landlord must also pay tenant(s) a "relocation fee" of up to $2,500, depending on the length of tenancy and the size of unit. The fee must be paid when the tenant leaves, or tenant can sue landlord for three times the fee plus attorney's fees. Landlord does not have to pay fee if tenant fails to leave at end of 90-day period or pays to relocate tenant to comparable housing elsewhere. Notice, if not accompanied by fee, must inform tenant of its amount and that it is payable when the tenant vacates. The notice cannot be given until city approval of the project is obtained, and a copy of the notice must be sent to the City Clerk.
Landlord wants to substantially remodel property.	Landlord must first obtain removal permit from city. For substantial remodeling, tenant gets right of first refusal when work done. Landlord must give tenant one year's notice. Landlord must also pay tenant(s) a "relocation fee" of up to $2,500, depending on the length of tenancy and the size of unit. The fee must be paid when the tenant leaves, or tenant can sue landlord for three times the fee plus attorney's fees. Landlord does not have to pay fee if tenant fails to leave at end of 90-day period or pays to relocate tenant to comparable housing elsewhere. Notice, if not accompanied by fee, must inform tenant of its amount and that it is payable when the tenant vacates. The notice cannot be given until city approval of the project is obtained, and a copy of the notice must be sent to the City Clerk. Landlord must petition Board for permission and in some cases must provide replacement housing during remodeling.

CAMPBELL

Name of Ordinance

Campbell Municipal Code, Title 6, Ch. 6.09, §§ 6.09.010 to 6.09.190.

Adoption Date

1983. Last amended 12/98.

Exemption

Rental units on lots with three or fewer units. (§ 6.09.030(n).)

Administration

Campbell Rental Dispute Program
Project Sentinel Mediation Services
1055 Sunnyvale-Saratoga Road, Suite 3
Sunnyvale, CA 94087
408-243-8565; and 888-331-3332
Website: www.ci.campbell.ca.us. The general city site includes the Municipal Code. The site for the Rental Dispute Program is www.housing.org/campbell_rent_dispute_resolution.htm.

Registration

Not required.

Individual Adjustments

Tenants affected by an increase can contest it by filing a petition within 45 days after notice of increase or notice to quit, or 15 days from effective date of rent increase or notice to quit, whichever is later, or lose the right to object to the increase. Disputes raised by tenant petition are first subject to "conciliation," then mediation. If those fail, either party may file a written request for arbitration by city "Fact Finding Committee." Committee determines whether increase is "reasonable" by considering costs of capital improvements, repairs, maintenance and debt service, and past history of rent increases. However, the Committee's determination is not binding. (§§ 6.09.050-6.09.150.)

Vacancy Decontrol

No restriction on raises after vacancy.

Eviction

Ordinance does not require showing of just cause to evict, so three-day and 30-day notice requirements and unlawful detainer procedures are governed solely by state law.

Just Cause

Not required.

Other features

Rent increase notice must state: "Notice: Chapter 6.09 of the Campbell Municipal Code provides a conciliation and mediation procedure for property owners and tenants to communicate when there are disputes over rent increases. (Rent increases can include a significant reduction in housing services.) To use this nonbinding procedure, the tenants shall first make a reasonable, good faith effort to contact the property owner or the property owner's agent to resolve the rent increase dispute. If not resolved, the tenant may then file a petition within 45 calendar days of this notice or 15 calendar days following the effective day of the increase, whichever is later. There may be other tenants from your complex receiving a similar rent increase, in which case, the petitions will be combined. For more information you should contact the City's designated Agent at 408-243-8565. Petitioning for conciliation cannot guarantee a reduction in the rent increase."

Note. Because this ordinance does not provide for binding arbitration of any rent increase dispute, it is not truly a rent control ordinance. Compliance with any decision appears to be voluntary only.

EAST PALO ALTO

Name of Ordinance

Rent Stabilization and Eviction for Good Cause Ordinance, Ordinance No. 076.

Adoption Date

11/23/83. Last amended 4/88.

Exception

Units constructed after 11/23/83, units owned by landlords owning four or fewer units in city, property rehabilitated in accordance with federal Internal Revenue Code § 174(k). (§ 5.)

Administration

Rent Stabilization Board
2277 University Avenue
East Palo Alto, CA 94303
650-853-3114; and 650-853-3109
Website: www.ci.east-palo-alto.ca.us. This is the general city site with access to the Municipal Code.

Registration

Required.

Vacancy Decontrol

State law (Civ. Code § 1954.53) supersedes the ordinance. Upon voluntary vacancy or eviction for nonpayment of rent, rents may be increased to any level following such vacancies. Once property is rerented, it is subject to rent control based on the higher rent.

Just Cause

Required (§ 13.A). This aspect of the ordinance applies even to new construction, which is otherwise exempt. Specific just cause to evict must be stated both in the notice and in any unlawful detainer complaint. (§ 13.B.)

Other Features

Landlord's complaint must allege compliance with both the implied warranty of habitability and the rent control ordinance, except for evictions for remodeling or demolition (§ 13.C). If remodeling, demolition, or moving self or a relative, on which eviction was based, doesn't occur within two months of the tenant's leaving, tenant can sue landlord to regain possession of property and recover actual damages (treble damages or $500 if reason willfully false). (§ 15.B.)

East Palo Alto's ordinance does not specifically allow eviction for illegal use of the premises, such as dealing drugs. Still, if the lease has a clause prohibiting illegal use of the premises, you can evict for breach of lease provision (see below). If there's no such lease provision, see an attorney about whether C.C.P. § 1161(4)s, allowance of an eviction for illegal activity, may "preempt" the local ordinance.

Reasons Allowed for Just Cause Evictions	Additional Local Notice Requirements and Limitations
Nonpayment of rent.	Ordinary Three-Day Notice to Pay Rent or Quit is used.
Breach of lease provision, following written notice to cease.	Three-Day Notice to Cure Covenant or Quit is used. Provision must be reasonable and legal and been accepted by the tenant or made part of the rental agreement. If the provision was added after the tenant first moved in, the landlord can evict for breach only if the tenant was told in writing that she didn't have to accept the new term. Ordinance forbids use of an unconditional notice.
Willful causing or allowing of substantial damage to premises and refusal to both pay the reasonable cost of repair and cease causing damage, following written notice.	Even though damage is involved an ordinary unconditional Three-Day Notice to Quit is not allowed. Only a three-day notice that gives the tenant the option of ceasing to cause damage and pay for the costs of repair, as demanded by the landlord, is allowed.

Reasons Allowed for Just Cause Evictions	Additional Local Notice Requirements and Limitations
Tenant refuses to agree to rental agreement or lease on expiration of prior one, where new proposed agreement contains no new or unlawful terms.	This applies only when a lease or rental agreement expires of its own terms. No notice is required. However, an improvised notice giving the tenant several days to sign the new agreement or leave is a good idea.
Tenant continues to be so disorderly as to disturb other tenants, following written notice to cease.	Even if the tenant is committing a legal nuisance for which state law would allow use of a Three-Day Notice to Quit, ordinance requires that three-day notice be in conditional "cease or quit" form.
Tenant, after written notice to cease, continues to refuse the landlord access to the property as required by Civ. Code § 1954.	If provision is in lease, use three-day notice giving tenant option of letting you in or moving. If not, and tenancy is month to month, use 30-day notice specifying reason, following written demand for access to property.
Landlord wants to make substantial repairs to bring property into compliance with health codes, and repairs not possible while tenant remains.	Under state law, eviction for this reason is allowed only if rental agreement is month to month. Thirty-day notice giving specific reason must be used. Landlord must first obtain all permits required for the remodeling, must provide alternative housing for the tenant if he has other vacant units in city, and must give evicted tenant right of first refusal to rerent after remodeling is finished. (Tenant given alternate housing may be evicted from it if he refuses to move into old unit after work is completed. § 13.A.10.)
Landlord wants to demolish property.	Under state law, eviction for this reason is allowed only if rental agreement is month to month. Thirty-day notice giving specific reason must be used. Landlord must first obtain all permits required for the remodeling, must provide alternative housing for the tenant if he has other vacant units in city, and must give evicted tenant right of first refusal to rerent after remodeling is finished. (Tenant given alternate housing may be evicted from it if he refuses to move into old unit after work is completed. § 13.A.10.) (Although ordinance requires "good faith" to demolish, a euphemism for not doing it because of rent control, the state Ellis Act severely limits cities refusing demolition permits on this basis.)
Landlord wants to move self, spouse, parent, grandparent, child, or grandchild into property.	Under state law, eviction for this reason is allowed only if rental agreement is month to month. Thirty-day notice giving specific reason must be used. Also, Thirty-day notice terminating month-to-month tenancy for this reason should specify name and relationship of person moving in.

FREMONT

Name of Ordinance

City of Fremont Residential Rent Increase Dispute Resolution Ordinance (RRIDRO), Ordinance No. 2253, Fremont Municipal Code, Title III, Chapter 19, §§ 3-1900–3-1955.

Adoption Date

7/22/97, last amended 5/2001.

Exception

None. Ordinance applies to "any housing unit offered for rent or lease in the city consisting of one or more units." (§ 3-1905.)

Administration

East Bay Community Mediation
22227 Redwood Road
Castro Valley, CA 94546-7043
510-733-4940
FAX: 510-733-4944
Website: www.ci.fremont.ca.us

Registration

Not required.

Rent Formula

No fixed formula; landlord must respond to Mediation Services within two business days and participate in good faith in conciliation, mediation, and/or fact-finding proceedings, or rent increase notice can be ruled void. (§§ 3-1925, 1930, 1935.) Also, only one rent increase is allowed in any 12-month period. (§§ 3-1910(d).)

Individual Adjustments

Tenants affected by an increase can contest it by contacting Mediation Services within 15 days. Disputes raised by tenant request are first subject to conciliation, then mediation. If those fail, either party may file a written request for determination of the dispute by a fact-finding panel. This panel determines if the increase is reasonable by considering costs of capital improvements, repairs, existing market rents, return on investment, and the Oakland/San Jose All Urban Consumer Price Index. Panel's decision is not binding, but if landlord fails to appear or fails to participate in good faith in conciliation, education, or fact-finding

process, that "shall void the notice of rent increase for all purposes." (§§ 3-1925(g), 1930(e), 1935(l).)

Rent Increase Notice Requirements

60 days' notice appears to be required for all rent increases, even those of 10% or less (§ 3-1915(c)). All tenants, on moving in, must be provided a notice informing them of the dispute resolution programs, and that they can receive a copy by calling City Office of Neighborhoods at 510-494-4500. All rent increase notices must show the name, address, and phone number of the responsible party [§ 3-1915(b)], and must also state the following in bold type:

> **"NOTICE: You are encouraged to contact the owner or manager [*list name*] of your rental unit to discuss this rent increase. However, chapter 19 of Title III of the Fremont Municipal Code provides a procedure for conciliation, mediation, and fact finding for disputes over rent increases. To use the procedure and secure additional information about the city ordinance, you must contact Mediation Services at 510-733-4945 within fifteen days following receipt of this notice."**

If this language is not included, the notice is not valid. (§ 3-1915(a)(d).)

Vacancy Decontrol

No restriction on raises after vacancy.

Eviction

Ordinance does not require showing of just cause to evict, so three-day and 30-day notice requirements and unlawful detainer procedure are governed solely by state law.

Note

Because this ordinance does not provide for binding arbitration of any rent increase dispute, it is not a true rent control ordinance. Compliance with any decision appears to be voluntary, except that if a city mediator or fact finder rules the landlord has failed to appear or act in "good faith" in any conciliation, mediation, or fact-finding proceeding, the rent increase notice can be ruled invalid. In this respect, the ordinance could, under certain circumstances, act as a sort of mild rent control.

HAYWARD

Name of Ordinance
"Residential Rent Stabilization," Ordinance No. 83-023 C.S.

Adoption Date
9/13/83. Last amended 1/2003.

Exceptions
Units first occupied after 7/1/79, units owned by landlord owning four or fewer rental units in the city. (§ 2(l).)

Administration
Rent Review Office
777 B Street, 4th Flr.
Hayward, CA 94541
510-583-4454
Website: www.ci.hayward.ca.us. Provides no rent control information. Municipal Code is accessible, but rent control ordinance is not part of Municipal Code and cannot be accessed online.

Registration
Not required.

Vacancy Decontrol
Rent controls are permanently removed from each rental unit after a voluntary vacancy followed by the expenditure by the landlord of $200 or more on improvements, and city certification of compliance with City Housing Code (Section 8).

Units still subject to controls (those for which there were no voluntary vacancies in preceding years) can be rerented for any rent amount, with property being subject to controls based on the higher rent.

Just Cause
Required. (§ 19(a).) This aspect of the ordinance applies even to voluntarily vacated property no longer subject to rent control. Specific good cause to evict must be stated in both the notice and in any unlawful detainer complaint. (§ 19(b).)

Special Features
Tenant may defend any eviction lawsuit on the basis of the landlord's failure to provide tenant with any of the information required under the ordinance. (§ 8(f).)

Reasons Allowed for Just Cause Evictions	Additional Local Notice Requirements and Limitations
Nonpayment of rent.	Ordinary Three-Day Notice to Pay Rent or Quit is used.
Breach of lease provision following written notice to cease.	Three-Day Notice to Cure Covenant or Quit is used. Provision must be reasonable and legal and have been accepted by the tenant or made part of the rental agreement. If the provision was added after the tenant first moved in, the landlord can evict for breach only if the tenant was told in writing that she didn't have to accept the new term. Notice must give the tenant the option of correcting the problem.
Willful causing or allowing of substantial damage to premises and refusal to both pay the reasonable cost of repair and cease causing damage, following written notice.	Even though damage is involved an ordinary unconditional Three-Day Notice to Quit is not allowed. Only a three-day notice that gives the tenant the option of ceasing to cause damage and pay for the costs of repair, as demanded by the landlord, is allowed.
Tenant refuses to agree to rental agreement or lease on expiration of prior one, where new proposed agreement contains no new or unlawful terms.	This applies only when a lease or rental agreement expires of its own terms. No notice is required. However, an improvised notice giving the tenant several days to sign the new agreement or leave is a good idea.
Tenant continues to be so disorderly as to disturb other tenants, following written notice to cease.	Even if the tenant is committing a legal nuisance for which state law would allow use of a Three-Day Notice to Quit, ordinance requires that three-day notice be in conditional "cease or quit" form.

Reasons Allowed for Just Cause Evictions	Additional Local Notice Requirements and Limitations
Tenant, after written notice to cease, continues to refuse the landlord access to the property as required by Civ. Code § 1954.	If provision is in lease, use three-day notice giving tenant option of letting you in or moving. If not, and tenancy is month to month, use 30-day notice specifying reason, following written demand for access to property.
Landlord wants to make substantial repairs to bring property into compliance with health codes, and repairs not possible while tenant remains.	Under state law, eviction for this reason is allowed only if rental agreement is month to month. Thirty-day notice giving specific reason must be used. Landlord must first obtain all permits required for the remodeling, and must give tenant notice giving him first chance to rerent after remodeling is finished. (No requirement for alternative housing.)
Landlord wants to demolish property.	Under state law, eviction for this reason is allowed only if rental agreement is month-to-month. Thirty-day notice giving specific reason must be used. Landlord must first obtain all necessary permits. (Although ordinance requires "good faith" to demolish, a euphemism for not doing it because of rent control, the state Ellis Act severely limits cities from refusing demolition permits on this basis.)
Landlord wants to move self, spouse, parent, child, stepchild, brother, or sister into property, and no comparable vacant unit exists in the property.	Under state law, eviction for this reason is allowed only if rental agreement is month-to-month. Thirty-day notice giving specific reason must be used. Landlord must first obtain all permits required for the remodeling, and must give tenant notice giving him first chance to rerent after remodeling is finished. (No requirement for alternative housing.) Thirty-day notice terminating month-to-month tenancy for this reason should specify name and relationship of person moving in.
Landlord wants to move in herself, and lease or rental agreement specifically allows this.	Termination procedure must be in accordance with lease provision. Thirty days' written notice is required to terminate month-to-month tenancy unless agreement provides for lesser period as short as seven days.
Tenant is using the property illegally.	Three-Day Notice to Quit is used.
Tenant continues, after written notice to cease, to violate reasonable and legal regulations applicable to all tenants generally, if tenant accepted regulations in writing in the lease or rental agreement, or otherwise.	If tenancy is not month to month and violation is very serious, use Three-Day Notice to Perform Covenant or Quit. If tenancy is month to month, use 30-day notice preceded by written warning.
Lawful termination of apartment manager's employment, where he or she was compensated with use of apartment.	This type of eviction is not covered in this book because the question of what notice is required is extremely complicated, depending in part on the nature of the management agreement. You should seek legal advice.

LOS ANGELES

Name of Ordinance

Rent Stabilization Ordinance, Los Angeles Municipal Code, Chapter XV, §§ 151.00–155.09.

Adoption Date

4/21/79. Last amended 5/2005.

Exceptions

Units constructed (or substantially renovated with at least $10,000 in improvements) after 10/1/78, "luxury" units (defined as 0, 1, 2, 3, or 4+ bedroom units renting for at least $302, $420, $588, $756, or $823, respectively, as of 5/31/78), single-family residences, except where two or more houses are located on the same lot. (§ 151.02. G, M.)

Administration

Los Angeles Housing Department
3550 Wilshire Boulevard, Suite 1500
Los Angeles, CA 90010; and
3415 S. Sepulveda Blvd., Suite 150
Los Angeles, CA 90034; and
6640 Van Nuys Boulevard
Van Nuys, CA 91405; and
690 Knox Street, Suite 125,
Torrance, CA 90502
For information regarding ordinance, call 800-994-4444 or 866-557-7368 (RENT).

Websites: www2.cityofla.org/LAHD for information on rent control and www.tenant.net/Other_Areas/ Calif/losangel/index.html. For the L.A. Municipal Code, navigate the city's main website at www.ci.la.ca.us. (See front of this appendix.)

Registration

Required.

Vacancy Decontrol

Landlord may charge any rent after a tenant either vacates voluntarily or is evicted for nonpayment of rent or breach of a rental agreement provision, or to substantially remodel. (Controls remain if landlord evicts for any other reason, fails to remodel after evicting for that purpose, or terminates or fails to renew a subsidized-housing lease with the city housing authority.) However, once the property is rerented, it is subject to rent control based on the higher rent. (§ 151.06.C.)

Just Cause

Required. (§ 151.09.) Every termination notice must state "the reasons for the termination with specific facts to permit a determination of the date, place, witnesses, and circumstances concerning the reason." (§ 151.09.C.1.) Tenant may not defend unlawful detainer action on the basis of lack of good cause or failure of the notice to state the reason if tenant has disobeyed a pretrial court order requiring him or her to deposit rent into court; see C.C.P. § 1170.5 and *Green v. Superior Court* (1974) 10 Cal. 3d 616. (§ 151.09.E.). State law requires use of a 60-day termination notice of month-to-month tenancy, instead of a 30-day notice, for this city, if the tenant has occupied the premises for a year or more.

Other Features

Tenant may defend on the basis that the landlord failed to register the property in accordance with the ordinance. (§ 151.09.F.)

Reasons Allowed for Just Cause Evictions	Additional Local Notice Requirements and Limitations
Nonpayment of rent.	Ordinary Three-Day Notice to Pay Rent or Quit is used.
Breach of lease provision, following written notice to cease. (Landlord may not evict based on breach of no-pets clause added by notice of change of terms of tenancy, where no such clause existed at the outset of the tenancy. § 151.09.D.)	Three-Day Notice to Cure Covenant or Quit is used. The ordinance requires that the tenant be given "written notice to cease," which precludes an unconditional Three-Day Notice to Quit, even if the breach can be considered uncorrectable.
Commission of a legal nuisance (disturbing other residents) or damaging the property.	Unconditional Three-Day Notice to Quit may be used.
Tenant is using the property for illegal purpose.	Unconditional Three-Day Notice to Quit may be used.
Tenant refuses to agree to rental agreement or lease on expiration of prior one, where new proposed agreement contains no new or unlawful terms.	This applies only when a lease or rental agreement expires of its own terms. No notice is required. However, an improvised notice giving the tenant several days to sign the new agreement or leave is a good idea, even though not required by ordinance or state law.
Tenant, after written notice to cease, continues to refuse the landlord access to the property as required by Civ. Code § 1954.	If provision is in lease, use three-day notice giving tenant option of letting you in or moving. If not, and tenancy is month to month, use 30-day notice specifying reason, following previous written demand for access to property.
Fixed-term lease has expired, and person occupying property is subtenant not approved by landlord.	Eviction on this basis is allowed only if person living there is not original tenant or approved subtenant. No notice is required. If lease has not expired and contains no-subletting clause, use Three-Day Notice to Quit to evict for breach of lease.
Landlord wants to move self, spouse, parent, child, or legally required resident manager into property. Landlord must pay relocation fee of $2,000-$2,500 to tenants except where moving legally required manager into property.	Only month-to-month tenant can be evicted on this ground. Landlord must serve tenant with copy of a form, the original of which must first be filed with the Community Development Department, that specifies the name and relationship of the person to be moving in.
Landlord wants to: (1) demolish the unit, or (2) undertake "Primary Renovative Work," under a "Tenant Habitability Plan" filed with the Housing Department, and the tenant is "unreasonably interfering" with that plan; or (3) substantially renovate the rental unit, where the landlord has complied with all necessary notices and relocation requirements, and the tenant has refused to cooperate with the landlord's plans.	Only month-to-month tenant can be evicted on this ground. Use 30-day notice specifying this reason. Landlord must serve tenant with copy of a filed Community Development Department form describing the renovation work or demolition.
Landlord seeks to permanently remove the unit from the rental housing market.	Only month-to-month tenant can be evicted on this ground. Use 30-day notice specifying this reason.

LOS GATOS

Name of Ordinance

Los Gatos Rental Dispute Mediation and Arbitration Ordinance, Los Gatos Town Code, Chapter 14, Article VIII, §§ 14.80.010-14.80-315.

Adoption Date

10/27/80. Last amended 3/2004.

Exception

Property on lots with two or fewer units, single-family residences, rented condominium units. (§ 14.80.020.)

Administration

Project Sentinel—Mediation Services
1055 Sunnyvale-Saratoga Road, Suite 3
Sunnyvale, CA 94087
408-720-9888 and 888-331-3332
Website: www.town.los-gatos.ca.us, official city website. Choose Town Government, then Town Codes. Rent control provisions are in Chapter 14, Article VIII. The site for the Rental Dispute Program is www.housing.org/los_gatos_rent_dispute_resolution.htm.

Registration

Not required. (However, a "regulatory fee" to pay for program is added to annual business license fee, when business license is required.)

Vacancy Decontrol

Landlord may charge any rent after a tenant vacates voluntarily or is evicted following Three-Day Notice for Nonpayment of Rent or other breach of the rental agreement. However, once the new rent for a vacated unit is established by the landlord and the property is rerented, it is subject to rent control based on the higher rent. (§ 14.80.310.)

Just Cause

Not required.

Other Features

Tenant faced with termination notice may invoke mediation/arbitration hearing procedure on eviction issue and stay landlord's eviction suit; if tenant wins mediation/arbitration hearing, eviction will be barred. (§ 14.80.205.)

OAKLAND

Name of Ordinance
"Ordinance Establishing a Residential Rent Arbitration Board," Oakland Municipal Code, Title 8, Ch. 8.22, §§ 8.22.010-8.22.200. See also Title 8, Ch. 8.22, §§ 8.22.300-8.22.480.

Adoption Date
10/7/80. Last amended 10/2003.

Exceptions
Units constructed after 1/18/84, buildings "substantially rehabilitated" at cost of 50% of that of new construction, as determined by Chief Building Inspector. (§ 8.22.030.)

Administration
Rent Adjustment Program
250 Frank H. Ogawa Plaza
Oakland, CA 94612
510-238-3721
FAX: 510-238-3691
Website: www.ci.oakland.ca.us or www.oaklandnet. com. Choose the Municipal Code and go to Title 8, Chapter 8.22; or, choose "Rent Ordinance"; and click "Go."

Registration
Not required.

Vacancy Decontrol
Landlord may charge any rent after a tenant vacates voluntarily or is evicted for nonpayment of rent. If tenant otherwise vacates involuntarily, landlord may not increase the rent for 24 months.

On eviction for reasons other than nonpayment of rent, ordinance allows increase of up to 12%, depending on rent increases over previous 12 months.

Once property is rerented, it is subject to rent control based on the higher rent.

Just Cause
Under a separate "Just Cause for Eviction" ordinance (Measure EE), enacted 11/5/2002, landlords may terminate a month-to-month rental agreement (or refuse to renew a lease) only when the tenant has failed to pay the rent (or has violated another important lease term), refused to enter into a written renewal of a rental agreement or lease, caused substantial damage, disturbed the peace and quiet of other tenants, engaged in illegal activities, or refused entry to the landlord when properly asked. Landlords may also terminate rental agreements or not renew leases when they want to live in the unit themselves (or intend it for a close family member), or to substantially renovate the unit. (See Municipal Code Title 8, Ch. 22 §§ 8.22.300-8.22.480.)

Other Features
Rent increase notices must be in a form prescribed by Section 8.22.070(H)(1), which requires tenant be notified of right to petition rent board. All Tenants, on moving in, must be provided a notice informing of their rights under the ordinance. (8.22.060.)

Landlord evicting to "rehabilitate" the property (presumably to obtain permanent exemption from controls) must obtain building permit before eviction.

PALM SPRINGS

Name of Ordinance

"Rent Control," Palm Springs Municipal Code, Title 4, Chapters 4.02, 4.04, 4.08, §§ 4.02.010-4.08.190.

Adoption Date

9/1/79. Last amended, by initiative, 12/94.

Exceptions

Units constructed after 4/1/79; owner-occupied single-family residences, duplexes, triplexes, and four-plexes; units where rent was $450 or more as of 9/1/79. (§§ 4.02.010, 4.02.030.)

Administration

Rent Review Commission
3200 E. Tahquitz Canyon Way
Palm Springs, CA 92262
760-778-8465
The city website is www.ci.palm-springs.ca.us.

Registration

Required. (§ 4.02.080.)

Vacancy Decontrol

Rent controls are permanently removed after tenant voluntarily vacates or is evicted for cause.

Just Cause

Landlords must show just cause to evict for units subject to rent control. After voluntary vacancy or eviction for cause, just cause requirement does not apply any more. (Section 4.08.060(j)(2).)

Reasons Allowed for Just Cause Evictions	Additional Local Notice Requirements and Limitations
Nonpayment of rent.	Ordinary Three-Day Notice to Pay Rent or Quit is used.
Breach of lease provision.	Three-Day Notice to Cure Covenant or Quit is used, or Three-Day Notice to Quit where breach cannot be cured, or improper subletting.
Creation or maintenance of a nuisance.	State law allows use of a Three-Day Notice to Quit.
Tenant is using the property illegally.	Three-Day Notice to Quit is used.
Landlord wants to move self, parent, child, grandparent, brother or sister, mother-in-law, father-in-law, son-in-law, or daughter-in-law into property.	Under state law, eviction for this reason is allowed only if rental agreement is month to month. Thirty-day notice giving specific reason must be used.

SAN FRANCISCO

Name of Ordinance
Residential Rent Stabilization and Arbitration Ordinance, San Francisco Administrative Code, Chapter 37.

Adoption Date
6/79. Last amended 8/8/2006.

Exceptions
Units constructed after 6/79; buildings over 50 years old and "substantially rehabilitated" since 6/79. (§ 37.2 (p).)

Administration
Residential Rent Stabilization and
Arbitration Board
25 Van Ness Avenue, Suite 320
San Francisco, CA 94102
415-252-4602, 415-252-4600 (recorded info);
FAX 415-252-4699
"Fax-Back" Service (fax a question, they fax you an answer): 415-252-4660
Website: www.ci.sf.ca.us/rentbd; or www.sfgov.org/site/rentboard_index.htm. Municipal Code/Administrative Code is available from the city official site, www.ci.sf.ca.us. Rent control laws (in superior format) and regulations are available from rent board site.

Registration
Not required.

Vacancy Decontrol
Landlord may charge any rent after a tenant vacates voluntarily or is evicted for cause. Once property is rerented for a year, it is subject to rent control based on the higher rent. (§ 37.3(a).)

Just Cause
Required. Every termination notice must state "the grounds under which possession is sought" and must advise the tenant that advice regarding the notice is available from the Board. (§ 37.9.)

Other Features
Tenant or Board may sue landlord, following either unsuccessful eviction attempt or successful eviction based on falsified reason, for treble damages and attorney's fees. (§ 37.9(e).) Landlord must file copy of tenancy termination notice (except Three-Day Notice to Pay Rent or Quit) with rent board within ten days after it is served on the tenant. (§ 37.9(c).) Must have just cause to remove certain housing services (such as parking and storage facilities) from a tenancy. (§ 37.2(r).)

Reasons Allowed for Just Cause Evictions	Additional Local Notice Requirements and Limitations
Nonpayment of rent.	Ordinary Three-Day Notice to Pay Rent or Quit is used.
Tenant "habitually pays the rent late or gives checks which are frequently returned ...."	This can only be used if tenancy is month to month, by using 30-day notice.
Breach of lease provision, following written notice to cease.	Three-Day Notice to Perform Covenant or Quit is used. Tenant must be given "written notice to cease," which precludes an unconditional Three-Day Notice to Quit, even if the breach is uncorrectible.
Commission of a legal nuisance (disturbing other residents) or damaging the property.	Unconditional Three-Day Notice to Quit may be used.
Tenant is using the property for illegal purpose.	Unconditional Three-Day Notice to Quit may be used.
Tenant refuses, after written demand by landlord, to agree to new rental agreement or lease on expiration of prior one, where new proposed agreement contains no new or unlawful terms.	This applies only when a lease or rental agreement expires of its own terms. No notice is required. However, a written notice giving the tenant at least three days to sign the new agreement or leave should be served on the tenant with the proposed new lease or rental agreement.
Tenant, after written notice to cease, continues to refuse the landlord access to the property as required by Civ. Code § 1954.	If provision is in lease, use three-day notice giving tenant option of letting you in or moving. If not, and tenancy is month to month, use 30-day notice specifying reason, following written demand for access to property.

Reasons Allowed for Just Cause Evictions	Additional Local Notice Requirements and Limitations
Landlord owning at least 25% interest (10% if bought before 2/91) wants to move self, parent, grandparent, child, grandchild, brother, sister, or spouse (including domestic partner) of any of the foregoing into the property. Note that spouses and domestic partners (those registered as such pursuant to the San Francisco Administrative Code Chapter 62.1 and 62.8) may aggregate their interests, but not tenants in common. Evictions for this reason are known as "owner move-in" evictions, or "OMI" evictions. They are the most contentious type of eviction and are often the subject of prolonged litigation. Before commencing an OMI eviction, you would be well advised to check the Ordinance and the Rent Board website, which is extremely helpful, for updates, details, and any added regulations.	Eviction for this reason is allowed only if rental agreement is month to month. Also, ownership must have been previously registered with Board. By popular vote in November 1998 (Proposition G), effective December 18, 1998, OMIs are not allowed as to: 1. Seniors 60 years of age or older who have lived in the rental for at least ten years; 2. Disabled or blind tenants who meet the Supplemental Security Income/California State Supplemental Program (SSI/SSP) criteria for disability, as determined by the Program or any other method approved by the Rent Board, who have lived in the rental for at least ten years; and 3. Tenants with a "catastrophic illness" (as certified by the tenant's primary care physician) who have lived in the rental for at least five years. There are several restrictions to allowable OMIs. The landlord must live in the same building as the unit that is the subject of the OMI (unless the landlord owns only one unit in the building). Only one "owner move-in" eviction is allowed for a single building. The unit that is the subject of the first OMI becomes the designated OMI unit for that building for the future. Landlords may not do an OMI as to a particular unit if there is a comparable vacant unit in the building, and must cease eviction proceedings if a comparable unit becomes available prior to recovering possession. For buildings of three or more units built before 6/79, the landlord must obtain a conditional use permit from the city planning department. Certain tenants will be entitled to a $1,000 relocation benefit from the landlord. The landlord or other qualified relative who occupies the recovered unit must move in within three months and reside there continuously for 36 months
Landlord wants to sell unit following condominium-conversion approval pursuant to separate city ordinance.	Allowed only if rental agreement is month to month. Ownership must have been previously registered with Board. Landlord must get all necessary approvals first. New tenants must stay there for a year.
Landlord wants to demolish the unit.	Allowed only if rental agreement is month to month. Ownership must have been previously registered with Board. Landlord must obtain all necessary permits first.
Landlord wants to rehabilitate the property or add capital improvements.	Allowed only if rental agreement is month to month. Ownership must have been previously registered with Board. Can't evict if rehab financed by city with "RAP" loans. If improvements are not "substantial rehabilitation" of building 50 or more years old, landlord must give tenant right of first refusal to reoccupy property when work is completed.
Landlord wants to permanently remove property from the rental housing market.	Allowed only if rental agreement is month to month. Ownership must have been previously registered with Board. Although the ordinance requires that the landlord must pay relocation compensation of $1,500-$3,000, the Court of Appeal ruled in a case involving Berkeley's ordinance that this requirement was illegal, as preempted by the state Ellis Act. (See *Channing Properties v. City of Berkeley* (1992) 11 Cal. App. 4th 88, 14 Cal. Rptr. 2d 32.)
Fixed-term lease has expired, and person occupying property is subtenant not approved by landlord.	No notice is required. Ordinance allows eviction on this basis only if person living there is not original tenant or approved subtenant. (If lease has not expired and contains no-subletting clause, use Three-Day Notice to Quit to evict for breach of lease.)

SAN JOSE

Name of Ordinance

San Jose Rental Dispute Mediation and Arbitration Ordinance, San Jose Municipal Code, Title 17, Chapter 17.23, §§ 17.23.010-17.23.770.

Adoption Date

7/7/79. Last amended 7/1/2003.

Exceptions

Units constructed after 9/7/79, single-family residences, duplexes, townhouses, and condominium units. (§ 17.23.150.)

Administration

San Jose Rental Rights and Referrals Program
200 East Santa Clara Street
San Jose, CA 95113
408-975-4480
Website: www.ci.san-jose.ca.us and www.sanjose. ca.gov. This is the general city site, which provides no rent control information. The telephone menu, however, at 408-975-4480, provides helpful information. Municipal Code is accessible. Rent control portions are in Title 17, Chapter 17.23.

Registration

Required.

Vacancy Decontrol

Landlord may charge any rent after a tenant vacates voluntarily or is evicted following Three-Day Notice to Pay Rent or Quit or other breach of the rental agreement. However, once the new rent for a vacated unit is established by the landlord and the property is rerented, it is subject to rent control based on the higher rent. (§ 17.23.190.)

Just Cause

Not required. Notice requirements and unlawful detainer procedures are governed solely by state law, except that 90 days' notice, rather than 60 days', is required to terminate a month to month tenancy if the tenant has lived there a year or more. (§ 17.23.610A.) Sixty days' notice is also required if the tenant is served with an offer to arbitrate. (§ 17.23.615.)

Other

All tenants, on moving in, must be provided a notice informing of their rights under the ordinance. (§ 17.23.030.) Rent increase notices must notify tenant of right to petition, time limits, and the city rent program's address and phone number. (§ 17.23.270.)

In addition, ordinance requires that 90-day notice of termination be given to a tenant of month-to-month tenancy that's lasted over a year, or a 60-day notice if served with an offer to arbitrate. We believe this provision is invalid as superseded by recent state law allowing a 60-day notice without an offer to arbitrate.

Important: Copies of Notices to Vacate must be sent to the city. (§ 17.23.760.)

SANTA MONICA

Name of Ordinance

Rent Control Charter Amendment, City Charter Article XVIII.

Adoption Date

4/10/79. Last amended 1/99.

Exceptions

Units constructed after 4/10/79; owner-occupied single-family residences, duplexes, and triplexes; single-family dwellings not rented on 7/1/84. (Charter Amendment (C.A.) §§ 1801(c), 1815; Regulation (Reg.) §§ 2000 and following, 12000 and following.) However, rental units other than single-family dwellings not rented on 7/1/84 must be registered and the exemption applied for.

Administration

Rent Control Board
1685 Main Street, Room 202
Santa Monica, CA 90401
310-458-8751
Email: rent_control@csanta-monica.org.
Websites: www.ci.santa-monica.ca.us/rentcontrol.

This is an excellent site. Includes rent control laws in "Charter Amendment and Regulations"—both of which are not in the Municipal Code. See also www.tenant. net/Other_Areas/Calif/smonica/rentctrl.html.

Registration

Required. (C.A. §§ 1803(q), 1805(h).)

Vacancy Decontrol

State law (Civ. Code § 1954.53) supersedes the ordinance. Upon voluntary vacancy or eviction for nonpayment of rent, rents may be increased to any level following such vacancies. Once property is rerented, it is subject to rent control based on the higher rent.

Just Cause

Required. Specific good cause to evict must be stated in the termination notice. (Reg. § 9001.)

Other Features

Landlord's complaint must allege compliance with rent control ordinance. (C.A. § 1806.)

Reasons Allowed for Just Cause Evictions	Additional Local Notice Requirements and Limitations
Nonpayment of rent.	Ordinary Three-Day Notice to Pay Rent or Quit is used.
Breach of lease provision.	Three-Day Notice to Perform Covenant or Quit is used. Ordinance requires that the tenant has "failed to cure such violation," which precludes an unconditional Three-Day Notice to Quit, even if the breach is uncorrectable.
Willful causing or allowing of substantial damage to premises, or commission of nuisance that interferes with comfort, safety, or enjoyment of the property, following written notice.	No requirement for alternative three-day notice giving tenant the option of correcting the problem. Three-Day Notice to Quit may be used.
Tenant is convicted of using the property for illegal purpose.	Three-Day Notice to Quit may be used, but only if tenant is actually convicted. This appears to mean that drug dealers can't be evicted unless first convicted. This provision may violate state law, which does not require a conviction. See C.C.P. § 1161(4). If you wish to evict for illegal use without a conviction, try it based on a violation of a lease provision that forbids illegal use of the premises. Otherwise, see a lawyer about making the argument that this part of the ordinance is preempted by state law.

Reasons Allowed for Just Cause Evictions	Additional Local Notice Requirements and Limitations
Tenant refuses to agree to rental agreement or lease on expiration of prior one, where new proposed agreement contains no new or unlawful terms.	This applies only when a lease or rental agreement expires of its own terms. No notice is required. However, an improvised notice giving the tenant several days to sign the new agreement or leave is a good idea.
Tenant, after written notice to cease, continues to refuse the landlord access to the property as required by Civ. Code § 1954.	If provision is in lease, use three-day notice giving tenant option of letting you in or moving. If not, and tenancy is month to month, use 30-day notice specifying reason, following written demand for access to property.
Fixed-term lease has expired, and person occupying property is subtenant not approved by landlord.	No notice is required. Eviction on this basis is allowed only if person living there is not original tenant or approved subtenant. (If lease has not expired and contains no-subletting clause, use Three-Day Notice to Quit to evict for breach of lease.)
Landlord wants to move self, parent, child, brother, sister, or spouse of foregoing into property.	Eviction for this reason is allowed only if rental agreement is month to month. Landlord must include on the termination notice the name of the current tenant, the rent charged, and the name, relationship, and address of person to be moving in. The notice must be filed with the Board within three days of service on the tenant. (Reg. § 9002(e).) The landlord must also offer any comparable vacant unit in the same building to the tenant and must allow the tenant to move back into the property if the relative does not occupy it within 30 days after the tenant moves out.
Landlord wants to demolish property, convert to condominiums, or otherwise remove property from rental market. (City's very strict ordinance has been modified by the state Ellis Act, which severely limits cities from refusing removal permits. See *Javidzad v. City of Santa Monica* (1988) Cal. App. 3d 524, 251 Cal. Rptr. 350.)	Eviction for this reason allowed only if tenancy is month to month. Although the ordinance requires a landlord to pay a relocation fee of up to $4,000, the Court of Appeal ruled in a case involving Berkeley's ordinance that this requirement was illegal, as preempted by the state Ellis Act. (See *Channing Properties v. City of Berkeley* (1992) 11 Cal. App. 4th 88, 14 Cal. Rptr. 2d 32.) That ruling appears to apply only in cases where the landlord just wants to remove the property from the housing market.

THOUSAND OAKS

Name of Ordinance

Rent Stabilization Ordinance, Ordinance Nos. 755-NS, 956-NS, 1284-NS.

Adoption Date

7/1/80. Last amended 5/20/97.

Exceptions

Units constructed after 6/30/80; "luxury" units (defined as 0, 1, 2, 3, or 4+-bedroom units renting for at least $400, $500, $600, $750, or $900, respectively, as of 6/30/80); single-family residences, duplexes, triplexes, and four-plexes, except where five or more units are located on the same lot. (§ III.L of 956-NS.)

Administration

Housing Redevelopment & Economic Division
2100 Thousand Oaks Boulevard,
Civic Arts Plaza, 2nd floor, Suite B
Thousand Oaks, CA 91362
805-449-2393

Website: www.ci-thousand-oaks.ca.us. This is the official city site, but it has no rent control information. The Municipal Code is accessible, but rent control ordinances are not available online.

Registration

Required. (§ XIV.)

Vacancy Decontrol

Rent controls are permanently removed after tenant voluntarily vacates or is evicted for cause.

Just Cause

Required. (§ VIII.) Termination notice must state specific reason for termination.

Reasons Allowed for Just Cause Evictions	Additional Local Notice Requirements and Limitations
Nonpayment of rent.	Ordinary Three-Day Notice to Pay Rent or Quit is used.
Breach of lease provision, following written notice to correct.	Three-Day Notice to Cure Covenant or Quit is used. Ordinance requires that the tenant be given "written notice to cease," which precludes an unconditional Three-Day Notice to Quit, even if the breach is uncorrectable.
Tenant continues to damage property or disturb other tenants, following written notice to cease.	Even if the tenant is causing nuisance or damage for which state law would allow use of a Three-Day Notice to Quit, ordinance requires that Three-Day notice be in alternative "cease or quit" form.
Tenant is using the property for illegal purpose.	Ordinance allows use of unconditional Three-Day Notice to Quit.
Tenant refuses, after written demand by landlord, to agree to new rental agreement or lease on expiration of prior one, where new proposed agreement contains no new or unlawful terms.	This applies only when a lease or rental agreement expires of its own terms. No notice is required. However, written notice giving the tenant at least three days to sign the new agreement or leave should be served on the tenant with the proposed new lease or rental agreement.
Tenant has refused the landlord access to the property as required by Civ. Code § 1954.	If provision is in lease, use Three-Day notice giving tenant option of letting you in or moving. If not, and tenancy is month to month, use 30-day notice specifying reason.

Reasons Allowed for Just Cause Evictions	Additional Local Notice Requirements and Limitations
Fixed-term lease has expired, and person occupying property is subtenant not approved by landlord.	No notice is required. Eviction on this basis is allowed only if person living there is not original tenant or approved subtenant. (If lease has not expired and contains no-subletting clause, use Three-Day Notice to Quit to evict for breach of lease.)
Landlord wants to substantially remodel, convert to condominiums, or demolish property.	Allowed under state law only if fixed-term tenancy has expired, or month-to-month tenancy is terminated by 30-day notice.
Landlord seeks to permanently remove the unit from the rental housing market.	Allowed under state law only if fixed-term tenancy has expired, or month-to-month tenancy is terminated by 30-day notice. (Although ordinance requires "good faith" to demolish, a euphemism for not doing it because of rent control, the state Ellis Act severely limits cities from refusing demolition permits on this basis.)

WEST HOLLYWOOD

Name of Ordinance

Rent Stabilization Ordinance, West Hollywood Municipal Code, Title 17, §§ 17.04.010-17.68.01, and Title 2, §§ 2.64.010-2.64.090.

Adoption Date

6/27/85. Last amended 2006. Frequently amended; call for details.

Exceptions

Units constructed after 7/1/79 and units where owner has lived for two or more years ("just cause" eviction requirements do apply, however). However, many exemptions must be applied for in application for exemption (see below). (§ 17.24.010.)

Administration

Department of Rent Stabilization and Housing
8300 Santa Monica Boulevard
West Hollywood, CA 90069
323-848-6450
Website: www.ci.west-hollywood.ca.us or www.weho. org. Click "City Government," then "Municipal Code."

Registration

Required. (§§ 17.28.010–17.28.050.)

Vacancy Decontrol

State law (Civ. Code § 1954.53) supersedes ordinance except where tenant evicted for reason other than nonpayment of rent.

On voluntary vacancy or eviction for nonpayment of rent, rents may be increased to any level on rerenting following such vacancies. (§ 17.40.020.)

On eviction for reasons other than nonpayment of rent, ordinance does not allow an increase.

Once property is rerented, it is subject to rent control based on the higher rent.

Just Cause

Required. (§ 17.52.010.) This aspect of the ordinance applies even to new construction, which is otherwise exempt from ordinance. Termination notice must state "with particularity the specific grounds" and recite the specific paragraph of ordinance under which eviction sought. State law requires use of a 60-day termination notice of month-to-month tenancy, instead of a 30-day notice, for this city, if the tenant has occupied the premises for a year or more.

Other Features

Copy of any unlawful detainer summons and complaint must be filed with Rent Stabilization Commission. Numerous procedural hurdles apply when evicting to move self or relative into property, and substantial relocation fee must be paid to tenant.

Reasons Allowed for Just Cause Evictions	Additional Local Notice Requirements and Limitations
Nonpayment of rent.	Ordinary Three-Day Notice to Pay Rent or Quit is used.
Failure to cure a lease or rental agreement violation within "a reasonable time" after receipt of written notice to cure it.	Three-Day Notice to Perform Covenant or Quit is used. Tenant must be given "a reasonable time" to correct the violation, which precludes an unconditional Three-Day Notice to Quit. Also, the tenant must have been "provided with a written statement of the respective covenants and obligations of both the landlord and tenant" before the violation. Giving the tenant a copy of the written lease or rental agreement should comply with this requirement. This ground is specifically not applicable if the violation is having another person living on the property in violation of the agreement if the person is a "spouse, domestic partner, child, parent, grandparent, brother, or sister" of the tenant. (Tenant, however, is required to notify landlord in writing of this fact and state the person's name and relationship, when that person moves in.)

Reasons Allowed for Just Cause Evictions	Additional Local Notice Requirements and Limitations
The tenant's spouse, child, "domestic partner," parent, grandparent, brother, or sister can be evicted if the tenant has left, unless that person lived in the unit for at least a year and the tenant died or became incapacitated.	State law allows eviction for this reason by three-day notice only if the tenant's having moved the other person in was a violation of the lease or rental agreement. Thirty-day notice can be used if tenancy is month to month.
Commission of a legal nuisance (disturbing other residents) or damaging the property.	Unconditional Three-Day Notice to Quit may be used.
Tenant is using the property for illegal purpose.	Unconditional Three-Day Notice to Quit may be used.
Tenant refuses, after written demand by landlord, to agree to new rental agreement or lease on expiration of prior one, if new proposed agreement contains no new or unlawful terms.	This applies only when a lease or rental agreement expires of its own terms. No notice is required under state law. However, tenant must have refused to sign a new one containing the same provisions as the old one; a written notice giving the tenant at least three days to sign the new agreement or leave should be served on the tenant with the proposed new lease or rental agreement.
Tenant continues to refuse the landlord access to the property as required by Civ. Code § 1954.	If provision is in lease, use three-day notice giving tenant option of letting you in or moving. If not, and tenancy is month to month, use 30-day notice specifying reason.
Person occupying property is subtenant (other than persons mentioned in 2 and 3 above) not approved by landlord. (No requirement, as in other cities, for lease to have expired.)	Thirty-day notice may be used if tenancy is month to month. Otherwise, Three-Day Notice to Quit may be used if lease or rental agreement contains provision against subletting.
Employment of resident manager, who began tenancy as such (not tenant who was "promoted" from regular tenant to manager) and who lived in manager's unit, has been terminated.	This type of eviction is not covered in this book because the question of what is required is extremely complicated, depending in part on the nature of the management agreement. You should seek legal advice.
Employment of resident manager, who was a regular tenant before "promotion" to manager, has been terminated for cause.	Landlord must give tenant 60-day notice, give copy of notice to city, and pay tenant a relocation fee. There are other restrictions as well. This type of eviction can be extremely complicated; see a lawyer.
Landlord wants to move in, after returning from extended absence, and tenancy was under lease for specific fixed term.	No notice is required under state law when fixed-term lease expires, and ordinance doesn't seem to require notice, either. However, written letter stating intent not to renew, or clear statement in lease, is advisable.
Landlord wants to move self, parent, grandparent, child, brother or sister into property, and no comparable vacant unit exists in the property.	Tenant must be given 90-day notice that states the name, relationship, and address of person to be moved in, and a copy of the notice must be sent to the Rent Commission. Landlord must also pay tenant(s) of 15 months or more a "relocation fee" between $1,500 and $2,500 ($3,000 for senior citizen or handicapped person), depending on size of unit. Tenant is liable for repayment of the fee if he has not moved at the end of the 90-day period. Person moved in must live in property for at least one year, or bad faith is presumed and tenant may more easily sue landlord for wrongful eviction. Not allowed if tenant is certified by physician as terminally ill.
Landlord wants to make substantial repairs to bring property into compliance with health codes, and repairs not possible while tenant remains.	Under state law, eviction for this reason is allowed only if rental agreement is month to month. Landlord must first obtain all permits required for remodeling. Thirty-day notice giving specific reason must be used.

Reasons Allowed for Just Cause Evictions	Additional Local Notice Requirements and Limitations
Landlord has taken title to single-family residence or condominium unit by foreclosure.	Tenant must be given 90-day notice that states the name, relationship, and address of person to be moved in, and a copy of the notice must be sent to the Rent Commission. Landlord must also pay tenant(s) of 15 months or more a "relocation fee" between $1,500 and $2,500 ($3,000 for senior citizen or handicapped person), depending on size of unit. Tenant is liable for repayment of the fee if he has not moved at the end of the 90-day period. Person moved in must live in property for at least one year, or bad faith is presumed and tenant may more easily sue landlord for wrongful eviction. Not allowed if tenant is certified by physician as terminally ill. (Vacancy decontrol provisions are not applicable if property is rerented following eviction.)

WESTLAKE VILLAGE

This small city (population 10,000) has a rent control ordinance that applies to apartment complexes of five units or more (as well as to mobile home parks, whose specialized laws are not covered in this book). However, the city never had more than one apartment complex of this size, and that one was converted to condominiums. Since there is therefore now no property (other than mobile home parks) to which the ordinance applies, we don't explain the ordinance here. ∎

2

How to Use the CD-ROM

The tear-out forms in Appendix 3 are included on a CD-ROM in the back of the book. This CD-ROM, which can be used with Windows computers, installs files that you use with software programs that are already installed on your computer. It is *not* a stand alone software program. Please read this appendix and the README.TXT file included on the CD-ROM for instructions on using the Forms CD.

Note to Mac users. This CD-ROM and its files should also work on Macintosh computers. Please note, however, that Nolo cannot provide technical support for non-Windows users.

How to View the README File

If you do not know how to view the file README.TXT, insert the Forms CD-ROM into your computer's CD-ROM drive and follow these instructions:

- Windows 98, 2000, Me, and XP: (1) On your PC's desktop, double click the My Computer icon; (2) double click the icon for the CD-ROM drive into which the Forms CD-ROM was inserted; (3) double click the file README.TXT.
- Macintosh: (1) On your Mac desktop, double click the icon for the CD-ROM that you inserted; (2) double click on the file README.TXT.

While the README file is open, print it out by using the Print command in the File menu.

Two different kinds of forms are on the CD-ROM:
- word processing (RTF) forms that you can open, complete, print, and save with your word processing program (see "Using the Word Processing Files to Create Documents," below), and
- forms in Portable Document Format (PDF) that can be viewed only with Adobe Acrobat Reader (see "Using PDF Files," below). Some of these forms have "fill-in" text fields and can be completed using your computer. You will not, however, be able to save the completed forms with the filled-in data. PDF forms without fill-in text fields must be printed out and filled in by hand or with a typewriter.

See Appendix 3 for a list of forms, their file names, and their file formats.

Installing the Form Files Onto Your Computer

Before you can do anything with the files on the CD-ROM, you need to install them onto your hard disk. In accordance with U.S. copyright laws, remember that copies of the CD-ROM and its files are for your personal use only.

Insert the Forms CD and do the following.

Windows 98, 2000, Me, and XP Users

Follow the instructions that appear on the screen. (If nothing happens when you insert the Forms CD-ROM, then (1) double click the My Computer icon; (2) double click the icon for the CD-ROM drive into which the Forms CD-ROM was inserted; and (3) double click the file WELCOME.EXE.)

By default, all the files are installed to the \Eviction Forms folder in the \Program Files folder of your computer. A folder called "Eviction Forms" is added to the "Programs" folder of the Start menu.

Macintosh Users

Step 1: If the "Eviction Forms CD" window is not open, open it by double clicking the "Eviction Forms CD" icon.

Step 2: Select the "Eviction Forms" folder icon.

Step 3: Drag and drop the folder icon onto the icon of your hard disk.

Using the Word Processing Files to Create Documents

This section concerns the files for forms that can be opened and edited with your word processing program.

All word processing forms come in rich text format. These files have the extension ".RTF." For example, the form for the Three-Day Notice to Pay Rent or Quit discussed in Chapter 3 is on the file 3-Day Notice Rent.rtf. All forms, their file names, and file formats are listed in Appendix 3.

RTF files can be read by most recent word processing programs including all versions of MS Word for Windows and Macintosh, WordPad for Windows, and recent versions of WordPerfect for Windows and Macintosh.

To use a form from the CD to create your documents you must (1) open a file in your word processor or text editor; (2) edit the form by filling in the required information; (3) print it out; (4) rename and save your revised file.

The following are general instructions. However, each word processor uses different commands to open, format, save, and print documents. Please read your word processor's manual for specific instructions on performing these tasks.

Do not call Nolo's technical support if you have questions on how to use your word processor.

Step 1: Opening a File

There are three ways to open the word processing files included on the CD-ROM after you have installed them onto your computer:

- Windows users can open a file by selecting its "shortcut" as follows: (1) Click the Windows "Start" button; (2) open the "Programs" folder; (3) open the "Eviction Forms" subfolder; (4) open the "RTF" subfolder; and (5) click on the shortcut to the form you want to work with.

- Both Windows and Macintosh users can open a file directly by double clicking on it. Use My Computer or Windows Explorer (Windows 98, 2000, Me, or XP) or the Finder (Macintosh) to go to the folder you installed or copied the CD-ROM's files to. Then, double click on the specific file you want to open.

- You can also open a file from within your word processor. To do this, you must first start your word processor. Then, go to the File menu and choose the Open command. This opens a dialog box where you will tell the program (1) the type of file you want to open (*.RTF); and (2) the location and name of the file (you will need to navigate through the directory tree to get to the folder on your hard disk where the CD's files have been installed).

Where Are the Files Installed?

Windows Users: RTF files are installed by default to a folder named \Eviction Forms\RTF in the \ Program Files folder of your computer.

Macintosh Users: RTF files are located in the "RTF" folder within the "Eviction Forms" folder.

Step 2: Editing Your Document

Fill in the appropriate information according to the instructions and sample agreements in the book. Underlines are used to indicate where you need to enter your information, frequently followed by instructions in brackets. Be sure to delete the underlines and instructions from your edited document. You will also want to make sure that any signature lines in your completed documents appear on a page with at least some text from the document itself.

Editing Forms That Have Optional or Alternative Text

Some of the forms have check boxes before text. The check boxes indicate:

- optional text, where you choose whether to include or exclude the given text
- alternative text, where you select one alternative to include and exclude the other alternatives.

If you are using the tear-out forms in Appendix 3, you simply mark the appropriate box to make your choice.

If you are using the Forms CD, however, we recommend that instead of marking the check boxes, you do the following.

Optional text

If you **don't want** to include optional text, just delete it from your document.

If you **do want** to include optional text, just leave it in your document.

In either case, delete the check box itself as well as the italicized instructions that the text is optional.

Alternative text

First delete all the alternatives that you do not want to include.

Then delete the remaining check boxes, as well as the italicized instructions that you need to select one of the alternatives provided.

Step 3: Printing Out the Document

Use your word processor's or text editor's "Print" command to print out your document.

Step 4: Saving Your Document

After filling in the form, use the "Save As" command to save and rename the file. Because all the files are "read-only," you will not be able to use the "Save" command. This is for your protection. *If you save the file without renaming it, the underlines that indicate where you need to enter your information will be lost, and you will not be able to create a new document with this file without recopying the original file from the CD-ROM.*

Using PDF Files

Electronic copies of useful forms from government agencies are included on the CD-ROM in Adobe PDF format. You must have Adobe Reader installed on your computer to use these forms. Adobe Reader is available for all types of Windows and Macintosh systems. If you don't already have this software, you can download it for free at www.adobe.com.

All forms, their file names, and file formats are listed in Appendix 3. The PDF form files were not created by Nolo.

Some of these forms have fill-in text fields. To create your document using these files, you must (1) open a file; (2) fill in the text fields using either your mouse or the tab key on your keyboard to navigate from field to field; and (3) print it out.

Note: While you can print out your completed form, you will *not* be able to save your completed form to disk.

Forms without fill-in text fields cannot be filled out using your computer. To create your document using these files, you must (1) open the file, (2) print it out, and (3) complete it by hand or typewriter.

Step 1: Opening a Form

PDF files, like the word processing files, can be opened one of three ways.

- Windows users can open a file by selecting its "shortcut" as follows: (1) Click the Windows "Start" button; (2) open the "Programs" folder; (3) open the "Eviction Forms" subfolder; (4) open the "PDF" folder; and (5) click on the shortcut to the form you want to work with.
- Both Windows and Macintosh users can open a file directly by double clicking on it. Use My Computer or Windows Explorer (Windows 98, 2000, Me, or XP) or the Finder (Macintosh) to go to the folder you created and copied the CD-ROM's files to. Then, double click on the specific file you want to open.
- You can also open a PDF file from within Adobe Reader. To do this, you must first start Reader. Then, go to the File menu and choose the Open command. This opens a dialog box where you will tell the program the location and name of the file

(you will need to navigate through the directory tree to get to the folder on your hard disk where the CD's files have been installed).

Where Are the PDF Files Installed?

Windows Users: PDF files are installed by default to a folder named \Eviction Forms\PDF in the \ Program Files folder of your computer.

Macintosh Users: PDF files are located in the "PDF" folder within the "Eviction Forms" folder.

Step 2: Filling in a Form

Use your mouse or the Tab key on your keyboard to navigate from field to field within these forms. Be sure to have all the information you will need to complete a form on hand, because you will not be able to save a copy of the filled-in form to disk. You can, however, print out a completed version.

NOTE: This step is only applicable to forms that have been created with fill-in text fields. Forms without fill-in fields must be completed by hand or typewriter after you have printed them out.

Step 3: Printing a Form

Choose Print from the Acrobat Reader File menu. This will open the Print dialog box. In the "Print Range" section of the Print dialog box, select the appropriate print range, then click OK.

Special Requirements for Motions and Declarations

The sample motions and declarations in this book are all printed on "pleading paper": 8½ x 11-inch paper with numbered lines and a vertical line on the left. The purpose of the numbers is to allow judges or lawyers to easily refer to portions of a document (for example, you might want to refer to "line 12 of Plaintiff's motion"). The RTF form files in this book use a legal template that includes these features. When you print your document, the line and numbers will show. Most recent versions of Microsoft Word support this pleading paper template.

If Your Word Processor Doesn't Support the Pleading Paper Format

If your word processor doesn't support the pleading paper format—that is, when you print out your document, the lines are not numbered on the left—you'll need to manually insert pages of lined pleading paper into your printer and print your motions and declarations on them. A blank sheet of pleading paper has been included as PLEADING. PDF.

As you might expect, there are rules regarding what should be typed on which lines. We've given you the relevant portions here. (California Rule of Court 201.) While you may find these ridiculously picky, ignore them at your peril. Officious clerks have been known to reject papers that don't comply.

You can read other relevant rules by going to the Judicial Council website at www.courtinfo.ca.gov/rules. Choose Title Two of the Rules.

California Rule of Court 201, provides in part:

Rule 201. Form of papers presented for filing

(a) [Definitions] As used in this rule:

(1) "Papers" includes all documents, except exhibits or copies of documents, that are offered for filing in any case; but it does not include Judicial Council and local court forms, records on appeal in limited civil cases, or briefs filed in appellate divisions.

(2) "Recycled" as applied to paper means "recycled paper product" as defined by section 42202 of the Public Resources Code.

(Subd (a) amended effective January 1, 2003; previously amended effective July 1, 1993, and January 1, 1994.)

(b) [Use of recycled paper; certification by attorney or party]

(1) The use of recycled paper is required for the following:

(A) All original papers filed with the court and all copies of papers, documents, and exhibits, whether filed with the court or served on other parties; and

(B) The original record on appeal from a limited civil case, any brief filed with the court in a matter to be heard in the appellate division, and all copies of such documents, whether filed with the court or served on other parties.

(2) Whenever the use of recycled paper is required by these rules, the attorney, party, or other person filing or serving a document certifies, by the act of filing or service, that the document was produced on paper purchased as recycled.

(Subd (b) amended effective January 1, 2003; adopted effective July 1, 1999.)

(c) [Size of paper, type style, and print color]

(1) All papers must be typewritten or printed or be prepared by a photocopying or other duplication process that will produce clear and permanent copies equally as legible as printing in type not smaller than 12 points, on opaque, unglazed paper, white or unbleached, of standard quality not less than 20-pound weight, 8½ by 11 inches.

(2) The typeface must be essentially equivalent to Courier, Times Roman, or Helvetica.

(3) The color of print must be blue-black or black.

(Subd (c) amended effective January 1, 2003; previously amended and relettered effective July 1, 1999; previously amended effective April 1, 1962, July 1, 1964, July 1, 1969, July 1, 1971, January 1, 1976, January 1, 1993, July 1, 1993, and January 1, 1994.)

(d) [Line spacing and numbering]

(1) Only one side of the paper may be used, and the lines on each page must be one and one-half spaced or double spaced and numbered consecutively.

(2) Descriptions of real property may be single spaced and footnotes, quotations, and printed forms of corporate surety bonds and undertakings may be single spaced and have unnumbered lines if they comply generally with the space requirements of (f).

(3) The left margin must be at least one inch from the left edge of the paper and the right margin at least ½ inch from the right edge of the paper.

(4) Line numbers must be placed at the left margin and separated from the text of the paper by a vertical column of space at least 1/5 inch wide or a single or double vertical line. Each line number must be aligned with a line of type or the line numbers must be evenly spaced vertically on the page. Line numbers must be consecutively numbered beginning with the number 1 on each page. There must be at least three line numbers for every vertical inch on the page.

(Subd (d) amended effective January 1, 2003; previously amended and relettered effective July 1, 1993, and July 1, 1999; previously amended effective January 1, 1999.)

(e) [Page numbering and hole punching]

(1) Each page must be numbered consecutively at the bottom.

(2) Each paper must consist entirely of original pages without riders, and must be firmly bound together at the top.

(3) Exhibits may be fastened to pages of the specified size and, when prepared by a machine copying process, must be equal to typewritten material in legibility and permanency of image.

(4) Each paper presented for filing must contain two pre-punched normal-sized holes, centered 2½ inches apart, and ⅝ inch from the top of the paper.

(Subd (e) amended effective January 1, 2003; previously amended and relettered effective July 1, 1993, and July 1, 1999; previously amended effective January 1, 1994.)

(f) [Format of first page] The first page of each paper must be in the following form:

(1) In the space commencing 1 inch from the top of the page with line 1, to the left of the center of the page, the name, office address, or, if none, residence address, telephone number, fax number, and email address (if provided), and State Bar membership number of the attorney for the party in whose behalf the paper is presented, or of the party if he or she is appearing in person; but the name, office address, telephone number, and State Bar membership number of the attorney printed on the page is sufficient. Inclusion of a fax number or email address on any document is optional, and its inclusion does not constitute consent to service by fax or email unless otherwise provided by law.

(2) In the first 2 inches of space between lines 1 and 7 to the right of the center of the page, a blank space for the use of the clerk.

(3) On line 8, at or below 3⅓ inches from the top of the paper, the title of the court.

(4) Below the title of the court, in the space to the left of the center of the page, the title of the case. In the title of the case on each initial complaint or cross-complaint, the name of each party must commence on

a separate line beginning at the left margin of the page. On any subsequent pleading or paper, it is sufficient in the title of the case to (1) state the name of the first party on each side, with appropriate indication of other parties, and (2) state that a cross-action or cross-actions are involved, if applicable.

(5) To the right of and opposite the title, the number of the case.

(6) Below the number of the case, the nature of the paper and, on all complaints and petitions, the character of the action or proceeding. In a case having multiple parties, any answer, response, or opposition must specifically identify the complaining, propounding, or moving party and the complaint, motion, or other matter being answered or opposed.

(7) Below the nature of the paper or the character of the action or proceeding, the name of the judge and department, if any, to which the case is assigned.

(8) Below the nature of the paper or the character of the action or proceeding, the word "Referee:" followed by the name of the referee, on any paper filed in a case pending before a referee appointed pursuant to Code of Civil Procedure section 638 or 639.

(9) On the complaint, petition, or application filed in a limited civil case, below the character of the action or proceeding, the amount demanded in the complaint, petition, or application, stated as follows: "Amount demanded exceeds $10,000" or "Amount demanded does not exceed $10,000," as required by Government Code section 72055.

(10) In the caption of every pleading and every other paper filed in a limited civil case, the words "Limited Civil Case," as required by Code of Civil Procedure section 422.30(b).

(11) If a case is reclassified by an amended complaint, cross-complaint, amended cross-complaint, or other pleading under Code of Civil Procedure section 403.020 or 403.030, the caption must indicate that the action or proceeding is reclassified by this pleading. If a case is reclassified by stipulation under Code of Civil Procedure section 403.050, the title of the stipulation must state that the action or proceeding is reclassified by this stipulation. The caption or title must state that the case is a limited civil case reclassified as an unlimited civil case, or an unlimited civil case reclassified as a limited civil case, or other words to that effect.

(Subd (f) amended effective January 1, 2003; adopted as subd (c) effective January 1, 1949; previously amended and relettered effective July 1, 1993, and July 1, 1999; previously amended effective January 1, 1978, July 1, 2000, January 1, 2001, and January 1, 2002.)

(g) [Footer] Except for exhibits, each paper filed with the court must bear a footer in the bottom margin of each page, placed below the page number and divided from the rest of the document page by a printed line. The footer must contain the title of the paper (examples: "Complaint," "XYZ Corp.'s Motion for Summary Judgment") or some clear and concise abbreviation. The title of the paper must be in at least 10-point type.

(Subd (g) amended effective January 1, 2003; adopted effective January 1, 1999 as subd (f); previously relettered effective July 1, 1999; previously amended effective July 1, 2000.)

(h) [Changes on face of paper—conformance of copies] Additions, deletions, or interlineations must be initialed by the clerk or judge at the time of filing. All copies served must conform to the original filed, including the numbering of lines, pagination, additions, deletions, and interlineations.

(Subd (h) amended effective January 1, 2003; adopted effective January 1, 1949 as subd (d); previously amended and relettered effective July 1, 1999; previously relettered as subd (g) effective January 1, 1999, and as subd (f) effective July 1, 1993.)

(i) [Several causes of action, defenses, etc.] Each separately stated cause of action, count, or defense must be separately numbered.

(Subd (i) amended effective January 1, 2003; adopted effective January 1, 1949 as subd (e); previously amended and relettered effective July 1, 1999; previously relettered as subd (h) effective January 1, 1999, and as subd (g) effective July 1, 1993; previously amended effective January 1, 1973.)

(j) [Acceptance for filing] The clerk of the court must not accept for filing or file any papers that do not comply with this rule, except:

(1) The clerk must not reject a paper for filing solely on the ground that it is handwritten or handprinted or that the handwriting or handprinting is in a color other than blue-black or black.

(2) For good cause shown, the court may permit the filing of papers that do not comply with this rule.

(Subd (j) amended effective January 1, 2003; previously relettered effective January 1, 1999; previously relettered as subd (h) effective January 1, 1966, July 1, 1974, and January 1, 1978; previously amended and relettered as subd (g) effective January 1, 1984; previously relettered as subd (i) effective July 1, 1993.)

(k) Except as provided, this rule does not apply to Judicial Council forms, local court forms, or forms for juvenile dependency proceedings produced by the California State Department of Social Services Child Welfare Systems Case Management System. ■

Tear-Out Forms

File Name	Form	Discussed in Chapter
3-Day Notice Rent.rtf	Three-Day Notice to Pay Rent or Quit	2
30-Day Notice.rtf	30-Day Notice of Termination of Tenancy	3
60-Day Notice.rtf	60-Day Notice of Termination of Tenancy	3
90-Day Notice.rtf	90-Day Notice of Termination of Tenancy	3
3-Day Notice Covenant.rtf	Three-Day Notice to Perform Covenant or Quit	4
3-Day Notice Quit.rtf	Three-Day Notice to Quit	4
sum130.pdf	Summons—Unlawful Detainer—Eviction*	6
ud100.pdf	Complaint—Unlawful Detainer*	6
cm010.pdf	Civil Case Cover Sheet*†	6
CIV 109.pdf	Civil Case Cover Sheet Addendum and Statement of Location	6
POS-010.pdf	Proof of Service of Summons*	6
CIV 107.pdf	Application and Order to Serve Summons by Posting for Unlawful Detainer	6
cp105.pdf	Prejudgment Claim of Right to Possession*†	6
PLEADING.pdf	Blank Pleading Paper	
CIV-100.pdf	Request for Entry of Default*†	7
ej130.pdf	Writ of Execution*†	7
CIV 096.pdf	Application for Issuance of Writ of Execution, Possession or Sale (Los Angeles only)	7
Declaration RDC.pdf	Declaration in Support of Default Judgment for Rent, Damages, and Costs (3-, 30-, 60-, or 90-Day Notice)	7
Declaration DC.rtf	Declaration in Support of Default Judgment for Damages and Costs (Violation of Lease)	7

* Be sure that the back of the forms you submit to the court are printed upside down, as they are on the appendix forms.

† These PDF files have blank text fields. Please refer to Appendix 2 for instruction on how to use PDF files with blank text fields.

File Name	Form	Discussed in Chapter
ud116.pdf	Declaration for Default Judgment by Court*†	7
ud110.pdf	Judgment—Unlawful Detainer*†	7
ud115.pdf	Stipulation for Entry of Judgment*†	8
ud150.pdf	Request/Counter-Request to Set Case for Trial—Unlawful Detainer*	8
Notice of Motion.rtf	Notice of Motion for Summary Judgment; Plaintiff's Declaration; Points and Authorities	8
Order Granting Motion.rtf	Order Granting Motion for Summary Judgment	8
Judgment.rtf	Judgment Following Granting of Motion for Summary Judgment	8
ud110s.pdf	Judgment—Unlawful Detainer Attachment*†	8
ej125.pdf	Application and Order for Appearance and Examination*†	9
Questionnaire.rtf	Questionnaire for Judgment-Debtor Examination	9
98251.pdf	Application for Earnings Withholding Order (Wage Garnishment)†	9
ej100.pdf	Acknowledgment of Satisfaction of Judgment†	9
Proof of Service.rtf	Proof of Service by Mail	10

---

* Be sure that the back of the forms you submit to the court are printed upside down, as they are on the appendix forms.

† These PDF files have blank text fields. Please refer to Appendix 2 for instruction on how to use PDF files with blank text fields.

Get the Form Online

Many of the court forms used in this book are written by the Judicial Council. These forms were current when this book went to press, but the Council revises them from time to time. You can use the Internet to confirm that you're using the most current form, and you can download and print any form (hardware and software permitting). The Judicial Council's Web address is www.courtinfo.ca.gov/forms.

- To make sure that you're using the most current Judicial Council form, check the form's title, number, and revision date (printed in the lower left-hand corner of the form). Go to the Council's Web page and choose to see the forms by numbers. If the revision date on the Web page next to the form's name and number is more recent than the one from the book, you'll need the new form.

- To download a Judicial Council form that you will complete online, by hand, or on a typewriter, choose the "Fillable" or "Non-Fillable Form" link. If you choose the "Fillable Form" option, you can fill the form out online and then print it, but you won't be able to save the completed file to your hard drive unless you have the expensive Adobe software called *Acrobat Approval* or *Adobe Acrobat*. If you choose the nonfillable version, selecting it will place it on your computer's desktop. You'll need software (Adobe *Acrobat Reader*) to open and print the form. You can download *Acrobat Reader* from the site.

Add a footer if you use the blank pleading paper. If you copy and use the blank pleading paper provided in this appendix, be sure to add a "footer" to the bottom. California Rules of Court 201(f) and 501(f) require all papers intended for filing in court to include page numbers (if the filing is over one page long) and a footer. The footer consists of a solid line at the bottom of the page below the page number, with the name of the paper or pleading below the line. Take a look at the footers in the appendix for an example.

Three-Day Notice to Pay Rent or Quit

To: _____ ,
　　　　　　　　　　　　　　　　(name)

Tenant(s) in possession of the premises at _____ ,
　　　　　　　　　　　　　　　　　　　　　　　(street address)

City of _____ , County of _____ , California.

Please take notice that the rent on these premises occupied by you, in the amount of $ _____ , for the period

from _____ to _____ , is now due and payable.

YOU ARE HEREBY REQUIRED to pay this amount within THREE (3) days from the date of service on you of this notice or to vacate and surrender possession of the premises. In the event you fail to do so, legal proceedings will be instituted against you to recover possession of the premises, declare the forfeiture of the rental agreement or lease under which you occupy the premises, and recover rents, damages, and costs of suit.

RENT IS TO BE PAID TO:

☐ the undersigned, or

☐ the following person: _____

AT THE FOLLOWING ADDRESS: _____

_____ , California, phone: (_____)_____ ;

IN THE FOLLOWING MANNER:

☐ In person. Usual days and hours for rent collection are: _____

☐ by mail to the person and address indicated above

☐ by deposit to account _____ at _____ , a financial institution

　　located within 5 miles of your rental at ,_____ California

☐ by electronic funds transfer procedure previously established.

Date: _____　　_____
　　　　　　　　　　　　　　　　　Owner/Manager

- -

Proof of Service

I, the undersigned, being at least 18 years of age, served this notice, of which this is a true copy, on _____ , _____ , one of the occupants listed above as follows:

☐ On _____ , _____ , I delivered the notice to the occupant personally.

☐ On _____ , _____ , I delivered the notice to a person of suitable age and discretion at the occupant's residence/business after having attempted personal service at the occupant's residence, and business, if known. On _____ , _____ , I mailed a second copy to the occupant at his or her residence.

☐ On _____ , _____ , I posted the notice in a conspicuous place on the property, after having attempted personal service at the occupant's residence, and business, if known, and after having been unable to find there a person of suitable age and discretion. On _____ , _____ , I mailed a second copy to the occupant at the property.

I declare under penalty of perjury under the laws of the State of California that the foregoing is true and correct.

Date: _____　　_____
　　　　　　　　　　　　　　　　　Signature

30-Day Notice of Termination of Tenancy

(Tenancy Less Than One Year)

To: _____,
(name)

Tenant(s) in possession of the premises at _____,
(street address)

City of _____, County of _____, California.

YOU ARE HEREBY NOTIFIED that effective 30 DAYS from the date of service on you of this notice, the periodic tenancy by which you hold possession of the premises is terminated, at which time you are required to vacate and surrender possession of the premises. If you fail to do so, legal proceedings will be instituted against you to recover possession of the premises, damages, and costs of suit.

_____

_____

_____

_____

_____

_____

_____

_____

Date: _____   _____
                                       Owner/Manager

Proof of Service

I, the undersigned, being at least 18 years of age, served this notice, of which this is a true copy, on _____, _____, one of the occupants listed above as follows:

☐ On _____, _____, I delivered the notice to the occupant personally.

☐ On _____, _____, I delivered the notice to a person of suitable age and discretion at the occupant's residence/business after having attempted personal service at the occupant's residence, and business, if known. On _____, _____, I mailed a second copy to the occupant at his or her residence.

☐ On _____, _____, I posted the notice in a conspicuous place on the property, after having attempted personal service at the occupant's residence, and business, if known, and after having been unable to find there a person of suitable age and discretion. On _____, _____, I mailed a second copy to the occupant at the property.

I declare under penalty of perjury under the laws of the State of California that the foregoing is true and correct.

Date: _____   _____
                                       Signature

60-Day Notice of Termination of Tenancy

(Tenancy of One Year or Longer)

To: _____,

(name)

Tenant(s) in possession of the premises at _____,

(street address)

City of _____, County of _____, California.

YOU ARE HEREBY NOTIFIED that effective SIXTY (60) DAYS from the date of service on you of this notice, the periodic tenancy by which you hold possession of the premises is terminated, at which time you are required to vacate and surrender possession of the premises. If you fail to do so, legal proceedings will be instituted against you to recover possession of the premises, damages, and costs of suit.

_____

_____

_____

_____

_____

_____

_____

_____

_____

_____

Date: _____   _____

Landlord/Manager

- -

Proof of Service

I, the undersigned, being at least 18 years of age, served this notice, of which this is a true copy, on _____,
_____, one of the occupants listed above as follows:

☐ On _____, _____, I delivered the notice to the occupant personally.

☐ On _____, _____, I delivered the notice to a person of suitable age and discretion at the occupant's residence/business after having attempted personal service at the occupant's residence, and business, if known. On _____, _____, I mailed a second copy to the occupant at his or her residence.

☐ On _____, _____, I posted the notice in a conspicuous place on the property, after having attempted personal service at the occupant's residence, and business, if known, and after having been unable to find there a person of suitable age and discretion. On _____, _____, I mailed a second copy to the occupant at the property.

I declare under penalty of perjury under the laws of the State of California that the foregoing is true and correct.

Date: _____   _____

Signature

90-Day Notice of Termination of Tenan

(Subsidized Tenancies)

To: _____
(name)

Tenant(s) in possession of the premises at _____
(street ad

City of _____, County of _____

YOU ARE HEREBY NOTIFIED that effective NINETY (90) DAYS from the date of servic
tenancy by which you hold possession of the premises is terminated, at which time yo
possession of the premises. If you fail to do so, legal proceedings will be instituted aga
premises, damages, and costs of suit.

_____

_____

_____

_____

_____

_____

_____

_____

Date: _____   _____
                                       Landlord/Manager

- -

Proof of Service

I, the undersigned, being at least 18 years of age, served this notice, of which this is a true
_____, one of the occupants listed above as follows:

☐ On _____, _____, I delivered the notice to the occup

☐ On _____, _____, I delivered the notice to a person
occupant's residence/business after having attempted personal service at the occupant's
_____, _____, I mailed a second copy to the occupa

☐ On _____, _____, I posted the notice in a conspicuo
attempted personal service at the occupant's residence, and business, if known, and aft
of suitable age and discretion. On _____, _____, I m
property.

I declare under penalty of perjury under the laws of the State of California that the foregoi

Date: _____   _____
                                       Signature

Three-Day Notice to Perform Covenant or Quit

To: _____,
(name)

Tenant(s) in possession of the premises at _____,
(street address)

City of _____, County of _____, California.

YOU ARE HEREBY NOTIFIED that you are in violation of the lease or rental agreement under which you occupy these premises because you have violated the covenant to:

_____

_____

_____

in the following manner:

_____

_____

YOU ARE HEREBY REQUIRED within THREE (3) DAYS from the date of service on you of this notice to remedy the violation and perform the covenant or to vacate and surrender possession of the premises.

If you fail to do so, legal proceedings will be instituted against you to recover possession of the premises, declare the forfeiture of the rental agreement or lease under which you occupy the premises, and recover damages and court costs.

Date: _____   _____
                                        Owner/Manager

- -

Proof of Service

I, the undersigned, being at least 18 years of age, served this notice, of which this is a true copy, on _____,
_____, one of the occupants listed above as follows:

☐ On _____, _____, I delivered the notice to the occupant personally.

☐ On _____, _____, I delivered the notice to a person of suitable age and discretion at the occupant's residence/business after having attempted personal service at the occupant's residence, and business, if known. On _____, _____, I mailed a second copy to the occupant at his or her residence.

☐ On _____, _____, I posted the notice in a conspicuous place on the property, after having attempted personal service at the occupant's residence, and business, if known, and after having been unable to find there a person of suitable age and discretion. On _____, _____, I mailed a second copy to the occupant at the property.

I declare under penalty of perjury under the laws of the State of California that the foregoing is true and correct.

Date: _____   _____
                                        Signature

Three-Day Notice to Quit

(Improper Subletting, Nuisance, Waste, or Illegal Use)

To: _____ ,
(name)

Tenant(s) in possession of the premises at _____ ,
(street address)

City of _____ , County of _____ , California.

YOU ARE HEREBY NOTIFIED that you are required within THREE (3) DAYS from the date of service on you of this notice to vacate and surrender possession of the premises because you have committed the following nuisance, waste, unlawful use, or unlawful subletting:

_____

_____

_____

_____

As a result of your having committed the foregoing act(s), the lease or rental agreement under which you occupy these premises is terminated. If you fail to vacate and surrender possession of the premises within three days, legal proceedings will be instituted against you to recover possession of the premises, damages, and court costs.

Date: _____   _____
                                                Owner/Manager

- -

Proof of Service

I, the undersigned, being at least 18 years of age, served this notice, of which this is a true copy, on _____ ,
_____ , one of the occupants listed above as follows:

☐ On _____ , _____ , I delivered the notice to the occupant personally.

☐ On _____ , _____ , I delivered the notice to a person of suitable age and discretion at the occupant's residence/business after having attempted personal service at the occupant's residence, and business, if known. On _____ , _____ , I mailed a second copy to the occupant at his or her residence.

☐ On _____ , _____ , I posted the notice in a conspicuous place on the property, after having attempted personal service at the occupant's residence, and business, if known, and after having been unable to find there a person of suitable age and discretion. On _____ , _____ , I mailed a second copy to the occupant at the property.

I declare under penalty of perjury under the laws of the State of California that the foregoing is true and correct.

Date: _____   _____
                                                Signature

SUMMONS
(CITACION JUDICIAL)
UNLAWFUL DETAINER—EVICTION
(RETENCIÓN ILÍCITA DE UN INMUEBLE—DESALOJO)

NOTICE TO DEFENDANT:
(AVISO AL DEMANDADO):

YOU ARE BEING SUED BY PLAINTIFF:
(LO ESTÁ DEMANDANDO EL DEMANDANTE):

FOR COURT USE ONLY *(SOLO PARA USO DE LA CORTE)*

You have **5 CALENDAR DAYS** after this summons and legal papers are served on you to file a written response at this court and have a copy served on the plaintiff. (To calculate the five days, count Saturday and Sunday, but do not count other court holidays. If the last day falls on a Saturday, Sunday, or a court holiday then you have the next court day to file a written response.) A letter or phone call will not protect you. Your written response must be in proper legal form if you want the court to hear your case. There may be a court form that you can use for your response. You can find these court forms and more information at the California Courts Online Self-Help Center (www.courtinfo.ca.gov/selfhelp), your county law library, or the courthouse nearest you. If you cannot pay the filing fee, ask the court clerk for a fee waiver form. If you do not file your response on time, you may lose the case by default, and your wages, money, and property may be taken without further warning from the court.

There are other legal requirements. You may want to call an attorney right away. If you do not know an attorney, you may want to call an attorney referral service. If you cannot afford an attorney, you may be eligible for free legal services from a nonprofit legal services program. You can locate these nonprofit groups at the California Legal Services Web site (www.lawhelpcalifornia.org), the California Courts Online Self-Help Center (www.courtinfo.ca.gov/selfhelp), or by contacting your local court or county bar association.

Tiene 5 DÍAS DE CALENDARIO después de que le entreguen esta citación y papeles legales para presentar una respuesta por escrito en esta corte y hacer que se entregue una copia al demandante. (Para calcular los cinco días, cuente los sábados y los domingos pero no los otros días feriados de la corte. Si el último día cae en sábado o domingo, o en un día en que la corte esté cerrada, tiene hasta el próximo día de corte para presentar una respuesta por escrito). Una carta o una llamada telefónica no lo protegen. Su respuesta por escrito tiene que estar en formato legal correcto si desea que procesen su caso en la corte. Es posible que haya un formulario que usted pueda usar para su respuesta. Puede encontrar estos formularios de la corte y más información en el Centro de Ayuda de las Cortes de California (www.courtinfo.ca.gov/selfhelp/espanol/), en la biblioteca de leyes de su condado o en la corte que le quede más cerca. Si no puede pagar la cuota de presentación, pida al secretario de la corte que le dé un formulario de exención de pago de cuotas. Si no presenta su respuesta a tiempo, puede perder el caso por incumplimiento y la corte le podrá quitar su sueldo, dinero y bienes sin más advertencia.

Hay otros requisitos legales. Es recomendable que llame a un abogado inmediatamente. Si no conoce a un abogado, puede llamar a un servicio de remisión a abogados. Si no puede pagar a un abogado, es posible que cumpla con los requisitos para obtener servicios legales gratuitos de un programa de servicios legales sin fines de lucro. Puede encontrar estos grupos sin fines de lucro en el sitio web de California Legal Services, (www.lawhelpcalifornia.org), en el Centro de Ayuda de las Cortes de California, (www.courtinfo.ca.gov/selfhelp/espanol/) o poniéndose en contacto con la corte o el colegio de abogados locales.

1. The name and address of the court is:
   (El nombre y dirección de la corte es):

CASE NUMBER: *(Número del caso):*

2. The name, address, and telephone number of plaintiff's attorney, or plaintiff without an attorney, is:
   (El nombre, la dirección y el número de teléfono del abogado del demandante, o del demandante que no tiene abogado, es):

3. *(Must be answered in all cases)* An **unlawful detainer assistant (Bus. & Prof. Code, §§ 6400–6415)** ☐ did **not** ☐ did for compensation give advice or assistance with this form. *(If plaintiff has received **any** help or advice for pay from an unlawful detainer assistant, complete item 6 on the next page.)*

Date: _____ Clerk, by _____, Deputy
(Fecha) *(Secretario)* *(Adjunto)*

(For proof of service of this summons, use Proof of Service of Summons *(form POS-010).)*
(Para prueba de entrega de esta citatión use el formulario Proof of Service of Summons, *(POS-010)).*

[SEAL]

4. **NOTICE TO THE PERSON SERVED:** You are served
   a. ☒ as an individual defendant.
   b. ☐ as the person sued under the fictitious name of *(specify):*
   c. ☐ as an occupant
   d. ☐ on behalf of *(specify):*
      under: ☐ CCP 416.10 (corporation)
      ☐ CCP 416.20 (defunct corporation)
      ☐ CCP 416.40 (association or partnership)
      ☐ CCP 415.46 (occupant)
      ☐ CCP 416.60 (minor)
      ☐ CCP 416.70 (conservatee)
      ☐ CCP 416.90 (authorized person)
      ☐ other *(specify):*

5. ☐ by personal delivery on *(date):*

Page 1 of 2

PLAINTIFF *(Name):*	CASE NUMBER:
DEFENDANT *(Name):*	

6. **Unlawful detainer assistant** *(complete if plaintiff has received any help or advice for pay from an unlawful detainer assistant):*

   a. Assistant's name:

   b. Telephone no.:

   c. Street address, city, and ZIP:

   d. County of registration:

   e. Registration no.:

   f. Registration expires on *(date):*

ATTORNEY OR PARTY WITHOUT ATTORNEY *(Name, State Bar number, and address):*

TELEPHONE NO.:   FAX NO. *(Optional):*

E-MAIL ADDRESS *(Optional):*

ATTORNEY FOR *(Name):* Plaintiff in Pro Per

SUPERIOR COURT OF CALIFORNIA, COUNTY OF
STREET ADDRESS:

MAILING ADDRESS:

CITY AND ZIP CODE:

BRANCH NAME:

PLAINTIFF:

DEFENDANT:

[ ] DOES 1 TO _____

COMPLAINT — UNLAWFUL DETAINER*	CASE NUMBER:
[ ] **COMPLAINT** [ ] **AMENDED COMPLAINT** *(Amendment Number):* _____	

Jurisdiction *(check all that apply):*

[ ] **ACTION IS A LIMITED CIVIL CASE**

Amount demanded [ ]   **does not exceed $10,000**

[ ]   **exceeds $10,000 but does not exceed $25,000**

[ ] **ACTION IS AN UNLIMITED CIVIL CASE (amount demanded exceeds $25,000)**

[ ] **ACTION IS RECLASSIFIED by this amended complaint or cross-complaint** *(check all that apply):*

     [ ] **from unlawful detainer to general unlimited civil (possession not in issue)**   [ ] **from limited to unlimited**

     [ ] **from unlawful detainer to general limited civil (possession not in issue)**   [ ] **from unlimited to limited**

1. PLAINTIFF *(name each):*

   alleges causes of action against DEFENDANT *(name each):*

2. a. Plaintiff is   (1) [ ]   an individual over the age of 18 years.   (4) [ ]   a partnership.

               (2) [ ]   a public agency.   (5) [ ]   a corporation.

               (3) [ ]   other *(specify):*

     b. [ ] Plaintiff has complied with the fictitious business name laws and is doing business under the fictitious name of *(specify):*

3. Defendant named above is in possession of the premises located at *(street address, apt. no., city, zip code, and county):*

4. Plaintiff's interest in the premises is   [ ] as owner   [ ] other *(specify):*

5. The true names and capacities of defendants sued as Does are unknown to plaintiff.

6. a. On or about *(date):*   defendant *(name each):*

     (1) agreed to rent the premises as a   [ ] month-to-month tenancy   [ ] other tenancy *(specify):*

     (2) agreed to pay rent of $ payable   [ ] monthly   [ ] other *(specify frequency):*

     (3) agreed to pay rent on the   [ ] first of the month   [ ] other day *(specify):*

     b. This [ ] written [ ] oral   agreement was made with

         (1) [ ] plaintiff.   (3) [ ] plaintiff's predecessor in interest.

         (2) [ ] plaintiff's agent.   (4) [ ] other *(specify):*

* NOTE: Do not use this form for evictions after sale (Code Civ. Proc., § 1161a).

Form Approved for Optional Use
Judicial Council of California
UD–100 [Rev. July 1, 2005]

COMPLAINT—UNLAWFUL DETAINER

Civil Code, § 1940 et seq.
Code of Civil Procedure §§ 425.12, 1166
www.courtinfo.ca.gov

American LegalNet, Inc.
www.USCourtForms.com

6. c. ☐ The defendants not named in item 6a are

    (1) ☐ subtenants.

    (2) ☐ assignees.

    (3) ☐ other (specify):

d. ☐ The agreement was later changed as follows (specify):

e. ☐ A copy of the written agreement, including any addenda or attachments that form the basis of this complaint, is attached and labeled Exhibit 1. (Required for residential property, unless item 6f is checked. See Code Civ. Proc., § 1166.)

f. ☐ (For residential property) A copy of the written agreement is **not** attached because (specify reason):

    (1) ☐ the written agreement is not in the possession of the landlord or the landlord's employees or agents.

    (2) ☐ this action is solely for nonpayment of rent (Code Civ. Proc., § 1161(2)).

7. ☐ a. Defendant (name each):

was served the following notice on the same date and in the same manner:

    (1) ☐ 3-day notice to pay rent or quit   (4) ☐ 3-day notice to perform covenants or quit

    (2) ☐ 30-day notice to quit   (5) ☐ 3-day notice to quit

    (3) ☐ 60-day notice to quit   (6) ☐ Other (specify):

b. (1) On (date): the period stated in the notice expired at the end of the day.

    (2) Defendants failed to comply with the requirements of the notice by that date.

c. All facts stated in the notice are true.

d. ☐ The notice included an election of forfeiture.

e. ☐ A copy of the notice is attached and labeled Exhibit 2. (Required for residential property. See Code Civ. Proc., § 1166.)

f. ☐ One or more defendants were served (1) with a different notice, (2) on a different date, or (3) in a different manner, as stated in Attachment 8c. (Check item 8c and attach a statement providing the information required by items 7a–e and 8 for each defendant.)

8. a. ☐ The notice in item 7a was served on the defendant named in item 7a as follows:

    (1) ☐ by personally handing a copy to defendant on (date):

    (2) ☐ by leaving a copy with (name or description):

    a person of suitable age and discretion, on (date): at defendant's

    ☐ residence ☐ business AND mailing a copy to defendant at defendant's place of residence on

    (date): because defendant cannot be found at defendant's residence or usual place of business.

    (3) ☐ by posting a copy on the premises on (date): ☐ AND giving a copy to a person found residing at the premises AND mailing a copy to defendant at the premises on

    (date):

        (a) ☐ because defendant's residence and usual place of business cannot be ascertained OR

        (b) ☐ because no person of suitable age or discretion can be found there.

    (4) ☐ (Not for 3-day notice; see Civil Code, § 1946 before using) by sending a copy by certified or registered mail addressed to defendant on (date):

    (5) ☐ (Not for residential tenancies; see Civil Code, § 1953 before using) in the manner specified in a written commercial lease between the parties.

b. ☐ (Name):

was served on behalf of all defendants who signed a joint written rental agreement.

c. ☐ Information about service of notice on the defendants alleged in item 7f is stated in Attachment 8c.

d. ☐ Proof of service of the notice in item 7a is attached and labeled Exhibit 3.

9. ☐ Plaintiff demands possession from each defendant because of expiration of a fixed-term lease.

10. ☐ At the time the 3-day notice to pay rent or quit was served, the amount of **rent due** was $

11. ☐ The fair rental value of the premises is $ per day.

12. ☐ Defendant's continued possession is malicious, and plaintiff is entitled to statutory damages under Code of Civil Procedure section 1174(b). *(State specific facts supporting a claim up to $600 in Attachment 12.)*

13. ☐ A written agreement between the parties provides for attorney fees.

14. ☐ Defendant's tenancy is subject to the local rent control or eviction control ordinance of *(city or county, title of ordinance, and date of passage):*

     Plaintiff has met all applicable requirements of the ordinances.

15. ☐ Other allegations are stated in Attachment 15.

16. Plaintiff accepts the jurisdictional limit, if any, of the court.

17. **PLAINTIFF REQUESTS**
    a. possession of the premises.
    b. costs incurred in this proceeding:
    c. ☐ past-due rent of $
    d. ☐ reasonable attorney fees.
    e. ☐ forfeiture of the agreement.
    f. ☐ damages at the rate stated in item 11 from *(date):*   for each day that defendants remain in possession through entry of judgment.
    g. ☐ statutory damages up to $600 for the conduct alleged in item 12.
    h. ☐ other *(specify):*

18. ☐ Number of pages attached *(specify):* _____

UNLAWFUL DETAINER ASSISTANT (Bus. & Prof. Code, §§ 6400–6415)

19. *(Complete in all cases.)* An unlawful detainer assistant ☐ did **not** ☐ did for compensation give advice or assistance with this form. *(If plaintiff has received **any** help or advice for pay from an unlawful detainer assistant, state:)*

     a. Assistant's name:
     b. Street address, city, and zip code:

     c. Telephone No.:
     d. County of registration:
     e. Registration No.:
     f. Expires on *(date):*

Date:

▶

_____
(TYPE OR PRINT NAME)

_____
(SIGNATURE OF PLAINTIFF OR ATTORNEY)

VERIFICATION

(Use a different verification form if the verification is by an attorney or for a corporation or partnership.)

I am the plaintiff in this proceeding and have read this complaint. I declare under penalty of perjury under the laws of the State of California that the foregoing is true and correct.

Date:

▶

_____
(TYPE OR PRINT NAME)

_____
(SIGNATURE OF PLAINTIFF)

ATTORNEY OR PARTY WITHOUT ATTORNEY *(Name, State Bar number, and address):*	*FOR COURT USE ONLY*

TELEPHONE NO.:   FAX NO.:

ATTORNEY FOR *(Name):*   Plaintiff in Pro Per

SUPERIOR COURT OF CALIFORNIA, COUNTY OF

    STREET ADDRESS:

    MAILING ADDRESS:

    CITY AND ZIP CODE:

    BRANCH NAME:

CASE NAME:

CIVIL CASE COVER SHEET	**Complex Case Designation**	CASE NUMBER:
[ ] **Unlimited** [X] **Limited**	[ ] **Counter** [ ] **Joinder**	
(Amount demanded exceeds $25,000) (Amount demanded is $25,000 or less)	Filed with first appearance by defendant (Cal. Rules of Court, rule 3.402)	JUDGE: DEPT:

Items 1–5 below must be completed (see instructions on page 2).

1. Check **one** box below for the case type that best describes this case:

Auto Tort
- [ ] Auto (22)
- [ ] Uninsured motorist (46)

Other PI/PD/WD (Personal Injury/Property Damage/Wrongful Death) Tort
- [ ] Asbestos (04)
- [ ] Product liability (24)
- [ ] Medical malpractice (45)
- [ ] Other PI/PD/WD (23)

Non-PI/PD/WD (Other) Tort
- [ ] Business tort/unfair business practice (07)
- [ ] Civil rights (08)
- [ ] Defamation (13)
- [ ] Fraud (16)
- [ ] Intellectual property (19)
- [ ] Professional negligence (25)
- [ ] Other non-PI/PD/WD tort (35)

Employment
- [ ] Wrongful termination (36)
- [ ] Other employment (15)

Contract
- [ ] Breach of contract/warranty (06)
- [ ] Collections (09)
- [ ] Insurance coverage (18)
- [ ] Other contract (37)

Real Property
- [ ] Eminent domain/Inverse condemnation (14)
- [ ] Wrongful eviction (33)
- [ ] Other real property (26)

Unlawful Detainer
- [ ] Commercial (31)
- [X] Residential (32)
- [ ] Drugs (38)

Judicial Review
- [ ] Asset forfeiture (05)
- [ ] Petition re: arbitration award (11)
- [ ] Writ of mandate (02)
- [ ] Other judicial review (39)

Provisionally Complex Civil Litigation (Cal. Rules of Court, rules 3.400–3.403)
- [ ] Antitrust/Trade regulation (03)
- [ ] Construction defect (10)
- [ ] Mass tort (40)
- [ ] Securities litigation (28)
- [ ] Environmental/Toxic tort (30)
- [ ] Insurance coverage claims arising from the above listed provisionally complex case types (41)

Enforcement of Judgment
- [ ] Enforcement of judgment (20)

Miscellaneous Civil Complaint
- [ ] RICO (27)
- [ ] Other complaint *(not specified above)* (42)

Miscellaneous Civil Petition
- [ ] Partnership and corporate governance (21)
- [ ] Other petition *(not specified above)* (43)

2. This case [ ] is [X] is not   complex under rule 3.400 of the California Rules of Court. If the case is complex, mark the factors requiring exceptional judicial management:
    a. [ ] Large number of separately represented parties   d. [ ] Large number of witnesses
    b. [ ] Extensive motion practice raising difficult or novel issues that will be time-consuming to resolve   e. [ ] Coordination with related actions pending in one or more courts in other counties, states, or countries, or in a federal court
    c. [ ] Substantial amount of documentary evidence   f. [ ] Substantial postjudgment judicial supervision

3. Type of remedies sought *(check all that apply):*
    a. [X] monetary   b. [X] nonmonetary; declaratory or injunctive relief   c. [ ] punitive

4. Number of causes of action *(specify):*

5. This case [ ] is [X] is not   a class action suit.

6. If there are any known related cases, file and serve a notice of related case. *(You may use form CM-015.)*

Date:

        ▶

_____   _____
(TYPE OR PRINT NAME)   (SIGNATURE OF PARTY OR ATTORNEY FOR PARTY)

NOTICE
- Plaintiff must file this cover sheet with the first paper filed in the action or proceeding (except small claims cases or cases filed under the Probate Code, Family Code, or Welfare and Institutions Code). (Cal. Rules of Court, rule 3.220.) Failure to file may result in sanctions.
- File this cover sheet in addition to any cover sheet required by local court rule.
- If this case is complex under rule 3.400 et seq. of the California Rules of Court, you must serve a copy of this cover sheet on **all** other parties to the action or proceeding.
- Unless this is a complex case, this cover sheet will be used for statistical purposes only.

Page 1 of 2

Form Adopted for Mandatory Use
Judicial Council of California
CM-010 [Rev. January 1, 2007]

CIVIL CASE COVER SHEET

Cal. Rules of Court, rules 3.220, 3.400–3.403;
Standards of Judicial Administration, § 19
www.courtinfo.ca.gov

INSTRUCTIONS ON HOW TO COMPLETE THE COVER SHEET

To Plaintiffs and Others Filing First Papers

If you are filing a first paper (for example, a complaint) in a civil case, you **must** complete and file, along with your first paper, the *Civil Case Cover Sheet* contained on page 1. This information will be used to compile statistics about the types and numbers of cases filed. You must complete items 1 through 5 on the sheet. In item 1, you must check **one** box for the case type that best describes the case. If the case fits both a general and a more specific type of case listed in item 1, check the more specific one. If the case has multiple causes of action, check the box that best indicates the **primary** cause of action. To assist you in completing the sheet, examples of the cases that belong under each case type in item 1 are provided below. A cover sheet must be filed only with your initial paper. You do not need to submit a cover sheet with amended papers. Failure to file a cover sheet with the first paper filed in a civil case may subject a party, its counsel, or both to sanctions under rules 2.30 and 3.220 of the California Rules of Court.

To Parties in Complex Cases

In complex cases only, parties must also use the *Civil Case Cover Sheet* to designate whether the case is complex. If a plaintiff believes the case is complex under rule 3.400 of the California Rules of Court, this must be indicated by completing the appropriate boxes in items 1 and 2. If a plaintiff designates a case as complex, the cover sheet must be served with the complaint on all parties to the action. A defendant may file and serve no later than the time of its first appearance a joinder in the plaintiff's designation, a counter-designation that the case is not complex, or, if the plaintiff has made no designation, a designation that the case is complex.

CASE TYPES AND EXAMPLES

Auto Tort
  Auto (22)–Personal Injury/Property
    Damage/Wrongful Death
  Uninsured Motorist (46) (*if the
    case involves an uninsured
    motorist claim subject to
    arbitration, check this item
    instead of Auto*)

**Other PI/PD/WD (Personal Injury/
Property Damage/Wrongful Death)
Tort**
  Asbestos (04)
    Asbestos Property Damage
    Asbestos Personal Injury/
      Wrongful Death
  Product Liability (*not asbestos or
    toxic/environmental*) (24)
  Medical Malpractice (45)
    Medical Malpractice–
      Physicians & Surgeons
    Other Professional Health Care
      Malpractice
  Other PI/PD/WD (23)
    Premises Liability (e.g., slip
      and fall)
    Intentional Bodily Injury/PD/WD
      (e.g., assault, vandalism)
    Intentional Infliction of
      Emotional Distress
    Negligent Infliction of
      Emotional Distress
    Other PI/PD/WD

Non-PI/PD/WD (Other) Tort
  Business Tort/Unfair Business
    Practice (07)
  Civil Rights (e.g., discrimination,
    false arrest) (*not civil
    harassment*) (08)
  Defamation (e.g., slander, libel)
    (13)
  Fraud (16)
  Intellectual Property (19)
  Professional Negligence (25)
    Legal Malpractice
    Other Professional Malpractice
      (*not medical or legal*)
  Other Non-PI/PD/WD Tort (35)

Employment
  Wrongful Termination (36)
  Other Employment (15)

Contract
  Breach of Contract/Warranty (06)
    Breach of Rental/Lease
      Contract (*not unlawful detainer
      or wrongful eviction*)
    Contract/Warranty Breach–Seller
      Plaintiff (*not fraud or negligence*)
    Negligent Breach of Contract/
      Warranty
    Other Breach of Contract/Warranty
  Collections (e.g., money owed, open
    book accounts) (09)
    Collection Case–Seller Plaintiff
    Other Promissory Note/Collections
      Case
  Insurance Coverage (*not provisionally
    complex*) (18)
    Auto Subrogation
    Other Coverage
  Other Contract (37)
    Contractual Fraud
    Other Contract Dispute

Real Property
  Eminent Domain/Inverse
    Condemnation (14)
  Wrongful Eviction (33)
  Other Real Property (e.g., quiet title) (26)
    Writ of Possession of Real Property
    Mortgage Foreclosure
    Quiet Title
    Other Real Property (*not eminent
      domain, landlord/tenant, or
      foreclosure*)

Unlawful Detainer
  Commercial (31)
  Residential (32)
  Drugs (38) (*if the case involves illegal
    drugs, check this item; otherwise,
    report as Commercial or
    Residential*)

Judicial Review
  Asset Forfeiture (05)
  Petition Re: Arbitration Award (11)
  Writ of Mandate (02)
    Writ–Administrative Mandamus
    Writ–Mandamus on Limited Court
      Case Matter
    Writ–Other Limited Court Case
      Review
  Other Judicial Review (39)
    Review of Health Officer Order
    Notice of Appeal–Labor
      Commissioner Appeals

**Provisionally Complex Civil Litigation
(Cal. Rules of Court Rules 3.400–3.403)**
  Antitrust/Trade Regulation (03)
  Construction Defect (10)
  Claims Involving Mass Tort (40)
  Securities Litigation (28)
  Environmental/Toxic Tort (30)
  Insurance Coverage Claims
    (*arising from provisionally
    complex case type listed above*)
    (41)

Enforcement of Judgment
  Enforcement of Judgment (20)
    Abstract of Judgment (Out of
      County)
    Confession of Judgment (*non-
      domestic relations*)
    Sister State Judgment
    Administrative Agency Award
      (*not unpaid taxes*)
    Petition/Certification of Entry of
      Judgment on Unpaid Taxes
    Other Enforcement of Judgment
      Case

Miscellaneous Civil Complaint
  RICO (27)
  Other Complaint (*not specified
    above*) (42)
    Declaratory Relief Only
    Injunctive Relief Only (*non-
      harassment*)
    Mechanics Lien
    Other Commercial Complaint
      Case (*non-tort/non-complex*)
    Other Civil Complaint
      (*non-tort/non-complex*)

Miscellaneous Civil Petition
  Partnership and Corporate
    Governance (21)
  Other Petition (*not specified above*)
    (43)
    Civil Harassment
    Workplace Violence
    Elder/Dependent Adult
      Abuse
    Election Contest
    Petition for Name Change
    Petition for Relief from Late
      Claim
    Other Civil Petition

CIVIL CASE COVER SHEET ADDENDUM AND STATEMENT OF LOCATION
(CERTIFICATE OF GROUNDS FOR ASSIGNMENT TO COURTHOUSE LOCATION)

This form is required pursuant to LASC Local Rule 2.0 in all new civil case filings in the Los Angeles Superior Court.

Item I. Check the types of hearing and fill in the estimated length of hearing expected for this case:

JURY TRIAL? ☐ YES   CLASS ACTION? ☐ YES   LIMITED CASE? ☐ YES   TIME ESTIMATED FOR TRIAL_____ ☐ HOURS/ ☐ DAYS

Item II. Select the correct district and courthouse location (4 steps – If you checked "Limited Case", skip to Item III, Pg. 4):

Step 1: After first completing the Civil Case Cover Sheet Form, find the main civil case cover sheet heading for your case in the left margin below, and, to the right in Column **A**, the Civil Case Cover Sheet case type you selected.

Step 2: Check **one** Superior Court type of action in Column **B** below which best describes the nature of this case.

Step 3: In Column **C**, circle the reason for the court location choice that applies to the type of action you have checked.
For any exception to the court location, see Los Angeles Superior Court Local Rule 2.0.

Applicable Reasons for Choosing Courthouse Location (see Column C below)

1. Class Actions must be filed in the County Courthouse, Central District.
2. May be filed in Central (Other county, or no Bodily Injury/Property Damage).
3. Location where cause of action arose.
4. Location where bodily injury, death or damage occurred.
5. Location where performance required or defendant resides.
6. Location of property or permanently garaged vehicle.
7. Location where petitioner resides.
8. Location wherein defendant/respondent functions wholly.
9. Location where one or more of the parties reside.
10. Location of Labor Commissioner Office.

Step 4: Fill in the information requested on page 4 in Item III; complete Item IV. Sign the declaration.

	A Civil Case Cover Sheet Category No.	**B** Type of Action (Check only one)	**C** Applicable Reasons - See Step 3 Above
Auto Tort	Auto (22)	☐ A7100 Motor Vehicle - Personal Injury/Property Damage/Wrongful Death	1., 2., 4.
	Uninsured Motorist (46)	☐ A7110 Personal Injury/Property Damage/Wrongful Death – Uninsured Motorist	1., 2., 4.
Other Personal Injury/Property Damage/Wrongful Death Tort	Asbestos (04)	☐ A6070 Asbestos Property Damage	2.
		☐ A7221 Asbestos - Personal Injury/Wrongful Death	2.
	Product Liability (24)	☐ A7260 Product Liability (not asbestos or toxic/environmental)	1., 2., 3., 4., 8.
	Medical Malpractice (45)	☐ A7210 Medical Malpractice - Physicians & Surgeons	1., 2., 4.
		☐ A7240 Other Professional Health Care Malpractice	1., 2., 4.
	Other Personal Injury Property Damage Wrongful Death (23)	☐ A7250 Premises Liability (e.g., slip and fall)	1., 2., 4.
		☐ A7230 Intentional Bodily Injury/Property Damage/Wrongful Death (e.g., assault, vandalism, etc.)	1., 2., 4.
		☐ A7270 Intentional Infliction of Emotional Distress	1., 2., 3.
		☐ A7220 Other Personal Injury/Property Damage/Wrongful Death	1., 2., 4.
Non-Personal Injury/Property Damage/Wrongful Death Tort	Business Tort (07)	☐ A6029 Other Commercial/Business Tort (not fraud/breach of contract)	1., 2., 3.
	Civil Rights (08)	☐ A6005 Civil Rights/Discrimination	1., 2., 3.
	Defamation (13)	☐ A6010 Defamation (slander/libel)	1., 2., 3.
	Fraud (16)	☐ A6013 Fraud (no contract)	1., 2., 3.

Non-Personal Injury/Property Damage/Wrongful Death Tort (Cont'd.)

A Civil Case Cover Sheet Category No.	B Type of Action (Check only one)	C Applicable Reasons -See Step 3 Above
Professional Negligence (25)	☐ A6017 Legal Malpractice	1., 2., 3.
	☐ A6050 Other Professional Malpractice (not medical or legal)	1., 2., 3.
Other (35)	☐ A6025 Other Non-Personal Injury/Property Damage tort	2.,3.

Employment

Wrongful Termination (36)	☐ A6037 Wrongful Termination	1., 2., 3.
Other Employment (15)	☐ A6024 Other Employment Complaint Case	1., 2., 3.
	☐ A6109 Labor Commissioner Appeals	10.

Contract

Breach of Contract/ Warranty (06) (not insurance)	☐ A6004 Breach of Rental/Lease Contract (not Unlawful Detainer or wrongful eviction)	2., 5.
	☐ A6008 Contract/Warranty Breach -Seller Plaintiff (no fraud/negligence)	2., 5.
	☐ A6019 Negligent Breach of Contract/Warranty (no fraud)	1., 2., 5.
	☐ A6028 Other Breach of Contract/Warranty (not fraud or negligence)	1., 2., 5.
Collections (09)	☐ A6002 Collections Case-Seller Plaintiff	2., 5., 6.
	☐ A6012 Other Promissory Note/Collections Case	2., 5.
Insurance Coverage (18)	☐ A6015 Insurance Coverage (not complex)	1., 2., 5., 8.
Other Contract (37)	☐ A6009 Contractual Fraud	1., 2., 3., 5.
	☐ A6031 Tortious Interference	1., 2., 3., 5.
	☐ A6027 Other Contract Dispute(not breach/insurance/fraud/negligence)	1., 2., 3., 8.

Real Property

Eminent Domain/Inverse Condemnation (14)	☐ A7300 Eminent Domain/Condemnation Number of parcels_____	2.
Wrongful Eviction (33)	☐ A6023 Wrongful Eviction Case	2., 6.
Other Real Property (26)	☐ A6018 Mortgage Foreclosure	2., 6.
	☐ A6032 Quiet Title	2., 6.
	☐ A6060 Other Real Property (not eminent domain, landlord/tenant, foreclosure)	2., 6.

Unlawful Detainer

Unlawful Detainer-Commercial (31)	☐ A6021 Unlawful Detainer-Commercial (not drugs or wrongful eviction)	2., 6.
Unlawful Detainer-Residential (32)	☐ A6020 Unlawful Detainer-Residential (not drugs or wrongful eviction)	2., 6.
Unlawful Detainer-Drugs (38)	☐ A6022 Unlawful Detainer-Drugs	2., 6.

Judicial Review

Asset Forfeiture (05)	☐ A6108 Asset Forfeiture Case	2., 6.
Petition re Arbitration (11)	☐ A6115 Petition to Compel/Confirm/Vacate Arbitration	2., 5.

CIV 109 03-04 (Rev. 03/06)
LASC Approved

**CIVIL CASE COVER SHEET ADDENDUM
AND STATEMENT OF LOCATION**

LASC, rule 2.0
Page 2 of 4

A Civil Case Cover Sheet Category No.	**B** Type of Action (Check only one)	**C** Applicable Reasons - See Step 3 Above
Writ of Mandate (02)	☐ A6151 Writ - Administrative Mandamus ☐ A6152 Writ - Mandamus on Limited Court Case Matter ☐ A6153 Writ - Other Limited Court Case Review	2., 8. 2. 2.
Other Judicial Review (39)	☐ A6150 Other Writ /Judicial Review	2., 8.
Antitrust/Trade Regulation (03)	☐ A6003 Antitrust/Trade Regulation	1., 2., 8.
Construction Defect (10)	☐ A6007 Construction defect	1., 2., 3.
Claims Involving Mass Tort (40)	☐ A6006 Claims Involving Mass Tort	1., 2., 8.
Securities Litigation (28)	☐ A6035 Securities Litigation Case	1., 2., 8.
Toxic Tort Environmental (30)	☐ A6036 Toxic Tort/Environmental	1., 2., 3., 8.
Insurance Coverage Claims from Complex Case (41)	☐ A6014 Insurance Coverage/Subrogation (complex case only)	1., 2., 5., 8.
Enforcement of Judgment (20)	☐ A6141 Sister State Judgment ☐ A6160 Abstract of Judgment ☐ A6107 Confession of Judgment (non-domestic relations) ☐ A6140 Administrative Agency Award (not unpaid taxes) ☐ A6114 Petition/Certificate for Entry of Judgment on Unpaid Tax ☐ A6112 Other Enforcement of Judgment Case	2., 9. 2., 6. 2., 9. 2., 8. 2., 8. 2., 8., 9.
RICO (27)	☐ A6033 Racketeering (RICO) Case	1., 2., 8.
Other Complaints (Not Specified Above) (42)	☐ A6030 Declaratory Relief Only ☐ A6040 Injunctive Relief Only (not domestic/harassment) ☐ A6011 Other Commercial Complaint Case (non-tort/non-complex) ☐ A6000 Other Civil Complaint (non-tort/non-complex)	1., 2., 8. 2., 8. 1., 2., 8. 1., 2., 8.
Partnership Corporation Governance(21)	☐ A6113 Partnership and Corporate Governance Case	2., 8.
Other Petitions (Not Specified Above) (43)	☐ A6121 Civil Harassment ☐ A6123 Workplace Harassment ☐ A6124 Elder/Dependent Adult Abuse Case ☐ A6190 Election Contest ☐ A6110 Petition for Change of Name ☐ A6170 Petition for Relief from Late Claim Law ☐ A6100 Other Civil Petition	2., 3., 9. 2., 3., 9. 2., 3., 9. 2. 2., 7. 2., 3., 4., 8. 2., 9.

Judicial Review (Cont'd.)

Provisionally Complex Litigation

Enforcement of Judgment

Miscellaneous Civil Complaints

Miscellaneous Civil Petitions

Item III. Statement of Location: Enter the address of the accident, party's residence or place of business, performance, or other circumstance indicated in Item II., Step 3 on Page 1, as the proper reason for filing in the court location you selected.

REASON: CHECK THE NUMBER UNDER COLUMN C WHICH APPLIES IN THIS CASE ☐1. ☐2. ☐3. ☐4. ☐5. ☐6. ☐7. ☐8. ☐9. ☐10.			ADDRESS:
CITY:	STATE:	ZIP CODE:	

Item IV. *Declaration of Assignment*: I declare under penalty of perjury under the laws of the State of California that the foregoing is true and correct and that the above-entitled matter is properly filed for assignment to the _____ courthouse in the _____ District of the Los Angeles Superior Court (Code Civ. Proc., § 392 et seq., and LASC Local Rule 2.0, subds. (b), (c) and (d)).

Dated: _____

_____
(SIGNATURE OF ATTORNEY/FILING PARTY)

PLEASE HAVE THE FOLLOWING ITEMS COMPLETED AND READY TO BE FILED IN ORDER TO PROPERLY COMMENCE YOUR NEW COURT CASE:

1. Original Complaint or Petition.

2. If filing a Complaint, a completed Summons form for issuance by the Clerk.

3. Civil Case Cover Sheet form CM-010.

4. Complete Addendum to Civil Case Cover Sheet form LASC Approved CIV 109 03-04 (Rev. 03/06).

5. Payment in full of the filing fee, unless fees have been waived.

6. Signed order appointing the Guardian ad Litem, JC form 982(a)(27), if the plaintiff or petitioner is a minor under 18 years of age, or if required by Court.

7. Additional copies of documents to be conformed by the Clerk. Copies of the cover sheet and this addendum must be served along with the summons and complaint, or other initiating pleading in the case.

CIV 109 03-04 (Rev. 03/06)
LASC Approved

CIVIL CASE COVER SHEET ADDENDUM
AND STATEMENT OF LOCATION

LASC, rule 2.0
Page 4 of 4

ATTORNEY OR PARTY WITHOUT ATTORNEY *(Name, State Bar number, and address):*	*FOR COURT USE ONLY*
TELEPHONE NO.: FAX NO. *(Optional):* E-MAIL ADDRESS *(Optional):* ATTORNEY FOR *(Name):* Plaintiff in Pro Per	

SUPERIOR COURT OF CALIFORNIA, COUNTY OF	
STREET ADDRESS: MAILING ADDRESS: CITY AND ZIP CODE: BRANCH NAME:	

PLAINTIFF/PETITIONER:	CASE NUMBER:
DEFENDANT/RESPONDENT:	

PROOF OF SERVICE OF SUMMONS	Ref. No. or File No.:

(Separate proof of service is required for each party served.)

1. At the time of service I was at least 18 years of age and not a party to this action.

2. I served copies of:

   a. ☐   summons

   b. ☐   complaint

   c. ☐   Alternative Dispute Resolution (ADR) package

   d. ☐   Civil Case Cover Sheet *(served in complex cases only)*

   e. ☐   cross-complaint

   f. ☐   other *(specify documents):*

3. a. Party served *(specify name of party as shown on documents served):*

   b. ☐   Person (other than the party in item 3a) served on behalf of an entity or as an authorized agent (and not a person under item 5b on whom substituted service was made) *(specify name and relationship to the party named in item 3a):*

4. Address where the party was served:

5. I served the party *(check proper box)*

   a. ☐   **by personal service.** I personally delivered the documents listed in item 2 to the party or person authorized to receive service of process for the party (1) on *(date):*   (2) at *(time):*

   b. ☐   **by substituted service.** On *(date):*   at *(time):*   I left the documents listed in item 2 with or in the presence of *(name and title or relationship to person indicated in item 3):*

       (1) ☐   **(business)** a person at least 18 years of age apparently in charge at the office or usual place of business of the person to be served. I informed him or her of the general nature of the papers.

       (2) ☐   **(home)** a competent member of the household (at least 18 years of age) at the dwelling house or usual place of abode of the party. I informed him or her of the general nature of the papers.

       (3) ☐   **(physical address unknown)** a person at least 18 years of age apparently in charge at the usual mailing address of the person to be served, other than a United States Postal Service post office box. I informed him or her of the general nature of the papers.

       (4) ☐   I thereafter mailed (by first-class, postage prepaid) copies of the documents to the person to be served at the place where the copies were left (Code Civ. Proc., § 415.20). I mailed the documents on *(date):*   from *(city):*   **or** ☐ a declaration of mailing is attached.

       (5) ☐   I attach a **declaration of diligence** stating actions taken first to attempt personal service.

Page 1 of 2

Form Adopted for Mandatory Use Judicial Council of California POS-010 [Rev. January 1, 2007]	**PROOF OF SERVICE OF SUMMONS**	Code of Civil Procedure, § 417.10

5. c. ☐ **by mail and acknowledgment of receipt of service.** I mailed the documents listed in item 2 to the party, to the address shown in item 4, by first-class mail, postage prepaid,

    (1) on *(date):*   (2) from *(city):*

    (3) ☐ with two copies of the *Notice and Acknowledgment of Receipt* and a postage-paid return envelope addressed to me. *(Attach completed Notice and Acknowledgement of Receipt.)* (Code Civ. Proc., § 415.30.)

    (4) ☐ to an address outside California with return receipt requested. (Code Civ. Proc., § 415.40.)

  d. ☐ **by other means** *(specify means of service and authorizing code section):*

    ☐ Additional page describing service is attached.

6. The "Notice to the Person Served" (on the summons) was completed as follows:
  a. ☐ as an individual defendant.
  b. ☐ as the person sued under the fictitious name of *(specify):*
  c. ☐ as occupant.
  d. ☐ On behalf of *(specify):*
    under the following Code of Civil Procedure section:

    ☐ 416.10 (corporation)   ☐ 415.95 (business organization, form unknown)
    ☐ 416.20 (defunct corporation)   ☐ 416.60 (minor)
    ☐ 416.30 (joint stock company/association)   ☐ 416.70 (ward or conservatee)
    ☐ 416.40 (association or partnership)   ☐ 416.90 (authorized person)
    ☐ 416.50 (public entity)   ☐ 415.46 (occupant)
                      ☐ other:

7. **Person who served papers**
  a. Name:
  b. Address:
  c. Telephone number:
  d. **The fee** for service was: $
  e. I am:
    (1) ☐ not a registered California process server.
    (2) ☐ exempt from registration under Business and Professions Code section 22350(b).
    (3) ☐ a registered California process server:
      (i) ☐ owner ☐ employee ☐ independent contractor.
      (ii) Registration No.:
      (iii) County:

8. ☐ **I declare** under penalty of perjury under the laws of the State of California that the foregoing is true and correct.

    or

9. ☐ **I am a California sheriff or marshal and** I certify that the foregoing is true and correct.

Date:

▶

_____   _____
(NAME OF PERSON WHO SERVED PAPERS/SHERIFF OR MARSHAL)   (SIGNATURE)

NAME, ADDRESS, AND TELEPHONE NUMBER OF ATTORNEY OR PARTY WITHOUT ATTORNEY:	STATE BAR NUMBER	*Reserved for Clerk's File Stamp*

ATTORNEY FOR (Name):   Plaintiff in Pro Per

SUPERIOR COURT OF CALIFORNIA, COUNTY OF

COURTHOUSE ADDRESS:

PLAINTIFF:

DEFENDANT:

APPLICATION AND ORDER TO SERVE SUMMONS BY POSTING FOR UNLAWFUL DETAINER	CASE NUMBER:

1. I am the ☐ plaintiff   ☐ plaintiff's attorney   ☐ other (specify):_____

2. I apply for an order pursuant to Code of Civil Procedure section 415.45 to permit service by posting of the summons and complaint on defendant(s). *Specify name(s):* _____
    _____
    _____
    _____
    _____

3. The complaint seeks possession of property location at: _____
    _____. The property is ☐ residential   ☐ commercial.

4. The notice to quit, or pay rent or quit, was served by: ☐ personal service   ☐ substituted service
    ☐ posting and mailing ☐ other *(specify)*:_____

5. At least three attempts to serve in a manner specified in Code of Civil Procedure, Article 3, (other than posting or publication) are required. List attempts to serve, if made by declarant, or attach declaration(s) of process server(s) stating attempts to locate and serve the defendants. If service not made, please explain.

DATE	TIME	REASON SERVICE COULD NOT BE MADE/REMARKS

☐ Declaration(s) of process server stating attempts to locate and serve the defendant(s) is attached and incorporated into this application by reference

CIV 107 10-03
LASC Approved

**APPLICATION AND ORDER TO SERVE SUMMONS
BY POSTING FOR UNLAWFUL DETAINER**

Code Civ. Proc., § 415.45
Page 1 of 2

6. Service ☐ has ☐ has not been attempted during regular business hours at the place(s) of employment of the defendant(s). If not, state reason: ☐ the place(s) of employment of the defendant(s) is not known. ☐ Other (specify): _____

_____

_____

7. Service ☐ has ☐ has not been attempted at the "residence" of the defendant(s). If not, state reasons: ☐ The place of residence of the defendant(s) is not known. ☐ Other (specify): _____

_____

_____

8. Other: _____

_____

_____

9. Did the plaintiff pay for help from a registered unlawful detainer assistant (Bus. and Prof. Code, §§ 6400-5415) who helped prepare this form? ☐ Yes ☐ No If yes, complete the following information: Name of Unlawful Detainer Assistant: _____; Telephone Number: (   ) _____ Address (Mailing address, city and Zip code): _____

_____

Registration #: _____; County of Registration: _____.

I declare under penalty of perjury under the laws of the State of California, that the foregoing is true and correct.

DATE	TYPE OF PRINT DECLARANT'S NAME	DECLARANT'S SIGNATURE

FINDINGS AND ORDER

THE COURT FINDS:

1. The defendant(s) named in the application cannot with reasonable diligence be served in any manner specified in Code of Civil Procedure, Article 3.

2. (a) A cause of action exists against the defendant(s) named in the application; **and/or** (b) defendant(s) named in the application has or claims an interest in real property in California that is subject to the jurisdiction of the court; **and/or** (c) the relief demanded in the complaint consists wholly or partially in excluding the defendant(s) from any interest in the property.

THE COURT ORDERS:

The defendant(s) named in the application may be served by posting a copy of the summons and complaint on the premises in a manner most likely to give actual notice to the defendant(s), and by immediately mailing, by certified mail, a copy of the summons and complaint to the defendant(s) at his/her last known address.

Dated: _____   _____   _____

Judicial Officer   Div/Dept.

CIV 107 10-03
LASC Approved

**APPLICATION AND ORDER TO SERVE SUMMONS
BY POSTING FOR UNLAWFUL DETAINER**

Code Civ. Proc., § 415.45
Page 2 of 2

CLAIMANT OR CLAIMANT'S ATTORNEY *(Name and Address)*:

TELEPHONE NO.:

FOR COURT USE ONLY

ATTORNEY FOR *(Name)*: Plaintiff in Pro Per

NAME OF COURT: SUPERIOR COURT OF THE STATE OF CALIFORNIA, COUNTY OF

STREET ADDRESS:

MAILING ADDRESS:

CITY AND ZIP CODE:

BRANCH NAME:

PLAINTIFF:

DEFENDANT:

PREJUDGMENT CLAIM OF RIGHT TO POSSESSION

CASE NUMBER:

Complete this form only if ALL of these statements are true:
1. **You are NOT named in the accompanying Summons and Complaint.**
2. **You occupied the premises on or before the date the unlawful detainer (eviction) Complaint was filed.**
3. **You still occupy the premises.**

(To be completed by the process server)
DATE OF SERVICE:

(Date that this form is served or delivered, and posted, and mailed by the officer or process server)

I DECLARE THE FOLLOWING UNDER PENALTY OF PERJURY:

1. My name is *(specify)*:

2. I reside at *(street address, unit No., city and ZIP code)*:

3. The address of "the premises" subject to this claim is *(address)*:

4. On *(insert date)*: [   ], the landlord or the landlord's authorized agent filed a complaint to recover possession of the premises. *(This date is the court filing date on the accompanying Summons and Complaint.*

5. I occupied the premises on the date the complaint was filed *(the date in item 4)*. I have continued to occupy the premises ever since.

6. I was at least 18 years of age on the date the complaint was filed *(the date in item 4)*.

7. I claim a right to possession of the premises because I occupied the premises on the date the complaint was filed *(the date in item 4)*.

8. I was not named in the Summons and Complaint.

9. I understand that if I make this claim of right to possession, I will be added as a defendant to the unlawful detainer (eviction) action.

10. *(Filing fee)* I understand that I must go to the court and pay a filing fee of $ or file with the court the form "Application for Waiver of Court Fees and Costs." I understand that if I don't pay the filing fee or file with the court the form for waiver of court fees within 10 days from the date of service on this form (excluding court holidays), I will not be entitled to make a claim of right to possession.

(Continued on reverse)

PREJUDGMENT CLAIM OF RIGHT TO POSSESSION
Code of Civil Procedure §§ 415.46, 715.010, 715.020, 1174.25

PLAINTIFF (Name):	CASE NUMBER:
DEFENDANT (Name):	

NOTICE: If you fail to file this claim, you will be evicted without further hearing.

11. *(Response required within five days after you file this form)* I understand that I will have *five days* (excluding court holidays) to file a response to the Summons and Complaint after I file this Prejudgment Claim of Right to Possession form.

12. **Rental agreement.** I have *(check all that apply to you)*:
   a. ☐ an oral rental agreement with the landlord.
   b. ☐ a written rental agreement with the landlord.
   c. ☐ an oral rental agreement with a person other than the landlord.
   d. ☐ a written rental agreement with a person other than the landlord.
   e. ☐ other *(explain)*:

I declare under penalty of perjury under the laws of the State of California that the foregoing is true and correct.

WARNING: Perjury is a felony punishable by imprisonment in the state prison.

Date:

. . . .
(TYPE OR PRINT NAME)

▶ _____
(SIGNATURE OF CLAIMANT) –

NOTICE: If you file this claim of right to possession, the unlawful detainer (eviction) action against you will be determined at trial. At trial, you may be found liable for rent, costs, and, in some cases, treble damages.

— NOTICE TO OCCUPANTS —

YOU MUST ACT AT ONCE if all the following are true:
   1. **You are NOT named in the accompanying Summons and Complaint.**
   2. **You occupied the premises on or before the date the unlawful detainer (eviction) complaint was filed.** *(The date is the court filing date on the accompanying Summons and Complaint.)*
   3. **You still occupy the premises.**

(Where to file this form)   You can complete and SUBMIT THIS CLAIM FORM WITHIN 10 DAYS from the date of service (on the reverse of this form) at the court where the unlawful detainer (eviction) complaint was filed.

(What will happen if you do not file this form)   If you do not complete and submit this form and pay a filing fee or file the form for proceeding in forma pauperis if you cannot pay the fee), YOU WILL BE EVICTED.

After this form is properly filed, you will be added as a defendant in the unlawful detainer (eviction) action and your right to occupy the premises will be decided by the court. *If you do not file this claim, you will be evicted without a hearing.*

ATTORNEY OR PARTY WITHOUT ATTORNEY *(Name, State Bar number, and address):*	*FOR COURT USE ONLY*
TELEPHONE NO.: FAX NO. *(Optional):* E-MAIL ADDRESS *(Optional):* ATTORNEY FOR *(Name):* Plaintiff in Pro Per	

SUPERIOR COURT OF CALIFORNIA, COUNTY OF

STREET ADDRESS:

MAILING ADDRESS:

CITY AND ZIP CODE:

BRANCH NAME:

PLAINTIFF/PETITIONER:

DEFENDANT/RESPONDENT:

REQUEST FOR **(Application)**	☐ **Entry of Default** ☐ **Clerk's Judgment** ☐ **Court Judgment**	CASE NUMBER:

1. TO THE CLERK: On the complaint or cross-complaint filed

   a. on *(date):*

   b. by *(name):*

   c. ☐ Enter default of defendant *(names):*

   d. ☐ I request a court judgment under Code of Civil Procedure sections 585(b), 585(c), 989, etc., against defendant *(names):*

      (Testimony required. Apply to the clerk for a hearing date, unless the court will enter a judgment on an affidavit under Code Civ. Proc., § 585(d).)

   e. ☐ Enter clerk's judgment

      (1) ☐ for restitution of the premises only and issue a writ of execution on the judgment. Code of Civil Procedure section 1174(c) does not apply. (Code Civ. Proc., § 1169.)

         ☐ Include in the judgment all tenants, subtenants, named claimants, and other occupants of the premises. The *Prejudgment Claim of Right to Possession* was served in compliance with Code of Civil Procedure section 415.46.

      (2) ☐ under Code of Civil Procedure section 585(a). *(Complete the declaration under Code Civ. Proc., § 585.5 on the reverse (item 5).)*

      (3) ☐ for default previously entered on *(date):*

2. **Judgment to be entered.**

	Amount	Credits acknowledged	Balance
a. Demand of complaint	$	$	$
b. Statement of damages *			
(1) Special	$	$	$
(2) General	$	$	$
c. Interest	$	$	$
d. Costs *(see reverse)*	$	$	$
e. Attorney fees	$	$	$
f. **TOTALS**	$	$	$

   g. **Daily damages** were demanded in complaint at the rate of: $ per day beginning *(date):*

   (* Personal injury or wrongful death actions; Code Civ. Proc., § 425.11.)

3. ☐ *(Check if filed in an unlawful detainer case)* **Legal document assistant or unlawful detainer assistant** information is on the reverse *(complete item 4).*

Date: ▶

_____   _____

(TYPE OR PRINT NAME)   (SIGNATURE OF PLAINTIFF OR ATTORNEY FOR PLAINTIFF)

FOR COURT **USE ONLY**	(1) ☐ Default entered as requested on *(date):* (2) ☐ Default NOT entered as requested *(state reason):* Clerk, by_____, Deputy

Page 1 of 2

Form Adopted for Mandatory Use
 Judicial Council of California
 CIV-100 [Rev. January 1, 2007]
    REQUEST FOR ENTRY OF DEFAULT
 (Application to Enter Default)
    Code of Civil Procedure,
 §§ 585–587, 1169 <br> www.courtinfo.ca.gov

PLAINTIFF/PETITIONER:	CASE NUMBER:
DEFENDANT/RESPONDENT:	

4. **Legal document assistant or unlawful detainer assistant (Bus. & Prof. Code, § 6400 et seq.).** A legal document assistant or unlawful detainer assistant ☐ did ☐ did **not** for compensation give advice or assistance with this form. *(If declarant has received **any** help or advice for pay from a legal document assistant or unlawful detainer assistant, state):*

   a. Assistant's name:
   b. Street address, city, and zip code:

   c. Telephone no.:
   d. County of registration:
   e. Registration no.:
   f. Expires on *(date):*

5. ☐ **Declaration under Code of Civil Procedure Section 585.5** *(required for entry of default under Code Civ. Proc., § 585(a)).* This action

   a. ☐ is ☐ is not on a contract or installment sale for goods or services subject to Civ. Code, § 1801 et seq. (Unruh Act).
   b. ☐ is ☐ is not on a conditional sales contract subject to Civ. Code, § 2981 et seq. (Rees-Levering Motor Vehicle Sales and Finance Act).
   c. ☐ is ☐ is not on an obligation for goods, services, loans, or extensions of credit subject to Code Civ. Proc., § 395(b).

6. **Declaration of mailing (Code Civ. Proc., § 587).** A copy of this *Request for Entry of Default* was

   a. ☐ **not mailed** to the following defendants, whose addresses are **unknown** to plaintiff or plaintiff's attorney *(names):*

   b. ☐ **mailed** first-class, postage prepaid, in a sealed envelope addressed to each defendant's attorney of record or, if none, to each defendant's last known address as follows:

   (1) Mailed on *(date):*   (2) To *(specify names and addresses shown on the envelopes):*

I declare under penalty of perjury under the laws of the State of California that the foregoing items 4, 5, and 6 are true and correct.
Date:

▶

_____   _____
(TYPE OR PRINT NAME)   (SIGNATURE OF DECLARANT)

7. **Memorandum of costs** *(required if money judgment requested).* Costs and disbursements are as follows (Code Civ. Proc., § 1033.5):

   a. Clerk's filing fees . . . . $
   b. Process server's fees . . . . $
   c. Other *(specify):* . . . . $
   d. . . . . $
   e. **TOTAL** . . . . $ _____

   f. ☐ Costs and disbursements are waived.

   g. I am the attorney, agent, or party who claims these costs. To the best of my knowledge and belief this memorandum of costs is correct and these costs were necessarily incurred in this case.

I declare under penalty of perjury under the laws of the State of California that the foregoing is true and correct.
Date:

▶

_____   _____
(TYPE OR PRINT NAME)   (SIGNATURE OF DECLARANT)

8. ☐ **Declaration of nonmilitary status** *(required for a judgment).* No defendant named in item 1c of the application is in the military service so as to be entitled to the benefits of the Servicemembers Civil Relief Act (50 U.S.C. App. § 501 et seq.).

I declare under penalty of perjury under the laws of the State of California that the foregoing is true and correct.
Date:

▶

_____   _____
(TYPE OR PRINT NAME)   (SIGNATURE OF DECLARANT)

REQUEST FOR ENTRY OF DEFAULT
(Application to Enter Default)

ATTORNEY OR PARTY WITHOUT ATTORNEY *(Name, State Bar number and address):*	
TELEPHONE NO.: FAX NO. *(Optional):*	
E-MAIL ADDRESS *(Optional):*	
ATTORNEY FOR *(Name):* Plaintiff in Pro Per	
[ ] ATTORNEY FOR [ ] JUDGMENT CREDITOR [ ] ASSIGNEE OF RECORD	

SUPERIOR COURT OF CALIFORNIA, COUNTY OF

STREET ADDRESS:

MAILING ADDRESS:

CITY AND ZIP CODE:

BRANCH NAME:

PLAINTIFF:

DEFENDANT:

WRIT OF	[ ] **EXECUTION (Money Judgment)** [ ] **POSSESSION OF** [ ] **Personal Property** [ ] **Real Property** [ ] **SALE**	CASE NUMBER:

1. **To the Sheriff or Marshal of the County of:**

   You are directed to enforce the judgment described below with daily interest and your costs as provided by law.

2. **To any registered process server:** You are authorized to serve this writ only in accord with CCP 699.080 or CCP 715.040.

3. *(Name):*

   is the [ ] judgment creditor [ ] assignee of record whose address is shown on this form above the court's name.

4. **Judgment debtor** *(name and last known address):*

   [ ] Additional judgment debtors on next page

5. **Judgment entered** on *(date):*

6. [ ] **Judgment renewed** on *(dates):*

7. **Notice of sale** under this writ
   a. [ ] has not been requested.
   b. [ ] has been requested *(see next page).*

8. [ ] Joint debtor information on next page.

   [SEAL]

9. [ ] See next page for information on real or personal property to be delivered under a writ of possession or sold under a writ of sale.

10. [ ] This writ is issued on a sister-state judgment.

11. Total judgment . . . . $

12. Costs after judgment (per filed order or memo CCP 685.090) . . . . $

13. Subtotal *(add 11 and 12)* . . . . $ _____

14. Credits . . . . $

15. Subtotal *(subtract 14 from 13)* . . . . $ _____

16. Interest after judgment (per filed affidavit CCP 685.050) (not on GC 6103.5 fees). . . $

17. Fee for issuance of writ . . . . $

18. **Total** *(add 15, 16, and 17)* . . . . $ _____

19. Levying officer:
    (a) Add daily interest from date of writ *(at the legal rate on 15)* (not on GC 6103.5 fees) of. . . . . . . $
    (b) Pay directly to court costs included in 11 and 17 (GC 6103.5, 68511.3; CCP 699.520(i)) . . . . $

20. [ ] The amounts called for in items 11–19 are different for each debtor. These amounts are stated for each debtor on Attachment 20.

Issued on *(date):*	Clerk, by _____ , Deputy	

NOTICE TO PERSON SERVED: SEE NEXT PAGE FOR IMPORTANT INFORMATION.

Form Approved for Optional Use
Judicial Council of California
EJ-130 [Rev. January 1, 2006]

WRIT OF EXECUTION

Code of Civil Procedure, §§ 699.520, 712.010,
Government Code, § 6103.5
www.courtinfo.ca.gov

PLAINTIFF:	CASE NUMBER:
DEFENDANT:	

— **Items continued from page 1**—

21. ☐ **Additional judgment debtor** (name and last known address):

22. ☐ **Notice of sale** has been requested by (name and address):

23. ☐ **Joint debtor** was declared bound by the judgment (CCP 989–994)
    a. on (date):   a. on (date):
    b. name and address of joint debtor: b. name and address of joint debtor:

    c. ☐ additional costs against certain joint debtors (itemize):

24. ☐ (Writ of Possession or Writ of Sale) **Judgment** was entered for the following:
    a. ☐ Possession of real property: The complaint was filed on (date):
        (Check (1) or (2)):
        (1) ☐ The Prejudgment Claim of Right to Possession was served in compliance with CCP 415.46.
                The judgment includes all tenants, subtenants, named claimants, and other occupants of the premises.
        (2) ☐ The Prejudgment Claim of Right to Possession was NOT served in compliance with CCP 415.46.
            (a) $ was the daily rental value on the date the complaint was filed.
            (b) The court will hear objections to enforcement of the judgment under CCP 1174.3 on the following
                dates (specify):
    b. ☐ Possession of personal property.
        ☐ If delivery cannot be had, then for the value (itemize in 9e) specified in the judgment or supplemental order.
    c. ☐ Sale of personal property.
    d. ☐ Sale of real property.
    e. Description of property:

NOTICE TO PERSON SERVED

WRIT OF EXECUTION OR SALE. Your rights and duties are indicated on the accompanying *Notice of Levy* (Form EJ-150).
WRIT OF POSSESSION OF PERSONAL PROPERTY. If the levying officer is not able to take custody of the property, the levying officer will make a demand upon you for the property. If custody is not obtained following demand, the judgment may be enforced as a money judgment for the value of the property specified in the judgment or in a supplemental order.
WRIT OF POSSESSION OF REAL PROPERTY. If the premises are not vacated within five days after the date of service on the occupant or, if service is by posting, within five days after service on you, the levying officer will remove the occupants from the real property and place the judgment creditor in possession of the property. Except for a mobile home, personal property remaining on the premises will be sold or otherwise disposed of in accordance with CCP 1174 unless you or the owner of the property pays the judgment creditor the reasonable cost of storage and takes possession of the personal property not later than 15 days after the time the judgment creditor takes possession of the premises.
► *A Claim of Right to Possession form accompanies this writ (unless the Summons was served in compliance with CCP 415.46).*

NAME, ADDRESS, AND TELEPHONE NUMBER OF ATTORNEY OR PARTY WITHOUT ATTORNEY	STATE BAR NUMBER	*Reserved for Clerk's File Stamp*

ATTORNEY FOR (Name):   Plaintiff in Pro Per

SUPERIOR COURT OF CALIFORNIA, COUNTY OF LOS ANGELES

COURTHOUSE ADDRESS:

PLAINTIFF:

DEFENDANT:

APPLICATION FOR ISSUANCE OF WRIT OF EXECUTION, POSSESSION OR SALE	CASE NUMBER:

I, _____ declare under penalty of perjury under the laws of the State of California:

1. I am the _____ in the above-entitled action.

2. The following ❑Judgment / ❑Order was made and entered on _____.
   ❑Judgment was renewed on _____.

3. Judgment/Order as entered/renewed provides as follows:

   Judgment Creditor: (name and address)

   Judgment Debtor: (name and address)

   Amount of Order and/or Description of Property:

4. ☐ (Unlawful Detainer Proceedings Only) The daily rental value of the property as of the date the complaint was filed is $_____.

5. ☐ This is an unlawful detainer judgment, and a Prejudgment Claim of Right to Possession was served on the occupant(s) pursuant to Code of Civil Procedure section 415.46. Pursuant to Code of Civil Procedure sections 715.010 and 1174.3, this writ applies to all tenants; subtenants, if any; named claimants, if any; and any other occupants of the premises.

6. ☐ This is a Family Law Judgment/Order entitled to priority under Code of Civil Procedure section 699.510.

7. This writ is to be issued to: ❑ Los Angeles County   ❑ Other (Specify):_____

APPLICATION FOR ISSUANCE OF WRIT OF EXECUTION, POSSESSION OR SALE

Case Title:	Case Number:

INSTRUCTIONS

Fill in date below showing total of amount ordered (do not show separate amounts for principal, fees and pre-judgment costs and interest), amount actually paid, date paid and whether applied to order and/or to accrued interest if accrued interest is claimed, and balance due. Due date of costs of enforcement is the date they were added to the judgment pursuant to a cost bill after judgment, not date incurred.

Failure to claim interest shall be deemed a waiver thereof for the purpose of this writ only.

ON INSTALLMENT ORDERS: EACH PAYMENT ORDERED AND DUE DATE MUST BE STATED SEPARATELY.
PERSON TO WHOM AMOUNT IS ORDERED PAID MUST SIGN DECLARATION.

TOTAL ORDERED PAID		ACTUALLY PAID			BALANCE DUE	
DUE DATE	AMOUNT	DATE PAID	ON ORDER	ON ACCRUED INTEREST	ON ORDER	ON ACCRUED INTEREST

There is actually remaining due on said order the sum of $_____ plus $_____ accrued costs plus $_____ accrued interest plus $_____ interest per day accruing from date of this application to date of writ, for which sum it is prayed that a writ of possession/sale/execution issue in favor of

_____
(Judgment Creditor)

and against _____
(Judgment Debtor)

to the County of _____

I declare under penalty of perjury under the laws of the State of California that the foregoing is true and correct.

Executed on _____

_____
(Signature)

APPLICATION FOR ISSUANCE OF WRIT OF EXECUTION, POSSESSION OR SALE

Name:
Address:

Phone:

Plaintiff in Pro Per

SUPERIOR COURT OF CALIFORNIA, COUNTY OF _____

_____ DIVISION

_____)   Case No. _____
    Plaintiff,   )
)   DECLARATION IN SUPPORT OF DEFAULT
    v.   )   JUDGMENT FOR RENT, DAMAGES, AND COSTS
)
_____)
    Defendant(s).   )
_____)   (C.C.P. SECS. 585(d), 1169)

I, the undersigned, declare:

1. I am the plaintiff in the above-entitled action and the owner of the premises at _____

_____, City of

_____, County of _____, California.

2. On _____, _____, defendant(s) rented the premises from me pursuant

to a written/oral *[cross out one]* agreement under which the monthly rent was $_____ payable in

advance on the _____ day of each month.

3. The terms of the tenancy *[check one]*:

    ☐ were not changed; or

    ☐ were changed, effective _____, _____, in that monthly rent was

validly and lawfully increased to $_____ by ☐ agreement of the parties and subsequent payment of

such rent; or

    ☐ *[month-to-month tenancy only]* service on defendant(s) of a written notice of at least 30 days, setting forth

the increase in rent.

4. The reasonable rental value of the premises per day, that is, the current monthly rent divided by 30, is

$_____.

5. Pursuant to the agreement, defendant(s) went into possession of the premises.

6. On _____, _____, defendant(s) were in default in the payment of rent in

the amount of $_____, and I caused defendant(s) to be served with a written notice demanding that

defendant(s) pay that amount or surrender possession of the premises within three days after service of the notice.

7. Defendant(s) failed to pay the rent or surrender possession of the premises within three days after service

of the notice, whereupon I commenced this action, complying with any local rent control or eviction protection

ordinance applicable, and caused Summons and Complaint to be served on each defendant. Defendant(s) have

failed to answer or otherwise respond to the Complaint within the time allowed by law.

8. Defendant(s) surrendered possession of the premises on _____, _____,

after entry of a clerk's Judgment for Possession and issuance of a Writ of Execution thereon.

9. The rent was due for the rental period of _____, _____, through

_____, _____. After this latter date, and until defendant(s) vacated the premises,

I sustained damages at the daily reasonable rental value of $_____, for total damages of

$_____.

10. I have incurred filing, service, and writ fees in the total amount of $_____ in this action.

11. If sworn as a witness, I could testify competently to the facts stated herein.

I declare under penalty of perjury under the laws of the State of California that the foregoing is true and correct.

DATED:_____, _____

_____
Plaintiff in Pro Per

Name:

Address:

Phone:

Plaintiff in Pro Per

SUPERIOR COURT OF CALIFORNIA, COUNTY OF _____

_____ DIVISION

_____)   Case No. _____
)
                Plaintiff,   )
)   DECLARATION IN SUPPORT OF DEFAULT
        v.   )   JUDGMENT FOR DAMAGES AND COSTS
)
_____)
)
                Defendant(s).   )   (C.C.P. SECS. 585(d), 1169)
)
_____)

I, the undersigned, declare:

   1. I am the plaintiff in the above-entitled action and the owner of the premises at _____

_____, City of

_____, County of _____, California.

   2. On _____, _____, defendant(s) rented the premises from me pursuant to a

written/oral [cross out one] agreement under which the monthly rent was $_____ payable in advance

on the _____ day of each month.

   3. The terms of the tenancy [check one]:

      ☐ were not changed; or

      ☐ were changed, effective _____, _____, in that monthly rent was validly

and lawfully increased to $_____ by

      ☐ agreement of the parties and subsequent payment of such rent; or

      ☐ [month-to-month tenancy only] service on defendant(s) of a written notice of at least 30 days, setting forth

the increase in rent.

4. The reasonable rental value of the premises per day, that is, the current monthly rent divided by 30, is

$_____.

5. Pursuant to the agreement, defendant(s) went into possession of the premises.

6. On _____, _____, I served defendant with a written 30-day/ 60-day

[cross out one] termination notice.

7. Defendant(s) was still in possession of the property after the period of the notice expired on

_____, _____, and stayed until _____, _____,

when the sheriff evicted him/her/them pursuant to a clerk's Judgment for Possession and issuance of a Writ of

Execution.

8. I sustained damages at the daily reasonable rental value of $_____ for _____ days

between _____, _____ and _____, _____

for a total of $_____.

9. I have incurred filing, service, and writ fees in the total amount of $_____ in this action.

10. If sworn as a witness, I could testify competently to the facts stated herein.

I declare under penalty of perjury under the laws of the State of California that the foregoing is true and correct.

DATED:_____, _____

_____

Plaintiff in Pro Per

ATTORNEY OR PARTY WITHOUT ATTORNEY *(Name, state bar number, and address):*	*FOR COURT USE ONLY*
TELEPHONE NO.: FAX NO. *(Optional):* E-MAIL ADDRESS *(Optional):* ATTORNEY FOR *(Name):* Plaintiff in Pro Per	

SUPERIOR COURT OF CALIFORNIA, COUNTY OF
STREET ADDRESS:
MAILING ADDRESS:
CITY AND ZIP CODE:
BRANCH NAME:

PLAINTIFF *(Name):*

DEFENDANT *(Name):*

DECLARATION FOR DEFAULT JUDGMENT BY COURT **(Unlawful Detainer—Code Civil Proc., § 585(d))**	CASE NUMBER:

1. My name is *(specify):*
   a. ☐ I am the plaintiff in this action.
   b. I am
      (1) ☐ an owner of the property   (3) ☐ an agent of the owner
      (2) ☐ a manager of the property   (4) ☐ other *(specify):*

2. The property concerning this action is located at *(street address, apartment number, city, and county):*

3. Personal knowledge. I personally know the facts stated in this declaration and, if sworn as a witness, could testify competently thereto. I am personally familiar with the rental or lease agreement, defendant's payment record, the condition of the property, and defendant's conduct.

4. Agreement was ☐ written ☐ oral as follows:
   a. On or about *(date):*   defendant *(name each):*

      (1) agreed to rent the property for a ☐ month-to-month tenancy ☐ other tenancy *(specify):*
      (2) agreed to pay rent of $ payable ☐ monthly ☐ other *(specify frequency):*
          with rent due on the ☐ first of the month ☐ other day *(specify):*

   b. ☐ Original agreement is attached *(specify):* ☐ to the original complaint.
      ☐ to the *Application for Immediate Writ of Possession.* ☐ to this declaration, labeled Exhibit 4b.
   c. ☐ Copy of agreement with a declaration and order to admit the copy is attached *(specify):*
      ☐ to the *Application for Immediate Writ of Possession.* ☐ to this declaration, labeled Exhibit 4c.

5. ☐ Agreement changed.
   a. ☐ More than one change in rent amount *(specify history of all rent changes and effective dates up to the last rent change)* on *Attachment* 5a (form MC-025).

   b. ☐ Change in rent amount *(specify last rent change)*. The rent was changed from $ to $, which became effective on *(date):*   and was made
      (1) ☐ by agreement of the parties and subsequent payment of such rent.
      (2) ☐ by service on defendant of a notice of change in terms pursuant to Civil Code section 827 *(check item 5d).*
      (3) ☐ pursuant to a written agreement of the parties for change in terms *(check item 5e or 5f).*

   c. ☐ Change in rent due date. Rent was changed, payable in advance, due on *(specify day):*   .
   d. ☐ A copy of the notice of change in terms is attached to this declaration, labeled Exhibit 5d.
   e. ☐ Original agreement for change in terms is attached *(specify):* ☐ to the original complaint.
      ☐ to the *Application for Immediate Writ of Possession.* ☐ to this declaration, labeled Exhibit 5e.
   f. ☐ Copy of agreement for change in terms with a declaration and order to admit the copy is attached *(specify):*
      ☐ to the *Application for Immediate Writ of Possession.* ☐ to this declaration, labeled Exhibit 5f.

Page 1 of 3

6. Notice to quit.
   a. ☐ Defendant was served with a
      (1) ☐ 3-day notice to pay rent or quit
      (2) ☐ 3-day notice to perform covenants or quit
      (3) ☐ Other (specify):
      (4) ☐ 3-day notice to quit
      (5) ☐ 30-day notice to quit
      (6) ☐ 60-day notice to quit

   b. ☐ The 3-day notice to pay rent or quit demanded rent due in the amount of (specify): $ for the rental period
      beginning on (date)   and ending on (date)   .

   c. ☐ The total rent demanded in the 3-day notice under item 6b is different from the agreed rent in item 4a(2) (specify history of
      dates covered by the 3-day notice and any partial payments received to arrive at the balance) on Attachment 6c (form
      MC-025).

   d. ☐ The original or copy of the notice specified in item 6a is attached to (specify):   ☐ the original complaint.
      ☐ this declaration, labeled Exhibit 6d. (The original or a copy of the notice MUST be attached to this declaration if not
      attached to the original complaint.)

7. Service of notice.
   a. The notice was served on defendant (name each):
      (1) ☐ personally on (date):
      (2) ☐ by substituted service, including a copy mailed to the defendant, on (date):
      (3) ☐ by posting and mailing on (date mailed):

   b. ☐ A prejudgment claim of right to possession was served on the occupants pursuant to Code of Civil Procedure section
      415.46.

8. Proof of service of notice. The original or copy of the proof of service of the notice in item 6a is attached to (specify):
   a. ☐ the original complaint.
   b. ☐ this declaration, labeled Exhibit 8b. (The original or copy of the proof of service MUST be attached to this declaration if not
      attached to the original complaint.)

9. Notice expired. On (date):   the notice in item 6 expired at the end of the day and defendant failed to comply
   with the requirements of the notice by that date. No money has been received and accepted after the notice expired.

10. The fair rental value of the property is $ per day, calculated as follows:
    a. ☐ (rent per month) x (0.03288) (12 months divided by 365 days)
    b. ☐ rent per month divided by 30
    c. ☐ other valuation (specify):

11. Possession. The defendant
    a. ☐ vacated the premises on (date):
    b. ☐ continues to occupy the property on (date of this declaration):

12. ☐ Holdover damages. Declarant has calculated the holdover damages as follows:
    a. Damages demanded in the complaint began on (date):
    b. Damages accrued through (date specified in item 11):
    c. Number of days that damages accrued (count days using the dates in items 12a and 12b):
    d. Total holdover damages ((daily rental value in item 10) x (number of days in item 12c)): $

13. ☐ Reasonable attorney fees are authorized in the lease or rental agreement pursuant to paragraph (specify):
    and reasonable attorney fees for plaintiff's attorney (name):   are $.

14. ☐ Court costs in this case, including the filing fee, are $

15. ☐ Declarant requests a judgment on behalf of plaintiff for:
    a. ☐ A money judgment as follows:

(1) ☐ Past-due rent (item 6b)	$	
(2) ☐ Holdover damages (item 12d)	$	
(3) ☐ Attorney fees (item 13)*	$	* ☐ Attorney fees are to be paid by (name) only.
(4) ☐ Costs (item 14)	$	
(5) ☐ Other (specify):	$	
(6) **TOTAL JUDGMENT**	$	

    b. ☐ Possession of the premises in item 2 (check only if a clerk's judgment for possession was **not** entered).
    c. ☐ Cancellation of the rental agreement. ☐ Forfeiture of the lease.

I declare under penalty of perjury under the laws of the State of California that the foregoing is true and correct.

Date:

_____   }   _____
          (TYPE OR PRINT NAME)   (SIGNATURE OF DECLARANT)

Summary of Exhibits

16. ☐ Exhibit 4b: Original rental agreement.

17. ☐ Exhibit 4c: Copy of rental agreement with declaration and order to admit the copy.

18. ☐ Exhibit 5d: Copy of notice of change in terms.

19. ☐ Exhibit 5e: Original agreement for change of terms.

20. ☐ Exhibit 5f: Copy of agreement for change in terms with declaration and order to admit copy.

21. ☐ Exhibit 6d: Original or copy of the notice to quit under item 6a (MUST be attached to this declaration if it is not attached to original complaint).

22. ☐ Exhibit 8b: Original or copy of proof of service of notice in item 6a (MUST be attached to this declaration if it is not attached to original complaint).

23. ☐ Other exhibits (specify number and describe):

ATTORNEY OR PARTY WITHOUT ATTORNEY *(Name, state bar number, and address):*	FOR COURT USE ONLY

TELEPHONE NO.:   FAX NO. *(Optional):*

E-MAIL ADDRESS *(Optional):*

ATTORNEY FOR *(Name):* Plaintiff in Pro Per

SUPERIOR COURT OF CALIFORNIA, COUNTY OF

STREET ADDRESS:

MAILING ADDRESS:

CITY AND ZIP CODE:

BRANCH NAME:

PLAINTIFF:

DEFENDANT:

JUDGMENT—UNLAWFUL DETAINER	CASE NUMBER:

☐ **By Clerk**   ☐ **By Default**   ☐ **After Court Trial**
☐ **By Court**   ☐ **Possession Only**   ☐ **Defendant Did Not Appear at Trial**

JUDGMENT

1. ☐ **BY DEFAULT**

   a. Defendant was properly served with a copy of the summons and complaint.

   b. Defendant failed to answer the complaint or appear and defend the action within the time allowed by law.

   c. Defendant's default was entered by the clerk upon plaintiff's application.

   d. ☐ **Clerk's Judgment** (Code Civ. Proc., § 1169). For possession only of the premises described on page 2 (item 4).

   e. ☐ **Court Judgment** (Code Civ. Proc., § 585(b)). The court considered

      (1) ☐ plaintiff's testimony and other evidence.

      (2) ☐ plaintiff's or others' written declaration and evidence (Code Civ. Proc., § 585(d)).

2. ☐ **AFTER COURT TRIAL.** The jury was waived. The court considered the evidence.

   a. The case was tried on *(date and time):*

      before *(name of judicial officer):*

   b. Appearances by:

      ☐ Plaintiff *(name each):*   ☐ Plaintiff's attorney *(name each):*

                                          (1)

                                          (2)

      ☐ Continued on *Attachment* 2b (form MC-025).

      ☐ Defendant *(name each):*   ☐ Defendant's attorney *(name each):*

                                            (1)

                                          (2)

      ☐ Continued on *Attachment* 2b (form MC-025).

   c. ☐ Defendant did not appear at trial. Defendant was properly served with notice of trial.

   d. ☐ A statement of decision (Code Civ. Proc., § 632) ☐ was not ☐ was requested.

Form Approved for Optional Use
Judicial Council of California
UD-110 [New January 1, 2003]

JUDGMENT—UNLAWFUL DETAINER

Code of Civil Procedure, §§ 415.46,
585(d), 664.6, 1169

JUDGMENT IS ENTERED AS FOLLOWS BY: ☐ **THE COURT** ☐ **THE CLERK**

3. **Parties.** Judgment is

    a. ☐ for plaintiff *(name each):*

       and against defendant *(name each):*

       ☐ Continued on *Attachment* 3a (form MC-025).

    b. ☐ for defendant *(name each):*

4. ☐ Plaintiff ☐ Defendant is entitled to possession of the premises located at *(street address, apartment, city, and county):*

5. ☐ Judgment applies to all occupants of the premises including tenants, subtenants if any, and named claimants if any (Code Civ. Proc., §§ 715.010, 1169, and 1174.3).

6. **Amount and terms of judgment**

    a. ☐ Defendant named in item 3a above must pay plaintiff on the complaint:

(1) ☐	Past-due rent	$
(2) ☐	Holdover damages	$
(3) ☐	Attorney fees	$
(4) ☐	Costs	$
(5) ☐	Other *(specify):*	$
(6)	**TOTAL JUDGMENT**	$

    b. ☐ Plaintiff is to receive nothing from defendant named in item 3b.

       ☐ Defendant named in item 3b is to recover costs: $

       ☐ and attorney fees: $.

    c. ☐ The rental agreement is canceled. ☐ The lease is forfeited.

7. ☐ **Conditional judgment.** Plaintiff has breached the agreement to provide habitable premises to defendant as stated in *Judgment—Unlawful Detainer Attachment* (form UD–110S), which is attached.

8. ☐ **Other** *(specify):*

    ☐ Continued on *Attachment* 8 (form MC-025).

Date: ☐ _____
                                   JUDICIAL OFFICER

Date: ☐ Clerk, by _____, Deputy

(SEAL)

CLERK'S CERTIFICATE *(Optional)*

I certify that this is a true copy of the original judgment on file in the court.

Date:

Clerk, by _____, Deputy

ATTORNEY OR PARTY WITHOUT ATTORNEY *(Name and state bar number, and address)*:	FOR COURT USE ONLY
TELEPHONE NO.: FAX NO. *(Optional)*: E–MAIL ADDRESS *(Optional)*: ATTORNEY FOR *(Name)*: Plaintiff in Pro Per	

SUPERIOR COURT OF CALIFORNIA, COUNTY OF
STREET ADDRESS:
MAILING ADDRESS:
CITY AND ZIP CODE:
BRANCH NAME:

PLAINTIFF:

DEFENDANT:

STIPULATION FOR ENTRY OF JUDGMENT **(Unlawful Detainer)**	CASE NUMBER:

1. IT IS STIPULATED by plaintiff *(name each)*:   and
   defendant *(name each)*:

2. ☐ Plaintiff ☐ Defendant *(specify name)*:   is awarded
   a. ☐ possession of the premises located at *(street address, apartment number, city, and county)*:

   b. ☐ cancellation of the rental agreement.   ☐ forfeiture of the lease.
   c. ☐ past due rent $
   d. ☐ total holdover damages $
   e. ☐ attorney fees $
   f. ☐ costs $
   g. ☐ deposit of $ ☐ See item 3.
   h. ☐ other *(specify)*:
   i. Total $ to be paid by ☐ *(date)*:   ☐ installment payments (see item 5)

3. ☐ Deposit. If not awarded under item 2g, then plaintiff must
   a. ☐ return deposit of $ to defendant by *(date)*:
   b. ☐ give an itemized deposit statement to defendant within three weeks after defendant vacates the premises
      (Civ. Code, § 1950.5).
   c. ☐ mail the ☐ deposit ☐ itemized statement   to the defendant at *(mailing address)*:

4. ☐ A writ of possession will issue immediately, but there will be no lockout before *(date)*:

5. ☐ AGREEMENT FOR INSTALLMENT PAYMENTS
   a. Defendant agrees to pay $ on the *(specify day)*   day of each month beginning
      on *(specify date)*   until paid in full.

   b. If any payment is more than *(specify)*   days late, the entire amount in item 2i will become immediately due and
      payable plus interest at the legal rate.

6. a. ☐ Judgment will be entered now.
   b. ☐ Judgment will be entered only upon default of payment of the amount in item 2i or the payment arrangement in item 5a.
      The case is calendared for dismissal on *(date and time)*   in
      department *(specify)*   unless plaintiff or defendant otherwise notifies the court.
   c. ☐ Judgment will be entered as stated in *Judgment —Unlawful Detainer Attachment* (form UD-110S), which is attached.
   d. ☐ Judgment will be entered as stated in item 7.

Form Approved for Optional Use
Judicial Council of California
UD-115 [New January 1, 2003]   **STIPULATION FOR ENTRY OF JUDGMENT**
(Unlawful Detainer)   Code of Civil Procedure, § 664.6

7. ☐ Plaintiff and defendant further stipulate as follows *(specify):*

8. a. **The parties named in item 1 understand that they have the right to (1) have an attorney present and (2) receive notice of and have a court hearing about any default in the terms of this stipulation.**

   b. Date:

   _____
   (TYPE OR PRINT NAME)

   ▶ _____
   (SIGNATURE OF PLAINTIFF OR ATTORNEY)

   _____
   (TYPE OR PRINT NAME)

   ▶ _____
   (SIGNATURE OF PLAINTIFF OR ATTORNEY)

   ☐ Continued on *Attachment* 8b (form MC-025).

   c. Date:

   _____
   (TYPE OR PRINT NAME)

   ▶ _____
   (SIGNATURE OF DEFENDANT OR ATTORNEY)

   _____
   (TYPE OR PRINT NAME)

   ▶ _____
   (SIGNATURE OF DEFENDANT OR ATTORNEY)

   _____
   (TYPE OR PRINT NAME)

   ▶ _____
   (SIGNATURE OF DEFENDANT OR ATTORNEY)

   ☐ Continued on *Attachment* 8c (form MC-025).

9. IT IS SO ORDERED.

Date:

_____
JUDICIAL OFFICER

ATTORNEY OR PARTY WITHOUT ATTORNEY *(Name, State Bar number, and address):*

FOR COURT USE ONLY

TELEPHONE NO.:　　　　　　　FAX No. *(Optional):*

E-MAIL ADDRESS *(Optional):*

ATTORNEY FOR *(Name):*　　Plaintiff in Pro Per

SUPERIOR COURT OF CALIFORNIA, COUNTY OF

STREET ADDRESS:

MAILING ADDRESS:

CITY AND ZIP CODE:

BRANCH NAME:

PLAINTIFF:

DEFENDANT:

| ☐ **REQUEST** ☐ **COUNTER-REQUEST** **TO SET CASE FOR TRIAL—UNLAWFUL DETAINER** ☐ **Plaintiff** ☐ **Defendant** | CASE NUMBER: |

1. ☐ **Plaintiff's request.** I represent to the court that all parties have been served with process and have appeared or have had a default or dismissal entered against them. I request that this case be set for trial.

2. **Trial preference.** The premises concerning this case are located at *(street address, apartment number, city, zip code, and county):*

    a. ☐ To the best of my knowledge, the right to possession of the premises is still in issue. This case is entitled to legal preference under Code of Civil Procedure section 1179a.

    b. ☐ To the best of my knowledge, the right to possession of the premises is no longer in issue. No defendant or other person is in possession of the premises.

3. **Jury or nonjury trial.** I request ☐ a jury trial ☐ a nonjury trial.

4. **Estimated length of trial.** I estimate that the trial will take *(check one):*

    a. ☐ days *(specify number):*　　　　b. ☐ hours *(specify if estimated trial is less than one day):*

5. **Trial date.** I am not available on the following dates *(specify dates and reasons for unavailability):*

UNLAWFUL DETAINER ASSISTANT (Bus. & Prof. Code, §§ 6400–6415)

6. *(Complete in all cases.)* An unlawful detainer assistant ☐ did **not** ☐ did for compensation give advice or assistance with this form. *(If declarant has received **any** help or advice for pay from an unlawful detainer assistant, complete a–f.)*

    a. Assistant's name:　　　　　　　　　　　c. Telephone no.:

    b. Street address, city, and zip code:　　　　d. County of registration:

    　　　　　　　　　　　　　　　　　　　　e. Registration no.:

    　　　　　　　　　　　　　　　　　　　　f. Expires on *(date):*

I declare under penalty of perjury under the laws of the State of California that the foregoing is true and correct.

Date:

▶

_____　　　　_____
(TYPE OR PRINT NAME)　　　　　　　　　　(SIGNATURE OF PARTY OR ATTORNEY FOR PARTY)

NOTICE

- An unlawful detainer case must be set for trial on a date not later than **20 days after the first request** to set the case for trial is made (Code Civ. Proc., § 1170.5(a)).
- If a jury is requested, $150 must be deposited with the court 5 days before trial (Code Civ. Proc., § 631).
- Court reporter and interpreter services vary. Check with the court for availability of services and fees charged.
- If you cannot pay the court fees and costs, you may apply for a fee waiver. Ask the court clerk for a fee waiver form.

Page 1 of 2

Form Adopted for Mandatory Use
Judicial Council of California
UD-150 [New January 1, 2005]

REQUEST/COUNTER-REQUEST TO SET CASE FOR TRIAL—UNLAWFUL DETAINER

Code of Civil Procedure, §§ 631,
1170.5(a), 1179a
www.courtinfo.ca.gov

PLAINTIFF:	CASE NUMBER:
DEFENDANT:	

PROOF OF SERVICE BY MAIL

Instructions: *After having the parties served by mail with the* Request/Counter-Request to Set Case for Trial—Unlawful Detainer, *(form UD-150), have the person who mailed the form UD-150 complete this* Proof of Service by Mail. *An **unsigned** copy of the* Proof of Service by Mail *should be completed and served with form UD-150. Give the* Request/Counter-Request to Set Case for Trial —Unlawful Detainer *(form UD-150) and the completed* Proof of Service by Mail *to the clerk for filing. If you are representing yourself, someone else must mail these papers and sign the* Proof of Service by Mail.

1. I am over the age of 18 and **not a party to this case.** I am a resident of or employed in the county where the mailing took place.
2. My residence or business address is *(specify):*

3. I served the *Request/Counter-Request to Set Case for Trial—Unlawful Detainer* (form UD-150) by enclosing a copy in an envelope addressed to each person whose name and address are shown below AND

   a. ☐ **depositing** the sealed envelope in the United States mail on the date and at the place shown in item 3c with the postage fully prepaid.

   b. ☐ **placing** the envelope for collection and mailing on the date and at the place shown in item 3c following ordinary business practices. I am readily familiar with this business's practice for collecting and processing correspondence for mailing. On the same day that correspondence is placed for collection and mailing, it is deposited in the ordinary course of business with the United States Postal Service in a sealed envelope with postage fully prepaid.

   c. (1) Date mailed:

   (2) Place mailed *(city and state):*

I declare under penalty of perjury under the laws of the State of California that the foregoing is true and correct:

Date:

▶

_____
(TYPE OR PRINT NAME)

_____
(SIGNATURE OF PERSON WHO MAILED *FORM UD-150*)

NAME AND ADDRESS OF EACH PERSON TO WHOM NOTICE WAS MAILED

	Name	Address *(number, street, city, and zip code)*
4.		
5.		
6.		
7.		
8.		
9.		

☐ List of names and addresses continued on a separate attachment or form MC-025, titled Attachment to Proof of Service by Mail.

REQUEST/COUNTER-REQUEST TO SET CASE FOR TRIAL—UNLAWFUL DETAINER

Name:

Address:

Phone:

Plaintiff in Pro Per

SUPERIOR COURT OF CALIFORNIA, COUNTY OF _____

_____ DIVISION

_____ Plaintiff, v. _____ Defendant(s). _____	) Case No. _____)) NOTICE OF MOTION FOR SUMMARY JUDGMENT;) PLAINTIFF'S DECLARATION; POINTS AND AUTHORITIES) (C.C.P. 437C, 1170.7))) Hearing Date: _____) Time: _____) Courtroom: _____

TO DEFENDANTS _____

AND THEIR ATTORNEY OF RECORD:

PLEASE TAKE NOTICE that on _____, _____, at _____ ____.M in the above-entitled Court, at _____,

City of _____, California, the above-named plaintiff

will move the Court for an Order granting summary judgment for possession of the subject premises herein, rent, damages, and costs in the above-entitled action.

This motion is made on the ground that defendants' defense has no merit and there exists no triable issue of fact as to plaintiff's cause of action, plaintiff having established that defendants are guilty of unlawfully detaining the subject premises following nonpayment of the rent due, service of a three-day notice to pay rent or quit, and failure to pay the rent or vacate the premises within the time given in the said notice.

This motion is based on this notice, the declaration of plaintiff attached hereto, the points and authorities

attached hereto, the pleadings, records, and files herein, and on such argument as may be presented at the hearing

on the motion.

DATED:_____, _____

_____
Plaintiff in Pro Per

DECLARATION OF PLAINTIFF

I, the undersigned, declare:

1. I am the plaintiff in the within action and the owner of the subject premises located at _____

_____, City of

_____, County of _____, California.

2. On _____, _____, defendant(s) rented the premises from me pursuant to

a written/oral agreement. The monthly rent was $_____ payable in advance on the _____

day of each month, the reasonable rental value of the premises per day being $_____.

3. Pursuant to the agreement, defendant(s) went into possession of the premises.

4. On _____, _____, defendant(s) were in default in the payment of rent in

the amount of $_____, and I served defendant(s) _____

_____ with a written notice demanding

that defendant(s) pay that amount or surrender possession of the premises within three days of service of the said

notice. A true copy of that notice is attached to the Complaint herein as Exhibit "B" thereto.

5. Prior to my service of the said three-day notice, defendant(s) had not notified me of any substantial defect in

the premises relating to the tenantability or habitability thereof.

6. Defendant(s) failed to pay the said rent or surrender possession of the said premises within three days of

service of the said notice, whereupon I commenced the instant action, complying with all applicable rent control

and/or eviction protection ordinances. Defendant(s) still remain in possession of the premises.

7. This rent was due for the rental period of _____, _____, through

_____, _____. After this latter date and to the present, I sustained

damages at the daily reasonable rental value indicated above in paragraph 2, for total damages in the amount of

$_____, and total rent and damages in the amount of $_____.

8. I have incurred service and filing fees in the total amount of $ _____ in the within action.

9. If sworn as a witness, I could testify competently to the facts stated herein.

I declare under penalty of perjury under the laws of the State of California that the foregoing is true and correct.

DATED:_____, _____

_____

Plaintiff in Pro Per

I.   PLAINTIFF'S MOTION FOR SUMMARY JUDGMENT IS PROPERLY BEFORE THE COURT.

In an unlawful detainer action a motion for summary judgment may be made on five days' notice. C.C.P. Sec. 1170.7. The time limits imposed by subdivision (a) of section 437c, as well as the requirement in subdivision (b) of a separate statement of material facts not in dispute, are not applicable to summary judgment motions in unlawful detainer actions. C.C.P. Sec. 437c(r).

The "separate statement" requirement for summary judgment motions does not apply to unlawful detainer actions. C.C.P. Section 437c, subdivision (q), states: "Subdivisions (a) and (b) shall not apply to actions brought pursuant to Chapter 4 (commencing with section 1159) of Title 3 of Part 3." The latter refers to the unlawful detainer statutes, and the requirement for a separate statement of facts is in section 437c(b). Thus, C.C.P. Section 437c(q) expressly states, though by an obscure reference to its own subdivision (b) and to C.C.P. Sections 1159 et seq., that unlawful detainer summary judgment motions do not require a separate statement of facts contended to be undisputed. While Rule 342, California Rules of Court, is silent on this issue, to construe such silence as requiring a separate statement of undisputed facts in unlawful detainer summary judgment motions, notwithstanding C.C.P. Section 437c(q), would allow a rule of court to supersede a statute, which is not permitted.

In all other respects, the motion is required to be granted on the same terms and conditions as a summary judgment motion under C.C.P. Sec. 437c, and such a motion must be decided solely on the affidavits or declarations filed. Ibid, subd. (c).

II.   PLAINTIFF HAS ESTABLISHED THE PRIMA FACIE ELEMENTS OF AN UNLAWFUL DETAINER ACTION FOR NONPAYMENT OF RENT.

Under section 1162(2) of the Code of Civil Procedure, a tenant or subtenant is guilty of unlawful detainer

> When he continues in possession … after default in the payment of rent … and three days' notice, in writing requiring its payment, stating the amount which is due, or possession of the property, shall have been served on him ….

Elements other than default in rent, service of the notice, the expiration of three days without payment, and the continuance in possession include the existence of a landlord-tenant relationship (Fredricksen v. McCosker (1956) 143 Cal. App. 2d 114) and proper contents of the notice (Wilson v. Sadleir (1915) 26 Cal. App. 357, 359).

1 Plaintiff's declaration establishes all these elements, so that plaintiff is entitled to summary judgment.

2 III. DEFENDANT(S) CANNOT PREVAIL UNDER A DEFENSE OF BREACH OF
         THE IMPLIED WARRANTY OF HABITABILITY.
3

4 Under the rule of Green v. Superior Court (1974) 10 Cal. 3d 616, the California Supreme Court held that in an

5 unlawful detainer action founded on nonpayment of rent, the tenant could assert as a defense that the landlord

6 breached an implied warranty to keep the premises habitable. The Court cited with approval the case of Hinson v.

7 Delis (1972) 26 Cal. App. 3d 62 in this regard. In Hinson, the tenant sued the landlord in a regular civil action for

8 breach of this implied warranty. After the trial court ruled in favor of the landlord, the Court of Appeal reversed,

9 holding that there existed such a warranty in the law, as to which, "The tenant must also give notice of alleged

10 defects to the landlord and allow a reasonable time for repairs to be made." Hinson at p. 70. When the Green

11 court held that the warranty of habitability established by the Hinson court could be asserted by the tenant as a

12 defense to an unlawful detainer action, as well as a basis for suit by the tenant, it did not modify or remove this

13 requirement of notice by the tenant to the landlord of the alleged defects by which the tenant seeks to withhold

14 rent. Therefore, the notice requirement also applies where the defense is asserted by the tenant in an unlawful

15 detainer action.

16 Plaintiff's declaration establishes that defendant(s) failed to give plaintiff notice of the alleged defects in the

17 premises. Unless a triable issue of fact exists in this regard, defendant(s) cannot assert this defense, as a matter of

18 law.

19 DATED:_____, _____

20   _____
                                                Plaintiff in Pro Per
21

22

23

24

25

26

27

28

PROOF OF PERSONAL SERVICE
(C.C.P. § 1011 (b))

I the undersigned, declare:

I am over the age of 18 years and not a party to the within action.

On _____, _____, I served the within Notice of Motion for Summary

Judgment, Declaration of Plaintiff, and Points and Authorities on defendant(s) by delivering true copies thereof to

each such defendant, or other person not less than 18 years of age, at defendants' residence address of

_____, City of

_____ , California, between 8:00 A.M. and 6:00 P.M.

I declare under penalty of perjury under the laws of the State of California that the foregoing is true and correct.

DATED:_____, _____   _____
                                            Signature

Name:

Address:

Phone:

Plaintiff in Pro Per

SUPERIOR COURT OF CALIFORNIA, COUNTY OF _____

_____ DIVISION

_____)   Case No. _____
            Plaintiff,   )
)   ORDER GRANTING MOTION
    v.   )   FOR SUMMARY JUDGMENT
)
_____)
            Defendant(s).   )
_____)

Plaintiff's motion for summary judgment came on for hearing in Department _____ of

the above-entitled Court on _____, _____, said plaintiff appearing in pro per

and defendant(s) _____ appearing by _____.

The matter having been argued and submitted,

   IT IS HEREBY ORDERED that plaintiff's motion for summary judgment for restitution of the premises the subject

of this action, rent and damages in the sum of $ _____, and costs of suit be, and the same is,

granted.

DATED:_____, _____

_____
Judge of the Superior Court

Name:
Address:

Phone:

Plaintiff in Pro Per

SUPERIOR COURT OF CALIFORNIA, COUNTY OF _____

_____ DIVISION

_____) Case No. _____
            Plaintiff,   )
) JUDGMENT FOLLOWING GRANTING
v.   ) OF MOTION FOR SUMMARY JUDGMENT
)
_____)
            Defendant(s).   )
_____)

The motion of plaintiff for summary judgment having been granted,

IT IS HEREBY ORDERED AND ADJUDGED that plaintiff have and recover from defendant(s) _____

_____

possession and restitution of the real property located at _____

_____, City of _____,

County of _____ , California, rent and damages in the sum of

$ _____, plus costs of suit in the sum of $ _____, for the total sum of $ _____.

DATED:_____, _____

                                        _____
                                        Judge of the Superior Court

PLAINTIFF:	CASE NUMBER:
DEFENDANT:	

JUDGMENT—UNLAWFUL DETAINER ATTACHMENT

7. ☐ **Conditional judgment.** Plaintiff breached the covenant to provide habitable premises to defendant.

    a. ☐ Defendant must pay plaintiff a reduced rent because of the breach in the amount and for the period shown below. *(Specify each defect on a separate line, the month or months (or other period) that the defect existed, and the percentage or amount of the reduced rent as a result of the defect to arrive at the reasonable value of the premises for the period that the defect or defects existed.)*

Month defect existed	Defect	Reasonable rental value is reduced by *(specify percentage)* or *(specify amount)*		Reduced monthly rent due
(1)		%	$	$
(2)		%	$	$
(3)		%	$	$
☐ Continued on *Attachment* 7a (form MC-025).				
		Total rent due in the 3-day notice is now *(specify):*		$

    b. ☐ Defendant is entitled to attorney fees *(specify):* $ and costs *(specify):* $

    c. ☐ Defendant is the prevailing party if defendant pays plaintiff *(specify total rent in item 7a, less any attorney fees and costs in item 7b):* $ by   p.m. on *(date):*   at *(address):*

    d. ☐ Judgment will be entered for defendant when defendant has complied with item 7c shown ☐ by defendant's filing of a declaration under penalty of perjury (see form MC-030), with proof of service on the plaintiff, OR ☐ at a hearing that has been set in this court as follows:

Date:	Time:	Dept.:	Room:

      (1) ☐ Defendant must continue to pay rent after expiration of the 3-day notice if the defendant continues in possession of the premises in the amount of $ per month. The total rent at item 7a is the corrected amount under the 3-day notice.

      (2) ☐ Plaintiff must repair the defects described in item 7a. The court retains jurisdiction over the case until those repairs are made. Rent remains reduced in the amount of *(specify monthly rent)* $ until the repairs are made.

      (3) ☐ Rent will increase to *(specify monthly rent)* $ the day after

          ☐ plaintiff files a declaration under penalty of perjury (see form MC-030), with proof of service on the defendant, stating that all the repairs have been made OR ☐ it is established that all the repairs have been made at a hearing set in this court as follows:

Date:	Time:	Dept.:	Room:

    e. ☐ Plaintiff is the prevailing party if defendant fails to comply with items 7c and 7d.

Form Approved for Optional Use
Judicial Council of California
UD-110S [New January 1, 2003]

JUDGMENT—UNLAWFUL DETAINER ATTACHMENT

Code of Civil Procedure, § 1174.2
Civil Code, §§ 1941, 1942.3

f. ☐ Judgment will be entered for plaintiff ☐ when plaintiff files a declaration under penalty of perjury (see form MC-030), with proof of service on the defendant, that the amount in item 7c has not been paid, OR ☐ at a hearing that has been set in the court as follows:

Date: Time: Dept.: Room:

(1) ☐	Past-due rent *(item 7a)*	$	
(2) ☐	Holdover damages*	$	
(3) ☐	Attorney fees *(item 7b)*	$	
(4) ☐	Costs *(item 7b)*	$	
(5) ☐	Other *(specify):*	$	
(6)	**TOTAL JUDGMENT**	$	

*Use one of the following formulas: From expiration of the 3-day notice to ☐ today's date ☐ date the premises were vacated *(specify number of days)* times

☐ *(specify reduced monthly rent $* times 0.03228 *(12 months divided by 365 days).)*

☐ *(specify reduced rent per month divided by 30): $*

= Total holdover damages

g. ☐ Plaintiff is awarded possession of the premises located at *(street address, apartment, city, and county):*

h. ☐ The rental agreement is canceled. ☐ The lease is forfeited.

8. ☐ **Other** *(specify):*

ATTORNEY OR PARTY WITHOUT ATTORNEY (Name, state bar number, and address):	FOR COURT USE ONLY
TELEPHONE NO.: FAX NO.: ATTORNEY FOR (Name): Plaintiff in Pro Per	

NAME OF COURT:
STREET ADDRESS:
MAILING ADDRESS:
CITY AND ZIP CODE:
BRANCH NAME:

PLAINTIFF:

DEFENDANT:

APPLICATION AND ORDER FOR APPEARANCE AND EXAMINATION	CASE NUMBER:

[ ] **ENFORCEMENT OF JUDGMENT**   [ ] **ATTACHMENT (Third Person)**
[ ] **Judgment Debtor**   [ ] **Third Person**

ORDER TO APPEAR FOR EXAMINATION

1. TO (name):
2. YOU ARE ORDERED TO APPEAR personally before this court, or before a referee appointed by the court, to
   a. [ ] furnish information to aid in enforcement of a money judgment against you.
   b. [ ] answer concerning property of the judgment debtor in your possession or control or concerning a debt you owe the judgment debtor.
   c. [ ] answer concerning property of the defendant in your possession or control or concerning a debt you owe the defendant that is subject to attachment.

Date: Time: Dept. or Div.:   Rm.:
Address of court [ ] shown above [ ] is:

3. This order may be served by a sheriff, marshal, registered process server, **or** the following specially appointed person (name):

Date:

_____
JUDGE OR REFEREE

This order must be served not less than 10 days before the date set for the examination.
IMPORTANT NOTICES ON REVERSE

APPLICATION FOR ORDER TO APPEAR FOR EXAMINATION

4. [ ] Judgment creditor   [ ] Assignee of record   [ ] Plaintiff who has a right to attach order
   applies for an order requiring (name):   to appear and furnish information
   to aid in enforcement of the money judgment or to answer concerning property or debt.
5. The person to be examined is
   a. [ ] the judgment debtor.
   b. [ ] a third person (1) who has possession or control of property belonging to the judgment debtor or the defendant or (2) who owes the judgment debtor or the defendant more than $250. An affidavit supporting this application under Code of Civil Procedure section 491.110 or 708.120 is attached.
6. The person to be examined resides or has a place of business in this county or within 150 miles of the place of examination.
7. [ ] This court is **not** the court in which the money judgment is entered or (attachment only) the court that issued the writ of attachment. An affidavit supporting an application under Code of Civil Procedure section 491.150 or 708.160 is attached.
8. [ ] The judgment debtor has been examined within the past 120 days. An affidavit showing good cause for another examination is attached.

I declare under penalty of perjury under the laws of the State of California that the foregoing is true and correct.

Date:

▶

_____   _____
(TYPE OR PRINT NAME)   (SIGNATURE OF DECLARANT)

(Continued on reverse)

Form Adopted for Mandatory Use Judicial Council of California AT-138, EJ-125 [Rev. July 1, 2000]	**APPLICATION AND ORDER** **FOR APPEARANCE AND EXAMINATION** (Attachment—Enforcement of Judgment)	Code of Civil Procedure, §§ 491.110, 708.110, 708.120

APPEARANCE OF JUDGMENT DEBTOR (ENFORCEMENT OF JUDGMENT)

NOTICE TO JUDGMENT DEBTOR   If you fail to appear at the time and place specified in this order, you may be subject to arrest and punishment for contempt of court, and the court may make an order requiring you to pay the reasonable attorney fees incurred by the judgment creditor in this proceeding.

APPEARANCE OF A THIRD PERSON
(ENFORCEMENT OF JUDGMENT)

(1) NOTICE TO PERSON SERVED   If you fail to appear at the time and place specified in this order, you may be subject to arrest and punishment for contempt of court, and the court may make an order requiring you to pay the reasonable attorney fees incurred by the judgment creditor in this proceeding.

(2) NOTICE TO JUDGMENT DEBTOR   The person in whose favor the judgment was entered in this action claims that the person to be examined pursuant to this order has possession or control of property which is yours or owes you a debt. This property or debt is as follows *(Describe the property or debt using typewritten capital letters)*:

If you claim that all or any portion of this property or debt is exempt from enforcement of the money judgment, you must file your exemption claim in writing with the court and have a copy personally served on the judgment creditor not later than three days before the date set for the examination. You must appear at the time and place set for the examination to establish your claim of exemption or your exemption may be waived.

APPEARANCE OF A THIRD PERSON (ATTACHMENT)

NOTICE TO PERSON SERVED   If you fail to appear at the time and place specified in this order, you may be subject to arrest and punishment for contempt of court, and the court may make an order requiring you to pay the reasonable attorney fees incurred by the plaintiff in this proceeding.

APPEARANCE OF A CORPORATION, PARTNERSHIP, ASSOCIATION, TRUST, OR OTHER ORGANIZATION

It is your duty to designate one or more of the following to appear and be examined: officers, directors, managing agents, or other persons who are familiar with your property and debts.

QUESTIONNAIRE FOR JUDGMENT-DEBTOR EXAMINATION

Date of Examination: _____, 20 _____

Part 1. Basic Identifying Facts

Your full name: _____

Any other names (including married/maiden names) used by you: _____

_____

Are you married?: _____ If so, give your spouse's full name: _____

If married, what other name(s) has your spouse used? _____

Your current residence (not P.O. box) address: _____

_____

Your telephone numbers: home: _____ work: _____

Do you have any children? _____ If so, give their names and ages, and state whether they live with you:

_____

_____

_____

Part 2a. Employment of Debtor

Are you employed? _____ Your employer's name and address: _____

_____

_____

How long have you worked for this employer? _____

What is your job classification? _____

Rate of pay? $_____ gross per month $_____ per hour. Hours per week you work for this employer: _____

What are your job duties? _____

Do you receive any kind of incentive payments or bonuses from your employer? _____

If so, state the conditions under which you get them, and when you get them:

_____

_____

_____

Part 2b. Employment of Spouse

Is your spouse employed? _____ Employer's name and address: _____

_____

_____

_____

How long has she/he worked for this employer? _____

What is his/her job classification? _____

Rate of pay? $_____ gross per month $_____ per hour. Hours per week she/he work for this employer: _____

What are his/her job duties? _____

Does she/he receive any kind of incentive payments or bonuses from the employer? _____

If so, state the conditions under which she/he gets them, and when she/he gets them: _____

_____

_____

_____

Part 2c. Other Employment of Debtor or Spouse

Your employer's name and address: _____

_____

_____

How long have you worked for this employer? _____

What is your job classification? _____

Rate of pay? $_____ gross per month $_____ per hour. Hours per week you work for this employer: _____

What are your job duties? _____

Do you receive any kind of incentive payments or bonuses from your employer? _____

If so, state the conditions under which you get them, and when you get them:

_____

_____

_____

Part 2d. Self-Employment of Debtor or Spouse

If you or your spouse is engaged in any type of full- or part-time self-employment, give the name and type of business, and

its location: _____

_____

_____

How long in this business? _____ Did you or your spouse start up or purchase it? _____

If started up, when? _____

If purchased, state the purchase price, date of purchase, and full names and addresses of sellers: _____

_____

_____

_____

Do you or your spouse have an accountant for this business? _____

Accountant's name and address: _____

_____

_____

Who prepares your business and personal income tax returns? _____

_____

Part 3. Cash, Savings or Checking Accounts, Safe Deposit Boxes

How much cash do you have on your person right now? _____

Do you or your spouse have a checking account? _____

If so, give bank, S&L, or credit union name and branch: _____

_____

Do you have a checkbook with you now? _____ If yes, give the account number(s): _____

Who is authorized to sign checks on the account? _____

_____

What is the current approximate balance? $_____ When did you make your last deposit? _____

Amount of last deposit: $_____ How often do you make deposits? _____

How often does your spouse make deposits? _____

When did you write your last check on that account? _____How much was the check for? $_____

Do you or your spouse have a savings account? _____

If so, give bank, S&L, or credit union name and branch: _____

_____

State the account number(s): _____

Who is authorized to withdraw funds? _____

_____

What is the current approximate balance? $ _____ When did you make your last deposit? _____

Amount of last deposit? $_____ When did you last make a withdrawal? _____

Do you have access to any business account for which you are an authorized signer? _____

Give the bank or S&L name, branch, and business name and address: _____

_____

Do you or your spouse have a safe deposit box? _____

Who has access to the box? _____

What property is kept in it? _____

_____

Give the box location and number: _____

_____

Part 4. Motor Vehicles

What motor vehicles do you and your spouse drive?

Vehicle 1: Make: _____ Model: _____ Year: _____

License Plate Number: _____ State: _____

Registered Owner(s): _____

_____

Where garaged? _____

Est. Value: $_____ Is it fully paid for? _____ If not paid for, state amount owed: $ _____

Name and address of lender/lienholder/legal owner: _____

_____

_____

Vehicle 2: Make: _____ Model: _____ Year: _____

License Plate Number: _____ State: _____

Registered Owner(s): _____

_____

Where garaged?_____

Est. Value: $_____ Is it fully paid for? _____ If not paid for, state amount owed: $ _____

Name and address of lender/lienholder/legal owner: _____

_____

_____

Do you or your spouse own any recreational vehicles, such as campers, trailers, boats, dirt bikes, and so on ? _____

If yes, give the following information:

Type of Vehicle: _____ Model: _____ Year: _____

License/Registration Number: _____ State: _____

Registered Owner(s): _____

_____

Where kept? _____

Est. Value: $_____ Is it fully paid for? _____ If not paid for, state amount owed: $ _____

Name and address of lender/lienholder/legal owner: _____

_____

_____

Part 5. Current Residence

Do you live in an apartment, single-family house, mobile home, condominium unit, or townhouse? _____

Do you rent or own your home? _____

Part 5a. If Debtor Rents

How much rent do you pay? $ _____ When paid? _____

How do you pay; check, cash, or money order? _____

Do you rent out any rooms? If so, state rents received and names of persons paying: _____

_____

_____

_____

State landlord's name, address, and phone: _____

_____

_____

_____

How long have you rented at this address? _____

Part 5b. If Debtor and/or Spouse Own Home

Who is listed as owner(s) on the deed to the property? _____

_____

When was the home purchased? _____ What was the purchase price? $_____

How much was the down payment? $_____ How much are the monthly payments? $_____

To what bank, S&L, or mortgage company are the monthly payments made? _____

_____

Who makes the actual payments? _____

How are the payments made: cash, check, or money order? _____

How much is still owed on the loan? $_____

How much do you think the property could sell for today? $_____

Is there a second deed of trust or second mortgage against the property? _____

For what amount? $_____ How much are the monthly payments? $_____

Who are these payments paid to? _____

Are there any other liens against the property? _____

If so, state the amounts, the names of the lienholders, and how the liens occurred: _____

_____

_____

Do you rent out any of the rooms in the residence? _____ If so, state rents received and names of persons paying:

_____

_____

Part 6. Real Property Other Than Home

Do you or your spouse own any real estate anywhere (other than any already discussed in 5b above)? _____

If yes, what kind of property is it? (vacant land? commercial property? and so on): _____

_____

_____

Is there a structure of any type on the land? _____ If yes, what kind? _____

Who is listed as owner(s) on the deed to the property? _____

When was the property purchased? _____

_____

What was the purchase price? $_____ How much was the down payment? $_____

How much are the monthly payments? $_____

To what bank, S&L, or mortgage company are the monthly payments made? _____

_____

_____

Who makes the actual payments? _____

How are the payments made: cash, check, or money order? _____

How much is still owed on the loan? $_____

How much do you think the property could sell for today? $_____

Is there a second deed of trust or second mortgage against the property? _____ For what amount? $_____

How much are the monthly payments? $_____

Who are these payments paid to? _____

Are there any other liens against the property? _____

If yes, state the amounts, the names of lienholders, and how the liens occurred: _____

_____

_____

_____

Do you receive any rents from the property? _____ If so, state rents received and names of persons paying:

_____

_____

_____

_____

Part 7. Other Property

Do you or your spouse own any stocks, bonds, or corporate securities of any kind? _____

If yes, state corporation name and address, type of holding, name(s) of owner(s), and value of holding(s):

_____

_____

_____

Do you or your spouse own any deeds of trust or mortgages on any real property or personal property? _____

If yes, state nature of property, location, nature of payments to you, and location of property:

_____

_____

_____

Are there any unsatisfied judgments in favor of you or your spouse? _____

If yes, state plaintiffs and defendants, amount of judgment, court, county, and judicial district:

_____

_____

_____

Do you or your spouse own any rings, watches, diamonds, other jewelry or antiques of any kind worth $100 or more?

_____

If yes, list property and value: _____

_____

_____

Do you or your spouse own any other personal property not already discussed, that is worth over $100? _____

If yes, list property and value: _____

_____

_____

In the past year have you or your spouse received any payments of money other than already discussed? _____

If yes, state amounts, dates received, reason money was received, and what happened to the money:

_____

_____

_____

Are you the beneficiary in any will? _____

If yes, state name and address of author of will, relationship of that individual to you, and type and value of property to be received: _____

_____

_____

_____

Part 8. Business Relations and Employment History

Are you or your spouse an officer, director, or stockholder of any corporation? _____

If yes, state corporation's name and address, nature of business, you or your spouse's position, and the nature and value of any shares of stock owned: _____

_____

_____

_____

For the past five years, list names and addresses of all businesses conducted by you and employment had by you, giving your position, duration of employment, and rate or amount of pay:

_____

_____

_____

_____

_____

_____

_____

_____

_____

_____

_____

_____

_____

_____

_____

_____

ATTORNEY OR PARTY WITHOUT ATTORNEY (Name and Address):	TELEPHONE NO.:	LEVYING OFFICER (Name and Address):

ATTORNEY FOR (Name): Plaintiff in Pro Per

NAME OF COURT, JUDICIAL DISTRICT OR BRANCH COURT, IF ANY:

PLAINTIFF:

DEFENDANT:

APPLICATION FOR EARNINGS WITHHOLDING ORDER (Wage Garnishment)	LEVYING OFFICER FILE NO.:	COURT CASE NO.:

TO THE SHERIFF OR ANY MARSHAL OR CONSTABLE OF THE COUNTY OF
OR ANY REGISTERED PROCESS SERVER

1. The judgment creditor (name):

requests issuance of an Earnings Withholding Order directing the employer to withhold the earnings of the judgment debtor (employee).

Name and address of employer   Name and address of employee

Social Security Number (if known):

2. The amounts withheld are to be paid to
   a. ☐ The attorney (or party without an attorney) named at the top of this page.
   b. ☐ Other (name, address, and telephone):

3. a. Judgment was entered on (date):
   b. Collect the amount directed by the Writ of Execution unless a lesser amount is specified here:
      $

4. ☐ The Writ of Execution was issued to collect delinquent amounts payable for the **support** of a child, former spouse, or spouse of the employee.

5. ☐ Special instructions (specify):

6. **(Check a or b)**
   a. ☐ I have not previously obtained an order directing this employer to withhold the earnings of this employee.
      —OR—
   b. ☐ I have previously obtained such an order, but that order (check one):
      ☐ was terminated by a court order, but I am entitled to apply for another Earnings Withholding Order under the provisions of Code of Civil Procedure section 706.105(h).
      ☐ was ineffective.

▶

....
(TYPE OR PRINT NAME)   (SIGNATURE OF ATTORNEY OR PARTY WITHOUT ATTORNEY)

I declare under penalty of perjury under the laws of the State of California that the foregoing is true and correct.

Date:

▶

....
(TYPE OR PRINT NAME)   (SIGNATURE OF DECLARANT)

Form Adopted by the
Judicial Council of California
982.5(1) [Rev. January 1, 1993]

APPLICATION FOR EARNINGS WITHHOLDING ORDER
(Wage Garnishment)

CCP 706.121

American LegalNet, Inc. | www.USCourtForms.com

ATTORNEY OR PARTY WITHOUT ATTORNEY *(Name, State Bar number, and address):*

After recording return to:

TELEPHONE NO.:

FAX NO. *(Optional):*

E-MAIL ADDRESS *(Optional):*

ATTORNEY FOR *(Name):*   Plaintiff in Pro Per

SUPERIOR COURT OF CALIFORNIA, COUNTY OF

STREET ADDRESS:

MAILING ADDRESS:

CITY AND ZIP CODE:

BRANCH NAME:

FOR RECORDER'S OR SECRETARY OF STATE'S USE ONLY

PLAINTIFF:

DEFENDANT:

CASE NUMBER:

ACKNOWLEDGMENT OF SATISFACTION OF JUDGMENT

☐ **FULL**   ☐ **PARTIAL**   ☐ **MATURED INSTALLMENT**

FOR COURT USE ONLY

1. Satisfaction of the judgment is acknowledged as follows:
   a. ☐ Full satisfaction
      (1) ☐ Judgment is satisfied in full.
      (2) ☐ The judgment creditor has accepted payment or performance other than that specified in the judgment in full satisfaction of the judgment.
   b. ☐ Partial satisfaction
      The amount received in partial satisfaction of the judgment is $
   c. ☐ Matured installment
      All matured installments under the installment judgment have been satisfied as of *(date):*

2. Full name and address of judgment creditor:*

3. Full name and address of assignee of record, if any:

4. Full name and address of judgment debtor being fully or partially released:*

5. a. Judgment entered on *(date):*
   b. ☐ Renewal entered on *(date):*

6. ☐ An ☐ abstract of judgment ☐ certified copy of the judgment has been recorded as follows *(complete all information for each county where recorded):*

   COUNTY   **DATE OF RECORDING**   **INSTRUMENT NUMBER**

7. ☐ A notice of judgment lien has been filed in the office of the Secretary of State as file number *(specify):*

NOTICE TO JUDGMENT DEBTOR: If this is an acknowledgment of full satisfaction of judgment, it will have to be recorded in each county shown in item 6 above, if any, in order to release the judgment lien, and will have to be filed in the office of the Secretary of State to terminate any judgment lien on personal property.

▶

Date:

_____
*(SIGNATURE OF JUDGMENT CREDITOR OR ASSIGNEE OF CREDITOR OR ATTORNEY**)*

Page 1 of 1

*The names of the judgment creditor and judgment debtor must be stated as shown in any Abstract of Judgment which was recorded and is being released by this satisfaction. ** A separate notary acknowledgment must be attached for each signature.

Form Approved for Optional Use
Judicial Council of California
EJ-100 [Rev. January 1, 2005]

ACKNOWLEDGMENT OF SATISFACTION OF JUDGMENT

Code of Civil Procedure, §§ 724.060,
724.120, 724.250

PROOF OF SERVICE BY MAIL

1

2   My address is_____

3   _____, California.

4   On _____, 20_____, I served the within:_____

5   _____

6

7

8   _____

9   by depositing true copies thereof, enclosed in separate, sealed envelopes, with the postage thereon fully prepaid, in the

10   United States Postal Service mail in_____ County, addressed as follows:

11   _____

12   _____

13   _____

14   _____

15   _____

16   _____

17   _____

18   _____

19   _____

20   _____

21   _____

22   I am, and was at the time herein-mentioned mailing took place, a resident of or employed in the County where

23   the mailing occurred, over the age of eighteen years old, and not a party to the within cause.

24   I declare under penalty of perjury under the laws of California and of the United States of America that the

25   foregoing is true and correct.

26   DATED: _____, _____

27   _____

28   Signature

Index

■

CATALOG

...more from Nolo

BUSINESS	PRICE	CODE
Business Buyout Agreements (Book w/CD-ROM)	$49.99	BSAG
The CA Nonprofit Corporation Kit (Binder w/CD-ROM)	$69.99	CNP
California Workers' Comp: How to Take Charge When You're Injured on the Job	$34.99	WORK
The Complete Guide to Buying a Business (Book w/CD-ROM)	$24.99	BUYBU
The Complete Guide to Selling a Business (Book w/CD-ROM)	$24.99	SELBU
Consultant & Independent Contractor Agreements (Book w/CD-ROM)	$29.99	CICA
The Corporate Records Handbook (Book w/CD-ROM)	$69.99	CORMI
Create Your Own Employee Handbook (Book w/CD-ROM)	$49.99	EMHA
Dealing With Problem Employees	$44.99	PROBM
Deduct It! Lower Your Small Business Taxes	$34.99	DEDU
Effective Fundraising for Nonprofits	$24.99	EFFN
The Employer's Legal Handbook	$39.99	EMPL
Essential Guide to Federal Employment Laws	$39.99	FEMP
Form a Partnership (Book W/CD-ROM)	$39.99	PART
Form Your Own Limited Liability Company (Book w/CD-ROM)	$44.99	LIAB
Home Business Tax Deductions: Keep What You Earn	$34.99	DEHB
How to Form a Nonprofit Corporation (Book w/CD-ROM)—National Edition	$49.99	NNP
How to Form a Nonprofit Corporation in California (Book w/CD-ROM)	$49.99	NON
How to Form Your Own California Corporation (Binder w/CD-ROM)	$59.99	CACI
How to Form Your Own California Corporation (Book w/CD-ROM)	$34.99	CCOR
How to Write a Business Plan (Book w/CD-ROM)	$34.99	SBS
Incorporate Your Business (Book w/CD-ROM)	$49.99	NIBS
Investors in Your Backyard (Book w/CD-ROM)	$24.99	FINBUS
The Job Description Handbook	$29.99	JOB
Legal Guide for Starting & Running a Small Business	$34.99	RUNS
Legal Forms for Starting & Running a Small Business (Book w/CD-ROM)	$29.99	RUNSF

Prices subject to change.

BUSINESS (CONT'D.)

	PRICE	CODE
LLC or Corporation?	$24.99	CHENT
The Manager's Legal Handbook	$39.99	ELBA
Marketing Without Advertising	$20.00	MWAD
Music Law (Book w/CD-ROM)	$39.99	ML
Negotiate the Best Lease for Your Business	$24.99	LESP
Nolo's Guide to Social Security Disability (Book w/CD-ROM)	$29.99	QSS
Nolo's Quick LLC	$29.99	LLCQ
The Performance Appraisal Handbook	$29.99	PERF
The Small Business Start-up Kit (Book w/CD-ROM)	$24.99	SMBU
The Small Business Start-up Kit for California (Book w/CD-ROM)	$24.99	OPEN
Starting & Running a Successful Newsletter or Magazine	$29.99	MAG
Tax Deductions for Professionals	$34.99	DEPO
Tax Savvy for Small Business	$36.99	SAVVY
Whoops! I'm in Business	$19.99	WHOO
Working for Yourself: Law & Taxes for Independent Contractors, Freelancers & Consultants	$39.99	WAGE
Working With Independent Contractors (Book w/CD-ROM)	$29.99	HICI
Your Crafts Business: A Legal Guide (Book w/CD-ROM)	$26.99	VART
Your Limited Liability Company: An Operating Manual (Book w/CD-ROM)	$49.99	LOP
Your Rights in the Workplace	$29.99	YRW

CONSUMER

	PRICE	CODE
How to Win Your Personal Injury Claim	$29.99	PICL
Nolo's Encyclopedia of Everyday Law	$29.99	EVL
Nolo's Guide to California Law	$24.99	CLAW

ESTATE PLANNING & PROBATE

	PRICE	CODE
8 Ways to Avoid Probate	$19.99	PRAV
Estate Planning Basics	$21.99	ESPN
The Executor's Guide: Settling a Loved One's Estate or Trust	$34.99	EXEC
How to Probate an Estate in California	$49.99	PAE
Make Your Own Living Trust (Book w/CD-ROM)	$39.99	LITR
Nolo's Simple Will Book (Book w/CD-ROM)	$36.99	SWIL

	PRICE	CODE
Plan Your Estate	$44.99	NEST
Quick & Legal Will Book (Book w/CD-ROM)	$19.99	QUIC
Special Needs Trust: Protect Your Child's Financial Future (Book w/CD-ROM)	$34.99	SPNT

FAMILY MATTERS

	PRICE	CODE
Always Dad	$16.99	DIFA
Building a Parenting Agreement That Works	$24.99	CUST
The Complete IEP Guide	$34.99	IEP
Divorce & Money: How to Make the Best Financial Decisions During Divorce	$34.99	DIMO
Divorce Without Court	$29.99	DWCT
Do Your Own California Adoption: Nolo's Guide for Stepparents and Domestic Partners (Book w/CD-ROM)	$34.99	ADOP
Every Dog's Legal Guide: A Must-Have for Your Owner	$19.99	DOG
Get a Life: You Don't Need a Million to Retire Well	$24.99	LIFE
The Guardianship Book for California	$34.99	GB
A Legal Guide for Lesbian and Gay Couples	$34.99	LG
Living Together: A Legal Guide (Book w/CD-ROM)	$34.99	LTK
Nolo's IEP Guide: Learning Disabilities	$29.99	IELD
Parent Savvy	$19.99	PRNT
Prenuptial Agreements: How to Write a Fair & Lasting Contract (Book w/CD-ROM)	$34.99	PNUP
Work Less, Live More	$17.99	RECL

GOING TO COURT

	PRICE	CODE
Beat Your Ticket: Go To Court & Win! (National Edition)	$21.99	BEYT
The Criminal Law Handbook: Know Your Rights, Survive the System	$39.99	KYR
Everybody's Guide to Small Claims Court (National Edition)	$29.99	NSCC
Everybody's Guide to Small Claims Court in California	$29.99	CSCC
Fight Your Ticket & Win in California	$29.99	FYT
How to Change Your Name in California	$29.99	NAME
Nolo's Deposition Handbook	$29.99	DEP
Represent Yourself in Court: How to Prepare & Try a Winning Case	$39.99	RYC
Win Your Lawsuit: A Judge's Guide to Representing Yourself in California Superior Court	$29.99	SLWY

HOMEOWNERS, LANDLORDS & TENANTS

	PRICE	CODE
California Tenants' Rights	$27.99	CTEN
Deeds for California Real Estate	$24.99	DEED
Every Landlord's Legal Guide (National Edition, Book w/CD-ROM)	$44.99	ELLI
Every Landlord's Guide to Finding Great Tenants (Book w/CD-ROM)	$19.99	FIND
Every Landlord's Tax Deduction Guide	$34.99	DELL
Every Tenant's Legal Guide	$29.99	EVTEN
For Sale by Owner in California	$29.99	FSBO
How to Buy a House in California	$29.99	BHCA
The California Landlord's Law Book: Rights & Responsibilities (Book w/CD-ROM)	$44.99	LBRT
The California Landlord's Law Book: Evictions (Book w/CD-ROM)	$44.99	LBEV
Leases & Rental Agreements	$29.99	LEAR
Neighbor Law: Fences, Trees, Boundaries & Noise	$26.99	NEI
Renters' Rights (National Edition)	$24.99	RENT

IMMIGRATION

	PRICE	CODE
Becoming A U.S. Citizen: A Guide to the Law, Exam and Interview	$24.99	USCIT
Fiancé & Marriage Visas (Book w/CD-ROM)	$34.99	IMAR
How to Get a Green Card	$29.99	GRN
Student & Tourist Visas	$29.99	ISTU
U.S. Immigration Made Easy	$39.99	IMEZ

MONEY MATTERS

	PRICE	CODE
101 Law Forms for Personal Use (Book w/CD-ROM)	$29.99	SPOT
Chapter 13 Bankruptcy: Repay Your Debts	$39.99	CHB
Credit Repair (Book w/CD-ROM)	$24.99	CREP
How to File for Chapter 7 Bankruptcy	$29.99	HFB
IRAs, 401(k)s & Other Retirement Plans: Taking Your Money Out	$34.99	RET
Solve Your Money Troubles	$19.99	MT
Stand Up to the IRS	$29.99	SIRS

PATENTS AND COPYRIGHTS

	PRICE	CODE
All I Need is Money: How to Finance Your Invention	$19.99	FINA
The Copyright Handbook: How to Protect & Use Written Works (Book w/CD-ROM)	$39.99	COHA
Copyright Your Software (Book w/CD-ROM)	$34.95	CYS

	PRICE	CODE
Getting Permission: How to License and Clear Copyrighted Materials Online and Off (Book w/CD-ROM)	$34.99	RIPER
How to Make Patent Drawings	$29.99	DRAW
The Inventor's Notebook	$24.99	INOT
Nolo's Patents for Beginners	$24.99	QPAT
Patent, Copyright & Trademark	$39.99	PCTM
Patent It Yourself	$49.99	PAT
Patent Pending in 24 Hours	$34.99	PEND
Patenting Art & Entertainment: New Strategies for Protecting Creative Ideas	$39.99	PATAE
Profit from Your Idea (Book w/CD-ROM)	$34.99	LICE
The Public Domain	$34.99	PUBL
Trademark: Legal Care for Your Business and Product Name	$39.99	TRD
Web and Software Development: A Legal Guide (Book w/ CD-ROM)	$44.99	SFT
What Every Inventor Needs to Know About Business & Taxes (Book w/CD-ROM)	$21.99	ILAX

RESEARCH & REFERENCE

Legal Research: How to Find & Understand the Law	$39.99	LRES

SENIORS

Long-Term Care: How to Plan & Pay for It	$19.99	ELD
Social Security, Medicare & Goverment Pensions	$29.99	SOA

SOFTWARE

Call or check our website at www.nolo.com for special discounts on Software!

Incorporator Pro	89.99	STNC1
LLC Maker—Windows..	$89.95	LLP1
Patent Pending Now!	$199.99	PP1
PatentEase—Windows	$349.00	PEAS
Personal RecordKeeper 5.0 CD—Windows	$59.95	RKD5
Quicken Legal Business Pro 2007—Windows	$109.99	SBQB7
Quicken WillMaker Plus 2007—Windows	$79.99	WQP7

Special Upgrade Offer

Save 35% on the latest edition of your Nolo book

Because laws and legal procedures change often, we update our books regularly. To help keep you up-to-date, we are extending this special upgrade offer. Cut out and mail the title portion of the cover of your old Nolo book and we'll give you 35% off the retail price of the New Edition of that book when you purchase directly from Nolo. This offer is to individuals only.

Order Form

Name

Address

City

State, Zip

Daytime Phone

E-mail

Our "No-Hassle" Guarantee

Return anything you buy directly from Nolo for any reason and we'll cheerfully refund your purchase price. No ifs, ands or buts.

☐ Check here if you do not wish to receive mailings from other companies

Item Code	Quantity	Item	Unit Price	Total Price

Method of payment

☐ Check   ☐ VISA

☐ American Express

☐ MasterCard

☐ Discover Card

Subtotal	
Add your local sales tax (California only)	
Shipping: RUSH $12, Basic $9 (See below)	
"I bought 3, ship it to me FREE!"(Ground shipping only)	
TOTAL	

Account Number

Expiration Date

Signature

Shipping and Handling

Rush Delivery—Only $12

We'll ship any order to any street address in the U.S. by UPS 2nd Day Air* for only $12!

*Order by noon Pacific Time and get your order in 2 business days. Orders placed after noon Pacific Time will arrive in 3 business days. P.O. boxes and S.F. Bay Area use basic shipping. Alaska and Hawaii use 2nd Day Air or Priority Mail.

Basic Shipping—$9

Use for P.O. Boxes, Northern California and Ground Service.

Allow 1-2 weeks for delivery.

U.S. addresses only.

For faster service, use your credit card and our toll-free numbers

Call our customer service group Monday thru Friday 7am to 7pm PST

Phone
1-800-728-3555

Fax
1-800-645-0895

Mail
Nolo
950 Parker St.
Berkeley, CA 94710

NOLO

Order 24 hours a day @ www.nolo.com

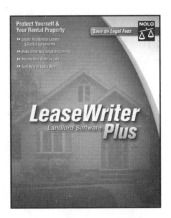

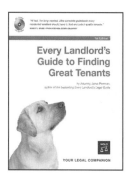
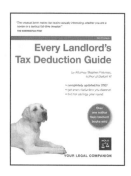